AF804162

Reforming the Law and Structure of the International Financial System

John H. Friedland

PRAEGER

Westport, Connecticut
London

Library of Congress Cataloging-in-Publication Data

Friedland, John H.
Reforming the law and structure of the international financial system / John H. Friedland.
p. cm.
Includes bibliographical references and index.
ISBN 1–56720–643–3 (alk. paper)
1. Financial institutions, International—Law and legislation. I. Title.
K4450.5.F75 2004
346′.08215—dc22 2003062259

British Library Cataloguing in Publication Data is available.

Copyright © 2004 by John H. Friedland

All rights reserved. No portion of this book may be reproduced, by any process or technique, without the express written consent of the publisher.

Library of Congress Catalog Card Number: 2003062259
ISBN: 1–56720–643–3

First published in 2004

Praeger Publishers, 88 Post Road West, Westport, CT 06881
An imprint of Greenwood Publishing Group, Inc.
www.praeger.com

Printed in the United States of America

The paper used in this book complies with the Permanent Paper Standard issued by the National Information Standards Organization (Z39.48–1984).

10 9 8 7 6 5 4 3 2 1

Copyright Acknowledgments

The author and publisher gratefully acknowledge permission to reprint the following:

Excerpts from *Eat the Rich* by P. J. O'Rourke. Copyright © 1998 by P. J. O'Rourke. Reprinted by permission of Grove/Atlantic, Inc.

"UK Corporate Governance and Disclosure" by John Friedland. Article first published in *International Journal of Disclosure and Governance*, vol. 1, no. 1, ISSN 1741–3591, October 2003. Published by Henry Stewart Publications, London, UK. Reprinted with the permission of Henry Stewart Publications.

Excerpts from An Open Letter to Joseph Stiglitz, by Kenneth Rogoff, Economic Counsellor and Director of Research, International Monetary Fund, July 2, 2002. Reprinted with the permission of the International Monetary Fund.

From "Sarbanes-Oxley: Certification, Financial Reporting and Economic Crime" by John H. Friedland, first published by Sweet & Maxwell Limited in *The Company Lawyer*, December 2002, pp. 384–88. Reproduced by agreement with Sweet & Maxwell.

Excerpts from Eliot Spitzer, "Editorial: Regulation Begins at Home," *New York Times*, November 17, 2003. Copyright 2003, Eliot L. Spitzer. Reprinted by permission.

I would like to thank Lawrence N. Friedland and Professor Barry A. K. Rider for encouraging me in this endeavor over the long haul.

Contents

Abbreviations

AAPA	American Association of Public Accountants
ACCA	Association of Chartered Certified Accountants
AG	Supervisory Boards of Stock Corporations
AIA	American Institute of Accountants
AICPA	American Institute of Certified Public Accountants
APB	Accounting Practices Board; *Auditing Practices Bulletin*
ASB	Accounting Standards Board
BIS	Bank for International Settlements
C&I	Consumer and Industrial
CAD	Capital Adequacy Directive
CBOT	Chicago Board of Trade
CBR	Conduct of Business Rules
CCAB	Cumulative Committee of Accounting Bodies
CCP	Central Counterparty
CEA	Commodities Exchange Act
CEO	Chief Executive Officer
CFMA	Commodities Futures Modernization Act of 2000
CFO	Chief Financial Officer
CFTC	Commodities Futures Trading Corporation
CGAA	Coordinating Group on Accounting and Auditing

CHIPS	Clearing House Interbank Payment System
CLS	Continuous Linked Settlement
CME	Chicago Mercantile Exchange
COB	Conduct of Business
CPSS	Committee on Payment and Settlement Systems
CSCI	Consolidated Supervision of Credit Institutions
CSD	Central Securities Depository
D&O	Directors and Officers
DCO	Derivatives Clearing Organization
DJIA	Dow Jones Industrial Average
DTCC	Depository Trust and Clearing Corporation
DTI	Department of Trade and Industry
DVP	Delivery versus Payment Basis
EAD	Exposure at Default
ECAI	External Credit Assessment Institutions
ECB	European Central Bank
ECJ	European Court of Justice
ECP	European Commercial Paper
EDGAR	Electronic Data Gathering Analysis and Retrieval
EEA	European Economic Area
EI	Exposure Indicator
EITF	Emerging Issue Task Force
EL	Expected Loss
EMU	Economic and Monetary Union
EP	European Parliament
ERISA	Employee Retirement Income Security Act
ERM	Exchange Rate Mechanism
ESCB	European System of Central Banks
ESOP	Employee Stock Ownership Plan
EU	European Union
Fannie Mae	Federal National Mortgage Association
FAS	Financial Accounting Standard
FASB	Financial Accounting Standards Board
FATF	Financial Action Taskforce
FCM	Futures Commissions Merchants

FDICIA	Federal Deposit Insurance Corporation Improvement Act of 1991
FERC	Federal Energy Regulatory Commission
fifo	first in first out
FRB	Federal Reserve Board
FRC	Financial Reporting Council
FRED	Financial Reporting Exposure Draft
FRN	Floating Rate Note
FRRP	Financial Reporting Review Panel
FSA	Financial Service Authority
FSF	Financial Stability Forum
FSLIC	Federal Savings and Loan Insurance Corporation
FSMA	Financial Services and Markets Act 2000
FTC	Federal Trade Commission
FTSE	Financial Times-Stock Exchange
GAAP	Generally Accepted Accounting Principles
GATT	General Agreement on Tariffs and Trade
GDP	Gross Domestic Product
Ginnie Mac	Government National Mortgage Association
GLB	Gramm-Leach-Bliley
HLI	Highly Leveraged Institutions
HLO	Highly Leveraged Organizations
IAS	International Accounting Standards
IASB	International Accounting Standards Board
IASC	International Accounting Standards Committee
IBRD	International Bank for Reconstruction and Development
ICAEW	Institute of Chartered Accountants of England and Wales
ICAS	Institute of Chartered Accountants of Scotland
ICC	Interstate Commerce Commission
IDB	Investigations and Discipline Board
IFC	International Finance Corporation
IFRS	International Financial Reporting Standard
IMF	International Monetary Fund
IOSCO	International Organization of Securities Commissions
IPO	Initial Public Offering

IRB	Internal Ratings Based Approach
IRCJ	Industrial Revitalization Corporation of Japan
IRS	Internal Revenue Service
ISD	Investment Services Directive
IT	Information Technology
ITE	Intra-Group Transactions and Exposure
JMU	Joint Monitoring Unit
LBO	Leveraged Buyout
LDC	Less Developed Countries
LED	Large Exposure Directive
LGD	Loss Given Default
LGE	Probability of Loss
LIED	Probability of Default on a Particular Loan
lifo	last in first out
LLR	Lender of Last Resort
LP	Listing Particulars
LPD	Listing Particulars Directive
LSE	London Stock Exchange
LTCB	Long Term Credit Bank
LTCM	Long Term Capital Management
M&A	Mergers and Acquisitions
MD&A	Management Discussion and Analysis
MITI	Ministry of Trade and Industry
MJDS	Multi-Jurisdiction Disclosure System
MOF	Ministry of Finance
MOSS	Market-Oriented and Sector Specific Talks
MOU	Memorandum of Understanding
MRP	Mutual Recognition of Prospectuses
NASD	National Association of Dealers
NASDAQ	National Association of Dealers Automated Quotations
NIF	Note Issuance Facilities
NPL	Nonperforming Loans
NSCC	National Securities Clearing Corporation
NSRO	Nationally Recognized Statistical Rating Organizations
NYSE	New York Stock Exchange

OCC	Options Clearing Corporation
OECD	Organization for Economic Cooperation and Development
OFC	Offshore Financial Centers
OFD	Own Funds Directive
OFR	Operating and Financial Review
OSI	Optimum Standard Issuance
OTC	Over the Counter
PCAOB	Public Company Accounting Oversight Board
PD	Probability of Default
PE	Probability of Loss Event
POB	Public Oversight Board
PSLRA	Private Securities Litigation Reform Act
PSR	Payment System Risk
R&D	Research and Development
Reg. FD	Fair Disclosure
RMB	Chinese Unit of Currency
RRAP	Report on the Regulation of the Accountancy Profession
RUF	Revolving Underwriting Facilities
RWA	Risk Weighted Assets
S&L	Savings and Loan
S&P	Standard and Poors
SBDI	EU Second Banking Directive
SBDII	EU Directive 2000/12
SDR	Special Drawing Rights
SEC	Securities and Exchange Commission
SECPCS	Securities Practice Committee
SEL	Securities and Exchange Law
SESC	Securities Exchange and Surveillance Commission
SIA	Securities Industry Association
SIB	Securities and Investments Board
SIPIC	Securities Investor Protection Insurance Corporation
SPE	Special Purpose Entity
SPV	Special Purpose Vehicle
SRD	Solvency Ration Directive
SRO	Self-Regulatory Organizations

SSI	Suspicious Activity Reports
SSS	Securities Settlement Systems
TFP	Total Factor Productivity
UCIT	Undertaking for Collective Investment Trusts
U.K.	United Kingdom
UKLA	United Kingdom Listing Authority
U.S.	United States
VAR	Value at Risk
WTFO	World Trade and Finance Organization
WTO	World Trade Organization
XBL	Extensible Binding Language
XML	Extra Markup Computer Language

Introduction

Since the collapse of Enron the extent and nature of financial regulation has already changed dramatically. Thus far, its effects have been limited to corporate governance and financial reporting. But the role played by U.S. banks has called into question a decade of deregulation that included the Gramm-Leach-Bliley Act ending, in large part, the separation of banking and investment banking in the United States. In the European Union (EU), an entirely new regime of capital market regulation began in 1986 with the United Kingdom creating its first securities regulator, followed by the EU single market for financial services, most of which was accomplished in the early 1990s, and the United Kingdom Financial Services and Markets Act 2000, which effectively ended self-regulation in the United Kingdom. In Japan, the inability of the government to require banks to realize bad debts from the 1980s era of speculation and lack of sound banking principles is at the top of the agenda for reform; Japan's Big Bang, a program of deregulation, has been a big bust, particularly in the continued structural weakness of the banking sector and the unwillingness to create a U.S.-style securities regulator.

International organizations play a major role in the international economy. Aside from the well-publicized role of the International Monetary Fund (IMF) and the World Bank in the Asia crisis for instance, the Bank for International Settlements (BIS) Committee on Banking and Supervisory Practices is a forum in which national regulators from G-10 countries formulate capital adequacy rules for banks and securities firms with mixed results. The International Organization of Securities Commissions (IOSCO) sets principles for international securities offerings and considers issues of systemic risk in securities markets, more often with generalized position papers, and has been effective in some areas while leaving other issues such as the risk posed by hedge funds at the stage of formulation.

If there were a common thread that ran through the world financial system today, it would certainly be financial reporting. While this theme is evident in securities regulation, it is also the underlying principle behind capital adequacy regulation of financial institutions. The proper writing down of underperforming bank assets is clearly a question of proper reporting and disclosure. The rules written by the BIS committee will ultimately reflect the degree of specificity that regulators feel able to impose on banks. However, onerous regulation may induce economic collapse. Meanwhile, the growth of the derivative markets continues apace with the aggregate turnover of exchange-traded derivative contracts reaching a notional amount of $169 trillion in 2002;[1] the latest figures for over-the-counter derivatives indicate that the stock of aggregate positions was $98 trillion.[2] Derivatives, as Long-Term Capital Management, Enron, and various other scandals have shown, pose a risk most often associated with banking and systemic risk issues. Despite efforts of the BIS committee to quantify such risk, the risk remains qualitative.

One can readily distinguish between capital market countries such as the United States and the United Kingdom and universal banking countries such as Germany or Japan where banks own shares and financing is dependent on long-term relationships between borrowers and lenders. London survives as a financial center, not because it is the capital of the United Kingdom, but because it is a global city with a nexus of lawyers, accountants, information technology (IT) consultants, and investment bankers and a long history of merchant law that has translated into a trusted regulatory regime and legal system.

But the United States remains the centerpiece of the international financial system. In 1995 the United States was still a net creditor nation (on the basis of foreign direct investment) and had just yielded its status as the largest net creditor nation; it is now the largest net debtor nation to the tune of almost $2 trillion. Before 1995, the United States was last a net debtor nation in 1916. The current account imbalance is the ultimate nightmare of international financial accounting. The possibility of sudden financial crisis looms over any attempt at the regulation of financial markets. The greatest problem in promoting prudent financial market regulation can be summarized as the disaster myopia hypothesis. The further removed we are from a financial crisis the less we believe in the possibility of a reoccurrence.[3]

Before delving into the regulations that shape the structure of financial markets in the United States, the EU, and Japan, we must consider the age-old question, why regulate? That paradigm of financial regulation, the Glass Steagall Act, is no longer. Was it ever justified in the first place or was it intended to punish money-centered banks for their undue influence in the 1920s? The problem was, as noted by the Senate Banking Committee's counsel, Ferdinand Pecora, National City stock salesmen "came to them clothed with all the authority and prestige of the magic name 'National City.'"[4] If a bank failed, the Feds would be required to stand behind the bank and its failed securities affiliate. Although different from a legal perspective, the fable poignantly recalls the probe currently being conducted into analysts at investment banks who issued buy recommendations and, in some instances, received their bonuses directly from the head of corporate finance. But the argument made by the Morgan bank, that it was strictly a wholesale bank and did not deal with retail customers, was not considered in the political climate of the era.

The market capitalization of the London Stock Exchange (LSE) is less than 20 percent of the New York Stock Exchange (NYSE), and Germany and France together are even less. Thus the impact of U.S. financial markets on EU financial markets is much greater than the impact of EU markets on the United States. The EU has become a military, trading, and financial union among European states. The internationalization of securities markets means that a more integrated European securities market is inevitable in the medium-term future, which will also strengthen the role of the euro as an international unit of reserve. The current era of financial regulation in Europe began with the Big Bang in London, which produced a U.S.-style Securities and Exchange Commission (SEC) beginning in 1986, ending a regime of self-regulation and culminating in the Financial Services and Markets Act 2000. U.K. concepts of corporate governance are roughly similar to those in the United States although less developed and more principle rather than rule oriented. In other European countries aside from the Netherlands, equity tends to be owned by a more closely knit ownership including families and banks. This reduces the liquidity of equity markets in the classic tradeoff of liquidity and control.[5] European financial markets reflect U.S. innovations and generally offer lower degrees of investor protection.

Capital adequacy of financial institutions, which in Europe, outside of the United Kingdom, more often means banks than securities firms, is an essential part of the international safety net. Unfortunately, Japan has managed to create a lax environment in this area by sidestepping developments in capital adequacy creating the risk of an international financial pandemic. Yet, the U.S. financial system is the hinge on which the entire system rests.

Increasingly, in the United States, financial regulation or the lack thereof has been more relevant as a determinant of overall credit than monetary policy or even fiscal stimulus. The deregulation of thrifts in the 1980s and the debt overhang resulting from junk bonds caused the liquidity crunch in the early 1990s. In the late 1990s, the lack of regulation of the initial public offering (IPO) market and financial accounting standards and the failure of bank supervisors to reign in bank underwriting of equity-linked bonds and consumer credit were perhaps more important than interest rate policy in creating the recession of 2001.

European markets suffered spillover effects but continue to face different problems, particularly the structural rigidity of labor markets. There have never been definitive advantages to economic and monetary union, and integration of financial services is proceeding at a slow pace within the EU. However, convergence of accounting standards is likely to facilitate the integration of EU capital markets, and the euro may gradually serve as a hedge against fluctuations in the dollar (or the dollar/yen rate) and may increase its function as an alternative official reserve currency, although it is unlikely to ever seriously challenge the role of the dollar as a parallel world currency.

Financial regulation has rarely been assigned a significant position among monetary authorities, and, in the United Kingdom, financial regulation is no longer the responsibility of the Bank of England, which is charged only with lender of last resort functions and monetary policy. In the United States, prudential supervision has never attracted sufficient attention from the chairman of the Federal Reserve Board (FRB). This is, in part, the heritage of John Maynard Keynes, who was highly skeptical of, or even indifferent to, the role played by financial regulation.[6]

The issue of accounting standards is evidence of how differently the same issues may play out in the EU and the United States. In the United States, the issue is driven by the financial corruption scandals, particularly those involving Enron and off-balance sheet financing, while in the EU there is a directive requiring all nations to adopt international accounting standards by 2005. While the United Kingdom will require minor adjustments (its system is similar to the United States'), other member states will have to move from historical cost-based accounting to mark-to-market accounting. Financial law and financial structure are inextricably interwoven. Deutche Telekom was the only pan-European securities offering, despite the various EU directives, including the Investment Services Directive and the Listing Particular Directive and the Mutual Recognition of Prospectuses Directive intended to facilitate pan-European offerings. However, harmonization of accounting rules will make this more likely in the future. Accounting in the EU is more opaque than U.S. accounting, but thus far scandals in Europe, including Vivendi and Parmelat, have not reached the same pitch as U.S. scandals. After Enron, corporate governance will receive more attention in Europe, but the continental model of illiquid and closely held corporations is unlikely to witness a sea change. The United Kingdom, an arm's length market, offers the most dynamic financial markets and the most developed legal and accounting systems in the EU and by far the largest capitalization of stock and bond markets including the largest eurobond market in Europe. Accordingly, I have chosen to focus on it rather than continental markets.

In the United States, the Sarbanes-Oxley Act will have an impact on financial accounting and alter concepts of corporate governance. This will likely affect the desire of CEOs to engage in empire building, which will tend toward altering the tendency to form conglomerates. Strict financial reporting standards will depress earnings, which will make raising capital more difficult, lessening investment in the short term. The use of credit rating, which may or may not reflect value, determines the net capital of accounting firms and bank portfolios definitively influencing strategy. Capital adequacy rules determine the nature of bank loans and their extent. These are but a few of the more obvious examples of interaction between the fundamentals of financial law and structure.

There could be many ways to organize this book. The chapter on U.K. financial services is first because the developments in the international regulation of capital adequacy in the 1980s informed the EU single market program in financial services and were incorporated almost completely in the Capital Adequacy Directive and the Investment Services Directive. The EU financial services program utilized the approaches of commonality, reciprocity, and, above all, harmonization (or convergence) of financial regulation. It may have made sense to begin with the 1982 Lesser Developed Country Crisis, the genesis of derivative instruments, and the securitization of assets in a U.S. context where it originally arose. Instead, this subject is treated in chapter 1, on U.K. financial services. The 1988 G-10 agreement on capital adequacy for banks, which arose because of these new instruments and had profound consequences internationally, led directly to the Capital Adequacy Directive of the European community.

Internal controls of banks are a particularly strict form of corporate governance. Capital adequacy rules for banks involve disclosure and financial reporting; in fact, it could be argued that all financial derivative accounting standards, whether bank or corporate (i.e., Enron) related, should be treated together, but banking is also special and plays a role in the safety and soundness of national financial systems, separate and apart from that played by corporations, which make significant use of derivatives.

While a thematic approach to the material might have been appropriate, this book utilizes a more traditional approach by dividing the topics between the EU/United Kingdom, the United States, Japan, and international organizations (Bank for International Settlements, IOSCO, IMF, International Bank for Reconstruction and Development [IBRD]). This approach rests on the view that financial regulation develops organically in national or regional (EU) settings or by explicit international agreement in which, for instance, G-10 countries send representatives. Finally, each system has several components—banking, securities regulation, and corporate governance—that interact within a domestic or regional context or within an international forum.

Financial accounting is the seamless web that unites the United States, the EU, and Japan. Yet, in the EU, financial accounting is the potential springboard for the integration of European securities markets; in Japan, it is the distant possibility of fair value accounting for companies in general, and banks in particular, that will eventually lead the economy to recovery. In all three blocs, bank and securities firm capital adequacy is essentially a question of financial measurement, on which the safety and soundness of the world financial system depends.

Chapter 1 considers U.K. financial services in the context of the EU single market for financial services and demonstrates how the peculiar national institutions and initiatives of the United Kingdom are integrated into the EU framework. Beginning in the late 1980s Europe began to prepare for the single European market, which was to take effect in 1992. In 1986, Parliament promulgated the Financial Services Act, which established the Securities and Investments Board (SIB) to oversee the self-regulatory organizations and exchanges that composed British securities markets. This was Britain's SEC. In 1988, the Committee on Banking and Supervisory Practices of the Group of 10 Countries, a committee of the Bank for International Settlements, established the Capital Adequacy Accord (G-10 agreement), which set forth capital adequacy standards for international banks. This became the basis of the Second Banking Directive of the European Union (then the European Economic Community). This was closely followed by the Investment Services Directive, in which there was close U.S. participation, since the United States wanted its investment banks to have greater flexibility in their capital, which they held for short-term trading purposes. Parliament passed the Financial Services and Markets Act 2000 and gave the newly created Financial Services Authority (FSA) regulatory authority over almost all deposit taking and securities issuing institutions, effectively separating monetary and regulatory functions. The attendant weaknesses of this approach in the event of systemic failure will be discussed. U.K. corporate governance reform, which is specifically labeled as "after Enron" and the EU directive on financial conglomerates, which arose in part because of Enron, are considered in chapter 6, "Reform," along with Sarbanes-Oxley.

Chapter 1 will also consider the future of the euro and Britain's possible entry into the Economic and Monetary Union (EMU). Britain's unwillingness to join, given the primacy of London's capital markets, means that the regulatory functions of the European System of Central Banks (ESCB) are extremely limited. Thus, the business of financial regulation has been carried out by the Banking and Supervisory Committee of the Bank for International Settlements, in which the United States is also an active participant.

Chapter 2 will elucidate the New Capital Adequacy Accord (the new G-10 accord), which has been in the making since 1995 and is not expected to be completed until 2006. Fundamentally, this allows for a more flexible, yet more prudent, approach to banking supervision, including internal hedging, supervision on a consolidated basis, interest rate risk, credit risk, and market risk. It will also consider the documents presented by IOSCO and will critique International Accounting Standards (IAS), which are in certain respects quite different from Generally Accepted Accounting Principles (GAAP). New standards issued by the International Accounting Standards Board are denoted as International Financial Report Standards such as IFRS 2 "Accounting for Share Payments" (February 2004). Offshore financial centers will also be reviewed with emphasis on new U.S. legislation, the Patriot Act. The functions of the IMF and the World Bank will be discussed in the context of the Asia crisis and the Latin American situation in 2002.

Chapter 3 will discuss payment, securities settlement, and clearing systems, generally boring subjects but quite exciting in the event of a meltdown. The specific roles of the SEC and the Commodities Futures Trading Corporation (CFTC) in the United States will be considered, and the CFTC's deregulation of energy futures will be briefly discussed as an example of the problems of deregulation in a clearing system, as will the comparison of money, security, and energy transactions.

All of the foregoing leads to chapter 4, "The Deteriorating Integrity of the U.S. Financial System." "Securities" covers Congress's passage of the Private Securities Litigation Act of 1995, which limits shareholder suits against corporations; the tenure of Arthur Levitt as SEC chairman and his attempts to take on the accounting industry; and SEC initiatives after Enron. "Banking" considers banking: Gramm-Leach-Bliley, which virtually eliminates Glass Steagall; a description of the quality of U.S. banking assets; and the consequences of the external deficit and the negative savings rate.

Chapter 5 considers corporate governance and financial reporting and includes a survey of issues in corporate governance, and the evolution of the accounting industry in the United States, and then considers a conceptual approach to issues in financial disclosure.

Chapter 6 is titled "Reform: Sarbanes-Oxley, Its Consequences, and the European Response" and contains the all-important provisions of the Sarbanes-Oxley Act. In general, the act overhauls securities laws by requiring certification by the chief executive officer (CEO) and chief financial officer (CFO) with criminal penalties and also requiring that the audit committee, rather than management, hire auditors. The act also mandates that a financial expert be a member of the audit committee, establishes an attorney's duty to report misconduct, prohibits loans to officers and directors, and establishes a new Public Company Accounting Oversight Board (PCAOB) for the accounting industry involved in preparing public offerings. Particular attention will be paid to the new economic crime resulting from improper reporting. The agenda for future reform is then laid out. United Kingdom post-Enron proposals for changes to corporate law are included here as is the proposed EU directive on the supervision of financial conglomerates.

Chapter 7 will consider the plight of Japan, which has a debt of 130 percent of gross domestic product (GDP) (the United States was griping when Japan's debt was 79 percent in 1992), which proves that Keynesian economics does not work in the absence of real tangible structural reform or that it is inapplicable to Japan, which continues to pass consumption taxes in the midst of huge spending bills. Japan is intent on maintaining its trade surplus and remains indifferent to the plight of consumers. The inability or refusal of Japan or Asia in general to develop a consumer society has led to an unsustainable U.S. trade deficit, unsustainable only in that it has developed into an unsustainable current account deficit.

Chapter 8 considers evolving trends in corporate governance. This includes: the implementation of Sarbanes-Oxley and related provisions in the United States; and United Kingdom proposals for director independence, reform of the accounting profession, and the criminalization of securities fraud that followed in the wake of Sarbanes-Oxley in the United States.

Consequently the conclusion, while summarizing the best direction for the EU, the United States, and Japan in standards of corporate governance and financial reporting, will also propose a complete restructuring of the Bretton Woods Agreement based on the necessity of medium-term balanced current accounts.

NOTES

1. Bank for International Settlements (BIS), "BIS Quarterly Review: International Banking and Financial Market Developments" (September 2002), p. 29.

2. Bank for International Settlements, "BIS Quarterly Review: International Banking and Financial Market Developments" (December 2001), p. 29.

3. Richard Herring, "Disaster Myopia in International Banking," Princeton Essays in International Finance no. 164 (1986), pp. 29–30.

4. Ferdinand Pecora, "Wall Street under Oath: The Story of Our Modern Money Changers," cited in Row Chernow, *The House of Morgan: An American Banking Dynasty and the Rise of Modern Finance* (Atlantic Monthly Press, 1990), p. 375.

5. *See* chapter 5, "Corporate Governance."

6. *See* conclusion notes 1 and 2 and accompanying text.

CHAPTER 1

United Kingdom Financial Services Regulation in the Context of EU Financial Market Regulation: The Financial Services Authority Über Alles?

By 1986, a European initiative in the financial services sector was inevitable. The United Kingdom cobbled together its various self-regulatory organizations (SRO) under one umbrella under the Financial Services Act 1986. By the mid-1990s, the existing structure was far too simplistic for the demands of the age and the regulators' powers were insufficient. These concerns gave birth to the Financial Services Authority (FSA), which began absorbing powers in 1996. By 1997, it had absorbed most securities regulation functions and become the regulatory supervisor of credit institutions. Eventually, it would absorb 22 SROs, including accounting and law (to the extent these involve financial services), insurance, investment trusts, building societies, and other things not nailed down. Its existence was fabricated piecemeal, culminating in the Financial Services and Markets Act 2000, the most comprehensive financial legislation known to man, giving the FSA dominion over all things financial, if not the beasts of the field. Its enactment has not been without confusion, and its implementation has been fraught with bureaucratic rigmarole, the most egregious of which is its habit of issuing consultative papers, incorporating by reference all other consultative papers, each covering a wide range of issues. Most troubling is that its nexus of concerns tend to reflect the bull market during which it originated (see for example, the amendment to the listing particulars).[1] In part, its enactment was clearly political, an attempt to define regulatory concepts in the European Union (EU) arena to ward off the leadership of other continental regulators, the United Kingdom having already proved irrelevant to the success or failure of the euro. Nonetheless, it should be noted that the city of London is still home to by far the deepest and most comprehensive capital markets in Europe, second only to Wall Street, and even surpassing Wall Street in forex and international bond issues; its regulators are the only European regulators with the breadth of knowledge to regulate such markets. Continental European regulators, particularly in the arena of securities markets, can only be said to pale in comparison.

In July 1988, the Group of 10 countries (G-10 countries) signed an agreement to abide by common rules for determining risk-based capital depending on the creditworthiness of the counterparty to transactions. This agreement, also known as the Basel Convergence Agreement (the G-10 agreement), forms the basis of the EU directives allowing for a single passport for banks throughout the EU. Compared to banks, investment services firms engaged in securities activities have traditionally held less, albeit more liquid, capital as a percentage of assets. Consequently, the EU Capital Adequacy Directive (CAD) will require less risk-based capital for security activities of banks and securities firms.

The Financial Services Act of 1986 required the securities activities of most banks and all other securities activities to be regulated by the Securities Investments Board (SIB) and self-regulatory organizations depending upon the form of security business in which a firm is engaged. This scheme was understandably considered a regulatory maze by European banks.

Regulation of financial services will never be global. Rather, globalization is a trend, along with regionalization best characterized by free trade associations such as the North American Free Trade Association, which stands at the other end of the continuum from an individual country's establishment of rules attempting to create a distinct national framework in spite of the tendency toward world financial integration. While global harmonization and mutual recognition of financial regulation continue apace, it is necessary to understand that national and regional regulators have distinct criteria that clash with global harmonization and mutual recognition.

As domestic markets give way to global markets, the EU has been at the forefront of enacting legislation that results in transnational regulation of financial institutions, the objective of which is the free movement of capital throughout the EU. The single market in financial services allows community-wide branching of credit institutions and investment services as well as provides for mutual recognition of listing particulars and prospectuses,[2] all of which are part of the European single market program.[3] This chapter will consider the way market risk in financial services is addressed in the context of EU law and will explore the conflict between national (member state) legal regulation and EU law, with emphasis on the law of the United Kingdom.

The United Kingdom has developed sophisticated regulatory structures in such diverse areas as consolidated supervision of banking, securitization, regulation of exchanges, and solvency of members of financial markets. The U.K.

regulatory structure, which is second only to the United States' in its comprehensive regulation of securities, entrenched its premiere position by enacting the Financial Services Act of 1986 in 1988. A major step was undertaken toward centralizing authority in establishing the Securities and Investments Board, which served as an umbrella organization for investment services self-regulatory organizations. A major obstacle to EU financial integration is the separate cultures of banking and investment banking in the United Kingdom and the limited continental experience with securities markets. While it is generally perceived that the single passport for credit institutions provided for by the EU Second Banking Directive (SBDI) established universal banking (i.e., banks that perform deposit and securities functions in the same corporate entity), this may not be the case. Furthermore, there may not be explosive growth in securities markets on the Continent in spite of the worldwide tendency toward pooled asset financing and away from tailored banking relationships, and continental banks may continue to perform mainly traditional banking functions.

THE LEGAL STRUCTURE OF THE EUROPEAN COMMUNITY

The EU has its origins in the Treaty of Rome, which promulgated four principles called the Four Freedoms: Freedom of Movement of Capital, Labor, Goods, and Services. In the context of financial services, certain provisions of the Treaty of Rome are particularly relevant: the provision allowing for the right of establishment in other member states,[4] the freedom to provide services throughout the EU,[5] and national (nondiscriminatory) treatment of member state institutions.[6]

The EU, even after the Single European Act,[7] which, although altering voting procedures from unanimity to qualified majority vote,[8] still allowed member states to opt out in cases of extreme national exigencies relating to noneconomic matters and fiscal matters,[9] differs significantly from the U.S. federal system; however, the EU involves measures of contractual obligations and systematic law not found in other international treaty organizations such as the General Agreement on Tariffs and Trade (GATT). Like the International Monetary Fund (IMF), the EU Council of Europe has a weighted voting policy and, as in the IMF, more powerful nations play a disproportionately larger part in deciding issues.

The Single European Act formalized the role of the European Parliament (EP) in the decision-making process of the EU. Under the new cooperation procedures that apply to the harmonization of laws, amendments to the Treaty of Rome proposed by the parliament must be taken into account by the EU Commission and now shares the right of codecision. However, ratification of an amendment that is not supported by the commission requires unanimous approval by the council.[10] The Single European Act also sets forth goals in other areas generally not included in the Treaty of Rome. In the monetary area, the Single European Act committed the member states to further cooperation and, if necessary, to institutional changes "in order to ensure the convergence of economic and monetary policy" and to the creation of a single European market for financial services.[11]

The council (consisting of ministers from the member states responsible for the legislation considered) is the legislative body that determines by qualifying majority vote whether commission recommendations will become law. Although the power of the European Court of Justice (ECJ) in interpreting the Treaty of Rome is not completely delineated, it is quite clear that the ECJ may mandate an approach for mutual recognition of products among member states.[12]

The powers of the European Parliament have been extended by subsequent treaties, particularly the Treaty of Amsterdam. Under the co-decision procedure, the EP shares equal power with the European Council. If these institutions disagree, a conciliation committee—made up of equal numbers of members of parliament and of the council, with the commission present—convenes, seeking a compromise on a text that the council and parliament can both subsequently endorse. If this conciliation does not result in an agreement, the parliament can reject the proposal outright by an absolute majority. The co-decision procedure, which strengthens the role of the EP as co-legislator, applies to a wide range of issues (39 legal bases in the EU treaty), such as the free movement of workers, consumer protection, education, culture, health, and trans-European networks.

The consultation procedure requires an opinion from the EP before the council can adopt a legislative proposal from the commission. Neither the commission nor the council is obliged to accept the amendments listed in the opinion of the EP. Once the EP has given its opinion, the council can adopt the proposal without amendments or adopt it in an amended form. However, the EP can refuse to give an opinion. The consultation procedure applies to agriculture (price review), taxation, competition, harmonization of legislation not related to the single market, industrial policy, aspects of social and environmental policy (subject to unanimity), most aspects pertaining to the creation of an area of freedom, security and justice, and adoption of general rules and principles for comitology. For the purpose of the approximation of laws and regulations, this procedure also applies to a new framework-decision instrument created by the Amsterdam Treaty under the third pillar.[13]

In March 1998 the EU formally launched the process that would make enlargement possible. It embraces the following 13 applicant countries: Bulgaria, Cyprus, the Czech Republic, Estonia, Hungary, Latvia, Lithuania, Malta, Poland, Romania, the Slovak Republic, Slovenia, and Turkey.[14] Negotiations with all countries except Turkey are underway, and 6 countries—Cyprus, the Czech Republic, Estonia, Hungary, Poland, and Slovenia—have already been recommended for inclusion by the European Commission.

EU law is accepted as prevailing over national law[15] and judgments and preliminary rulings of the ECJ based on community law are binding and enforceable and have direct effect in member states.[16]

In *EC Commission v. Germany*,[17] the ECJ, while striking down a German law requiring permanent establishment of insurance carriers in order to provide services, did find that, in the case of insurance, host country controls were permissible in the public interest. This ruling can be extended to other areas including banking and, to a lesser extent, to investment services that require similar investor protection measures. In the area of investment services in the United Kingdom, such investor protection measures appear in the form of conduct of business rules (CBR).[18]

The judicial process in the EU has not been the leitmotif of vast changes in law as is the case in the United States[19] and will only supplement in a broad, objective, purposive way the progressive consensual process of creating a single market. In this regard, in spite of the supremacy of EU law over municipal law, EU law stands midway between the sort of judicial process that occurs within a municipal legal system and that which occurs under an international organization, such as the law of the International Monetary Fund, in which weighted voting and administrative decisions are frequently eschewed in favor of consensus building.

EU law at the highest level is by way of directives, liberally worded documents enacted by the council pursuant to a commission recommendation, that are intended to be implemented in the national law of the member states by way of national legislation. The commission has the exclusive right to propose directives, but their implementation is governed by the principle of subsidiarity, which is precisely defined in the proposed treaty on European Union[20] and is part of the common law of the EU. Directives do not in themselves have direct effect in the member states, and variance in the wording of the implementation of directives in national legislation may create discrepancies among member state laws. However, directives are conceptually binding, and all national laws are subject to review by the ECJ.

FINANCIAL SYSTEMS IN THE UNITED KINGDOM AND GERMANY

The principal difference in the financial arena between Germany and the United States and the United Kingdom is that Germany is a universal banking country—a country in which banks perform most investment service functions, while the U.K. financial system is a hybrid of the universal banking system and the U.S. system, which separates banking from investment services, although this separation has been largely eliminated.[21] Other continental countries have a system that tends toward universal banking and also have the high leverage that typifies the absence of non-bank-dominated securities markets within such countries.[22] As shall be discussed in "Corporate Governance in the EU" later in this chapter, the United Kingdom has a separate regulatory structure to govern investment services, and the Investment Services Directive (ISD) is directed largely to U.K. concerns.

The gap between the economic systems of countries with high leverage, that is, high debt to equity ratio, such as Germany and Japan, and low-leverage countries, such as the United States and the United Kingdom, makes international agreement all the more difficult.[23] In Germany, two-thirds of all liabilities arise from borrowing from banks, whereas in the United Kingdom the figure is one-quarter.[24] In Germany, three-fourths of bonds are bank-issued bonds (debts initially taken on board by banks as borrowers) whereas the comparable figure for the United Kingdom is one-tenth.[25] The result in Germany and other universal banking countries (which are invariably those with high leverage) is that banks dominate the securities markets and are able to set the prime rate for lending to prime borrowers. That rate will in all likelihood be higher than that charged in the London interbank market and the eurobond market and will be particularly higher than the commercial paper rate.[26]

In universal banking countries, banks may practice additional monitoring supervision because they frequently own large equity stakes[27] in the borrowers. Borrowers are recompensed to an extent by the fact that in these countries a lower dividend is usually required than in capital market countries such as the United Kingdom and the United States. The result is a higher price to earnings ratio for the shares in universal banking countries than in capital market countries. Under the Basel convergence, which sets capital risk weighting for international banks, banks are entitled to count toward capital 45 percent of the difference between the book value and market value of the securities that they own,[28] thereby further rewarding them for their lower income-producing securities.

The high leverage in universal banking countries and Japan (which is not a universal banking country) cannot be adequately accounted for by tax considerations[29] or the advantage of debt over equity. Apparently, the ineffable investor-company relationships are the only possible answer. In general, three factors characterize such systems: (1) the simultaneous holding of debt and equity claims; (2) the similar proportion of debt and equity; and (3) government policy.[30] German and Japanese banks have traditionally held significant equity holdings[31] and equity shares (about one-third Japanese and two-fifths German shares are held by nonfinancial enterprises),[32] thereby creating significant cross-holdings.[33]

Frequently, national laws enhance the distinction in national economic systems within the EU, for example, in the arena of takeovers. The proposed takeover directive[34] will ostensibly regulate the terms and conditions of takeovers in the EU. In the United Kingdom, takeovers are regulated by the Takeover Panel, which is a self-regulatory (i.e., nongovernmental) body, and hostile takeovers are, proportional to the economy, almost as prevalent as in the United States.

French and German law confer particular rights on employees and their representatives. In France, employees, trade unions, and workers' councils have the right to be consulted about a range of corporate activities.[35] In Germany, representatives of employees and trade unions have 50 percent of the seats on the supervisory boards of stock corporations (AGs) having more than 2,000 employees. In addition, workers' councils have rights relating to terms of employment and dismissal, and members of the supervisory board can be replaced only with a 75 percent vote of the shareholders.[36] French companies are able to place serious restrictions on transfers of shares and voting rights of shareholders.[37] These issues are discussed in detail in "Corporate Governance in the EU" below.

REGULATION OF INTERNATIONAL BANKING

The International Debt Crisis and the Birth of Derivative Instruments

The regulation of international banking—as well as of other financial services—took on new dimensions in the 1980s. The current dialogue on banking regulation has been carried out at an international level. The urgency of international actions, like the coordination of exchange rate policy in the monetary sphere proper, was precipitated by the proliferation of new financial instruments in the wake of overexposure of international banks, particularly U.S. banks, to less developed countries (LDC). In 1982, the illiquidity of U.S. loans to LDC created a need for additional financing for banks,[38] thereby enhancing the eurobond market, as distinct from the syndicated loan market.

Commercial banks are perhaps the major source of international liquidity. The ratio of their capital to assets is a measure of their solvency. In order to bolster their supply of capital, banks issued floating rate notes in the Euromarket, creating the threshold activity for the eurobond market and ultimately enabling corporate borrowers to issue debt at far lower rates than in syndicated loans. While banks earned reasonable profit margins on bond underwriting, they were subject to competition from securities houses. The process of disintermediation continued and led to the emergence of the European commercial paper (ECP) market, discussed below.[39] The LDC crisis also caused the development of off-balance sheet financing techniques, mostly as a self-induced response by banks to the insolvency of their loans and also in response to government regulation. These methods were successful in reducing the assets appearing on banks' balance sheets, thus freeing up capital that could then be used for other purposes, generating new fees.

The purpose of financial regulation is to provide a legal framework that will lessen the possibility of shock in the financial system; however, it may be that regulation can occur only after crisis. Prudential supervision is dedicated to the opposing concept. The 1982 shock has left in its wake a bewildering array of financial instruments that required complex and insightful regulation. The debt crisis created the rush toward off-balance sheet financing and caused the expansion of the eurobond market. Banks required new sources of capital, which they obtained in large measure through use of the floating rate note (FRN), which consists of a perpetual sector and a dated sector. But the market was in large measure driven by banks needing to service floating rate business and lacking the requisite capital because of the debt crisis.[40] This market collapsed in 1986 amid fears that the Basel Committee would not allow perpetual notes to be considered part of capital under its capital adequacy solvency measure. (In fact, these notes were allowed to be considered part of tier-two capital.)[41] A second reason for the collapse was the expansion of the ECP market, which imported the U.S. commercial paper concept. There were several advantages to ECP: the turnaround time was two days as opposed to seven, and A-rated companies could often borrow at sub-Libid levels as opposed to higher sales commanded by medium-term FRNs[42] (particularly if the ECP was enhanced by note issuance facilities [NIFs] or revolving underwriting facilities [RUFs]), and ECP did not require direct underwriting, therefore making it less expensive than FRNs to issue.[43]

European commercial paper came into existence because the banking crisis had called into question the creditworthiness of banks and lenders. A-rated companies came to be considered better credit risks than banks, thereby giving corporate borrowers an advantage over their intermediaries.[44] This disintermediation process poses grave dangers for the international banking system as it causes both a qualitative and a quantitative deterioration of banking loan portfolios.[45]

The geometric rise in international capital market volume has contributed significantly to interdependence in the international economic system. This is especially true with regard to the growth of derivative instruments, including interest rate[46] and currency swaps[47] and financial futures.[48]

Dollar denomination of new financial instruments[49] enshrines the dollar as the world's central currency. This fact, taken together with the United States' lead in financial innovation and deregulation, rules out any unilateral EU initiative in financial market regulation, as U.S. exchanges and the dollar denomination of financial instruments continue the pattern of U.S. domination of financial markets and, consequently, financial regulation. But the United States and the EU, in the late 1980s, were about to embark on new terrain in international regulation.

The EU Single Market in Banking: The Basel Convergence and the Second Banking Directive

By the mid-1980s, not only exposure to LDC risk but the off-balance sheet financing that had followed in its wake had aroused international concern.

Thus, it became apparent to the Anglo-American regulators that something had to be done in the way of relevant regulation. The Anglo-American agreement led to the G-10 Agreement,[50] which is far and away the most important agreement in the international financial arena since Bretton Woods.[51] On December 30, 1989, the EU concluded the SBDI, the Solvency Ratio Directive (SRD) and the Own Funds Directive (OFD), which is largely based on the G-10 agreement.[52]

The underlying principle of the G-10 agreement and these directives is a capital adequacy ratio for banks of 8 percent capital to assets, with assets being risk-weighted.[53] The G-10 agreement, the SBDI, and its corollary directives (the SRD and the OFD)[54] are broadly similar, although the G-10 agreement concerns only international banks while the SBDI and its corollary directives concern all EU banks. The only real difference in the risk weights attached to assets is regarding claims against domestic central government securities and against official sector institutions within the country or within Organization for Economic Cooperation and Development (OECD) countries. This discretion is afforded by the G-10 agreement, while the SRD weights central government obligations at a 0 percent weight.[55]

In their determination of what constitutes a bank's capital (defined as "Own Funds" in the EU directive), the G-10 agreement and the EU banking directives are fairly similar; however, some important distinctions do emerge. Both the G-10 agreement and the SRD require 8 percent of capital to assets ratio by the end of 1992. Both the SBDI and G-10 agreement allow different kinds of hybrid capital instruments, including noncumulative preferred stock and subordinated term debt, to be included within capital,[56] although only to a maximum of 50 percent of the core (tier-one) capital element. The OFD also allows general provisions and reevaluation reserves to be included to 100 percent of tier-one capital[57] and certain kinds of fixed term cumulative preferred and subordinated loan capital to a point of 50 percent tier-one capital.[58] What within the G-10 agreement is described as hybrid debt capital instruments (i.e., perpetual debt instruments in the United States) would be treated similarly under Article 3 of the OFD, in which capital freely available to the credit institution is included as tier-one capital.

Under the G-10 agreement and the OFD, subordinated term debt of over five years' duration will be counted as tier-two capital. To debt of five years or less, a discount of 20 percent per year will be applied. Both the G-10 agreement and the OFD require the deduction of certain categories of investment, including goodwill, from capital.[59] Under both the G-10 agreement and the SRD, loan loss reserves are limited to 1.25 percent of tier-two capital.[60]

The differences between the G-10 agreement and the OFD are difficult to spot; however, here are a few examples. The OFD will allow only the inclusion of interim profits, that is, current year earnings, if such amount is net of any foreseeable charge or dividend.[61] The G-10 agreement has a two-tier system of capital. The first tier consists primarily of a bank's paid-up capital and disclosed reserves while the second tier of capital includes general provisions, that is, general loan loss reserves and reevaluation reserves, which include hidden reserves and shares of transferable securities that may be marked up to their market value with a discount of 55 percent of the difference between historic cost book value and market value.[62] There are no undisclosed reserves under EU law but, because banks own marketable securities, there is considerable unrealized market value of shares held at book value.[63]

Transferable securities must be held either as financial fixed assets or as part of a portfolio trading book.[64] This is, in fact, the first formulation under EU law of a trading book option important under the CAD, which is discussed below.[65] The higher value adjustment for capital adequacy purposes appears to state that under EU regulation a member state may include the full market value of transferable securities as tier-one capital; in contrast, the G-10 agreement requires a 55 percent discount.

The risk weights of capital as well as the capital to assets ratio are all products of compromise, but they serve as a starting point for further international agreement, particularly with respect to off-balance sheet assets. Under both the SRD and the G-10 agreement, exposure to the private sector is listed at 100 percent weight. Under both the SRD and the G-10 agreement a standby letter of credit will require a 50 percent risk weighting.[66] One to four family residential mortgages bear a 50 percent weight under both the SRD and the G-10 agreement.[67] As far as swaps contracts are concerned, a 0.5 percent weight is attached to interest rate swaps and 5 percent to currency swaps multiplied by the risk-weighted category of the counterparts as an add-on to replacement cost, although a higher weighting can be opted for, which will not require a previous replacement cost component.[68] Novation will allow a netting of hedged positions whereas assignment or participation agreements will not. Under both the G-10 agreement and SBDI, non-OECD government debts are rated at 100 percent risk, hardly likely to provide liquidity for developing countries.[69] Thus, the document has severe economic implications beyond the G-10 agreement and suggests the interlinking of trade, monetary, and financial law. Instruments that are traded on an exchange and marked to market are exempted under the G-10 agreement. The G-10 agreement relegates many off-balance sheet items to 50 percent risk weights multiplied by the risk weight attached to the counterparty.[70] Certain risk participations will incur a weight with respect to the residual liability. Several aspects of banking regulation including deposit insurance, interest rate ceilings on deposits, and reserve requirements are not included in the subject matter covered by the SBDI and its corollary directives.

Other forms of residual liabilities will evoke different treatment in different EU countries. One example is securitization. Securitization, the process whereby loans or receivables are pooled and then sold for the purpose of moving assets off balance sheets to improve the capital adequacy of the seller, is not directly addressed by the G-10 agreement or the SBDI. Such receivables must have a reasonably ascertainable cash flow and include mortgages and credit card receivables. The United Kingdom requires consolidated reporting under the 1989 Companies Act (therefore requiring on-balance sheet treatment) of securitized assets where a parent has over 50 percent interest in the subsidiary or control thereof.[71] This use made of the EU Eighth Company Law Directive[72] is illustrative of the manifold ways in which EU financial law is incorporated into member state legal systems; U.K. law is particularly important in this regard as the United Kingdom is the European leader in financial services and financial innovation.[73] Securitization is discussed in detail in "The FSA before the Financial Services and Markets Act" later in this chapter.

Two real problems emerge when evaluating financial innovation. First, banking traditionally involved rule of thumb pricing, but the subtlety of today's instruments defies proper pricing.[74] NIFs, for instance, may seriously jeopardize a bank's liquidity because the time at which such facilities will be drawn is unknown, although a material adverse change clause may provide some protection for banks. Second, no overall strategy exists for assessing interest rate risk on overall portfolio investment, according to the Bank for International Settlements (BIS) report on banking innovation.[75]

The SBDI requires implementation in the member state in which the credit institution is authorized. Complex amendments of national legislation are therefore necessary. In the United Kingdom, the implementation of the SBDI has been addressed in a consultative document issued by the Treasury and the Department of Trade and Industry (DTI).[76] Specifically, a single authorization covering all the activities listed in Annex B of the SBDI for banks and their OFD (Article 18) subsidiaries is needed to make use of the passport to do business elsewhere in the EU. This requires that different authorizations granted by various U.K. supervisory authorities be replaced by a single authorization by the Bank of England, so that the Bank of England can exercise authority over non-deposit-taking activities carried out by credit institutions elsewhere in the EU. Later, the Financial Services Authority assumed dominion over credit institutions. However, there will continue to be interaction between the responsibilities of the bank and those of other U.K. regulators.[77] It was also necessary to make this authorization the exclusive route for passportable institutions to carry on annex activities in other member states. A new definition of subsidiary undertaking and the current definition of parent undertaking must be introduced into legislation.[78] The current definition of subsidiary is much narrower than the term used in the directive. It was also necessary to redefine deposit-taking institutions under Section 3 of the Banking Act of 1987. Primary legislation may be needed to make the 1987 Banking Act consistent with the European Communities Act of 1972 in regard to the question of punishable offenses that relate to the powers of banking supervisors to obtain information and carry on investigations.[79]

The SBDI requires effective market access to third country markets[80] (which is mirrored in the ISD).[81] This is also the principle articulated in the financial services component of the Uruguay Round.[82]

INVESTMENT SERVICES: THE FINAL FRONTIER

Prospectus and Listing Particular Directives

The ISD includes the right of establishment and the freedom to provide services as guaranteed by the Treaty of Rome.[83] Most important, member states may require that certain transactions relating to services be carried out on a regulated market, provided the investor is a habitual resident or established in that member state and the transaction involves an instrument dealt in on a regulated market.[84]

Additional EU legislation relating to securities exchanges includes a directive making mandatory mutual recognition of listing particulars (LP),[85] which amends earlier directives the goal of which was the harmonization of listing particulars.[86] Another directive provides for the mutual recognition of prospectus requirements for unlisted securities, except certain eurosecurities not generally the subject of an advertising campaign (the Mutual Recognition of Prospectuses [MRP] Directive).[87] The largely unregulated eurobond market will remain unregulated.

The cumulative effect of the various LP and MRP directives is that

1. listing particulars for exchanges of member states must comply with the minimum requirement of the Listing Particulars Directive (LPD), must be drawn up and approved by the competent authorities in member states, and must be recognized as listing particulars in all member states;
2. where official listing is not sought, offers to the public (however defined) must, unless they fall within the exceptions in the MRP, comply with the minimum requirement of the MRP, and public offering prospectuses drawn up to the requirements of the LPD and approved must be recognized both as listing particulars and as public offering prospectuses in all member states.[88]

Notably, the MRP directive does not define "offer to the public"; thus, this definition under U.K. law would be governed by Part 5 of the Financial Services Act of 1986. The absence of this definition is not in itself a major failing of the EU legislation as it is intended to allow freedom of each member state to determine in its own terms what an offer to the public is or what minimum policing requirements are. The DTI, in its consultative document, essentially says that the prudential standards for issuance of securities that are not the subject of a public offering will be fulfilled by the requirement under Section 57 of the Financial Services Act of 1986 that authorized persons approve the content of advertisements.[89] Authorization is also the principal standard under the Financial Services and Markets Act (2000), which supercedes the Financial

Services Act of 1986.[90] Listed securities that are public offers will have to comply with the MRP directive.

The MRP goes beyond the offer-for-sale-type situations envisaged by the definition of secondary offer[91] and would cover a situation in which a share was offered to the public several years later[92] (Section 160 of the Financial Services Act of 1986 might also cover such a situation). It is certainly to be queried as to whether the absence of any clear restriction on public resale under U.K. or EU law represents a gap in investor protection. Furthermore, offers of short-dated debentures are not deemed to be offers to the public.[93]

The MRP directive list of exclusions is far larger than that provided for under U.S. securities law.[94] Disclosure requirements under the MRP directive[95] are considerably less specific than comparable disclosure requirements under Sections 5 and 11 of the U.S. Securities and Exchange Act. Under the MRP, there is mutual recognition by all member states; however, member states may require the prospectus to include information specific to the market of the country in which the public offer is being made, concerning, in particular, the income tax system, the financial organizations retained to act as paying agent for the issuer in that country, and the way in which notices to investors are published.[96] In the case of an offering for transferable securities that are to be admitted to official listing on a stock exchange, the prospectus must comport with the LPD and at the same time be adapted to the circumstances of a public offer.[97] This information is more detailed than that required under the MRP directive.[98] The MRP directive must be contrasted with U.S. prospectus requirements and liability for failure to disclose material information. Even to the extent that the United Kingdom has interpreted its domestic disclosure laws through a judicial line of decisions, these will be irrelevant to a non-U.K. firm doing business in the United Kingdom, which will be held instead to the disclosure requirements of the MRP (together with the domestic law of another member state that may, under a conflict of law approach, be interpreted by a U.K. court) with appeal to the ECJ. This level of investor protection is lower than that afforded by the U.S. courts' 60 years' history of interpreting the disclosure requirements of the Securities and Exchange Acts.

The LPD and the MRP are feasible only to the extent of the harmonization and mutual recognition of accounting principles used in the preparation of financial statements. Of the directives enacted on the harmonization of accounting principles, the most important are the Fourth Directive of Company Law[99] and the Seventh Directive of Company Law.[100] The Fourth Directive of Company Law presents a compromise between the legalistic (statute-based) approach to accounting and financial reporting in continental Europe and the true and fair value approach prevailing in the English-speaking countries. It allows for a choice among many alternative treatments and gives member states options after implementation.[101] There are no requirements for cash flow statements or statements of changes in shareholders' equity. The income statement may be shown in four different forms, each of which is laid down in a separate article of the Fourth Directive of Company Law.[102] For measuring assets and liabilities, the Fourth Directive of Company Law uses the term "valuation rules."[103]

The Seventh Directive of Company Law requires consolidated financial statements for related companies. Fundamentally, the Seventh Directive of Company Law requires consolidation where either the parent or the subsidiary is a limited liability company (i.e., a corporation), regardless of the location of its registered office. The legal concept of control, which is broadly defined, determines the obligation to consolidate. Article 13 of the Seventh Directive of Company Law specifies conditions allowing exclusion from the EU consolidation obligation.[104] Article 14 of the directive allows exclusion from consolidation if there are demonstratively dissimilar activities at the subsidiary level. Article 7 of the Seventh Directive of Company Law provides for mandatory exemption from consolidation of EU parents' undertakings that are themselves 100-percent-owned subsidiaries of another EU parent. Where the ultimate parent is an EU undertaking, exemption from some consolidation is possible.[105] Where the parent is headquartered outside the EU, exemption from EU subconsolidations may be allowed.[106] Articles 16 to 23 of the Seventh Directive of Company Law address consolidation methods.[107] Article 34 deals with disclosure and involves considerable detail, including the disclosure of persons, registered offices of all related entities, and a full description of consolidated net turnover broken down by categories of activity and geographical markets and tax considerations reflected in the financial statement.

The directive concerning annual financial and consolidated statements of financial institutions is an extension of the Fourth and Seventh Directives of Company Law,[108] is tailored to financial institutions, adds other considerations, such as marking to market any instruments that are part of a trading portfolio, and begins to consider new financial instruments (particularly in forward transactions). The United Kingdom has implemented the Fourth and Seventh Company Directives of Company Law through the Companies Acts of 1981, 1985, and 1989.[109] The one principal change is the requirement for geographic segment reporting.[110]

The ISD requires member states to enable access to membership to exchanges located within their borders.[111] The mutual recognition of listing particulars mandates the minimum as well as maximum conditions to which issuers will be subject.[112]

The Capital Adequacy Directive for Securities Firms and Credit Institutions

The CAD is analogous to the various banking directives regulating capital. It is founded on the assumption that securities firms and securities activities of banks have short-term credit exposure and most of the instruments traded are marked to market. Generally, the directive regulates position risk and provides an overall safeguard for systemic risk. Position risk is the risk from the net position of the securities firm, and the capital requirement is 8 percent, which is considered general risk. Also, an additional 2 percent to 4 percent risk weighting will be assigned against gross equity positions depending upon the diversification of the portfolio in order to capture specific risk. Interest rate risk is also divided into specific and general risk, depending upon the issuer.[113]

These approaches enshrine what is entitled the building block approach, under which different kinds of risk are added together. The earlier comprehensive approach looked at a securities position less arithmetically and in one stage rather than at two positions. The Committee on Banking and Supervisory Practices, which has been chaired by the United States under the auspices of the Bank for International Settlements and the International Organization of Securities Commissions (IOSCO), is the principal forum in which these issues are being discussed.

The definition of a qualifying issuer of equity or debt allows regulators to consider securities that are neither listed nor rated as qualifying items, taking into account the characteristics of certain markets.[114] Article 7 aims to provide a detailed regulatory framework for the supervision of market risks on a consolidated basis pursuant to the approach envisioned in the directive on consolidated supervision of credit institutions (CSD).[115] The CAD preempts the CSD where the group does not contain credit institutions.[116] Groups not containing credit institutions may waive the principles of compulsory consolidation if certain strict conditions are met.[117] Specifically, entities of a group located in a single member state may offset their positions, even though they do not comply with capital requirements on a solo basis. Such offset is allowed if some entities of a group are established in another member state and comply with the CAD requirements on a solo basis.[118]

Under Article 14, a review clause is established to allow incorporation of developments in the work of the Basel group of banking supervisors and IOSCO, which is carrying out parallel work in the area of capital adequacy.[119] Under Annex 3 of the CAD, institutions may apply different weights for calculating capital requirements against foreign exchange risks in order to take into account the existence of groups of currencies characterized by high degrees of correlation, most notably in the exchange rate mechanism (ERM). Under the CAD, the trading book is made mandatory for both credit institutions and investment services[120] and the rules laid down in the SRD are also applicable to investment firms in respect of their non-trading book.[121] Alternative regulatory capital (i.e., capital that is related to the trading book) is defined in a very similar fashion. Under the CAD, credit institutions and investment firms may use tier-three capital up to 150 percent of tier-one capital as defined in the Own Funds Directive. However, credit institution utilization of tier three beyond 150 percent of tier-one capital as defined in the Own Funds Directive requires authorization from the competent authorities, while the application of the 250 percent of tier-one ceiling involves compulsory deduction of illiquid assets.[122] The provisions for large exposures in the CAD are fairly similar to those in the Large Exposure Directive (LED)[123] for credit institutions, with some adaptations. Exposures to a single client or a group of connected clients arising solely from the trading book may exceed the limit contained in the LED subject to several conditions: (1) for a period of 10 days an additional holding of own funds is required;[124] (2) after the 10th day, additional capital, the amount of which is linked to the size of the excess, must be set aside;[125] and (3) overall limits on individual and aggregate exposures must be respected.[126]

The CAD offered major incentives for firms to move many assets from their bankbook to their trading book, or, alternatively, to issue debt and equity securities (i.e., to securitize their assets) in order to achieve the lower risk ratings for position risk at the higher gearing allowed for trading books (tier-three capital). Consider a short-term loan to a nongovernmental entity[127] or short-term commercial paper. Even a mortgage that bears only a 50 percent risk weighting may be preferable to hold as part of a securitized trading portfolio.[128]

Tier-three capital, as distinguished from tier-two capital, includes the net profits or losses for the year to date[129] and subordinated loan capital having an original maturity of at least two years (versus at least five years maturity requirement with discounts thereafter for tier-two capital). Thus, the advantages of tier-three capital are its maturity period and the fact that it can be up to 250 percent of tier-one capital for own funds of credit institutions.[130]

The trading book option of the CAD applies only to certain activities of investment firms. The specific assignment of risk has been addressed by the building block approach (general and specific risk), and the netting requirements (of long and short positions) are supplemented by a new system that breaks down a long futures position,[131] for example, to a combination of a loan maturing on the delivery date of a futures contract and the holding of an underlying security. (Options are treated similarly.)[132] A broadly diversified stock index future that hedges underlying equities will have a 0 percent specific risk weighting while the underlying equities will attract a 2 percent specific risk. Member states are responsible for ensuring that additional capital is maintained to cover situations where indexes do not move in uniformity with underlying positions.

A formulation is set forth for underwriting positions that are subscribed by third parties, reducing net positions for the first five working days of an underwriting, and unsettled transactions that do not cause exposure to a firm shall have no capital requirement.[133] Large exposure to a particular client or group of connected clients is limited to 25 percent.[134]

Firms would not be subject to consolidated supervision if they deduct participation and other investments from their own funds.[135] Certain assets may have been held for a long time but if they are traded it will be difficult to categorize such assets.[136]

Consolidated Supervision

Another important distinction between the OFD and the G-10 agreement is in the treatment of subsidiaries. The OFD requires national regulators to deduct from capital all investments by banks in other banks (including equity and bonds) that exceed 10 percent of capital. G-10 requires banks to apply a 100 percent weight to such investments, thereby forcing banks to keep 8 percent of capital on hand against such risks,[137] a requirement less than one-tenth as strenuous as the OFD requirement that all investments by banks that exceed 10 percent in other nonconsolidated banks (including equity and bonds) be deducted from capital;[138] but, the G-10 agreement includes all non-consolidated subsidiaries, not just those over 10 percent.

No definition of consolidation is given in the G-10 agreement, highlighting the distinction between an international agreement and a legal regime. The SBDI is subject to an earlier (1983) Consolidated Supervision Directive requiring consolidated supervision of credit institutions.[139] The supervision of credit institutions on a consolidated basis has been supplemented by a second directive on the Consolidated Supervision of Credit Institutions Directive, which involves consolidation of banking groups, including financial holding companies.[140] However, it was the 1983 directive that began the process of consolidated supervision. The clearest statement regarding which institutions are to be consolidated appeared in the 1986 directive (the Eighth Directive on Company Law on the annual and consolidated accounts of banks and other financial institutions),[141] which provides rules of consolidation derived in large measure from the Seventh Directive of Company Law.[142]

The 1983 directive states that a credit institution having a 50 percent ownership participation in another credit institution or financial institution "shall require either full or pro rata consolidation of the financial institutions concerned."[143]

Under the SRD the solvency ratio of credit institutions that are parent undertakings shall be calculated on a consolidated basis by the method laid down in the two consolidated supervision directives.[144] The authorities responsible for authorizing and supervising a parent undertaking may also require the calculations of an unconsolidated ratio with respect to the parent undertaking. When the subsidiary of a parent is authorized in another state, the competent authorities of the member state in which the subsidiary is located shall require the calculation of a subconsolidated or unconsolidated ratio.[145] However, provided the commission is informed, competent authorities may delegate the responsibility for supervising solvency to the competent authorities that have authorized and supervised the parent undertaking.

Where the SRD and the SBDI utilize the traditional approach of consolidated supervision (they also create the subconsolidated or unconsolidated supervision), these directives are contrary to the doctrine embodied in the Basel Concordat of 1975[146] and the later Basel Concordat of 1981,[147] under which the subsidiary is the responsibility of the state in which it is located.[148]

Under the SBDI, no credit institution may have qualifying holdings exceeding 15 percent of its own funds in an undertaking that is neither a credit institution nor a financial institution;[149] the total amount of a credit institution's qualifying holdings, meaning direct or indirect holdings of more than 10 percent,[150] may not exceed 60 percent.[151] Credit institutions shall be given 10 years to comply with the qualifying holdings,[152] and compliance shall be on a consolidated basis.[153]

The Large Exposure Directive limits credit institutions on a consolidated basis to exposure to a client or a group of connected clients to 25 percent of own funds.[154] Credit institutions may not incur large exposures that in the aggregate exceed 800 percent of own funds (large exposures are defined as 10 percent of own funds).[155]

Within Europe differences exist regarding deposit insurance. Because the alternative to deposit insurance is very often a bailout by the lender of last resort (LLR), the emphasis on the LLR will vary depending on the degree of deposit insurance available.

Liquidity under the Basel Concordat of 1975 and the revised Basel Concordat of 1981[156] is generally considered to be the responsibility of the host member state, and the SBDI did not depart from this approach; however, different EU member states have different liquidity requirements.[157] Frequently, the regulator will have different rules governing the liquidity of domestic and foreign banks.

The CSD,[158] together with the LED,[159] provides a framework for EU regulation of financial conglomerates. The LED, in general, limits exposure of any credit institution to any single borrower to 25 percent of risk-based capital. The CSD basically extends the concept of consolidated supervision to unregulated entities of financial conglomerates. The CSD expands the consolidated supervision approach of the EU banking directives to include the consolidation of credit institutions to all banking groups including those whose parent undertakings are not credit institutions. Consolidation is applied to almost all banking groups.[160] Matching provisions to those in the SRD exist for the subconsolidated ratio of the subsidiary in another member state[161] and for bilateral agreement to delegate responsibility for supervision of such a subsidiary.[162]

Where credit institutions authorized in two or more member states have their parent in the same financial holding company, supervision on a consolidated basis shall be exercised by the competent authorities of the member state in which the financial holding company is set up.[163] If no subsidiary is authorized in the member state where the financial holding company is set up, the competent authorities shall reach agreement on who shall exercise supervision. In the absence of such agreement, supervision shall be exercised by the authorities that authorized the credit institution with the greatest balance sheet.[164]

In general, the need for supervision of financial conglomerates is mandated by the fact that many financial conglomerates include entities that are not subject to regulation. While some of these unregulated entities may be engaged in nonfinancial activities, others may be conducting financial activities or have close involvement with a group of companies engaged in financial activities. Leasing, consumer credit, bridge lending, foreign exchange, and swaps are examples of financial activities that do not require authorization in many G-10 countries.[165]

Consolidation exists in three contexts: financial reporting (i.e., the Seventh and Eighth Directive of Company Law), consolidated supervision, and consolidation of capital ratios, the latter two forms being contained in the 1983 and 1992 consolidation supervision directives, the SRD and the CAD. The CSD applies to groups with at least one bank, although it makes reference to the Capital Adequacy Directive and preserves the trading book option. The BIS framework for supervision of financial conglomerates formed the basis for the EU-proposed directive on the supplementary supervision of financial conglomerates, which is discussed in chapter 6.

Conduct of Business Regulation, the Investment Services Directive Proposal, and Other EU Legislation

The ISD, under the rationale of *EC Commission v. Germany*,[166] is presumed to exempt investor protection from the scheme of home country control of branching.[167] This exception covering CBR may be so large as to swallow the rule of the ISD; Articles 10 and 11 concern the conduct of business rules that are in the control of the host country as discussed above.[168] Specifically, Article 10 requires adequate arrangements for funds belonging to investors to be safeguarded, monitoring requirements, and requirements to protect clients' interests from conflict of interest. Article 11 even applies, where appropriate, to non-core services and includes additional conduct of business rules, including adequate disclosure, the avoidance of conflict of interest, and the positive duty to act with due skill, care, and diligence.

Article 12 requires that an investment firm inform investors which compensation fund or equivalent protection will apply with respect to transactions envisaged. This is a notable position given the complex conflict of laws that have traditionally applied in financial affairs.

A directive on Undertaking for Collective Investment Trusts (UCIT) (in U.S. parlance, open-ended mutual funds controlled by a trust indenture rather than by corporate governance) provides for EU sale even if standards are more stringent in the country of the customer than in the home country of the trust. Restrictions will not apply if the UCIT is headquartered in another member country.[169] Even if prospectus requirements are harmonized and eventually mandatory recognition is required, UCIT's advertising would still have to be approved by an authorized person under the U.K. Financial Services Act and conform to host country marketing and advertising standards under the UCIT's directive. The difference between marketing and advertising standards and conduct of business rules is obscure at best.[170]

While the need for segregation of clients' money and securities might therefore be obviated (under the ISD, credit institutions need only segregate noninstitutional clients' securities),[171] there are other CBR such as cold calling, advertising (particularly cross-border advertising), proper and timely execution of trades, and soft commission arrangements that drive up the cost of other commissions and tie-ins that are unrelated to solvency. Many CBR can be harmonized internationally.[172]

The U.K. Financial Services Act of 1986 created the most advanced structure for securities regulation in Europe; London today is the center of the Euromarket. The U.K. Financial Services Act of 1986 goes one step beyond the First Banking Directive and provides for automatic authorization of any member state investment firm "carrying on business in the U.K." not "having a permanent establishment in the U.K."[173] While member state investment firms were thus authorized, they also became subject to all rules of the SIB or relevant SRO whether or not they were members of the SRO.[174]

The ISD allowed branching for investment services defined broadly. Services are defined as (1) reception and transmission of orders on behalf of investors in relation to one or more of the instruments listed in Section B and the execution of such orders other than for one's own account; (2) dealing in any of the instruments listed in Section B for the brokers' own account; (3) managing portfolios of investments in accordance with mandates given by investors on a discretionary client-by-client basis where certain instruments are included; or (4) underwriting in respect of issues of any of the instruments or the placing of such issues.[175]

Many of the key provisions of the ISD are contained in the conditions for taking up business[176] requiring each member state to make access available to the investment firms subject to authorization granted by the home member state. Article 4 requires that the identities of the shareholders or members be known by the competent authorities of the home member state. The ISD requires approval for qualified holdings, which means direct or indirect holdings in investment firms representing 10 percent or more of the capital or the voting rights—additional thresholds include 20 percent, 33 percent, or 50 percent under Article 9, regardless of what approval is required for SROs. In the case of branches of investment firms that have registered home offices outside the community, member states shall not apply provisions that result in treatment more favorable than that accorded to branches of investment firms that have registered home offices in member states.[177] The directive contains rigorous provisions relating to the treatment accorded to community investment firms in third countries mirroring those in the SBDI.[178]

THE FSA BEFORE THE FINANCIAL SERVICES AND MARKETS ACT

Securitization

The Bank of England was the regulatory authority for institutions under the Banking Act of 1987 until June 1, 1998, when the FSA became the regulator overseeing banks.[179] The Guide to Banking Supervisory Policy published that month supersedes all notices of the Bank of England. Chapter SE sets out the FSA policy on securitization of banking assets.[180] Securitization is the packaging of substantially similar assets, such as mortgages, credit card receivables, or other income yielding assets, generally of high quality, that are packaged into a tradable form, often with the help of credit enhancements. The structure involves the sale of the assets by the originator to a special purpose vehicle (SPV), which usually issues debt securities equal to the purchase price and fees and pays the purchase price to the originator, usually a bank, who is motivated by the desire to free up capital to use in other ventures. The guide, in conformity with European directives, applies only to U.K. incorporated banks acting in the capacity of originator, servicing agent, sponsor, or repackager.[181]

The guide sets out its objectives: (1) the relevant transaction achieves the intended effect of passing rights and obligations from the seller to the buyer—by way of a clean break; (2) all parties to the transaction fully understand the risks assumed or retained by them; and (3) any material risks to buyers or sellers are properly treated in the FSA supervision of banks.

The FSA believes that these objectives are best achieved by

- the immediate legal separation of the seller from the assets and their new owner (or the effective economic separation in the case of transfer by subparticipation);
- as far as possible, the complete economic separation of the seller from the assets and their new owner;
- presentational or moral separation of the seller from the assets and their new owner; and
- capital or other coverage of the retained risks.[182]

An originator may provide credit enhancement facilities for an SPV if it deducts the full amount of the credit enhancement from capital or it must include the full amount of the assets in its capital, and the choice must be made at the outset.[183] A distinction is made between first-tier loss credit enhancement and second-tier loss credit enhancement (analogous to reinsurance in the event that the first tier is depleted). This distinction is not relevant for originators, but it is relevant for sponsors and repackagers.[184] There is a subtle distinction between sponsor and repackager. A sponsor sells directly into a conduit without the assets directly appearing on its balance sheets whereas a repackager warehouses assets on its balance sheet.[185]

The FSA sets out four methods of transfer: (1) novation, (2) assignment (both notified and unnotified), (3) declaration of trust, and (4) subparticipation. The declaration of trust seems to be the preferred method since it circumvents restrictions in loan agreements[186] and was added to the final draft.[187] The forms of credit enhancement include subordinated loan or note, overcollateralization, where more assets are transferred to the issuer than the value of the notes issued, and spread accounts to trap excess spreads rather than transferring them to the originator.[188]

The guide draws a sharp distinction between credit and liquidity facilities. Liquidity facilities are intended to smooth over timing differences in payment of principal and interest and ensure payments in the event of market disruptions. Guide requirements for liquidity facilities include arm's length terms and normal credit review, nonutilization or reduced utilization if the SPV assets have declined in quality, and limitation in amount and duration.[189] An originator or servicing agent may not provide liquidity facilities as it is deemed to be funding and, thus, would not achieve a clean break.[190] Sponsors or repackagers may provide liquidity facilities, but the name of the bank may not be disclosed in the offering material.[191] An originating bank may structure a transaction to allow further tranches to be placed into the scheme, provided that the asset quality is not materially altered.[192] The guide also contains special rules regarding revolving credit. Revolving credit periods are ones in which the investor's share of principal payments is reinvested in further assets and the amortization period in which the investor's share of principal repayment is used to pay down the investor's interest in the pool. The guide seeks to avoid early exit by the investor and makes special provisions for early amortization resulting from noneconomic triggers only (such as tax or insolvency events). The guide also highlights the risks to banks and requires heightened systems requirements and increased liquidity and capital planning strategy.[193] A further limitation on a repackager is that if the bank, via its balance sheet, repackages assets that are not investment grade third party instruments, the bank will be treated as an originator unless the bank originates less than 10 percent of the sub-investment grade assets.[194] Additional restrictions on the originator include no ownership or control of any interest in the SPV, although it may have one director,[195] and the SPV must make no reference to the originator. The originator may underwrite or deal in shares of the SPV at arm's length when 90 percent are sold to third parties.[196]

Language in the guide suggests that "the FSA expects to be consulted when a bank proposes to act in any one of these roles (i.e., originator, servicer, sponsor, or repackager)."[197] Section 3 of the guide indicates that the FSA will be concerned with systems, operation and liquidity risks, and remaining capital base. The guide indicates that the bank may impose limits on the extent to which assets may be securitized in terms of total volume and/or the types of assets securitized in comparison to the total asset base of the bank; thus, even if the technical requirements of securitization are met, the FSA may regard the assets as carrying additional risks for the originator.[198]

Asset securitization highlights the issues of EU and international standards for complex financial transactions. The rules outlined in the guide are the most comprehensive in Europe and may rival those of the United States. The U.K. market for securitization dwarfs that of any other nation except the United States. Between 1988 and 1998, the United Kingdom had $74 billion of securitization compared with $31 billion for France.[199] What impact this new legislation will have on business is unclear. Will banks seek to change the status of their incorporation, or will U.K. banks lose business to less regulated regimes? In France and Spain, it is still possible to securitize assets by transferring them to SPVs incorporated elsewhere, and, generally, the provisions that apply to securitizations locally do not apply offshore except through consolidated supervision under the Basel framework discussed in chapter 2, although France has dealt with accounting treatment of local and offshore securitizations.[200]

Derivatives and Treatment of Depository Institutions

The capital treatment of credit derivatives demonstrates the interim treatment of complex derivative instruments that European countries have been employing while awaiting the final new G-10 accord from the Committee on Banking and Supervisory Practices. A credit derivative is essentially an arrangement that allows one party to transfer the credit risk of an instrument—usually a bond—in exchange for a fixed payment. The seller runs the obvious market risk, and the buyer runs the risk of the seller's default. In July 1998, the German Federal Banking Supervisory Office issued a draft circular[201] following the French Commission Bancaire[202] and the FSA.[203] The German Supervisory Office noted that, in total return swaps, both the buyer and the seller can be affected by counterparty default. It also felt that the potential covering cost corresponds to the share related price risk of the bond; therefore, there should be an equity add-on factor.[204] According to the Commission Bancaire if the issuer is investment grade, only interest rate add-ons should apply to the seller and credit add-ons to the buyer. If the issuer is less than investment grade, equity add-ons shall apply to the seller and commodity add-on factors to the buyer.[205] In the FSA release, interest rate add-ons shall apply to the buyer and equity add-ons shall apply if the buyer is less than investment grade. Although an ancillary EU directive specifies that an annex 8 will be added to the CAD containing the legal framework for internal models,[206] the language of both the CAD and the ancillary directive is only hortatory and awaits the action of the Basel Committee.

A related issue is raised by an FSA publication in which the FSA declared that it would consider depository institutions low impact, middle impact, or high impact.[207] It concludes that 80 percent of institutions are low impact, 19 percent are medium impact, and 1 percent is high impact.[208] However, this 1 percent has a 64 percent share of the market. What the FSA is doing is stating the obvious. Banks that take retail deposits and are national in scope need to be closely monitored. But is it also setting up a political position to protect small banks in the framework of the Basel Committee, which will apply to all financial institutions.

THE FINANCIAL SERVICES AND MARKETS ACT 2000

The Financial Services and Markets Act 2000 (FSMA) is the most comprehensive legislation of its kind ever enacted, far surpassing the Securities and Exchange Acts in terms of its prescriptive terms and definitions. Unfortunately, it was enacted at the high tide of a bull market and addressed concerns that were optimistically framed. Thus, it may turn out to be fated to be antiquated at the outset and come to be viewed as analogous to the last great cavalry charge. It is particularly notable in how little attention it gives to listing particulars and financial disclosure in general and there are no provisions for disciplining auditor or accounting firms, only individuals, unlike the U.S. Sarbanes-Oxley Act.[209]

Part 1 of the FSMA defines the Financial Services Authority as the regulator, establishes general duties, and enunciates the four principles that are the regulatory objectives: market confidence, public awareness, the protection of consumers, and the reduction of financial crime.[210] In a Labourite tinge, the FSA has the duty to form a practitioners' panel and a consumers' panel and is further required to consider the recommendations of both panels.[211] There are certain cases in which the Treasury is given the right to make independent inquiries and appoint panels.[212] In a charming reminder of the derogation of royal power, the general activity—engaging in securities—is classified as a general prohibition.[213] Next are authorized persons acting beyond their scope[214] and restrictions on financial promotion.[215] It is only then that we are treated to a definition of regulated investments.[216] But this brief punctuation in the litany of prohibitions is followed by "offences"[217] and "enforceability of agreements," which generally consider those prohibited agreements that are not enforceable.[218]

Finally, in Part 3, we reach the definition of authorization, which is as important under U.K. law as the definition of a security is under U.S. law. (However, the infamous quack test—if it quacks it's a security—doesn't apply.) There are many activities that don't require authorization, but insofar as dealing with the public is concerned, pretty much all activities require authorization. U.K. law is broadly similar to U.S. law in its exemptions and private offering exemptions. Offerings to fewer than 35 people are not considered an offering within the meaning the FSMA.[219] Part 4 and Part 5 concern the conduct of regulated activities by authorized persons, including the application process,[220] approvals,[221] and conduct,[222] and last, but by no means least for lawyers, actions for damages.[223] Part 6 concerns listing particulars, and includes the official list,[224] requirements for listing,[225] and listing particulars, which include general and supplemental duties of disclosure.[226] Here the general requirements for prospectuses are also set forth[227] and include a special section on prospectus requirements in instances where there is no listing,[228] general requirements for sponsors including a great little compendium, "public censure of sponsors,"[229] compensation for false or misleading listing particulars,[230] and statutory penalties for breach of listing particular rules.[231] Rules are set forth for an advertisement in connection with a listing.[232] Part 7 concerns control of business transfers, or mergers and acquisitions (M&A) in American speak. Part 8 is titled "Penalties for Market Abuse," which is separate and distinct from liability for false and misleading statements under listing particulars[233] (more similar to fraud on the market). Part 9 establishes the Financial Services and Markets Tribunal. Part 10, titled "Rules and Guidance," establishes the Financial Services Authority general rulemaking authority and certain specific authorities including insurance business rules and restrictions on unit trusts.[234] This part contains rules on price stabilization, prevention of money laundering, and financial promotion.[235] This part also contains its own action-for-damages section.[236] Chapter 2 establishes the concept of regulatory guidance as we've seen it in the securitization rules,[237] and Chapter 3 involves competition scrutiny. Other regulatory concepts include information gathering;[238] control over authorized persons;[239] incoming firms: intervention by regulator (non-U.K. firms);[240] as always, regulation of Lloyds;[241] and provision of financial services by members of the professions[242] and regulation of mutual societies.[243] Part 15 establishes the Financial Services Compensation Scheme.[244] Closely related is an entire insolvency regime for regulated persons.[245] The Ombudsman Scheme is a fund for complaints and makes awards.[246] Collective Investment Schemes are regulated under Part 17.[247] There are special rules for the European Economic Area (EEA) (EU firms),[248] which are required access under the UCIT Directive,[249] and special rules applying to individually recognized overseas schemes.[250] (One hopes with all these schemes having been dutifully reported that the word has a different meaning than the one accorded it in American English). Part 22 provides for the appointment of auditors and sets terms and conditions for the disqualification of auditors. It also makes it unlawful to provide false and misleading information to auditors and actuaries.[251] This section is indicative of how, although the FSMA was ahead of contemporaneous U.S. legislation, it lags behind Sarbanes-Oxley.[252] There are no provisions for disqualifying firms of auditors or chartered public accountants, no requirement of disclosures regarding conflict of interests à la Andersen, and no restrictions on such conflicts. Most issues relating to corporate governance, auditing, and financial reporting are under the auspices of the Department of Trade and Industry, which is discussed in "Corporate Governance in the United Kingdom" below.

Specifics

As with any new legislation, the FSMA is largely untested. Certain provisions have drawn notice. Chief among these is the new prohibition against unsolicited advertising, which unites the previous complex language of the Financial Services Act 1986 prohibitions against cold calling and unsolicited inducements to invest.[253] The FSMA is quite clear in stating, "A person must not in the course of business communicate an offer or inducement to engage in investment activity" unless such a person is an authorized person. The U.K. Treasury produced a proposal for one-off real-time communications exemptions and non-real-time communication exemption.[254] This proposal provides that if certain conditions are met, the solicitation will be exempt. These conditions include that the offer be tailor-made to the recipient or class of recipients in "the expectation of joint engagement in investment activity" and that it be tailored for "the particular circumstances of the recipient" and that it not "be part of a coordinated promotional strategy." As one commentator notes, this last term, particularly, is vague; there would be better ways to safeguard businesses that are attempting to raise their own capital.[255] The solicitation must be solicited, but this condition is met if the solicitor asks permission to discuss an investment. Under the draft order, there is a general exemption for non-real-time communications made from a place outside the United Kingdom to persons outside the United Kingdom provided there is no U.K. hyperlink[256] (this is an Internet-related provision). If a U.K. investor telephones an overseas broker, there is nothing to forbid the broker from returning the call provided that warnings about dispute resolution and compensation schemes are provided. The government also proposed exemptions for high net worth individuals in solicited real-time communications and unsolicited non-real-time communications, but these exemptions will rely on certification by an authorized person.[257]

While these particular exemptions may appear picayune when considering the entire architecture of the FSMA, they are a good starting point considering that the conduct of business rules is the exclusion to the European-wide passport bestowed by the LPD and the MRP Directive. It is not incidental that authorization is the touchstone of the FSMA as it was for the Financial Services Act 1986. It is within this sphere that the United Kingdom has virtual autonomy. The term "conduct of business rules" is a wide term of art embracing advertising, authorization of investment firms, market conduct on recognized exchanges, and takeover activity. For instance, at one extreme is market abuse, which relates to behavior on exchanges per se. In the Revised FSA Guide on Market Conduct, the FSA states that market conduct is dependent on the market in question and the participant within that market. It explicitly states in its final version of its policy statement on market abuse that stabilization does not amount to market abuse and that disclosure in derivatives markets is not required to be made in certain instances where that knowledge is traditionally used to hedge positions in equity markets.[258] Thus, the code articulates a regular user test, and market abuse will be present in the context of an artificial transaction unless the regular user would find "the legitimate purpose of the behavior as a commercial rationale" and "the way in which the behavior was engaged in as proper [sic]."[259] The code of market conduct and the offense of market abuse result in a continuous disclosure regime in which major events that may result in price movements, such as the resignation of directors, announcements of mergers, or any major announcement, must be disclosed at a press conference or on a Web site within hours. In this respect U.K. law is more stringent than the Securities and Exchange Commission (SEC) periodic, current disclosure regime. However, it should be noted that, although a private right of action for market abuse exists in theory, no such action has been brought. The dearth of private actions in general results from the difficulty of bringing a class action suit and severe limitations on contingent fees for attorneys.

The FSA has published a Conduct of Business Rules sourcebook, which culls its various consultation papers.[260] The FSA sets out its purpose as consolidating the various rules formally administered by the SROs[261] and defines its approach as being one that is characterized by both harmonization and differentiation.[262] While these principles and guidance concepts for the conduct of business (COB) are perhaps easier to negotiate than SRO rules, one should begin to ask whether conduct of business is such a broad term exception to the single market as to swallow the rule.

Block one is principles, systems and controls, and general provisions.[263] The code of market conduct concerns interprofessional dealing, but there are aspects of it such as Chinese walls that apply to both general business and professional business.[264] While this account will dispense with treatment of Lloyd's, which is covered here, we should recall that the U.K. self-vaunted system of regulation did little to arrest financial scandal in that arena. In a paradigm of complexity, collective investment trusts (which are not covered here in detail) are regulated in terms of marketing and advertising by the COB sourcebook, but, in what will be certain to bewilder the European setting out to conquer the U.K. mutual fund business, Chapter 10 of the COB covers the requirements for management of a collective investment trust and Chapter 11 sets out the responsibilities of trustees and depositories of the same. We are informed that these requirements are additional to those in Chapter 7.[265] If these were Japanese customs regulations, there would be hell to pay at the WTO.

There is a prohibition against soft commissions and inducements, and the rules were amended to forbid a regulated person from paying an unregulated person.[266] That such a prohibition could have gone through so many regulatory reviews really makes one question whether the principal purpose of these rules is the regulation of the conduct of business or the restraint of EU-wide business. In order to understand the regulatory structure, it is necessary to have recourse to each of the previous documents, to read this document. The FSA has retained the client classification system in earlier circulars, which provides different levels of protection to customers depending on their level of sophistication and includes an intermediate level.[267]

Two of the mantras of CBR in all the SROs were know your customer and suitability. One essential aspect of CBR is clients' money, which is to be placed in a designated account.[268] The segregation of clients' money is always a more complex matter than it appears and the compensation scheme,[269] like the Securities Investor Protection Insurance Corporation (SIPIC) in the United States, is intended to supplement these rules. It always seems that, even in an orderly liquidation of a securities firm, clients' money is at risk. This risk can occur through either legal means, when the money is for securities that are in the midst of settlement[270] (most frequently characterized as delivery versus payment,[271] for instance), or illegal mingling of accounts. In addition to the basic COB manual, there are separate manuals on authorization, supervision, and enforcement.[272] But the question of passporting rights for EU firms is directly addressed in a consultative paper misleadingly titled "Supervision and Authorisation Manuals."[273] This document purports to be feedback on various consultative documents and chapters of the authorization and supervision manuals and contains important verbiage on the EEA passport rights that were made pursuant to secondary legislation.[274] This release tells one where to find the provisions dealing with U.K. firms wishing to use EEA passports and EEA firms wishing to change their branches in the United Kingdom or close branches. Naturally, the provisions relating to EEA initial passports are in a separate section.[275] One is reminded of the Soviet Union in the good old days where there were plenty of laws to which only the prosecutors and judges had access. Here everyone has access to the laws if he or she has the perseverance to delve into them. The purpose appears to be one of deliberate obfuscation so that the FSMA and the various rules as interpreted by the FSA consultative documents would only be comprehensible to U.K. practitioners washed by the rivers and blessed by the sun of home.

In 1997, regulatory supervision of the United Kingdom Listing Authority (UKLA) was transferred from the London Stock Exchange to the FSA. The belated enabling legislation is Part 6 of the FSMA, which generally considers listings,[276] and suspension and discontinuation of listings,[277] listing particulars,[278] prospectuses,[279] sponsors (something akin to an underwriter who must be authorized),[280] compensation for false and misleading listing particulars,[281] penalties for breach of listing rules[282] (as opposed to penalties for false and misleading particulars), and approval of advertisements by the competent authority[283] (the UKLA). Of the contents of the listing particulars, beyond assets, liabilities, and financial position, the only relevant language in the FSMA is that "Regard must be had (in particular)" to (a) the nature of the securities and their issuer, (b) the nature of the persons likely to acquire them, (c) the fact that certain matters may reasonably be expected to be within the knowledge of professional advisors of a kind that people likely to acquire the securities would be expected to consult, and (d) any information available to investors or their professional advisors as a result of requirements imposed on the issuer by a recognized exchange. Pronouncements (b) and (c) are sufficiently Delphic as to cause one to question the meaning intended by the drafter of the legislation.

In the amendments to the listing particulars,[284] the FSA sets forth a number of technical changes and requires the issuer, when it prepares consolidated accounts, to set forth both its own and consolidated accounts together with earning per share and consolidated profits or loss per share for the last three years.[285] If in the last three years the number of shares has changed, the statement must be reconciled to provide comparability and must include comparability of dividends.[286] An opinion of officers and directors is required as to interim statements[287] and in cases where the financial or trading position of a group has undergone a significant change, a description or appropriate negative statement is required.[288] Unlike U.S. law, these listing particulars really entail a true and fair override where the accounts do not entail an accurate representation of the financial position of the company.[289] Issuers must provide a cash flow or application of funds statements for three years and basic financial information[290] for each business in which the book value of the undertaking represents 10 percent of the consolidated profits or loss or 10 percent of the consolidated net assets of the group. A large loophole exists since information may be omitted where the undertaking doesn't publish annual accounts.[291]

Mergers and acquisitions are divided into three classes ranging from class 3 to class 1 with class 1 being the most onerous.[292] Related party transactions are interesting in that, like U.S. requirements, they involve disclosure and must be reported in the annual statement, but, additionally, the United Kingdom Listing Authority must be informed in writing and provided with an independent opinion assuring the UKLA that the terms are fair.[293] This approach, which involves a greater degree of administrative oversight, suggests a definitive difference from the U.S. approach. It recalls the administrative role played by the FSA in reviewing securitizations.[294] Also, related party transactions occurring within 12 months are to be aggregated.[295] The amendment to the listing particulars also contains the model code on transactions in securities by directors, employees, and persons connected with them.[296] Chapters 25 and 27 concern innovative high-growth companies and strategic investment companies without a three year history of operation. (Don't ask what happened to Chapter 26.) Under the LP Directive[297] and the international foreign disclosure standards[298] that form the basis for listing in the

United Kingdom subject to certain supplemental information,[299] three years of audited financial accounts are required in order to qualify. However, the UKLA has created separate standards for particular kinds of companies. Companies intending to list under this exception must have made an offering of at least £20 million and have a market capitalization of £50 million.[300] The company must provide a detailed business plan with particular emphasis on plans for future sales, new products, and new methods of business. It must, in a separate section, set out risk factors: the competitors in the market; an explanation of capital expenditure plans and an undertaking by directors and related persons not to dispose of securities or, if there is no such undertaking, a statement to that effect; an independent report where the products are unproven; and, in all cases, a full disclosure of patents and intellectual property.[301] A company listing under this exception must report quarterly on a group basis.[302] The requirements for strategic investment companies are similar but tailored to that product and require that the company have at least five investments, none of which should account for more than 20 percent of total amount invested or 25 percent of value.[303]

Section 119 of the FSMA requires the FSA to issue a consultative paper containing guidance on the offense of market abuse, which has resulted in two consultative papers.[304] Where there is fraud and criminality, the Serious Frauds Office, the police, and the DTI will be responsible for taking action in the courts. Under the Code of Market Conduct, the FSA may bring civil actions against anyone guilty of the civil offense of market abuse rather than the criminal offense of market manipulation. The offense involves abusive behavior in relation to a qualifying investment and could involve failure to disclose acquisition or disposal of shares under Section 198 of the Company Act of 1985.[305] The FSMA enacts a tripartite definition of market abuse: (1) misusing market information not generally available to the relevant market; (2) misleading the market; and (3) distorting the market, if a regular user would consider the information relevant, if he or she would be misled or would believe that the information distorts the market, or if he or she would be regarded by the regular user as a failure to observe a standard of behavior expected from a person in that position.[306] The government may bring criminal charges under the Criminal Justice Act of 1993 for insider dealing or bring civil charges under another section of the FSMA.[307] As opposed to the criminal offense, which requires intent or, at least, recklessness, the civil offense of market abuse is gauged by effects. Conduct does not amount to market abuse if it is permitted under the Takeover Code, by stabilization, or if the person has done due diligence and does not believe that the offense constitutes market abuse. Other factors to be considered by the FSA in its policy guidance in assessing a penalty is how serious the market disruption is and whether the offense involves intent or recklessness. Observing Chinese walls and not directly acting on information creates a rebuttable presumption. Obligations to disclose or disclosure of legal transaction are also excepted from the definition of market abuse.[308] Currently, an EU directive on insider trading and market manipulation is in the offing.[309]

Civil liability for fraudulent statements contained in a prospectus has been recognized in U.S. law for over a hundred years. In *R. v. Bates*, the court, in interpreting the Prevention of Frauds Act of 1939, determined that the offense of recklessness did not require dishonesty in the forecasting of future events and could consist of "a high degree of negligence without dishonesty."[310]

Thus, the law in this regard is more expansive than contemporary U.S. law regarding forecasts under the Private Securities Litigation Reform Act (PSLRA), which requires scienter.[311] In *R. v. Caldwell*, the definition of "recklessness" was expanded to include failure to give the risk of misleading sufficient thought when the obviousness of the risk is apparent.[312] Although Section 47 of the Financial Services Act of 1986 and Section 391 of the FSMA allow criminal charges without scienter,[313] a fact that is grounds for complaint by at least one commentator, the civil offense is more clearly entrenched in U.K. law than the similar but less inclusive case law in the United States. However, the greater expansiveness of market abuse when compared with the making of a material misstatement in an offering, prospectus, or advertisement, should be considered. The belated disclosure of the annual financial statement and the biannual reports, when compared with the quarterly reports of the United States, means that other kinds of disclosure may be more important in moving markets, in particular, announcements and voluntary disclosure. The market abuse regime reflects the reality of the nature of disclosures that are likely to induce purchasers of securities. The increased emphasis on periodic and occasional disclosure in the United States[314] means a divergence between U.S. and U.K. regulation, although 10b-5 includes statements that involve market abuse rather than only material misstatements in prospectuses and annual and quarterly statements. But the evolution of corporate governance standards, including the evolution of audit committee responsibilities and probable increased attention to financial reporting, discussed later in "Corporate Governance in the United Kingdom" in this chapter and particular post-Enron initiatives discussed in chapter 6 will, in all probability, increase attention to financial disclosure and open the tap if not the floodgates of litigation.

CORPORATE GOVERNANCE AND FINANCIAL REPORTING

Corporate Governance in the EU

Bank domination of financial markets in universal bank countries discussed above has several consequences for corporate governance.

The two most distinctive features of corporate governance in Germany are the role workers play on corporate boards and the influence of universal banks that lend to firms, act as market makers, underwrite shares, hold equity positions, and exercise proxy votes for shares owned by others.[315] Changes in corporate control tend to be exercised behind closed doors by banks and large block-holders rather than through market-based takeovers.[316] There have only been a handful of hostile takeovers since World War II.[317] The authors of one article on the subject of German corporate finance state, "It appears reasonable to speak of a distinctive continental European model of capitalism stressing social consensus."[318] Universal banks have a competitive advantage in obtaining proxies since they provide the vast majority of retail brokerage outlets and, since shares are in bearer form, shareholders require bank custodial service; it is a small step to allow banks to control the proxy.[319] In 1986, a study showed that if the three largest banks had voted as a block, including equity positions held by each other and proxies held, they would have controlled a majority of shares in each other, despite the fact that they directly owned only a trivial amount of shares in each other.[320] Universal banks are particularly able to exert control in companies with dispersed ownership, where no large block holding exists.[321]

Another feature of the German corporate finance system is the prevalence of shares with multiple votes (preferred shares). Although German corporation law does not allow this practice today, many firms are grandfathered.[322] Cross-shareholdings are also prominent in Germany. The best-known web is Alliance AG.[323] Pyramiding, where company *a* owns a share in company *b*, which owns a share in company *c*, is also common in Germany.

In a study of board-level linkages among German industrial and financial corporations, there were 453 primary and 1,175 secondary interlocks among directors sitting on supervisory boards of Germany's 325 largest corporations, with banks displaying the greatest number of linkages.[324] Thus, fundamentally high-leverage countries have economic systems that do not partake of the same values as does the profit-motivated portfolio investor of capital market countries.[325]

In a sample of 198 companies, only 9 had no large block-holder (4.5 percent), and 165 had at least one block-holder with a stake of 25 percent or more.[326] Only about 20 percent of firms count banks as block-holders, and the blocks are typically smaller than average.[327] In Germany, one major shareholder owns a majority interest in 64.2 percent of listed companies, in Italy 56.1 percent, in Belgium 63.7 percent, compared to in the United Kingdom, where only 2.4 percent of listed companies have one majority shareholder.[328] The extent of ownership by large shareholders in continental Europe implies that capital markets operate entirely differently and are characterized by high leverage, bank intermediation through loans and eurobonds, and less developed arm's length equity markets. This leads to a tradeoff between liquidity and control in which liquidity is sacrificed for the benefits afforded by ownership and control being concentrated in the same individual or group. Additionally, even where shareholding is more dispersed, banks operate as depository trustees and vote shares. Thus, in Germany, for instance, the percentage of companies controlled by a small group of institutions is far higher than 65 percent of listed companies. Only 17.5 percent of companies have no holder with 25 percent of outstanding equity. Thus, the distinction between bank-dominated capital markets and arm's length securities markets characterized by dispersed equity ownership is more pronounced in the EU than it is, for example, in the United States and Japan. This latter distinction will be addressed in chapter 7. But many of the characteristics of Japanese securities markets are present in continental Europe. In the Anglo-Saxon world, there is a separation of ownership and control, which results in an agency problem, first discussed in Berle and Means in 1932. These issues will be considered in depth in chapter 5. But this distinction accounts for the greater emphasis on corporate governance procedures in the United Kingdom than in most continental countries, Belgium and the Netherlands being the exceptions. These countries are the only ones with securities markets proportional to the size of their population, are in the Anglo-Saxon mold, and have developed arm's length securities markets.

Therefore, it is not surprising that most corporate governance codes are voluntary. The greatest legal difference between member states of the EU is the corporate legal structure of the board of directors. Company law in Austria, Luxembourg, Sweden, and Germany allows employees the right to elect members of a supervisory board who frequently appoint members of the managing board. The CEO and chairman of the board functions are usually divided.[329] In the United Kingdom, the Combined Code, which is linked to the London Stock Exchange listing rules, now recommends separation.[330] Thus the structure of the board of directors is two-tiered with a supervisory board retaining certain responsibilities and a managing board retaining others. In the parlance of corporate governance, employees are stakeholders.[331] According to a report prepared by Weil Gotschal and Manges for the European Commission, member states have different rights and remedies for shareholders, rights for shareholders in the event of a merger, and different proxy solicitation and notice of meeting rules. An EU takeover statute is in the works[332] but its implementation into domestic law is likely to vary widely, and these variations within the EU may pose a barrier to further integration of securities markets.[333]

The United Kingdom and recently Ireland and France require disclosure of remuneration for key employees and directors.[334] Conflicts of interests tend to be addressed in codes. The Brussels Stock Exchange Code requires disclosure of all conflicts in the annual report and calls for arm's length transactions between companies and a major shareholder. The OECD code emphasizes disclosure, and the Draft German Cromme Code reminds directors of their responsibility not to compete with the company and calls for the immediate disclosure of conflicts to the chairman of the supervisory board and other members of the management board.[335] The use of nominating committees for the appointment of directors is favored in the U.K. Hampel Report and the

French Vienot Report.[336] The German Panel Rules urges boards to include "a sufficient number of independent persons who have no current or former business association with the company's group."[337] Praeda Report from Italy, not noted for its stellar corporate governance,[338] notes that nonexecutive directors outnumber executive directors and placed emphasis on "truly independent directors."[339] In France, the law limits the proportion of paid employees on a board to a third, but the Viennot Report recommends that one-third of directors be truly independent.[340]

Most codes make it the responsibility of the chairman to see that the members of the board or the supervisory board have adequate information.[341] Various codes specify that the nomination, audit, and remuneration committees be composed of a certain number of independent directors.[342] Many codes discuss the process of executive remuneration, and the U.K. Combined Code has specified a process.[343] Codes also tend to specify a process for the evaluation of management and boards.[344] Codes also place heavy emphasis on board oversight of preparation of financial reports, auditing, and internal controls.[345]

Since most codes are voluntary,[346] compliance is uneven. In the Netherlands, only 56 percent of companies complied with the Peters Report principles.[347] Of course, there is compliance, and then there is compliance. In the United Kingdom, one survey found that only 9 percent of listed companies had fully complied with the recommendations of the Combined Code.[348] Outside the United Kingdom, where a large shareholder or a small coterie of financial institutions control corporations, the rights of minority shareholders are, of necessity, limited. While a Corporate Governance Directive, which will highlight such issues as audit committees, may eventually be in the offing in the post-Enron era, the legal structure for enforcement is likely to remain weak in continental Europe. Yet, there will inevitably be a gradual attempt to access equity markets by such companies, implying a slow process toward corporate governance reform. But, monitoring through close supervision by a controlling shareholder or group is an alternative to arm's length securities markets. Certainly, such companies will always be limited by access to the liquidity provided by arm's length equities markets, but they also avoid the agency problem posed by the separation of ownership and control. These issues will be revisited in chapter 5.

Corporate Governance in the United Kingdom

The FSA is nearly absent from the dialogue about financial reporting and corporate governance. Under the current U.K. process, financial reporting and auditing exist in semiautonomous quasi-governmental organizations. In the United Kingdom, the transformation of the Auditing Practices Committee into the Auditing Practices Board by act was accomplished by the Companies Act 1989; and, the formulation of accounting standards was delegated to the Accounting Standards Board (ASB), a body nominally independent of the accounting profession.

The Company Law Review Steering Committee produced a consultative document under the aegis of the Department of Trade and Industry that considered all issues relating to the modernization of company law.[349] First, the issue of scope is addressed, which is the scope of the directors. Directors are to be under an obligation to achieve the success of the company for the benefit of the shareholders in the long term by taking into account all relevant considerations including the need to sustain ongoing relationship with employees, customers, suppliers, and others.[350] Additionally, companies must publish as part of the annual report an operating and financial review (OFR), which discusses the performance and future plans of the company, taking into account the relationship with employees, suppliers, and customers. This responsibility would be a statutory version of the current OFR, which is encouraged by the Accounting Standards Board. Proposals for two-tier boards were considered but adjudged ill advised; the stakeholder or social entity view is rejected or modified in a pluralist conception.[351]

The definition of director is extended to include shadow directors, those on whose instructions directors are intended to act. The directors' duties include maintaining a degree of loyalty to exercise his duties in the interest of the shareholders, which may require him or her to take into account the "Company's need to foster business relationships with stakeholders and the community and a reputation for high standards of business conduct,"[352] independence of judgment, good faith, and the duty to disclose any conflict of interest.[353] The comment says that a director will not be liable if he or she acts in good faith.[354] This seems to dismiss a negligence standard. However, the obligation to act with care, skill, and diligence, which would create a standard equal to professional negligence, imposes a higher duty on the finance director, for instance, than other directors if he has more skill in this arena.[355] Although there is no business judgment defense in England, Wales, and Scotland (the law will not be applicable in Northern Ireland), U.K. courts have been reluctant to review commercial decisions.[356] However, Section 310 of the Companies Act 1985 allows directors and companies to purchase liability insurance, a practice that is maintained in the consultative document.[357] The Financial Aspects of Corporate Governance (Cadbury Committee) issued a Code of Practice in 1992 covering the board's role, executive compensation, and duties of the board to present a balanced view of the company's performance. The code was directed to publicly listed companies.[358] In 1995, the Greenwood Committee issued a code that reiterated the Cadbury Committee's point of view. In 1996, the Hampel Committee issued a Combined Code that included the position on accounting and executive compensation and also included positions on management shareholder relations in general, and also a specific section on institutional investors. It was implemented in part through changes in the listing requirements in a general disclosure duty under the listing rules since 1998.[359] In general, the Combined Code calls for a company to be run by its board of directors for an audit and remuneration committee composed of a majority of nonexecutive directors. The code also makes recommendations about separating the CEO and chairman of the board functions. Most companies have a majority of independent directors as recommended by the Combined Code, and 87 percent have separated the CEO and chairman functions.[360] Additional safeguards include requiring shareholder approval for any transaction involving more than 25 percent of corporate assets. Although the evidence of takeovers is mixed, the Steering Committee report tends heavily toward maintaining the protections afforded by the takeover control. The market for corporate control is considered an additional shareholder protection in that the chapter is entitled "The Board and the Capital Market and the Market for Corporate Control."[361]

The next chapter considers the position of beneficial shareholders without legal control, the rights of shareholders as a group, and the rights of minority shareholders to act independently of the board.[362] There was general agreement on the proposal that companies bear the cost of circulating shareholder proposals.[363] Chapter 5 is entitled "Corporate Governance: Reporting and Accounting" and melds the subjects of corporate governance and financial accounting. The basis of company reporting is the Fourth and the Seventh Directives of Company Law of the EU.[364] The Company Act of 1989 recognized the Accounting Standards Board and its pronouncements, particularly its two new concepts: the mandatory cash flow statement and the recommended Operating and Financial Review, which requires a company to prepare revised accounts where existing ones do not meet the requirements of the act.[365] The Steering Committee proposed that a statutory prelim be sent to all investors within 70 days after the end of the financial year and a full report be sent to all shareholders (rather than the current prelim) to all investors who have not downloaded one.[366] The Steering Committee proposes a performance report together with a cash flow statement to replace the existing profit and loss statement, and a mandatory OFR and an extended definition of related entities through a wider definition of subsidiary and holding company.[367]

There is already a statutory fine for preparing misleading accounts with knowledge or recklessness. The proposal of the Law Committee is to extend the statutory scope of the Company Law to make anyone who has knowingly or recklessly been involved in the preparation of misleading financial statements subject to criminal sanctions.[368] But the danger is to "lead to an overemphasis on American-style legalistic interpretations and ever more complex and detailed rules."[369] It is also recommended that there be an administrative power of the DTI and the Financial Reporting Review Panel (FRRP) to require companies to restate accounts and allow a judicial appeal from this requirement.[370]

Among the items to be covered in the new mandatory OFR would be market changes, new product introduction or services introduction, changes in market, turnover and margins, new product acquisition and disposal, and the company's drivers, including a review of each division and how it has measured up to objectives. To the extent material: customer supplier dependencies, technological change, market competition, financial risks, health and environmental concerns, projects to enhance brands, tangibles and intangibles, research and development (R&D), and training.[371] Directors would not be expected to make "forward looking statements,"[372] while they are given a safe harbor to do so in the United States.[373] The new OFR should be applied to all large public companies and groups of companies should be subject to auditor review of those parts that can appropriately be audited.[374] The report also considers international accounting standards (which will now be mandated in 2005)[375] and electronic reporting (whether it should be mandatory) and distribution of information via the Internet (should rules be mandatory and standardized?).[376] The role of auditors is the final consideration for large companies. An exemption from liability for forward-looking statements—to directors and auditors—is proposed in this section.[377] While the Steering Committee discusses auditor independence, no firm view emerges, and the issue is handed off to European regulation and the Ethics Standard Board (which was enacted the year prior to this report).[378] However, the Steering Committee proposes to add new legislation to overrule case law and provide that auditors owe a duty of care to shareholders while at the same time eliminating Section 310 of the Companies Act 1985, which forbids auditors from entering into any contract to limit liability subject to shareholder approval. The Auditing Practice Board standards would provide a framework for limited liability.[379] The law should be clarified so that firms are liable for fraud, breach of duty by their directors and employees, and third parties such as auditors should be entitled to invoke such imputed liabilities against the company; companies should have a duty to bring to the attention of auditors matters within their knowledge that are material to an audit.[380] The remaining chapters of the report are related to implementation in smaller public and all private companies. The final report of the Steering Committee on Company Law was presented in 2000 and included draft legislation. The DTI is to propose legislation in the 2002 session of parliament.

In 1991, the Auditing Practices Committee was reconstituted as the Auditing Practices Board.[381] The net effect was a quasi-independent body where the London Stock Exchange and the Bank of England are involved in picking the chairman of a body that issues standards in its own name and of which half the members are non-auditors. Agenda papers are available to the public, but the public is excluded from meetings. Some continued to press for an independent regulatory body while others rejected the plan as inadequate, "half-hearted," and a "sham." In the opinion of one commentator, the U.K.

state and capitalist classes have a long history of compromises, and the non-auditors "co-opted onto the Accounting Practices Board (APB)" were primarily company directors. In the event of failure, the problems can easily be attributed to the accountancy bodies rather than the state or the capitalist system. Of 766 auditors who resigned in 1988–92, only 19 resigning auditors provided a reason for their resignation, which, in their opinion, the shareholders and creditors needed to know.[382] A proposal for reform of the U.K. Companies Acts suggests that stakeholders who are providers of human capital should be considered as a class whose interest is affected by auditor resignation; there should be a formal regulatory mechanism that routinely investigates situations in which there is prima facie evidence to doubt that an auditor has made full disclosure; auditors should be subjected to a statutory duty of care to shareholders and those creditors who can establish that auditing was responsible for losses; the incoming auditor should have statutory right of access to the files and working papers of the outgoing auditor; the audit committee should have a statutory right to auditor files; and the details of any discussion between incoming and outgoing auditors should be filed by companies.[383]

The proposals for reforming corporate governance including increased responsibility for the audit committee and new ideas about regulation of the accounting and auditing profession are discussed in chapter 6 so that they can be compared to those of Sarbanes-Oxley.

EUROPEAN ECONOMIC AND MONETARY UNION AND A EUROPEAN CENTRAL BANK

On February 7, 1992, the EU memorialized negotiations undertaken within the intergovernmental conferences on European monetary and political union begun in December 1990 at the Rome Summit and ended in Maastricht in December 1991. This treaty, entitled Treaty on European Union,[384] enunciates an economic and monetary policy for the EU.[385]

One of the most important provisions for the establishment of a European central bank is that member states shall avoid excessive government deficits. Punitive measures are enumerated, including the requirement that member states concerned make a non-interest-bearing deposit to the community until the excessive deficit has been redressed. An excessive deficit[386] will be found where the ratio of all government debt to gross domestic product exceeds 60 percent. The EU may also impose fines.[387] Denmark and the United Kingdom have protocols to the treaty that enable these member states to refrain from implementing the third stage of the treaty, that is, a single currency and a European central bank, to which they would derogate their monetary policy.[388]

The primary object of the European Central Bank (ECB) is to maintain price stability.[389] The ECB has the exclusive right to issue bank notes within the eurozone.[390] In the protocol of the statutes, the ECB is guaranteed independence from national authorities.[391] The governing council consists of the members of the executive board and the governors of the national central banks,[392] and vote is by simple majority. Only where a decision concerns bank capital will votes be weighted according to national bank shares.[393] The ECB is also charged with prudential supervision of the financial system of credit institutions and of the financial system in general.[394]

The delegation of powers to the ECB under the treaty in the areas of prudential supervision and exchange rate policy is not clear. No clear mandate is given in the area of prudential supervision. Article 105 of the treaty reads in pertinent part that

> The Council may, acting unanimously on a proposal from the Commission and after consulting the ECB and after receiving the assent of the European Parliament, confer upon the ECB specific tasks concerning policies relating to the prudential supervision of credit institutions and . . . other financial institutions with the exception of insurance undertakings.[395]

Under Article 104, the ECB is barred from lending directly to governments or buying securities from them. This ban on monetary financing makes it questionable whether the ECB is permitted to engage in open market operations. According to one estimate, if the ECB's domestic assets were to grow at 5 percent a year, and all of its purchases were of Italian government debt, purchases would be no more than 2 percent of the debt stock.[396] So, open market operations would not monetize national debts.

When countries join a monetary union, they forego the use of monetary and exchange rate policies to stabilize national economies. Without such tools, the only remaining tool is fiscal policy. Because the EU budget is small, stabilization programs will have to be carried out at the national level without jeopardizing the fiscal stance of the EU as a whole.[397] There are pros and cons to a monetary union vis-à-vis a federal system. Whenever economic activity falls in a particular U.S. state relative to other states, its residents' federal tax payments fall and they receive more federal payments; this is not the case in a monetary union.[398] In addition to restrictions on excessive budget deficits discussed above,[399] the treaty contains a no-bailout clause.[400] The EU budget could become more flexible in due course if certain programs were shifted from the national to the EU budget, particularly unemployment insurance.[401] This would depend on the willingness of rich member countries to underwrite the costs of adjustment in economically less developed member countries. But, as U.S. experience has shown, off-balance sheet expenditures may be less politically sensitive.

The EU commission detailed what it considers to be the prime benefits of economic and monetary union (EMU).[402] In its view, the very purpose of an international regime is to set rules that apply to all participating countries and that can be maintained without hegemony. The commission remarks that the flaw of the Bretton Woods System is that the leadership was given to one particular country (i.e., the United States), independent of the quality of its policy.[403]

Here is the impetus behind EMU. Although it is impossible to quantify the current role of the dollar, EMU and an ECB would undoubtedly limit the unilateral ability that the United States enjoys to monetize its deficit. The Maastricht Treaty even enunciates a procedure for the Council of Ministers[404] and the ECB to subscribe to an international monetary regime such as Bretton Woods.[405] This is the kernel of EMU. Consider the clout carried by the EU in the GATT. If EMU had been in place in early 1992, it is not clear that the U.S. Federal Reserve Bank could have lowered short-term interest rates without creating a dollar crisis.

The goal of price stability may have been appropriate to the 1980s, but conflicting goals of financial stability and economic growth may prove more important in the future. (The exchange rate mechanism survived throughout the 1980s because of an EU consensus on the primacy of price stability.) A short-term economic policy of price stability cannot serve as the foundation of EU monetary and financial law. The language of the statute that commits the ECB to price stability may be anathematic to the lender of last resort function that a central bank must play. The role played by a central bank in a financial crisis is foreclosed under a strict interpretation of the statute.[406] Although national central banks must be involved in lender of last resort operations, an integrated financial market poses the possibility of EU-wide contagion.[407] The tension between monetary policy and the lender of last resort function is all too clear.

A European Monetary Union inevitably reduces the costs of transactions for EU financial institutions operating within the eurozone. Directly, there will be fewer charges for foreign currency risk, and, indirectly, financial institutions would be able to assess the value of banking and security issues in their own currency.

The potential role of an ECB in the arena of prudential supervision is not readily apparent. Aside from its coordination of financial regulation, its attitude toward the bailing out of financially troubled institutions as a supplement to deposit insurance would be important in determining its functions. Even more important would be the role it would play in relation to the securities markets and the securitized markets (commercial paper and mortgage-backed securities). The possibility of an ECB that would not respond to liquidity crunches in securities markets is something to consider. Continental banking supervisors are not used to an independently functioning securities market requiring injections of liquidity through the easing of short-term interest rates, as was necessary in the United States in the 1987 market break. The willingness to perform this function is a sine qua non of a successfully functioning ECB, which will provide support for all EU securities markets, particularly those in the United Kingdom, which, as of this date, are the only ones that form a sector independent from the banking sector. The role of the central bank in providing credit to the securities markets is discussed in greater detail in chapter 3 in relation to the United States.

The question of the European Central Bank's authority in prudential supervision can most optimistically be described as open. The Treaty of Maastricht posed difficult hurdles for the ECB to become lead European regulator.[408] (These are embodied in the ECB statute annexed to the treaty.)[409] The emptiness of these provisions, unless there is a unanimous decision by the Council of Europe, a highly unlikely proposition, assures that each nation in Europe will perform its own LLR functions and redistribution of wealth will occur through other means within the EU. More importantly, it assures that, insofar as Europe is concerned, the Bank for International Settlements is the forum that will determine the new capital adequacy regime.

The Bank of England retains an LLR function under a memorandum of understanding between the Treasury, the Bank of England, and the FSA.[410] However the advisability of separating prudential supervision and monetary policy could only have been undertaken in anticipation of eventual monetary union. The risk for each nation that joins the euro is that domestic banking crises cannot be resolved by lowering interest rates. Greenspan lowered interest rates in response to the world economic crisis of 1998 and lowered them again after September 11. Volcker lowered interest rates in 1987 after the market crash and achieved astounding results. Yet, the United Kingdom is better off than other nations that suffer domestic rather than pan-European banking crises, since at least it controls its own monetary policy. Yet, in the era of globalization, it is common knowledge that, when Wall Street sneezes, everyone gets a cold. Within the EU, the risk of a domestic banking crisis limited to one country has not been adjudged significant enough to outweigh the benefits of monetary union.

In EU Directive Directive 2000/12[411] (hereinafter SBDII), the European Union found it necessary to restate the second banking directive with minor emendations. Recital 23 provides for a contact group of host country regulators. SBDII departs from its predecessor in two significant respects. In SBDI, the host country had control of liquidity issues. In SBDII this reach of host country control is extended to monetary policy.[412] One important addition to this directive, however, is home country control over the deposit insurance scheme.[413] In *Germany v. The European Parliament and Council*,[414] Germany sought to annul Directive 94/19, the Directive for Deposit Schemes,[415] because certain host countries did not provide as much deposit insurance as did Germany; the ECJ found against Germany, so SBDII assuages Germany's concerns. SBDII also takes a new approach in allowing cross-border banking services without a permanent establishment[416] and allows for the provision of investment services such as acting as securities brokers, the buying and selling of investment securities, and the arrangement of alternate funding for clients in capital markets.[417] Thus the structure of SBDII, as one commentator notes, would tend toward the formation of a single regulator for both banking and investment services.[418] The joint supervision now exercised by the FSA would fit neatly into this pattern. Banking and securities activities are regulated by one entity in almost all European countries, although insurance is separately regulated in a great number. The ESCB's (European System of Central Banks) potential stock as the regulator par excellence took a nosedive when the United Kingdom, the EU's acknowledged leader in the prudential supervision of complex capital markets, decided to apportion monetary policy and prudential supervision, creating the FSA to become the sole regulator for prudential supervision, of all financial firms and related businesses.

THE FSA, THE ACCOUNTING STANDARDS BOARD, AND THE EU

During the French presidency of the European Commission in 2000, the former head of the European Monetary Institute, Baron Alexandre Lamfalusy, was appointed to deliver a report on the further integration of EU financial markets, particularly securities markets. The Lamfalusy Report delivered on February 15, 2001, recommends a single national regulator for each financial system but stops short of recommending an EU financial regulator and submits additional guidelines to be implemented by 2003.[419] The report proposed that legislation being considered by the European Parliament and the council be in framework form and vetted by a newly created securities committee (level 2) that would be given technical rulemaking powers, in eurospeak, a comitology committee.[420] The Lamfalusy Report also envisaged the creation of a regulators committee that would work with the Securities Committee and the commission and would develop common standards and practice in the EU (level 3), and a fourth level that would entail more vigorous enforcement of legislation by the commission. The securities and regulators committees were established as advisory committees by decisions of the commission in June 2001 and began to consider proposed market abuse and prospectus directives.[421]

The FSA has hardly been silent on the issue. Clive Briault of the FSA, who has spoken both on his own and in a report for the FSA, concluded that the current minimal state of cross-border business did not justify a transnational regulator.[422] The EU and Financial Committee concluded in the Brouwer Report, "The existing institutions arrangements provide a coherent and flexible arrangement for safeguarding financial stability in Europe. No institutional changes are deemed necessary."[423] Briault identifies harmonization of a "weights and measures" kind involving accounting and trading platforms, but he also stresses the importance of "high level core standards." He stresses the importance of regulatory objectives such as the regulatory objectives of the FSA. The attention to levels, which are broad principles like the core principles of securities regulation adopted by IOSCO,[424] are, in fact, a complete irrelevance to the business of securities regulation. There appears to be a class of bureaucrats that is totally seduced by the verbiage of FSA pamphleteering such as that contained in "A Regulator for a New Millennium." Meanwhile, the firms affected by regulations are struggling to keep up with an ever more insular vocabulary.

Yet the official response to the Committee of Wise Men is far more balanced. The report is convinced of the benefits that could accrue from an integrated European securities market. The report notes that, as a percentage of GDP, only the United Kingdom and the Netherlands have equity markets that approach the size of the U.S. market, while France and Germany have markets one-third the size on a GDP basis.[425] The report identifies clearing and settlement as contributing to 80 percent of the cost difference between Europe and the United States and also notes that restrictions on pension fund investment in equities is a major stumbling block to the success of European equities markets.[426] It identifies two main areas of concern: a single passport for issuers and harmonization of accounting standards.[427] Very troublesome are the FSA's four major problems with the implementation of directives: the two biggest problems that they identify are the directives themselves, which are not adequate for market needs, and the reservation of right to the member states in the name of consumer protection—general good provisions. Specifically, there are different continuous reporting and disclosure requirements and different processes for Internet offers.[428] Furthermore, the FSA claims the transparency rules are out of date and need to be revisited,[429] and there is uncertainty about the legal treatment of collateral in various member states.[430] On balance, the report overplays the technological issues, especially infrastructure, which are arriving at a rapid pace, and underplays the importance of international accounting standards. This is par for the course for a regulator born of a bull market. Without harmonized accounting standards, an integrated European securities market is an impossibility.

Since 1978, the Fourth Directive of Company Law[431] began harmonizing financial reporting standards, reflecting the concerns of different member states. The United Kingdom argued forcefully for the inclusion of a "true and fair view," which created particular problems for some member states since the concept was unfamiliar and resulted in particular problems of translation for them; the inclusion of a detailed format reflected the German chairmanship of the early drafting since such prescriptive formats were unknown in the United Kingdom or Ireland prior to the directive.[432] In the United Kingdom and Ireland, a "true and fair view" may be used to override specific accounting rules, whereas this is not the case in Germany, and there is a range of interpretations in the member states.[433]

The Fourth Directive of Company Law sets out a framework for valuation: the company must be presumed to be a going concern without evidence to the contrary, methods of valuation must be applied consistently from one period to another, and valuation must be prudent, meaning only profits made may be included in financial statements, all foreseeable liabilities and potential losses must be taken into account as of the balance sheet date, and account must be taken of depreciation.[434] Expenses may be reported as a type of expenditure such as the purchase of goods or wages or by function cost of goods depending upon administrative function. Generally, historical cost accounting must be employed, although companies are allowed to value tangible fixed assets by replacement cost or other methods to take account of inflation and may revalue tangible fixed assets and financial assets.[435] Fixed assets with a useful life must be written off; goodwill and R&D must generally be written off over five years; current assets must be valued at purchase or production cost;[436] and inventory must be valued as first in first out (fifo) or last in first out (lifo).[437] Member states are permitted to use the equity method for holdings in affiliated companies.[438] The accrual method is specified,[439] and incomplete payments must be amortized no later than the payment of the debt.[440] Deferred taxes may be recognized. Provisions for contingencies must not be greater than the amount required.

The Seventh Directive of Company Law[441] defines groups that must be consolidated for financial statements. There are more than 50 accepted forms of consolidation, which represents a political compromise.[442] Subsidiaries are defined as companies where voting control is exercised, or there is a dominant influence established, by contract.[443] Merger accounting is permitted where payments equal less than 10 percent of the nominal value of shares issued; minority interests must be shown separately, but all income must be consolidated.[444] Goodwill on consolidation must be recognized or amortized, and negative goodwill is taken into account only when realized.[445] One EU directive and an EU regulation have begun to alter the potential for an EU securities market by creating the framework for EU accounting standards based on International Accounting Standards (IAS) (see chapter 2). The directive concerns fair value accounting, and member states are to "permit or require" companies to comply with the terms of the directive.[446] The directive cites the desire to implement International Accounting Standards as its rationale.[447] Derivative contracts are defined as contracts that are not used to meet purchase or sale requirements and are not commodity contracts intended for delivery.[448] The definition is further restricted by defining the instruments concerned as those that are held as part of a trading portfolio or are derivative contracts.[449] Items may qualify for derogation if they are held under a fair value hedge accounting system.[450] Where an item is accounted for under fair value accounting, assumptions behind the valuation model used, per category of financial instrument and for each category, information about the instrument must be disclosed.[451] For fixed financial assets carried at values above fair value, where the option to revalue at fair value has not been used, the book value and fair value of each asset or class of assets and the reasons for not applying fair value, including the reasons that book value will be recovered, must be disclosed.[452] In relation to the company's use of financial instruments and where material, a company is obliged to explain its financial risk management policies and its exposure to price risk, liquidity risk, and cash flow risk. The directive comes into force in 2004.[453] However, it is unclear what the "permit or require" language entails.

On May 27, 2002, the European Parliament and council issued a regulation on the adoption of International Accounting Standards by 2005.[454] By the end of 2002, the commission shall decide upon the "applicability of the international accounting standards in existence upon entry into force of this regulation." Article 4 requires consolidated accounting for company accounts for those companies traded on a regulated exchange within the EU.[455]

CONCLUSION

The FSA has a decidedly Janus-faced approach to Europe. While the response indicates several areas where improvements are possible, it appears at times to scuttle the whole approach, such as in its broadside on directives, per se. However, this much is not surprising from an agency that represents an uneasy truce between bowler hats and cool Britannia. The United Kingdom has little enough to fear from Frankfurt or Paris as competitors. In the end, the city of London is the loser from the failure of the EU to develop an integrated securities market. The potentialities for the expansion of existing capital markets to fuel growth in the EU, which has yet to entirely shake off eurosclerosis, are enormous. Prime Minister Blair has announced a referendum on U.K. participation in the euro. An affirmative vote would be the most critical factor in encouraging U.K. leadership in the financial services arena.

The FSA is a mid-1990s style regulator, unarmed for the forward march into financial reporting and disclosure issues. The SEC, particularly after Sarbanes-Oxley, has its tentacles deeply into this area. While the FSA has authority over accountants within its disciplinary ambit, the Department of Trade and Industry is responsible for proposals to Parliament for improving corporate law and all areas relating to the FRRP and the audit panel.

Paranoia about Europe, which infects the FSA in its pronouncements, is also partly a result of the dysfunctional nature of the regulator. One commentator describes the FSMA as "a monster piece of legislation" and wonders whether the FSA is itself a monster.[456] That is a fair question, but he concludes that it should not be judged in the short term. However, its manner of doing business has gotten off on the wrong foot. While it is appropriate to gather so many regulatory functions into one agency, there will have to be a functional separation into clearly delineated areas in order for the FSA to succeed in the long run. Naturally, it will take a long time to develop an esprit de corps and a sense of mission; part of the problem is that, unlike the SEC, it was not born of troubled times and consequently did not benefit from the attention of the best of minds. Despite its manifold faults, the SEC is able to deliver cogent self-contained releases on a consistent basis, whatever detriments its policies suffer from. The FSA seems confused and hurried, as though, if it issues hundreds of consultative papers, it can rival the 70-year history of the SEC. There is no cogent presentation of any issue, including SRO reform, market abuse, disclosure requirements, or takeovers. The policy cobbles together previous policies of which it is but the continuation. It is imperative that the FSA conduct a comprehensive policy and organizational review. It would be best served doing so in the context of a plan for integrating Europe's fractured securities markets.

NOTES

1. *See* note 284 *infra* and accompanying text.

2. The principal directives relating to eurofinancial integration are the Consolidated Supervision of Financial Institutions (*see infra* note 158); the Second Banking Directive (O.J. Eur. Comm. L.386, p. 1, et seq.); the Own Funds Directive (O.J. Eur. Comm. L.124, p. 16 89/299/EEC); and the Solvency Ratio Directive (O.J. Eur. Comm. L.386 [1989], p. 14); the Investment Services Directive (*see infra* note 81); and its corollary, the Capital Adequacy Directive (*see infra* note 113). *See also* the Mutual Recognition of Prospectus Requirements (*see infra* note 87) and Mutual Recognition of Listing Particulars (*see infra* notes 85 and 86). The Second Banking Directive (SBD) and the Investment Services Directive (ISD) are the core of the single market in financial services. Liberalization in the insurance sector has not kept pace with that in the financial sectors. The Second Non-Life Directive (87/357/EEC, 31 O.J. Eur. Comm. [no. L.172] [1988]) and the Second Life Directive (Comm [88] 729 Final [December 23, 1988]) did not provide for community-wide branching. The Second Non-Life Directive enabled a single market in insurance (*see* Sydney Key, "Financial Integration in the European Community," Federal Reserve Board of Governors, International Discussion Paper no. 349 [1989], pp. 120, 123–24).

The Third Directive on Life Assurance (92/96 EEC [November 1992]), which amends the Second Life Directive, and the Third Directive on Non-Life Assurance (92/96 EEC [June 1992]), which amends the Second Non-Life Directive, establishes the right of community-wide branching for assurance undertakings whose head office is in the community. While provisions of these directives are broadly similar to the SBD and utilize authorization as a touchstone, these directives are specifically crafted to the particulars of the insurance industry.

3. The Investment Services Directive and the Capital Adequacy Directive did not come into effect until 1996.

4. Treaty of Rome, Article 52, Common Mkt. Rep. (CCH) ¶ 1402.

5. *Ibid.*, Article 59, et seq. Common Mkt. Rep. (CCH) ¶¶ 1502–41.

6. *Ibid.*, Article 7, Common Mkt. Rep. (CCH) ¶ 191.

7. Single European Act, Articles 13 and 16. Treaties Establishing the European Communities (Luxembourg, Office of the Official Publication of the European Communities, 1987).

8. *Ibid.*, Article 18 (voting is weighted by population of the member state with 54 [out of 72] required). Also cited as Single European Act, Article 18 adding Article 100A to the Treaty of Rome, Common Mkt. Rep. (CCH) ¶ 21070.

9. *Ibid.*, Article 18(2), *see also* Article 8(4) and (5).

10. *See* note 12 *infra.*

11. *Ibid.*, Article 20, ¶ 21190, adding a new Article 102A to the Treaty of Rome.

12. In *Cassis de Dijon*, the court found that Germany could not prohibit the import of liquor that was lawfully produced and sold in France solely because its alcoholic label was too low for it to be deemed a liquor under German law (Case 120-78 [1979] ECR 649). Common Mkt. Rep. (CCH) ¶ 8543 (1979).

13. Treaty Establishing the European Union (Amsterdam Consolidated Version), Official Journal of the Eur. Comm. C-340 (November 11, 1997) pp. 0173–0306; Title 11, Chapter 2, "Provisions Common to Several Institutions," Sections 251 to 253. The cooperation procedure allows the European Parliament (EP) to improve proposed legislation by amendment. This requires an opinion and involves two readings by the EP, giving its members ample opportunity to review and amend the commission's proposal as well as the council's preliminary position. The commission indicates which amendments it accepts before forwarding its proposal to the council. This results in a common position of the council. At second reading, the council is obliged to take into account those amendments of the EP that were adopted by an absolute majority insofar as they have been taken on board by the commission. The Treaty of Amsterdam has simplified the various legislative procedures by significantly extending the codecision procedure, which is in practice almost replacing the cooperation procedure. As a consequence, the cooperation procedure applies to very few cases (two Economic and Monetary Union [EMU] provisions).

The assent procedure applies to those legislative areas in which the council acts by unanimous decision, limited, since the Amsterdam Treaty, to the organization and objectives of the Structural and Cohesion Funds. The EP's assent is also required for important international agreements concluded between the Union and a nonmember country or group of countries, such as the accession of new member states and association agreements with third countries (absolute majority of the EP's total membership required). Since the Maastricht Treaty, the EP has a limited right of legislative initiative in that it has the possibility of asking the commission to put forward a proposal. As one of the two arms of the budgetary authority, the EP is involved in the budgetary procedure from the preparation stage, notably in laying down the general guidelines and the type of spending.

Appeals to the Court of Justice

In cases of alleged violation of the Treaty by another institution, the EP has the right to institute proceedings before the Court of Justice. This may take the following forms:

- the right to intervene, i.e., to support one of the parties to the proceedings, in cases before the Court;

- in an action for "failure to act," the Parliament may institute proceedings against an institution before the Court for violation of the Treaty;
- for the purpose of protecting its prerogatives, the EP may bring an action to annul an act of another institution. The EP may be the defending party in an action against an act adopted under the co-decision procedure or when one of its acts is intended to produce legal effects *vis-à-vis* third parties.

14. At its summit in Luxembourg in December 1997, the European Council decided that the enlargement process should encompass

- the European Conference, a multilateral framework bringing together ten central European countries, Cyprus and Turkey, which was launched on 12 March 1998;
- the accession process, covering ten central European countries and Cyprus, which was launched on 30 March 1998;
- the accession negotiations, which the European Council decided to open on 31 March 1998 with six countries, as recommended by the European Commission: Cyprus, the Czech Republic, Estonia, Hungary, Poland and Slovenia. (http://europa.eu.int/comm/enlargement/enlargement.htm; last visited October 21, 2002)

See generally, Commission of the European Communities, "Toward the Enlarged Union: Strategy Paper and Report of the European Commission on the Progress toward Accession by Each of the Candidate Countries" (September 10, 2002).

15. Z. Costa, Ente Nazionale Per L'Energia Elettrica (Case 6/64) (1964) ECR 585, CMLR 425. Common Mkt. Rep. (CCH) ¶ 8023.

16. Treaty of Rome, *supra* note 4, Article 187, Common Mkt. Rep. (CCH) ¶ 4712; Article 192, Common Mkt. Rep. (CCH) ¶ 4915.

17. *EC Commission v. Germany* (Case 205/84), (1987 Common Mkt. L. Rev. 69). *See also EC Commission v. France* (Case 220/83) (1987 Common Mkt. L. Rev. 113). *Insurance Services v. EC Commission v. Denmark* (Case 252/83) (1987 Common Mkt. L. Rev. 169).

18. *See* "Conduct of Business Regulation, the Investment Services Directive Proposal, and Other EU Legislation." *Infra* note 6.

19. Michael S. Raab, "The Transparency Theory: An Alternative Approach to Glass-Steagall Issues," *Yale L. J.* 97 (1988): pp. 603, 607. *See also*, letter of Brian Smith, Chief Counsel of the OCC (April 12, 1983) Rep. 1M (1983–84 Transfer Binder) Fed. Banking L. Rep. (CCH) § 88.421 at 77.544, granting approval for bank's sale of pass-through certificates backed by FHA-insured mortgages. Donald Langevoort, "Statutory Obsolescence and the Judicial Process: The Role of the Courts in Federal Banking Regulation," *Mich. L. Rev.* 85 (1987): pp. 672, 690–91.

20. Treaty on European Monetary and Economic Union (printed in full by Agence Europe, No. 1759/60, Feb. 7, 1992), Article 3(b), which states that in areas that do not fall within the exclusive competence of the community, it shall take action "in accordance with the principles of subsidiarity only if and insofar as the objectives of the proposed actions cannot be sufficiently achieved by the member states and can therefore by reason of the scaled efforts of the proposed action be better achieved by the community."

21. *See* chapter 4, "Gramm-Leach-Bliley . . . ," and accompanying text.

22. *See* George Zavvos, "Banking Integration in 1992: Legal Issues and Policy Implications," *Harv. Int'l. L. J.* 31 (1990): pp. 463, 481.

23. Ratios of Gross Debt to Total Assets (market value*):

Countries	1970	1975	1980	1985	1986	1987
Low leverage						
United States	.45	.52	.50	.50	.49	.51
United Kingdom	.51	.64	.63	.52	.48	.48
High leverage						
Japan	.86	.83	.84	.73**	.63	.59
Germany	.72	.76	.81	.71	.70	.77

These ratios are now considerably lower in all countries because of higher price earnings ratios.

*Private nonfinancial corporations (all producing enterprises for Germany) with total assets calculated as gross debt plus equity at market value.

**Break in the series.

Sources: National flow-of-funds statistics and BIS estimates. BIS, "58th Annual Report" at 85.

The high leverage of Germany, Japan, France, and Italy as opposed to the United States is in large measure indicative of the predominant universal banking system employed in these countries. The United Kingdom and the United States are the only countries employing capital market systems, although Japan has a few aspects of the capital market system, including a Glass-Steagall type separation. *See* chapter 7, notes 21, 22, 57, and accompanying text.

24. M. Clarich, "German Banking System: Legal Foundation and Recent Trends," European University Institute Working Paper 87/269, p. 5.

25. *Ibid. See also* "Monthly Report of the Deutsche Bundesbank," (August 24, 1984).

26. *See* notes 42–44 *infra*, and accompanying text.

27. Deutsche Bank, for example, owns 25 percent of the equity of Daimler-Benz.

28. *See infra* note 66 and accompanying text.

29. Bank for International Settlements (BIS), "59th Annual Report" (June 12, 1989), at 85.

30. *Ibid.*

31. *Ibid.*, at 84–85.

32. *Ibid.*, at 85.

33. *Ibid.*, at 87. In Japan, the main bank of a typical group of nonfinancial enterprises *(Kereitsu)* nowadays provides between one-fifth and one-third of the group's borrowings. For detailed description, *see* chapter 7, "The *Keiretsu*" and "The Role of Institutional Investors as Monitors."

34. "Common Position of the European Council No. 1 / 2001 of June 19, 2000, with a View to Adopting a Directive of the European Parliament and the Council on Company Law concerning Takeover Bids," O.J. Eur. Comm. C023 (Jan. 24, 2000).

35. *Ibid.*, at 205.

36. *Ibid.*, at 207.

37. *Ibid.*, at 207.

38. Foreign loans of U.S. banks went from $14 billion in 1970 to $405 billion at the end of 1982 (Robert Triffin, "The Paper Exchange Standard: 1971–19??" in *International Monetary Cooperation: Essays in Honor of Henry C. Wallach*, Princeton Essays in International Finance no. 69, 70, 81 [1987]. These loans resulted from OPEC deposits and capital inflows created by the rising deficit. One consequence was the necessity of U.S. banks to relend funds placed on deposit). When U.S. bankers awoke to discover the illiquidity of their loans they decreased their lending from $110 billion in 1982 to $1 billion in 1985. In 1986, to avoid suspension of interest payments by debtors, they increased lending by $59 billion *(ibid.)*.

Default by sovereign debtors beginning in 1981 was caused by the prevailing high rate of interest that resulted from inflation caused by the tripling of oil prices in 1979–80. Here the relation of commodity prices to currency and the relation of both to the soundness of the international banking system is brought into relief.

See also Jack M. Guttentag and Richard Herring, "Accounting for Losses on Sovereign Debt: Implications for New Lending," Princeton Essays in International Finance no. 172 (1989), p. 19, where the authors show an increase in outstanding loans to public borrowers and banks for Latin America from $49 billion in June 1982 to $61 billion in December 1987 in U.S. banks' exposure. Meanwhile, the statistics of the International Monetary Fund (IMF) (appearing in the report of the Deutsche Bundesbank) show a growth to $477 billion at the end of 1988 ("Report of the Deutsche Bundesbank for the Year 1988," p. 77). These figures are mismatched from the beginning but may be explained by loans made by unconsolidated subsidiaries. Exposure to Brady 15 loans was over 100 percent of stated capital in 1982 and has been reduced to approximately 70 percent for nine money-centered banks on the more favorable statistics (Guttentag and Herring, *supra* this note, at 19).

Banks internationally and American banks in particular were frantic to raise capital in 1982. Devices included the sale-leaseback of corporate headquarters so as to realize the market value of property that was held at book value. J. Guttentag and R. Herring, "Disaster Myopia in International Banking," Princeton Essays in International Finance no. 164 (1986), pp. 29–30.

39. There have been many explanations of why U.S. and U.K. bankers led the way in making loans to developing countries, most of the explanations tending toward the psychological rather than the economic. Broadly, these explanations can be grouped under the rubric of "moral hazard." If several of the major money center banks make a certain type of loan of sufficient magnitude, bankers become aware that the national government will be the de facto insurer of such loans. Furthermore, bankers in the United States share the propensity of other corporate executives to look at a very short-term horizon given the mobility within the U.S. corporate structure. Second, like investment bankers, the primum mobile for bankers is not the long-term quality of the loans made but rather the fees generated and paid up front by the transactions. An additional contributing factor may be disaster myopia—the temporal distance between bankers and the last experience of a financial panic. It is important to note that financial crises develop in financial markets, that is, London and New York as well as Singapore and Hong Kong.

40. For a description of the decline of the FRN market and the rise of ECP, *see* BIS, "58th Annual Report," at 108–9, 127–28.

41. *Ibid.*

42. J.G.S. Jeanneau, "Structural Changes in World Capital Markets and Eurocommercial Paper," Bank of England, Discussion Paper no. 37 (February 1989).

43. *Ibid.*, at 21 and 33.

44. *Ibid. See also* Ralph Bryant, *International Financial Intermediation* (Brookings Institution, 1987), pp. 6–10.

45. *Ibid.*, at 33. In 1988, net new issues of eurobonds showed a 25 percent increase over 1987 at $138 billion, below the peak of $160 billion in 1986 (BIS, "59th Annual Report," *supra* note 29, at 122); however, this picture is vastly distorted by the part played by Japanese euroequity warrants. By 1989, over 50 percent of bonds floated in the first half of the year were Japanese and 60.3 percent of dollar issues were Japanese. Deutschemark issues expanded from DM 12.9 to DM 22.2 billion *(ibid.)*. Together the Swiss franc, the yen, and the DM accounted for 32 percent of the currency denomination of eurobond issues (*ibid.*, at 123).

The eurobond market has been shrinking steadily in terms of its truly international dimension and has become transformed at least partially into an offshore market for Germany and Japan. However, the denomination of Japanese euroequity warrants in U.S. dollars raises interesting questions about the nature of the word "offshore" as contrasted with the word "international." Although dollar equity warrants are not permitted in Japan (*Financial Times*, March 10, 1990), the intricate network of Euromarkets serves to repatriate Japanese trade surplus to Japan; the period of heavy U.S. activity on the Euromarket took place because of the need to finance foreign subsidiaries of U.S. corporations.

The U.S. International Lending Supervision Act of 1983 required banks to establish Allocated Transfer Risk Reserves (ATRRs) for countries if the government determined that a country's loans were value impaired (49 Fed. Reg. 5591 [1984]). In practice, in part because of the unfavorable tax treatment of such reserves, ATRRs were never imposed for major debtor countries. (Guttentag and Herring, *supra* note 38, at 10–12. Substantial discretion is allowed and ATRRs have never been established for the larger debtors.) Citibank's $3 billion special reserve in 1987 was allowed as a deduction yielding a tax-deferred write-off, provided the loss was realized over a several-year period thereafter (*ibid.*, at 36). Tax benefits might be as much as $600 million where the loss is charged off against income for the year it is realized, and the Bank of England has imposed a forbidding matrix system requiring provisioning of up to 70 percent against less developed countries (LDC) loans (The "Bank of England Sets New Debt Provisioning Guidelines: 35%–50% Provisioning," *Fin. Reg. Rep.* 19 [February 1990]).

46. BIS, "Developments in International Banking," Q. Rep. 33 (February 1990).

47. *Ibid.*, at 34.

48. BIS, "59th Annual Report," *supra* note 29, at 108.

49. Japanese predominance in international banking assets is undercut by U.S. predominance in off-balance sheet financing discussed *infra*. For example, 65 percent of interest rate swaps are denominated in dollars. Nearly 90 percent of eurocommercial paper is denominated in dollars. "Developments in International Banking," *supra* note 46, at 33.

50. Committee on Banking Regulation and Supervisory Practices, "International Convergence of Capital Measurement and Capital Standards" (July 1988). Banking Law Rep. (CCH) ¶ 5403.

51. *See* Bryant, *supra* note 44, at 140–44.

52. The Capital Adequacy Agreement adopted at Basel is only one of several regulatory frameworks that might have been adopted. These standards were developed in the United Kingdom and Basel in 1981. Traditionally, a capital to assets solvency ratio was used without regard to risk. (Richard Dale, *Regulation of International Banking* 131 [1986]. *See also* William Lovett, "Moral Hazard in International Banking," *Ohio St. L.J.* 49 [1989]: p. 1365.) The general loan loss provision had, however, been the mainstay of national banking systems. While the United Kingdom had employed reserve requirements for domestic banking purposes, it did not do so with regard to international banking, a field in which it was, and has continued to be, the world's leading host. In 1978–80, Paul Volcker, newly appointed head of the Federal Reserve Board (FRB), voiced a great deal of concern about solvency in eurobanking and urged an international banking reserve requirement *(ibid.)*. However, the United Kingdom did not oblige, fearing the loss of international business. The result was the establishment of the U.S. International Banking Facilities (IBF), allowing U.S. businesses abroad to compete on equal terms with other banks in the Euromarket *(ibid.)*, i.e., without reserves.

53. G. Zavvos, "The Integration of Banking Markets in the EEC. The Second Banking Directive," *J. Int'l. Banking L.* 2 (1988): p. 53; M. Gossling, "The Capital Adequacy Framework—An Introduction," *J. Int'l. Banking L.* 6 (1988): p. 243.

54. *Supra* note 2.

55. G-10 Agreement, *supra* note 50, § 2.11(35), and SRD directive, *supra* note 2 at Article 6(2) and (4).

56. *Ibid.*

57. Own Funds Directive, *supra* note 2 at Article 6 1-A.

58. *Ibid.*, § B.

59. G-10, *supra* note 50, Annex I(C), and Own Funds Directive, *supra* note 2, Article 2(10).

60. G-10 Agreement, *supra* note 50 at Article l(b)(iii)(21), and SRD, *supra* note 2 at Article (2)(1)(4), originally included without restriction but subject to additional limitation, presumably in keeping with G-10. (Although loan loss reserves for specific loans are not to be included in general loan loss reserves, such inclusion has been effectively the result because the nature of loan loss provisioning in the EU and Japan makes no clear distinction between general and specific loan loss reserves. [Interview with FRB staff.] These anomalous approaches to loan loss reserves will yield different results for the United States and the United Kingdom, on the one hand, and universal banks in the EU and Japan, on the other hand. Even more important, however, may be the requirement of specific provisioning for less than fully collateralized loans. [*See* chapter 2, notes 217–18.])

61. Own Funds Directive, *supra* note 2, Article 2(2).

62. G-10, *supra* note 50, at Article l(b)(ii)16–17.

63. *See* chapter 2, *infra* note 216, for a discussion of Germany's proposal to allow the inclusion of these kinds of revaluation reserves for banks with a tier-one capital ratio of at least 5 percent, and with other reserves. (Two definitions of certain funds within Article 2 of the Own Funds Directive require expansion: revaluation reserves [within the meaning of Article 3 of Council Directive 78/660/EEC 0.1. no. L.222 (August 14, 1978) pp. 11, 22] and value adjustments. [Within the meaning of 37(2) of Directive 86/635/EEC O1 Eur. Comm. no. L.372 (December 31, 1986) p. 1. Articles 35, 36.] Revaluation reserves relates to concepts of consolidation and permits certain

intergroup financial transactions allowing simpler treatment of assets within a consolidated group.)

64. *Ibid.*, Article 35.

65. "Consolidated Supervision."

66. SRD *Supra* note 2, at Annex I, and G-10 *supra* note 50, at Annex 3(I).

67. Under Article 2, subparagraph 4 of the SRD, *supra* note 2, Germany, Denmark, and Greece may apply a 50 percent weighting to assets secured by mortgages and completed residential property, and on office or multipurpose commercial property provided that the sum borrowed does not exceed 60 percent of the value of the property in question.

68. SRD *Supra* note 2, Annex 2, and G-10, *supra* note 50, at Annex 3.

69. SRD *Supra* note 2, Article 6(a)(5) and (d)(I) and (3); G-10 *supra* note 50, Annex 2.

70. G-10 agreement, *supra* note 50, at Annex 3.

71. *Companies Act of 1989, Clause 5, inserting a new § 227 in the Companies Act of 1985 and Clause 19 inserting a new § 257 in the 1985 Act. See also* Bank of England, Banking Supervision Division (BSD 1989/1/1 "Loan Transfers and Securitization").

72. *Infra* note 141.

73. In the United States, commercial banks are monitored by federal financial institutions and examination councils. *See* "Asset Securitization," *supra* note 115 at 664. When asset sales involve recourse, such sales are treated as on-balance sheet liabilities except for mortgage-backed securities that are government-insured. (Actually, they are on-balance sheet but receive a 0 percent risk weight. [*Ibid.*]) If the securities representing the indebtedness are interest-only or principal-only strips, the strips will be treated as 100 percent risk. Final Rule Amendment to Regulations H and Y, 75 Fed. Reserve Bull. 157 and Appendix (1989). Capital Adequacy Guidelines for Risk Based Measures. Bank holding companies are governed by Generally Accepted Accounting Principles (GAAP), and thus asset transfers involving recourse and sales or financing treatment are determined by Financial Accounting Standards Board Statement no. 77 (FASB 77), which provides more lenient terms to treat asset sales as sales if (1) transferor surrenders future economic control of the future economic benefits relating to the receivables; (2) transferor can reasonably estimate its obligation under the recourse provisions; or (3) the transferee cannot return the receivables to the transferor except pursuant to the recourse provisions. (*Ibid.*) (In France, the equity investment in a Fond Common de Creance [FCC] by credit institutions operating through mutual investment funds may hold only up to 5 percent of the issue. The French legislation also contains certain investor protection measures, which are lacking in the U.S. and the U.K. legislation. The Commission des Operations des Bourses is responsible for overseeing establishment and the by-laws of the Fond Common de Creance.) J. B. Devade and P. Boys, "Securitization: Another Step toward Developing the French Market," *J. Int'l. Banking Fin. L.* 5 [1989]: pp. 218–19. Another interpretation of the Second Banking Directive [SBD] by the Banking Supervision Division of the Bank of England is worthy of notice. Cash collateral will receive a 100 percent risk weighting where the cash depositor is not of the same local domicile as the branch or subsidiary of the bank [BSD 1989/1, note 10], presumably because the charge of the bank over the deposit may be subject to collateral attack in the domicile of the cash depositor. Because other factors such as choice of law and floating jurisdiction must be evaluated, the regulation appears simplistic.

74. BIS, "Recent Innovations in International Banking" (1986), at 199.

75. *Ibid.*, at 229.

76. *Implementing the Second Banking Coordination Directive in the U.K.: A Consultative Document Issued by HM Treasury and the Dept. of Trade Industry* (July 1992).

77. *Ibid.*, at 8.

78. *Ibid.*, at 12.

79. Primary legislation was needed to make the 1987 Banking Act consistent with the European Communities Act of 1972 in regard to the question of punishable offenses that relate to the powers of banking supervisors to obtain information and carry on investigations.

80. SBD, *supra* note 2, Article 7.

81. Council Directive 93/22/EEC of 10 May 1993 on Investment Services in the Securities Field, O.J. Eur. Comm. L.141 11/06/1993 pp. 0027–0046.

82. In the context of the midterm review of the Uruguay Round of General Agreement on Tariffs and Trades (GATT) negotiations held in Montreal in December 1988, the concept of effective market access relating to host country treatment of foreign financial institutions emerged. (*See* the statement by Trade Ministers of the Trade Negotiations Committee of the GATT Uruguay Round [Montreal, December 8, 1988] p. 2). "Effective market access appears to encompass two different concepts: national treatment and . . . progressive liberalization" *(ibid.)*.

83. ISD, *supra* note 81, Title 5, Article 14.

84. *Ibid.*, Title 5, Article 14, ¶ 3. One of the most contentious debates surrounding the Investment Services Directive (ISD) concerned the publication of information with the timely screen-driven report of all information, which makes it difficult for a market maker to operate efficiently. The compromise agreed on required publication at the start of each day's trading on the market of the weighted average price, the highest and the lowest price, and the volume dealt with on the regulated market in question, and for continuous order-driven and quote-driven markets, publication at the end of each hour's trading of similar weighted average price, and volume for a six-hour trading period, and every 20 minutes of the weighted average price, and the highest and lowest price on the regulated market in question for a two-hour period. (*Ibid.*, Article 21.)

85. 87/345 EEC, O.J. Eur. Comm. L.185 (1987), p. 81.

86. 79/279/EEC.

87. Directive Coordinating the Requirements for the Drawing Up, Scrutiny, and Distribution of the Prospectus to Be Published When Transferable Securities Are Offered to the Public. (Mutual Recognition of Prospectus Requirements Directive), 90/211/EEC, O.J. Eur. Comm. L.112 (1990).

88. Department of Trade and Industry, "Listing Particulars and Public Offer Prospectuses, Implementation of Part 5 of the Financial Services Act of 1986 and Related EC Directives" (July 1990).

89. *Ibid.*

90. Act of Parliament, Financial Services and Markets Act 2000 (Elizabeth II, chapter 8).

91. *Ibid. See also* Financial Services Act of 1986 § 160.

92. *Ibid. See also* MRP, *supra* note 87, Article 1.1.

93. *Ibid. See also* Companies Act of 1985, § 79-2.

94. (a) Where securities are offered to persons in the context of their trade or occupations; (b) where securities are offered to a restricted circle of persons; (c) where

the selling price of transferrable securities does not exceed 40,000 ECU; (d) where the transferrable securities offer can be acquired only for a consideration of at least ECU 40,000 per investor and to transferrable securities of the following types: (1) to transferable securities offered at individual denominations of at least ECU 40,000; (2) to units issued by collective undertakings other than those of the closed-end type; (3) to transferrable securities issued by the state or regional authority; (4) to transferrable securities offered in connection with a takeover bid; (5) to transferrable securities offered in connection with a merger; (6) to securities allotted free of charge to the holders of shares; (7) to shares and transferrable securities equivalent to shares offered in exchange for shares of the same company; (8) to transferrable securities offered by employers for the benefit of employees; (9) to transferrable securities resulting from the conversion of convertible debt securities or warrants to shares; (10) to transferrable securities issued with a view to obtain the means necessary to achieve their disinterested objectives by nonprofit-making bodies recognized by the state; (11) to U.S. securities that are not the subject of a generalized campaign of advertising or canvassing.

95. The minimum contents of the prospectus includes information regarding (a) those responsible for the prospectus' names of the functions; (b) the number of securities being issued and the rights attached to them, income withheld at source, date of entitlement to dividends, person underwriting or guaranteeing the offer, restrictions on free transferability, establishments serving as paying agents, and the price of securities or the method of payment, procedures for the exercise of rights of preemption; (c) information about the issuer, including place of incorporation, applicable legislation, capital, groups of undertakings to which the issuer belongs, in the case of shares—any shares not representing capital, the amount of authorized capital, duration of the authorization, and indication of shareholders who directly or indirectly exercise or could exercise control of the management of the issuer; (d) the issuer's principal activities, description of its principal activities (dependence on patents and licenses and contracts of these are of fundamental importance, and any legal proceedings having an effect on the issuer); (e) the issuer's assets and liabilities, financial position, profits and losses, audited and consolidated accounts, interim accounts, name and person responsible for auditing; (f) issuer's administration, management, and supervision; (g) to the extent that such information will have an impact on the issuer, recent developments on its business and prospects (the most significant recent trends concerning the issuer's business since the end of the preceding financial year and information on the issuer's prospects for at least the current financial year). (MRP Directive, Section 3, Article 11.)

96. *Ibid.*, Article 21, 1 and 2.

97. *Ibid.*, Preamble.

98. Listing Particulars Directive 80/390/EEC, Section 2, Articles 8, 9.

99. 78/660/EEC.

100. 83/349/EEC.

101. Gerhard Mueller, "1992 and Harmonization Efforts in the EC," in Frederic Choi, *Handbook of International Accounting*, Chapter 12.1 (Frederick Choi, ed., 1991).

102. The expenditure format, Article 2.1-vertical form, Article 24-horizontal form and the operational format, Article 25-vertical form and Article 26-horizontal form.

103. Fundamental accounting choices include historical costs, growing concern, prudence, accrual accountancy, and consistency. Each category of assets and liabilities

is to be valued separately. Consistency must be present and departure from basic principles is permitted only in certain cases and must be specified.

The most important specific measurement requirements of the Fourth Directive include (1) property, plant, and equipment: fixed assets with limited useful economic life must be depreciated by systematic annual charges to operations. If a member country allows any special tax incentives that result in excessive depreciation, the companies must disclose the nature and amount of the charge; (2) intangible assets; (3) intercorporate investments; (4) inventories to be valued at the lower of cost or market-lifo (last in first out) or fifo (first in first out) or weighted average may be used; (5) current assets—to be valued at the lower of cost or market; (6) liabilities—long-term debt, if issued at a discount, a reasonable amount of amortization is required; (7) organization; (8) inflation accounting—either (a) reevaluation of tangible fixed assets or (b) replacement cost for plant equipment and inventory or (c) valuation of all financial statement items. Article 47(2)(a)(b) of the directive allows member states the option to permit preparation of publication of only abridged balance sheets and abridged notes; all EU member states have used this option in whole or in part. (Fourth Directive, *supra* note 99, Article 47/2[a][b].) *See also*, Ernst and Whinney, International Series, "The Fourth Directive European Company Law" (1980); Deloitte, Haskins, and Sells (Europe), "The Fourth Directive Company Accounts (1978) and Price Waterhouse, E. C. Bulletin, Special Issue "Fourth E. C. Directive" (1987).

104. Article 13 includes (1) an undertaking that is of negligible importance; (2) severe long-term restrictions, such as currency control; (3) disproportionate expenses or undue delay unavoidable with regard to the information; (4) shares of enterprise held exclusively for subsequent resale. (*Supra* note 156, at Chapter 12.16.)

105. Under the following circumstances, exemption from subconsolidation is possible: (1) annual financial statements of the exempted undertaking and of all its subsidiaries are consolidated in the financial statements of a larger undertaking; (2) consolidated financial statements of larger undertakings are drawn up in accordance with the Seventh Directive; (3) such consolidated statements are published in a manner prescribed by the law of the member country that governs that undertaking; and (4) notes to the financial statement of the exempted undertaking disclose the name and registered offices of the parent that draws up the consolidated financial statement and indicate that it is exempted from the requirements of the Seventh Directive.

106. Exemptions may be allowed if (1) the annual statements of the exempted undertaking and all of its subsidiaries are consolidated in the financial statement of a larger undertaking, (2) the consolidated financial statements are drawn up in accordance with the Seventh Directive or an equivalent manner (this would include U.S. Generally Accepted Accounting Principles [GAAP]), and (3) such consolidated financial statements are audited by appropriately authorized persons.

107. The following are essential requirements: (1) line by line consolidation, (2) conformity to the requirements of the Fourth Directive, (3) specifying applicable accounting principles, (4) disclosure of purchase accounting methods and pooling of interest methods, (5) application of the equity method of accounting to investments and associated affiliated companies, (6) allowing positive goodwill to be either amortized over five years or written off directly to owner's equity. Article 31 addresses negative goodwill.

108. 86/635/EEC. This directive was implemented in 1991. (*See generally* Price

Waterhouse, E. C. Bulletin, Special Supplement, "EEC Seventh Directive-Consolidated Financial Statements" [1983].)

109. *See* Lee Radebaugh, "Segmental and Foreign Operations Disclosure," in *Handbook of International Accounting*, chapter 23 (Frederick Choi, 1991).

110. *Ibid.* One effect of the Companies Act of 1989 is to permit settlement of securities and foreign currency transactions notwithstanding insolvency. Furthermore, the new Companies Act will also provide a process under which a defaulting counterparty will not be able to cherry pick among its various contracts and to disavow the one it does not want. Counterparty default will in general be given a higher priority than previously through additional safeguards. Cooperation between the bankruptcy trustee and the relevant regulatory and exchange official is mandated. (*Companies Acts of 1989, §§ 159–163.*) These new provisions will bring U.K. protection in line with that afforded in the United States.

111. ISD, *supra* note 81, at Article 10.

112. *See supra* note 85 and accompanying text.

113. Council Directive of 93/6/EEC of March 15, 1993, on the Capital Adequacy of Investment Firms and Credit Institutions O.J. Eur. Comm. L.146, pp. 0001–0026, Nov. 6, 1993 Annex I-Position Risk.

114. *Ibid.*, Article 2(2).

115. 92/30/EEC.

116. *Op. cit.*, Article 7, 3–7.

117. *Ibid.*, 4–6.

118. *Ibid.*, 12 and 13.

119. *Ibid.*, Article 14. A simplified approach for risk on derivative instruments particularly applicable to small firms is set forth in Annex 1, 11–9.

120. *Ibid.*, Article 2(f).

121. *Ibid.*, Article 4(1)(iii).

122. *Ibid.*, Annex 5, (6) and (7).

123. *See infra* note 154.

124. *Op. cit.*, Annex 6, (8)(2).

125. *Ibid.*

126. *Ibid.*, Annex 6, (8)(3 and 4). Five hundred percent of own funds or 600 percent after 10 days.

127. A long-term loan will have interest rate risk under the trading book option but not under the Solvency Ratio Directive (SRD), therefore it may be propitious to keep such a loan in the banking book.

128. Although an adjustable rate mortgage, which is prevalent in Europe, would be preferable to hold in the trading book.

129. Own Funds, *supra* note 2, Annex 5, (2)(ii).

130. Own Funds are defined in Directive 89/270/EEC; O.J. Eur. Comm. no. L.124, Annex 5 (1989), p. 16.

131. CAD, *supra* note 113, Annex I, Position Risk, (4) and (5).

132. *Ibid.*, Annex I (35–38). Stock index futures that are perfectly matched with underlying equities attract no general risk, depending on the extent of diversification (a Standard and Poors [S&P] 500 index versus an oil index) will attract a specific risk of 2 percent or 4 percent. Positions that are not offset will, like any other long or short position, attract an 8 percent general risk weighting (as well as a specific risk weighting).

133. *Ibid.*, Annex 2, Settlement and Counterparty Risk.

134. *Ibid.*, Article 5 applying the Large Exposure Directive, *supra* note 154, to securities firms, except that exposures to clients that arise on the trading book are calculated by including the excess of institutions' long positions over short positions in all the financial instruments issued by the client, plus underwriting of equity for the client deducting subunderwriting position and the exposures to other transactions and agreements for counterparty risk. *Ibid.*, Annex 6, (2). Competent authorities may authorize the limits to be exceeded provided that (1) the excess arises entirely on the trading book, and (2) the firm meets an additional capital requirement calculated by selecting those components that attract the highest specific risk requirement for up to 10 days. For the 10-day period, the additional capital requirement is 200 percent of these components. (*Ibid.*, Annex 6 [8] [1 and 2].) The limit is between 200 percent and 900 percent, but during the 10-day period, exposure must not exceed 500 percent. Any excesses for more than the 10-day period must not exceed 600 percent.

135. *Ibid.*, Annex 5, (6).

136. Because it is the lender of last resort function of central banks that provides the banking safety net, it would be difficult to limit the safety net to nonsecurities activities. Furthermore, deposit insurance would have to be similarly limited. Even so, it is hard to envision a situation where failure of a bank's trading book operation would not lead to a bank run unless there was an effective Chinese wall. Even if activities were segregated into a subsidiary and capital deducted, without Chinese walls, banks could make loans to their securities affiliates and related issuers. Such practice is not possible in the United Kingdom where the Bank of England continues to monitor such transactions informally. Yet France's system was similar to the United Kingdom's, and prior to the *petit Bang* of 1988, a Chinese wall existed between banking and trading activities. (C. D. Deboissieu, "The French Banking Sector in Light of European Financial Integration" in *European Banking in the 1990's*, J. Dermins, ed.) In all likelihood the U.K. concept of segregating the securities activities of banks is the result of the lower capital requirements for broker dealers in the United Kingdom. Such segregation is not prevalent in universal banking systems because securities firms, distinct from banks, have been of minimal importance or even nonexistent in universal banking systems. (*See* "Financial Systems in the United Kingdom and Germany.")

137. G-10, *supra* note 50, at Article l(c)(24)(ii).

138. Own Funds, *supra* note 2, at Article 2(1)(12–13).

139. Council Directive of 13 June 1983 on the supervision of credit institutions on a consolidated basis (83/350/EEC), 26 0.1. Eur. Comm. (no. L.193) (1983), p. 18.

140. *See* note 158, *infra*.

141. O.J. no. L.372, 1 (1986).

142. *See* note 100, *supra* and accompanying text. Member state banks that currently have subsidiaries in other member states may well close them down as they would then be subject to the full regulatory requirements one more time than is necessary, and branches may become comparatively more advantageous.

143. The integration of this EU directive into U.K. financial law illustrates the possibilities for misapplication of EU law. The Banking Supervision Division of the Bank of England policy statement distinguishes between consolidated supervision and consolidation of financial returns. (Bank of England, Banking Supervision Division/ 1986/3.) This distribution is essential to understanding consolidated supervision as opposed to the consolidation supervision of capital ratios. In 1983, continental banking supervisors were implementing the same ratios for banking and securities activities,

while the United Kingdom was implementing more permissive ratios for securities firms. (*See infra* notes 237 and 238.) The approach of the EU directives on capital adequacy of banking institutions as contained in the Capital Adequacy Directive (CAD) and the trading book option, which banks may use for their securities activities, means that the consolidation of a securities subsidiary of a parent bank involved the consolidation of its trading book with the bank's trading book at the same capital adequacy ratio, not at the higher investment book level.

144. SRD, *supra* note 2, Article 3(iii).

145. *Ibid.*, Article 3(5).

146. BIS and Committee on Banking Regulations and Supervisory Authority of the Group of 10 Countries, *Basel Concordat of 1975.*

147. BIS and Committee on Banking Regulations and Supervisory Authority of the Group of 10 Countries, *Basel Concordat of 1981.*

148. *Ibid.*

149. SBD, *supra* note 2, Article 12(1).

150. *Ibid.*, Article (10). Other thresholds for qualified holdings requiring the holder to inform competent authorities about increases and decreases in position are reached at 20 percent, 33 percent, and 50 percent (*ibid.*, Article 11).

151. *Ibid.*, Article 12(2). But member states are not required to apply limits to holdings in insurance companies (*ibid.*, Article 12[3]).

152. *Ibid.*, Article 12(7).

153. *Ibid.*, Article 12(6).

154. The transitional period is seven years and ended in 2001 ("Communication from Commission to the European Parliament") pursuant to Article 149.2(b) of the Treaty of Rome, relating to the current position adopted by the council with a view to the adoption of the directive on monitoring the control of large exposures of credit institutions. Article 4(1).

155. (*Ibid.*) The background of the Large Exposure Directive (LED) dates back to the 1984 failure of the firm of Johnson Mathey, which created upheaval in the U.K. banking system, ultimately leading to the Banking Act of 1987. (Graham Penn, *Banking Supervision: The Banking Act of 1987: Regulation of the U.K. Banking Sector under the Banking Act of 1987* [Butterworth's Legal Pub., 1989], pp. 14–15.) At that time, the Bank of England employed a two-tiered regulatory system. In reaction to the First Banking Directive, the Banking Act of 1979 had provided statutory regulation for deposit-taking credit institutions but continued to supervise other institutions (recognized banks) like Johnson Mathey on a more informal basis. At the time of its failure, Johnson Mathey had surpassed the recommended 10 percent limitations on loans to nonbanking affiliates. (*Ibid.*) The Banking Act of 1987 made the 10 percent guideline statutory, requiring postnotification and prenotification at 25 percent, (*ibid.*) instituted a Banking Supervision Division that is required to report annually regarding compliance with the act, and eliminated the two-tiered system. Like the failure of Continental in the United States, the failure of Johnson Mathey revealed noncompliance with the recommended limits on affiliated loans. The Large Exposure Provision of the Second Banking Directive (SBD) limits to 15 percent exposure to an individual participation that is not a financial institution and total nonfinancial participations to 60 percent. (SBD, *supra* note 1, at Article 11.) These two kinds of provisions—the SBD on participations and the LED on loans—are fundamentally developments toward statutory banking regulation to minimize systematic risk first introduced in the United States

in the Banking Act of 1987. (Graham Penn, *Banking Supervision: The Banking Act of 1987* [Butterworth 1989], pp. 14–15.)

156. Ernest Baltersperger and J. Dermins, *European Banking: Prudential and Regulatory Issues in European Banking, supra* note 136.

157. *Ibid.*

158. 92/30/EEC April 6, 1992; O.J. Eur. Comm. no. L.110 52 (1992).

159. *Supra* note 154.

160. Excluded are those banking groups in any of the following situations: (1) an undertaking is included and situated in a third company where legal impediments exist to the transfer of information; (2) the undertaking that should be included is of negligible interest (i.e., smaller than ECU 10 million or 1 percent of the total balance sheet); (3) in the opinion of the competent authorities responsible, consolidation would be misleading. *Ibid.*, Article 3(3).

161. *Ibid.*, Article 3(8).

162. *Ibid.*, Article 8(9).

163. *Ibid.*, Article 4(2).

164. *Ibid.*, Article 4(2). Where the liability of a parent undertaking is limited to a share of capital, there shall only be proportional consolidation. (*Ibid.*, Article 5[1–2].) Yet, consolidations may be complete depending upon control exercised. (*Ibid.*, Article 5[4].) Control is determined by significant influence, single management, or dominant management. Member states are to negotiate agreements with third countries to promote consolidated supervision of credit institutions that have their parent undertaking in a third country and credit institutions in a third country that have their parent undertaking in the community. (*Ibid.*, Article 8[1].) Under the 1992 Consolidated Supervision Directive (CSD), supervision is of financial holding companies and their subsidiaries. Mixed activity holding companies are required to provide information to regulators and are subject to on-the-spot verification of information. (CSD, *supra* note 139, Article 6[1][2].) The provisions in the Capital Adequacy Directive (CAD) for consolidated supervision of investment firms that do not contain a credit institution include similar provisions to those in the Solvency Ratio Directive (SRD) and the CSD. Member states may waive the applications of the requirements on an individual or a subconsolidated basis to an institution that as a parent undertaking is subject to supervision on a consolidated basis and to any subsidiary of such institution that is subject to their authorization and supervision. (CAD, *supra* note 113, Article 7[7].) The same right of waiver is granted where the parent undertaking is a financial holding company with its head office in the same member state. Competent authorities may delegate their responsibility for supervising the subsidiary's capital adequacy and large exposure to the authorities responsible for the parent undertaking. (*Ibid.*, Article 7[9].) Authorities may allow the offsetting of net positions in the trading book of one institution with positions in the trading book of another institution, foreign exchange positions in one institution to offset foreign exchange positions in another institution within the group (*ibid.*, Article 7[10]) and similar offsetting of these positions in third countries where capital adequacy rules are basically equivalent. (*Ibid.*, Article 7[11].) When a group does not include a credit institution, competent authorities may waive supervision on a consolidated basis, provided that each investment firm in such a group (1) uses the same definition of "Own Funds" as is required in the directive (*ibid.*, Article 7[4]. Own Funds defined in Annex 5 [9]); (2) meets the capital requirements imposed on a solo basis; and (3) sets up systems to monitor and control the sources of capital

within the group. (*Ibid.*, Article 7[4].) However, should the waiver be given, authorities must be notified of the risks that could undermine financial positions and may take measures to limit transfers of capital from such firms to group entities. (*Ibid.*, Article 7[5].) Particular measures shall be taken to monitor risks of large exposures.

The CAD provides many exceptions to consolidated supervision and by allowing for the offsetting of net positions, consolidated supervision seems only to help the firm reduce its capital requirements. Nonetheless, the import of the consolidated supervision rule is that consolidated supervision may be waived only where a firm receiving the waiver of supervision complies with the rules of the directive. Therefore, it is quite likely that all unregulated affiliates and subsidiaries of investment firms, together with unregulated affiliates of credit institutions, must comply with capital adequacy standards. This is in sharp contrast with the situation in the United States, where, although bank holding company structures are subject to rigid supervision, affiliates of securities firms may be completely unregulated. (*See* chapter 3, *infra* notes 71–74, and accompanying text.)

165. *Ibid.*, at 5.

166. *See supra* note 17.

167. This is a view derived from several components. *See* The Securities Association, *The Investment Services Directive* (1990); SIB, "Conduct of Business Regulation: The International Dimension." Speech given by David Walker, Chairman of the Securities and Investments Board at the 14th Annual Conference of IOSCO in Venice on September 20, 1989.

168. ISD, *supra* note 81, Article 10 and Article 11.

169. O.J. Eur. Comm. L.375 (1985), 851611/EEC.

170. *Ibid.*, Article 44. *See also* Key, *supra* note 2, at 119, but the marketing and advertising of Undertaking for Collective Investment Trusts (UCITs) remain under host country control.

171. *Financial Times*, March 13, 1990, at 1.

172. As David Walker, the Chairman of Securities and Investments Board (SIB), remarked at an International Organization of Securities Commissions (IOSCO) meeting in 1989. (Walker, *infra* note 167, at 7, 8.) Examples of specific problems posed by the international organization of securities markets are, according to Walker (1) advertising and cross-border selling techniques, (2) proper prioritization of client business, (3) higher risks of market manipulation, and (4) preferential soft-commission arrangements. (*Ibid.*) Also, stabilization practices vary widely between exchanges. The amenability of these problems to EU and international cooperation is questionable.

173. Financial Services Act of 1986 § 31B.

174. The Securities Association, *infra* note 295. While it was quite clear that investment firms are able to be regulated by either the Securities and Investments Board [SIB] or the relevant self-regulatory organization [SRO], according to their preference, foreign banks and investment companies have chosen to be regulated by SROs as opposed to the SIB. [Phone interview with staff member of SIB.] One possible explanation for this preference is that the common fund for compensation to investors is spread out over the several thousand members of a particular SRO and must be absorbed by the 60 or so members that are directly authorized by the SIB, and the SIB members include U.K. clearing house banks and building societies which, of course, have a phenomenal potential exposure.

175. The instruments listed in Section B include transferrable securities, units in

collective investment trusts, money market instruments, financial futures contracts, forward interest agreements, interest rate currency, and equity straddles, and options on any of the above (ISD, *supra* note 81).

176. *Ibid.*, Title 2, Article 3.

177. *Ibid.*, Article 5.

178. *Ibid.*, Article 6.

179. On May 20, 1997, the U.K. Chancellor of the Exchequer announced that responsibility for banking supervision was to be transferred to an enlarged Securities and Investment Board, which would also subsume the three self-regulatory agencies (SROs). On October 28, 1997, in "Pathfinder Prospectus," the Financial Services Authority (FSA) came into being. In the Bank of England Act 1998, the responsibilities for banking supervision were transferred to the FSA. A Draft Financial Markets and Services Bill was published by the Treasury on July 30, 1998. The FSA then published "Meeting Our Responsibilities," a blueprint of how it proposed to proceed. The Financial Services and Markets Act 2000 became an act of Parliament.

180. The Guide to Banking Supervisory Policy supercedes the Banking Supervision Division Notices of the Bank of England: BSD/1989/1\d/1992/3 and S&S/1996/8. *See generally*, Steve Curtis, "A Practical Guide to the New FSA Rules for Securitisations and Loan Transfers," *Journal of International Banking Law* (1999): p. 260.

181. The Guide, Section 1.2.

182. The Guide, Section 2.2.

183. The Guide, Section 6.2.4.

184. The Guide, Section 7.4, paragraph 9. Under Section 6.2.3, any credit enhancement must be structured in accordance with certain principles; otherwise, the Financial Services Authority (FSA) will not recognize a clean break: (1) it must be limited in amount and duration; (2) There must be no recourse beyond the fixed contractual obligations provided for in the facility; (3) The facility must be separately documented from any other facility in the bank; (4) Subject to increase in the event of substitution or replenishment, the transaction should be undertaken at the initiation of the scheme; (5) The details of the facility should be disclosed in the relevant offering circular or other documentation; (6) Payment of any fee or other income for the facility must not be further subordinated beyond what is expressly provided for in the payment entitlement provisions.

185. Definitions under the Guide, *see also* Laura Stuart and Gareth Old, "The FSA Rules for Securitisation and Loan Transfers—A User's Guide," *Journal of International Banking Law* (2000): p. 211.

186. Curtis, "A Practical Guide to New FSA Rules," *supra* note 180.

187. Laura Stuart, "Revisions to the FSA Guide: Securitization and Asset Transfers," *Journal of International Banking Law* (2000): p. 87.

188. Stuart and Old, "FSA Rules for Securitisation," *supra* note 185, p. 213.

189. The Guide, Section 6.3.2. *See also* Curtis, "A Practical Guide to Securitisations," *supra* note 180.

190. The Guide, Section 6.3.3.

191. The Guide, Section 7.5. The sponsor or repackager may provide bridge loans provided the term is three months or less, and the loan must have senior secured status.

192. The Guide, Section 5.2.3.

193. Stuart and Old, "The FSA Rules for Securitisation," *supra* note 185, p. 214.

194. *Ibid.*, (Stuart and Old), p. 211.
195. *Ibid.*, (Stuart and Old), p. 212.
196. The Guide, Chapter TU.
197. The Guide, Section 2.2.
198. The Guide, Section 3.6.
199. *Legal Business*, October 1998, p. 40 cited in Curtis, "A Practical Guide to the New FSA Rules," *supra* notes 180.
200. Regulation 93-06 of December 21, 1993, cited in Curtis, "A Practical Guide to the New FSA Rules," *supra* note 180.
201. Peter Scherer and Frederico Torzo, "The Capital Treatment of Derivatives in Europe," *Journal of International Banking Law* (1999): p. 144.
202. Commission Bancaire, "Traitment prudentiel des instruments derives de credit" (1998).
203. Financial Services Authority, "Credit Derivatives" (July 1998).
204. *Ibid.*, p. 149.
205. *Ibid.*
206. Directive 98/31/EEC of the European Parliament and the Council of June 22, 1998 amending Council Directive 96/6/EEC on the capital adequacy of investment firms and credit institutions. O.J. L.204/13.
207. Financial Services Authority, "Building the New Regulatory" (December 2000).
208. *Ibid.*, p. 12.
209. *See* chapter 6, "The Sarbanes-Oxley Act. . . ."
210. The Financial Services and Markets Act 2000, Part 1, Sections 1–6 2000 Chapter c.8.
211. *Ibid.*, Sections 8–11.
212. *Ibid.*, Sections 14–18.
213. *Ibid.*, Part 2, Section 19.
214. *Ibid.*, Section 20.
215. *Ibid.*, Section 21.
216. *Ibid.*, Section 22.
217. *Ibid.*, Sections 22–25.
218. *Ibid.*, Sections 26–30.
219. *Ibid.*
220. *Ibid.* Part 4, Sections 40–43 and 55 et seq.
221. *Ibid.*, Sections 59–63.
222. *Ibid.*, Sections 64–70.
223. *Ibid.*, Section 71.
224. *Ibid.*, Part 6, Section 74.
225. *Ibid.*, Sections 75–78.
226. *Ibid.*, Sections 79–83.
227. *Ibid.*, Sections 84–87.
228. *Ibid.*, Section 87.
229. *Ibid.*, Sections 88–89.
230. *Ibid.*, Section 90.
231. *Ibid.*, Sections 91–94.
232. *Ibid.*, Section 98.
233. *See infra* notes 305, 306, 309, and accompanying text.
234. *Op. cit.*, Part 10, Chapter 1, Sections 138–43.

235. *Ibid.*, Sections 144–47.
236. *Ibid.*, Section 150.
237. *See* note 180, *supra.*
238. *Op. cit.*, Part 11.
239. *Ibid.*, Part 12.
240. *Ibid.*, Part 13.
241. *Ibid.*, Part 19.
242. *Ibid.*, Part 20.
243. *Ibid.*, Part 21.
244. This part establishes the manager of the scheme and the priority of right in certain persons insolvencies.
245. *Op. cit.*, Part 24.
246. Part 16.
247. Part 17. These schemes are divided into closed end and open ended and into a separate category of authorized unit trusts and open-ended investment companies.
248. *Ibid.*, Part 17, Sections 264–69.
249. *See* note 170, *supra* and accompanying text.
250. *Op. cit.*, Sections 270–82.
251. *Ibid.*, Part 22, Section 346.
252. *See* chapter 6, "The Sarbanes-Oxley Act. . . ."
253. John Crossthwait, "Financial Services and Markets Act: A Critical Assessment of the New Financial Promotion Proposals," *Journal of International Financial Markets* (2001).
254. HM Treasury Financial Promotion Third Consultation Document (October 2000).
255. *Op. cit.*, at 4.
256. *Ibid.*, at 6.
257. *Ibid.*, at 9.
258. FSA, Code of Market Conduct, April 30, 2001, issued pursuant to Section 119 of the FSMA. *See also* Karen Connoly, "Revised FSA Code of Market Conduct," *Journal of Financial Markets* (2001): p. 51.
259. *Ibid.*, at 53.
260. FSA, "Conduct of Rules Sourcebook," reporting the main issues from CP 45 Conduct of Rules Sourcebook; CP 57 Conduct of Rules Supplement and in part from CP 61 The Regulation of Stakeholder Pensions.
261. *See* the introduction of this chapter.
262. *Op. cit.*, at 3.2 and 3.3.
263. v 4.3 and 4.4.
264. *Ibid.*, 4.4–4.9.
265. *Ibid.*, 4.15–4.17.
266. *Ibid.*, 5.
267. *Ibid.*, 5.15 et seq. Originally set forth in CP 43 and 57.
268. *Ibid.*, 5.87 to 5.111 subject to special provisions for collateral and foreign jurisdictions.
269. *See supra* note 234.
270. *See* chapter 3, "Securities Settlement Systems (SSS)."
271. *Conduct of Rules Sourcebook, supra* note 260 at A.86–90. Mirror provisions apply to custody during settlement. The Financial Services Authority (FSA) had originally

thought of proposals involving segregation, but these proved too cumbersome to implement.

272. *See* e.g., FSA, CP 64, "The Supervision Manual," for a discussion of the supervision manual to be distinguished from the consultative paper of the same name.

273. FSA, "Authorisation and Supervision Manual" (October 2001) (feedback on CP 63 and 64 and chapters of the Authorisation and Supervision Manual).

274. Regulations 2001, SI 2001, no. 2511.

275. *Op. cit.*, identifying Chapter 5 of the Authorization Manual explaining how firms can utilize European economic area (EEA) passport rights under Schedule 3 and 4 of the FSMA.

276. *Ibid.*, Sections 74–76.

277. *Ibid.*, Sections 77–78.

278. *Ibid.*, Sections 79–83.

279. *Ibid.*, Sections 84–87.

280. *Ibid.*, Sections 87–89.

281. *Ibid.*, Section 90.

282. *Ibid.*, Section 91.

283. *Ibid.*, Section 98.

284. FSA, "Amendments to the Listing Particulars" (July 2001).

285. *Ibid.*, 6E 3 and 4.

286. *Ibid.*, 6E 5 and 6.

287. *Ibid.*, 6E 7.

288. *Ibid.*, 6E 8.

289. *Ibid.*, 6E 9.

290. *Ibid.*, 6E 10–11.

291. *Ibid.*

292. *Ibid.*, 6E 10 generally.

293. *Ibid.*, 11.8.

294. *See* note 182–98, *supra* and accompanying text.

295. *Op. cit.* 11.9.

296. *Ibid.*, 16.18 and Appendix.

297. *See supra* note 1.

298. *See* chapter 2, note 137, et seq. and accompanying text.

299. *Supra* note 210.

300. Amendments to Listing Particulars, *supra* note 284 at 25.3.

301. *Ibid.*, 25.6–11.

302. *Ibid.*, 25.13.

303. *Ibid.*, 27.5.

304. FSA, Draft Code of Market Abuse (2000), Consultative Paper no. 76. The directive will include a definition of inside information and market manipulation (Article 1) and disclosure requirements of issuers (Article 6) and Article 6(4) of the proposed directive will concern analyst conflict of interests and considers factors on how relevant research should be presented and factors that would require the disclosure of conflicts of interest. The specific provisions of the Market Abuse Directive are expected to take 18 months to hammer out. Currently, various EU countries have minimal research analyst disclosure requirements that focus on ownership by the analyst's firms of shares in the company and board of directors' interlocks. (The Committee of European Securities Regulators, "CESR Consultation on Possible Implementing Mea-

sures of the Proposed Market Abuse Directive" [CESR/02/089b, July 5, 2002]; *See also* appended consultation paper, "CESR's Advice on Possible Implementing Measures for the Proposed Market Abuse Directive" [CESR/02/089b].) In the United Kingdom, certain limitations on analysts are contained in FSA, "Price Sensitive Information Guide," which states that analysts should refrain from divulging price sensitive information that would cause the company to breach the listing rules, and companies are cautioned not to answer analyst questions that would result in divulging price sensitive information. This is a near equivalent of U.S. regulation FD, *see* chapter 4, note 19.

305. *See* Rosalind Wright, "Market Manipulation and Market Abuse: The Criminal, the Civil, and the Regulatory Interface," *Journal of International Financial Markets* (2001): p. 19.

306. Financial Services and Markets Act 2000, Section 118.

307. Section 397, reiterating Section 47 of the Financial Services Act of 1986; The FSMA empowers the Department of Trade and Industry (DTI) to give guidance as to when civil charges should be brought in lieu of criminal charges.

308. Julien Herbst and Kate McCaw, "Statutory Exceptions and Defenses: What Protection Is Available," *Company Lawyer*, pp. 206–212 (2001).

309. Council Common Position with a View to Adopting a Directive of the European Parliament of the Council on Insider Dealing and Market Manipulation, O.J. Eur. Comm. (228 E p. 0019 [Sept. 25, 2002]).

310. *R. v. Bates*, 2 All E.R 852 (1952).

311. *See* chapter 4, notes 4–6.

312. 1 All E.R. 961 (1981).

313. *See also* M. Gale, "Fraud in the Sale of Securities," *Company Lawyer* (2001).

314. *See* chapter 4, notes 105–25, and accompanying text.

315. William Emmons and Frank Shmid, "Universal Banking, Control Rights, and Corporate Finance in Germany," Federal Reserve Bank of St. Louis Review (July–August 1998), p. 19.

316. *Ibid.*, p. 20.

317. *Ibid.*

318. *Ibid.*, p. 22.

319. *Ibid.*, p. 26; banks must renew their proxies every 15 months.

320. *Ibid.*, citing Gottshalk.

321. *Ibid.*, p. 40.

322. *Ibid.*, p. 31; a prominent example is Siemens AG in which the founding family owned 6.94 percent of the capital but controls 14.03 percent of the votes on special issues (as of October 1996).

323. *Ibid.*, p. 33.

324. Rolf Ziegler, Donald Dender, and Herman Biehler, "Industry and Banking in the German Corporate Network" in *Networks of Corporate Power: A Comparative Analysis of 10 Countries* (Franz Stockman, et al., eds., 1985), pp. 91–111.

325. *Ibid.*, High leverage countries are characterized by extremely high price/earnings ratios, which are estimated at over 60 for Japan (about 4 or 5 times as high as would prevail in the U.S. or U.K. markets). (*Ibid.*, at 81.) One reason for this high leverage is that companies in Japan own considerable amounts of land (*ibid.*) which, given the current capital gains rate and low real estate taxes, means that few parcels of land are actually sold, and, when they are sold, are at an exorbitant price. A leverage buyout will typically involve a debt/asset ratio of 80 percent to 95 percent (*ibid.*, at 88)

but all bondholders will be arm's-length portfolio investors. But the risk inherent in the structure involves the new financial instruments such as resets, p.i.k.s., swaps, interest rate caps, futures, and options.

326. *Ibid.*

327. *Ibid.*

328. "Comparative Study of Corporate Governance Codes Relevant to the EU and its Member States," On Behalf of the European Commission, Internal Markets, Directorate General; Prepared by Weil, Gotschal and Manges (January 2002), Table K, citing F. Barca and M. Becht, *The Control of Corporate Europe* (Oxford University Press, 2001).

329. *Ibid.*, Executive Summary, Employee Representation.

330. U.K., London Stock Exchange, Committee on Corporate Governance, Combined Code: Principles of Corporate Governance and Code of Best Practice (June 1998), A.2.1 "A decision to combine the posts of Chairman and Chief Executive Officer in one person should not be publicly justified." By contrast, the Praeda Report (Italy) and the Olevincia Report (Spain) state that it is the practice in these countries to legally combine the roles.

331. *See infra* notes 352–53 and chapter 5, notes 22–26, and accompanying text.

332. *See supra* note 34 and accompanying text.

333. *Op. cit.*, Executive Summary, Shareholder Rights and Participation Mechanisms.

334. *Ibid.*, p. 48.

335. *Ibid.*, p. 49.

336. *Ibid.*

337. *Ibid.*, p. 53.

338. *See* chapter 5, note 10.

339. *Ibid.*, p. 54.

340. *Ibid.*, p. 54. There are a number of obvious criteria for determining independence, including to be employed in any capacity, be related, employed with a professional advisor, have a service contract, hold a position with a charitable company to which the firm makes contributions, benefit from related party transactions, cross-directorships, be on the board of a significant customer or supplier, or serve as the director of a significant competitor. (P.I.R.C Voting Guidelines, U.K., Part 2, p. 5. The definition in the Viennot II Report [France] and the German Panel Rules are far less restrictive.)

341. *Ibid.*, p. 61. These include the Olevincia Report (Spain), the Praeda Report (Italy), the Viennot II Report (France), The Combined Code (Belgium).

342. The Dual Code (Belgium) calls for a majority of independent directors. The Viennot Code (France) calls for a third. The German Panel Rules favor the use of supervisory committees for these functions.

343. *Op. cit.*

344. *Ibid.*, pp. 65–66.

345. *Ibid.*, pp. 66–67. E.g., Praeda Report (Italy), Peters Report (Netherlands), Hampel Report (United Kingdom), Viennot I Report (France), The European Guidelines, and the Danish Shareholders Association Guidelines call for the auditors to be elected by the shareholders.

346. Excepting the United Kingdom where the Combined Code is in effect.

347. Tilberg Economic Institute, "Monitoring Compliance with Corporate Governance in the Netherlands" (1998).

348. "Report on Corporate Governance relevant to the Member States," *supra* note 328, citing a January 2000 database study by Company Reporting, U.K.
349. The Company Law Steering Committee, "Modern Company Law for a Competitive Economy: Developing the Framework," consultative document (March 2000). This is the second stage in the consultative process. The first stage was the strategic framework consultative document published in February 1999.
350. *Ibid.*, Chapter 2, par. 2.21.
351. *Ibid.*
352. *Ibid.*, Chapter 3, 3.40.1.
353. *Ibid.*, 3.40.2 and 3.
354. *Ibid.*, 3.50.
355. *Ibid.*, 3.68.
356. *Ibid.*, 3.70.
357. *Ibid.*, 3.75.
358. *Ibid.*, 3.112 and 3.113.
359. *Ibid.*, 3.114-2-115.
360. *Ibid.*, 3.151.
361. *Ibid.*, 3.162 et seq.
362. *Ibid.*, Chapter 4, Part 2.
363. *Ibid.*, 4.51.
364. *See supra* notes 99 and 100.
365. *Op. cit.*, par. 5.16; Companies Act of 1989, sec. 245 a-c.
366. *Ibid.*, par. 5.23.
367. *Ibid.*, par. 5.51 and 5.52.
368. *Ibid.*, par. 5.63.
369. *Ibid.*, par. 5.63.
370. *Ibid.*, par. 5.67.
371. *Ibid.*, par. 5.88.
372. *Ibid.*, par. 5.90.
373. *See* chapter 4, note 11.
374. *Op. cit.*, par. 5.98–5.102.
375. *See infra* note 454.
376. *Generally*, 5.21 to 5.28.
377. Steering Committee Report, *supra* note 349 at par. 5.128.
378. *Ibid.*, par. 5.135–5.137.
379. *Ibid.*, par. 5.146 et seq.
380. *Ibid.*, Question 5.29.
381. Prem Sikka, "The Politics of Restructuring the Standard Setting Bodies: The Case of the Auditing Practices Board" WP 01/ 02 (University of Exeter, 2001).
382. *Ibid.*, p. 24.
383. Prem Sikka, "Keeping Auditors in the Dark" (Association for Accounting and Business Affairs, 1999).
384. European Union, Treaty on Economic and Monetary Union (printed in full by Agenca Europe no. 1759/60, Feb. 7, 1992).
385. *Ibid.*, Title 6.
386. *Ibid.*, Protocol on the Excessive Deficit Procedure.
387. *Ibid.*, Title 6, Economic and Monetary Policy, Article 104C, ¶ 11.

388. *Ibid.*, Protocol on Certain Provisions Relating to the United Kingdom and Northern Ireland and Protocol on Certain Provisions Relating to Denmark.

389. *Ibid.*, Article 104, ¶ 1.

390. *Ibid.*, Article 105A, ¶ 1.

391. Protocol on the Statute of European System of Central Banks and of the European Central Bank, Article 7.

392. *Ibid.*, Article 10.

393. *Ibid.*

394. *Ibid.*, Article 25.

395. *Ibid.*, Article 105. Additionally, Article 25 of the statute establishing the European Central Bank (ECB) says the ECB "may" offer advice that is less than previous drafts would have accorded. One commentator has noted, "No one could have built a higher set of hurdles." Peter Kennen, *EMU after Maastricht* (Group of Thirty) (Washington, D.C., 1992), p. 23.

396. *Ibid.*, at 54.

397. *Ibid.*, p. 67.

398. One study found that net changes in federal receipts amount to 40 cents per dollar. (X. Sali-i-Martin and Jeffrey Sachs, "Fiscal Federalism and the Optimum Currency Area," NBER Working Paper no. 3855 [Cambridge: National Bureau of Economic Research, 1991]) but other authors take issue with this study. *See also* Kennen, *supra* note 395, at 66–67.

399. *See* note 158, *supra*, and accompanying text.

400. *Treaty on Economic and Monetary Union*, *supra* note 384, Article 104b.

401. *See* C. Wyplosz, "Monetary Union and Fiscal Policy Discipline," in *The Economics of EMU*, European Economy, Special Edition 1 (1991).

402. European Economy, Commission of the European Communities, Directorate-General for Economic and Financial Affairs, "One Market, One Money: An Evaluation of the Potential Benefits and Costs of Forming an Economic and Monetary Union," no. 44 (October 1990).

403. *Ibid.*, at 196.

404. *See supra* note 9 and accompanying text.

405. Treaty on Economic and Monetary Union, *supra* note 384, Article 109.

406. *See* D. Folkerts-Landau, *Systematic Financial Risk in Payments Systems*, in "Determinants and Systematic Consequences of International Capital Flows," International Monetary Fund, Occasional Paper no. 77 (1991), and D. Folkerts-Landau and P. M. Garber, "The European Central Bank: A Bank or a Monetary Policy Rule," NBER Working Paper no. 4016 (1992).

407. P. A. Chiappori, C. Mayer, D. Neven, and X. Vives, "The Microeconomics of Monetary Union" in *Monitoring European Integration: The Making of Monetary Union* (1991).

408. Article 105(5). The European System of Central Banks (ESCB) shall contribute to the smooth conduct of policies pursued by the competent authorities relating to the prudential supervision of credit institutions and the stability of the financial system.

Article 105(6). The Council may, acting unanimously on a proposal from the Commission and after consulting the ECB and after receiving the assent of the European Parliament, confer upon the ECB specific tasks concerning policies relating to the prudential supervision of credit institutions with the exception of insurance undertakings.

409. Article 25(1) and (2) enabling the European Central Bank (ECB) to undertake prudential supervision in accordance with Article 105(6) of the treaty.

410. MoU of October 28, 1997, paragraphs 11–13. *See generally* Rosa Maria Lastra, "Banking Regulation in the 1990s." If the problem originates within the purview of Financial Services Authority (FSA) oversight, then the FSA is the lead regulator although the funds come from the Bank of England. If the problem is in the payment system, the Bank of England is the lead operator, but the Chancellor of the Exchequer has the option of refusing support.

411. O.J. L.126/1.

412. *Ibid.*, Article 27.

413. Subject to membership in a fund with a minimum of 25,000 euro insurance.

414. Case C. 233-94(19 97), E.C.R. 1-2405.

415. O.J L.135/5 (1994).

416. *Ibid.*, Article 20.

417. *Ibid.*, Annex 1.

418. Sideek Mohamed, "A Single Regulator for the EC Financial Market," *JIBL* (2001): p. 203.

419. Final Report of the Committee of Wise Men on Regulation of the European Securities Market, European Commission (February 2001).

420. Comitology Procedures are governed by 1999/468/EEC, which sets up the procedure for such rule-making committees.

421. Michael McKee, "The Proposed EU Market Abuse Directive," *Journal of International Financial Markets* (2001): p. 137.

422. Clive Briault, "The Rationale for a Transnational Regulator," FSA Occasional Paper no. 2 (1999).

423. H. Brouwer, "Report on Financial Stability" (EU Economic and Financial Committee, Brussels, April 2000).

424. *See* chapter 2, note 135, and accompanying text.

425. Response by the U.K. Financial Services Authority to the Committee of Wise Men on the Regulation of Securities Markets (September 27, 2000), p. 7.

426. *Ibid.*, p. 8.

427. *Ibid.*, p. 9.

428. *Ibid.*, pp. 14–19.

429. *Ibid.*, p. 22.

430. *Ibid.*, p. 23.

431. Fourth Directive, *supra* note 99.

432. Clare Roberts, Pauline Weetman, and Paul Gordon, *International Financial Accounting: A Comparative Approach*, p. 215.

433. *Ibid.*, p. 216.

434. Fourth Directive, *supra* note 99 Article 31.

435. *Ibid.*, Article 33.

436. Article 35 to 39.

437. *Ibid.*, Article 40.

438. *Ibid.*, Article 59.

439. *Ibid.*, Article 31.

440. *Ibid.*, Article 41.

441. *Supra* note 100.

442. *International Financial Accounting*, *supra* note 432, p. 221.

443. *Op. cit.*, Article 1–4.

444. *Ibid.*, Article 20–23.

445. *Ibid.*, Article 30–31. Goodwill should be calculated on the date of first consolidation or the date of purchase.

446. Directive regarding the valuation rules for consolidated and annual accounts of certain types of companies as well as banks. May 22, 2001.

447. *Ibid.*, at (11).

448. *Ibid.*, amending Directive 77/660/EEC, Article 1, par 2.

449. *Ibid.*, par. 3.

450. *Ibid.*, par. 5.

451. *Ibid.*, par. 42d.

452. *Ibid.*, par. 43(1)14.

453. *Ibid.*, Article 4.

454. Regulation of the European Parliament and the European Council Interinstitutional File 2001/0044 May 27, 2002; companies applying another set of internationally accepted accounting standards traded on the exchanges of a nonmember state may, at the option of a member state, have until 2007 to conform to the regulations (11).

455. Under Article 10, companies listing only debt securities shall have until 2007 to comply.

456. Andrew Campbell, "The Financial Services and Markets Acts 2000 by Alistair Alcock: Review," *JIBL* (2001): p. 167.

CHAPTER 2

International Financial Organizations

The Bank for International Settlements, the International Organization of Securities Commissions, the International Accounting Standards Board, the International Monetary Fund, the International Bank for Reconstruction and Development, or

BIS IOSCO IASB IMF IBRD

THE BANK FOR INTERNATIONAL SETTLEMENTS

The Bank for International Settlements (BIS) was founded in 1930, and under the Hague Agreement was granted all the privileges and immunities of an international organization necessary to carry out its function. It administered the ill-fated Dawes and Young loans to Germany in the 1920s and continues to administer international loan agreements. During World War II, it operated continuously under a U.S. president with two Nazis as his subordinates. The BIS building has no outward sign of identification. The BIS is located in a very modest structure said by *Time* magazine to be between a tea shop and a hairdresser.[1]

The BIS has 50 member nations. Its board of directors is comprised of 17 nations. The governors of the Banks of England, Belgium, France, Germany, and Italy and the chairman of the Federal Reserve Board (FRB) are ex officio members who appoint a member of the same nationality to the board. In addition, there are 9 member states that are elected and appoint members to the board on a rotating basis. In addition to acting as a forum for international financial regulators and supervisors, the bank acts as a trust agent in international transactions.[2] The bank had a balance sheet total of 76 billion gold francs and 3 billion in its own funds and reserves which, expressed in U.S. dollars, amount to $149 billion of assets and $7 billion of own funds and reserves.[3] Its committees include the Group of 10 central banks, which commenced when these nations decided to lend beyond the International Monetary Fund (IMF) quotas, the Committee on Banking and Supervisory Practices, and the Global Committee and the Global Financial Forum. It also sponsors many joint forums such as the Committee on the Supervision of Conglomerates, which is sponsored with the International Organization of Securities Commissions (IOSCO) and the International Accounting Standards (IAS). This chapter will be primarily concerned with the Committee on Banking and Supervisory Practices and the new G-10 accord and the Joint Forum on the Supervision of Conglomerates.

THE COMMITTEE ON BANKING AND SUPERVISORY PRACTICES

The New Capital Adequacy Accord[4]

Banking groups are to be supervised on a consolidated basis even where the holding parent company is a nonbank. Banking supervisors will determine whether a minority stake in a bank should be consolidated depending upon whether, and to what extent, its capital is available to the parent.[5] Where unconsolidated, the investment of the parent in the subsidiary will be deducted from the capital of the parent.[6] Investment in insurance subsidiaries is generally to be deducted from capital, although the regulator should consider the overall conglomerate structure. In certain instances, there may be a surplus investment in an insurance subsidiary in which case, subject to tax and other legal considerations, if it is available to the banking parent, it may be included in capital.[7] Minority stakes in noninsurance financial institutions will generally be deducted from capital except in the instance of a subsidiary in which other shareholders are willing to assume responsibility. Pro rata consolidation is permissible at some threshold level with the European community thresholds being between 20 and 50 percent. Cross-holdings intended to inflate capital are deductible. Investments in nonfinancial companies must not exceed 15 percent of a bank's capital or 60 percent in the aggregate.[8] These strictures don't seem so imposing to U.K. or U.S. banks, but Deutchebank had to divest some of its holdings in Daimler Benz, and the 60 percent aggregate might still concern Japanese banks. All deductions will be 50 percent from tier-one and 50 percent from tier-two capital.[9]

The first pillar is classified as credit risk. Claims on sovereigns will now depend on the debt rating of the sovereign and will range from 0 percent to

150 percent (of 8 percent).[10] In general, banks will be subject to a credit rating that is one category less favorable than that of the sovereign. Thus, if the claim on the sovereign were 0 percent as it is for most Organization for Economic Cooperation and Development (OECD) countries, the bank would be weighted at 20 percent. Under option two, the banking supervisor might determine the external credit rating of the bank itself, and loans under three months have preferential treatment with a floor of 20 percent.[11] Claims on securities firms are to be treated the same as banks provided they are subject to the new G-10 agreement. In April 2002, the Federal Reserve Board lowered the risk weighting for claims on qualifying securities firms from 100 percent to 20 percent.[12] Claims on corporations are to be determined in accordance with the rating of the corporate bond.[13] This is a big fillip for banks since loans to corporations attracted a 100 percent risk weighting under the 1988 Accord (G-10 agreement). There are no changes in regard to real estate—residential is 50 percent risk weighted and commercial is 100 percent risk weighted. However the new category of 150 percent risk weighting applies to securitization tranches rated B plus to B minus and all claims more than 90 days past due.[14] A credit conversion factor of 20 percent will be applied for a commitment that is less than one year, a 50 percent factor for greater than one year, and 100 percent for banks posting their own collateral (this last condition seems to be an advantage for banks in not being a deduction from capital).[15] National supervisors are responsible for determining whether a financial institution or issue meets the tests for an external credit assessment institution.[16] The criteria include disclosure, credibility, transparency, and resources. Under credit risk, the 1988 Accord also defines collateral and includes the volatility of the collateral and the volatility of the market price of the asset collateralized and currency risks.[17] These vary depending upon the duration of a bond and whether an equity is traded on a main exchange. There are conditions set forth, including legal issues of insolvency, that will determine whether a loan that collateralizes buyer or seller protection will enable the reduction of certain credit swaps to 10 percent risk weighting.[18]

The crux of the new Basel accord is the Internal Ratings Based Approach (IRB), a discussion of which begins under the first pillar.[19] This is divided into the foundation approach and the advanced approach. Institutions adopting the IRB must adopt it throughout the banking group; for the advanced approach, banks must assess the capital required for two years from the commencement of the new Basel accord and at no time will their capital commitment fall below 90 percent of the initial floor. This approach is available only for government and corporate exposures.[20] Banks adopting this approach include the probability of default (PD), the loss given default (LGD), and the sum of nonretail risk weighted assets (RWA), deriving from these three measures a negative or positive adjustment for single borrower risk exposures. For mismatches, the risk weight will be the difference between the exposure of the borrower of the original maturity and the exposure of the guarantor.[21] For undrawn credit facilities, a 75 percent conversion factor (naturally this will depend on the identity of the borrower) will be applied under the foundation approach whereas there is considerably more flexibility under the advanced approach. For commodity futures, interest and exchange rate futures, the rules of the 1988 Accord remain—replacement cost plus add-on.[22]

For corporate exposures, all exposures to one corporation must have the same rating, although transaction-specific factors can be taken into account in the LGD. Banks opting for this approach must have a minimum of six categories for performing loans and two for nonperforming loans.[23] The directors and management must have specific systems in place, including complete documentation and assumptions and theory behind IRB assessments, and internal and external audits are required, and the bank must have an internal credit risk-control unit solely concerned with IRB.[24] Banks must demonstrate appropriate information technology (IT), a three-year history of internal modeling, and perform appropriate stress tests. Banks must use track LGDs for each of their internal grades and include all collection and associated costs.[25] The LGD must be included in all reports to management and must be considered in pricing credit risk in each grade.[26] A bank must measure LGD for each LGD grade.[27] Banks must measure exposure at default (EAD) over at least a seven-year period.[28]

For retail exposures, similar criteria apply except that PD and LGD estimates must be used. Netting is allowed for individual borrowers. There is an additional regulatory requirement of isolating segments: segmentation by product type, i.e., credit card or residential mortgage; by borrower risk; by delinquency; and by vintage (that is, the date of the loan's origination[29]). An LGD and a PD must be provided for each segment.[30]

Rules for sovereign debt are identical to those for corporate debt; however, the floor of 0.003 percent does not apply to sovereign debt. Under the foundation approach, the LGD is 75 percent for subordinated debt and 50 percent for debt without clearly identifiable collateral,[31] and the rules for bank exposure are exactly the same as those for corporate exposure.[32]

Rules for IRB granularity are intended to identify the idiosyncratic risk of banks, the most typical of which is large exposures to a single borrower.[33] If two entities have strong corporate interrelationships and high default correlation, they should be treated as a singular entity for the purpose of this subsection.

Asset securitization appears to be slightly different from the U.K. version.[34] The legal forms required to achieve a clean break are identical to U.K. law, and the cleanup calls, while less precise than the U.K. law, are quite determinative. However, the law seems to allow the issuer to serve as the servicing agent and does not require the same conduit structure. The originator may provide credit enhancement, which is a charge against capital. As in the United Kingdom, a second credit enhancement facility may be treated as a credit substitute; however, here the originator may provide short-term liquidity facilities and undrawn cash facilities. Banks as investors will draw a risk weighting that is analogous to the rating of the tranche;[35] an unrated tranche draws a 100 percent risk weighting. The relevant LGD and PD risk weights attach to each tranche as determined by an External Credit Assessment Institution (ECAI)[36] for banks investing in securitizations of other banks; however, currently, the treatment is the same under the foundation and advanced approach insofar as the originator is concerned. The only outstanding issue is whether banks that retain tranches can use the LGD and PD approach.[37] If there is recourse to the originator in any tranche, the entire amount will be deducted from capital.[38]

Operational risk is defined as the risk of direct or indirect loss resulting from inadequate or failed internal processes or from external events. The definition includes legal risk but not strategic or reputational risk.[39]

There are three approaches: (1) the standardized approach, (2) the internal measurement approach, and (3) in the future, the loss distribution approach. Banks may use different methods for different businesses but must not revert. Under the basic approach, banks must hold a specific percentage of gross income or annual assets under management against operational risk.[40] Under the internal measurement approach, there is an exposure indictor (EI) for each business, which then has a probability of loss (LGE) and a probability of loss event (PE), the product of which equal the EL, the expected loss.[41] The product of gamma and EL is the amount deducted from capital. Yes, I'm serious.

Finally, we come to the end of pillar 1—credit risk with Trading Book issues;[42] in the Trading Book banks must mark to market. To account for market risks, this section replaces the 1996 Amendment to the new G-10 accord, which has already been incorporated into domestic law. The United States implemented the market risk provisions of the new G-10 accord framework in 1997.[43] Where marking to market is impossible, marking to model is the preferred approach; this involves the extrapolation of a market price from all available market data. Depending on the rating and maturity of the government bond to BBB minus, the charge is 0 to 1.25 percent and 8 percent for unrated bonds. An 80 percent specific risk charge will be applied to that side of the counterparty transaction that assumes the risk of uncertainty and the charge on the other side of the equation will be 0.

The second pillar is banking supervision. As I read this document, it seems to suggest that bank supervisors should do their job. It also points to the truism that bank supervisors insist that banks hold additional capital as a buffer since banking is not an exact science. No kidding. Basically, this section stands for the proposition that banking supervisors are as fond of words as they are of econometrics. There are four core principles of banking supervision, but they basically relate to the fact that banks should have enough capital on hand to do their business, and, if regulators don't think they do, the regulators should do something about it.

The disclosure requirements are manifold and cover all pillar 1 credit issues as well as market risk and interest rate shocks and sector analysis of retail banking on at least a semiannual basis. The disclosure requirements are fulsome: they include the different subsidiaries of a financial banking group, voting and control, consolidation and deduction from capital for unconsolidated subsidiaries and nonbanking business,[44] innovative tier-one capital instruments, unrealized gains and losses, and influence of deferred taxes. Additionally, banks must disclose use of special purpose vehicles (SPVs) and trigger events,[45] particularly with reference to complex hybrid instruments. There are several quantitative disclosure requirements about credit risk, broken down by sector, country, maturity, past due and impaired loans, and allowance for credit losses;[46] In addition, IRB reporting banks must disclose modeling assumptions, PD, LGD, or EAD risk weighting. Banks must also disclose credit risk mitigation techniques, their total exposures, including maturity mismatches, the type of regulatory methodologies they have chosen, credit instrument risk, capital requirements for operational and interest rate risk,[47] total capital requirements, and the percentage of total capital to total required capital and the amount of economic capital devoted to different businesses, products, transactions, and organizational unit.[48] The new G-10 accord is a paradigm of complete disclosure.

At the same time as it released the new G-10 accord, the bank released four supporting documents: the consultative documents on credit risk,[49] operations risk,[50] the IRB approach,[51] and interest rate risk,[52] the first three of which, in my judgment, add not an iota to the new G-10 accord but bespeak volumes about the committee's intention to write copiously and prodigiously in the hope that repetition will get the job done. But the consultative document on interest rate risk, after raking the same coals as the new G-10 accord itself, adds additional insight in the form of other methodologies that can be employed in measuring interest rate risk. The document specifies that supervisors should be particularly attentive to outlier banks where the shock described above (under one of the two tests, the simpler one being 200 basis points) leads to a 20 percent decline in the sum of tier-one and tier-two capital in the banking book.[53] There are two fundamental approaches outlined, the earnings approach and the economic value approach. Instruments where repricing cannot be determined, such as mortgages with an option for early repayment, must be assigned to a time band based on the banker's experience.[54] When analysis is used to assess the impact on current earnings, it is referred to as gap analysis, but it does not take into account basis risk, which considers the impact of interest rate changes on different instruments or the timing of payments in the new interest rate environment. Simulations are either static or dynamic in which case they simulate the behavior of bank's customers, depositors, and how the bank will administer these changes. One of the best-known dynamic simulation models is the Monte Carlo method.[55]

Overall, the new G-10 accord is a new species of financial regulation. In lowering the risk weighting of corporate bonds and applying rating agency evaluation to government and corporate bonds and asset-backed securities, it reflects the reality of the world financial system. Most importantly the sector-by-sector reporting and capital requirements in retail banking are particularly timely in an era of exorbitant consumer debt. However, the different kinds of indicators make the structure of the agreement top-heavy. One is appalled by the thought of bank CEOs who didn't get there by their performance in econometrics, running around getting in sound bites about ELs, PDs, LGEs, ECAIs, granularity, and the host of other measurements that are not altogether necessary. In particular, the granularity section recalls Keynes's injunction against formulas in economics. The infiltration of econometrics into this important process, which might determine the future of the international financial system, is too important to be left in the hand of insular supervisors, responding to lobbyists. The absence of any legislative process such as the European Parliament or even the European Commission, which includes ex-politicians, poses the prospect of regulatory capture, although Congress in the United States does not seem to have had the public interest uppermost in its mind.[56] I, for one, am uneasy that the IRB will be used to obfuscate rather than elucidate the fair and accurate view of bank financing. As a lawyer, a group not represented in the Committee on Banking and Supervisory Practices, I am troubled by the overlapping definitions of various IRB terms. In some instances, there is a question as to which risk of the various alphabets a particular instrument attracts. The constant and unnecessary repetition of similar principles that can hardly be differentiated begs the question: who writes this stuff anyway? Howard Davies, the wily chairman of the U.K. Financial Services Authority (FSA), has said that the regulators, while not proficient in English, are knowledgeable about economics.[57] One is apt to concur with the first part of his statement.

IOSCO

The International Organization of Securities Commissions lacks both the illustrious history of the Bank for International Settlement and its elitist structure; it was founded in 1973, yet, there is no doubt that the moving force behind its momentous impact is a coterie of nations and securities commissioners despite its open membership. However, in its joint pronouncements, it is overshadowed by the Committee on Banking and Supervisory Practices, and in particular by the Federal Reserve Board and the New York Federal Reserve Bank, which chaired the study on cross-sectoral comparison, the UR-text comparing insurance, banking, and securities regulation prepared with the BIS and the International Accounting Standards. Among IOSCO's most important solo acts are the study on Transparency and Market Fragmentation

(2001), which seeks to ensure that trades clear at the same price in all markets; as well as the Core Principles of Securities Regulations, which whittles securities regulations down to 30 core principles; and finally the International Disclosure Standards for Cross Border Offerings and Foreign Issuers, which is comparable, perhaps, to the new G-10 accord in that it is in use in most major capital markets, including in the United States, the United Kingdom, and Germany to different degrees, except it relates only to foreign issuers whereas the capital adequacy rules relate to all deposit-taking institutions.

Finessing the Transparency and Market Fragmentation Report, as this book generally will not concentrate on the mechanics of nitty-gritty market mechanisms in the ordinary workaday world including stabilization, market making, off-exchange trading, best execution, and a host of other important issues that are to be eschewed in favor of systemic importance defined as those that can bring down the whole shebang; we will begin with the cross-sectoral comparison, which compares the theories behind banking, securities, and insurance regulation and move from the general to the particular. There are a host of insights in this study, the most important of which is that the host country plays a role in securities regulation whereas it plays a de minimis role in the regulation of deposit-taking institutions. It is obvious that the great hazard faced by banks is the mismatch between their short-term deposit and their long-term loan, whereas the largest risks faced by securities firms is their proprietary positions and the collateral they have either borrowed or provided.[58] In plain English, this means their temptation to intermingle client funds or to lend clients too much in one fashion or another (not a question of simple margins even on derivative instruments). The issue with life and life insurers is simply described as technical provisions and the investment book. On a sliding scale, insurance firms hold provisions, banks hold loans loss reserves, which are similar to provisions as well as capital, and securities firms hold capital since their assets can be marked to market.[59] Evidence also suggests that insurance firms hold many times their minimum capital (except for Equitable Life UK) while large banks might only hold 150 percent of their minimum required capital).[60] One reason for the study is the growing problem of cross-sectoral risk transfer.[61] The recent passage of Gramm-Leach-Bliley in the United States highlights this concern; however, in my view, insurance firms such as Travelers are more likely to provide strength to banks than to cause problems. One of the problems with the status quo of financial regulation is that regulators are too often fighting last year's battles, as the cliché goes. The new proposed EU directive on the supervision of financial conglomerates, discussed in chapter 6, provides the most advanced regulatory approach.

The cross-sectoral comparison contains juicy tidbits. For instance, selling short; sale repurchase agreements make up a great deal of a securities firm's liabilities. Equity usually equals 5 percent of total funds, long-term debt another 10 percent, and other short-term debt instruments an additional 10 percent[62] (this is unlikely to count for regulatory capital). Firms use value-at-risk models,[63] frequently incorporated traumatic stress events such as the 1987 crash, to determine adequate capital. However, even without making reference to the complete irrelevance of the past in probability theory, I would suppose these amounts are probably downplayed based on my horse sense. Market risk together with liquidity risk are the most important risks for securities firms, according to this report.[64] Naturally, but credit risk in the form of counterparty risk isn't insubstantial, particularly in the form of netting arrangement, now being taken up under the Commodities Futures Modernization Act in the United States.[65]

The cross-sectoral report states the obvious in remarking that the securities sector has the shortest time frame and explains discounts on each instrument (haircuts) as derived from its perceived degree of liquidity.[66] The prime focus of banking supervision is to prevent systemic risk while the focus of securities regulation is consumer protection. Also, in general, because of the short-term nature of securities obligations, in that they are marked to market, a securities firm that is in the process of failing is liquidated in the United States, for instance, under Chapter 7 of the bankruptcy code, not taken through reorganization.[67]

Putting aside the jargon about other objectives, the report is quite correct in asserting the primacy of customer protection and the segregation of clients' moneys and assets. Given the fast-paced nature of the business, an emphasis on books and records is particularly important.[68] Capital rules for securities firms depend on the individual instruments that they hold. This subject has been considered in several places in this book.[69] In the United States, the practical limit is that firms must hold 5 percent of customer funds.[70] The EU and United States have different approaches.[71] Under the trading book option (as opposed to bonds declared to be held to maturity) of the new G-10 accord, as partially enacted and definitively practiced, a bond is treated as the sum of positions of general market risk and specific counterparty risk, and this would be true under the EU directive.[72] However, in the United States, the haircut is intended to account for devaluation during a firm's liquidation. Based on a survey conducted by IOSCO, the world's very largest securities firms—American and British—are operating with 1.2 to 1.3 times the required capital,[73] which means that they've handicapped the game far beyond the regulators' perception, in my view.

In a securities firm, regulators really aren't concerned with consolidated supervision, since their main concern is winding up the regulated entity and safeguarding clients' money.[74] But unregulated affiliates of securities firms are not to be neglected, nor are those affiliates that in the United States are regulated by the Commodities Futures Trading Corporation (CFTC), since futures activity can have an enormous impact on securities activity, but this subject will be dealt with in chapter 3. There are several approaches to how to consolidate banking/securities/insurance entities, with one caveat.[75] In all jurisdictions, securities firms are stand-alone entities, since they must have all their capital on hand; in the United States, banks' ownership of securities firms is strictly regulated under Gramm-Leach-Bliley,[76] so the issue only arises in insurance-banking combinations. The stylized balance sheet for securities firms indicates the source of potential risks in showing written options at 229 percent of firm's equity; financial futures and forward settlement agreements at 249 percent of firm's equity and swaps, presumably mostly interest rate; and currency swaps, at 1,228 percent of firm's balance sheet.[77] While in ordinary times these are hardly amounts to make one nervous, the possibility of a shock, particularly a joint interest rate currency shock and a precipitous decline in the futures market, is the arena that cannot be accounted for.

In international speak (BIS, IOSCO), a sector transfer risk is really a misnomer. What the gang means is regulatory capital arbitrage. In their parlance, what should be termed transfer risk is known as intragroup transfer risk and euphemistically entitled intragroup transactions and exposure (ITEs).[78] This report identifies the following interconnections: (1) cross-shareholding; (2) central management of risk within the conglomerate; (3) guarantees, letters of credit, loans, and commitments; (4) trading on behalf of another group member; (5) management of assets such as pension funds and back office support; (6) exposure to major shareholders; (7) placement of client assets with other companies within the group; (8) purchase and sale of assets with other group companies; and (9) transfers to shift third-party-related risks within the group.

This ITE paper is disconcerting. It has a great deal of touchy-feely language, noting that ITEs should be monitored through the regulated entity, and that the joint forum report on capital adequacy deals with the issues. One has the sense that there is little grasp of ITEs among regulators except to note that some conglomerates follow business sector/legal entity lines and others do not. On the consumer side, the kind of tie-in arrangement prohibited by the Bank Holding Company Act in the United States gives one a sense of the power of conglomerates. But what evil lurks in the possibilities of hiding liabilities is impossible to know. In a Pollyanish statement, the paper urges public disclosure. Enron shows the possibilities that lurk within unconsolidated SPVs, but the accounting nightmares that occur in unconsolidated risks of a regulated entity with unregulated affiliates are difficult to fathom. Exposures to a client in one company may appear minimal but, taken as a whole, the conglomerate may rise or fall on the price of oil or the price of rice in China. One never knows, does one? Here again, reformation of existing accounting principles requiring consolidation of risks, a term undefined in the current annals of accounting on a conglomerate level, would provide a starting point. However, where one of the entities is a regulated financial entity special accounting and disclosure rules should apply. Now that financial holding companies can acquire banks in the United States,[79] the possibilities for contagion of the banking sector have been expanded, no matter which vantage point one takes. Securities firms in the United States have unregulated entities whose dealings may never be fathomed; however, the CFTC Securities and Exchange Commission (SEC) split compounds the issue. In the EU, problems in a manufacturing sector can impact the financial sector, but, strangely, this is less likely to involve contagion. In Japan, the damage done by cross-holdings may never be fully accounted for, but the current estimation is well over a trillion dollars in outright monies required to prop up the banking system as well as untold loss of growth amounting to several trillion more.[80] In the interest of political finesse and in the service of formalism, regulators in this instance have shown a continued fascination with consolidation in hundreds of pages of documents with only this brief 12-page paper on all the clever ways, regardless of consolidation, that risks can be transferred between entities. Consolidation is a mantra among financial regulators proving that consistency is the hobgoblin of small minds. Until financiers can either be induced or inducted into public service, our Maginot line will be insular regulators who most often, as in the case of the legal department of the Federal Reserve, are spared the vicissitudes of this world and hired only out of law school.[81]

In a blithe complement to the risk management paper,[82] the Joint Forum issued a cross-sectoral paper on core principles[83] in which they sought, once again, to add to the comparative literature of financial regulation. Here, we are informed that securities regulators, unlike their brethren, have a host of additional responsibilities, including the regulation of collective investment trusts, secondary markets, clearance and settlement systems, disclosure by issuers, exchanges, conduct of business issues,[84] and SROs, and consequently a broader jurisdiction that emphasizes market discipline through disclosure of enforcement actions (would that it were so for the SEC).[85] The paper emphasizes the increasingly international component of securities markets.[86] There is a very seminal bit of equivocation and when Burnham Wood to Dunsinane Hill doth come we'll know why. The securities regulators do indeed have the broadest powers of regulation for violation of the securities law vis-à-vis nonregulated persons, but to classify such powers as comprehensive[87] is disingenuous. This really has to do with the unsuspecting public, not with protecting the international market against systemic risk. There are loads of unregulated entities associated with securities firms or, in the United States, regulated by the archenemy of the SEC, the CFTC, which, for instance, deregulated energy futures and turned the lights out in California,[88] and interest rates and currency traders and off-shore hedge funds who say, "Qu'est-que c'est regulation?" (even if their secretaries have to fill out a few forms). The new proposed EU directive on the supervision of financial conglomerates does not address unregulated affiliates.[89]

Next along this benighted IOSCO path, if we have wended our way through the perils of the joint forum, is IOSCO's paper, "Sound Practices for Managing Liquidity."[90] The paper identifies liquidity risk as arising on September 11 as the result of operational risk. Credit risk and market risk are other causes of liquidity risk. The goal of firms generally is to have sufficient liquidity to deal with financial crises without selling assets or to have a liquidity cushion.[91] There is a technical distinction between liability risk, which arises from obligations from unsecured funding, to third parties and asset risk, which arises from maturity of assets and their use of collateral. Security firms use the term to mean both, thereby incorporating all available cash and near cash assets.[92] Liquidity is also to be distinguished from capital (particularly regulatory capital) since a firm may have liquid assets but be low on regulatory capital or have sufficient capital for regulatory purposes but be low on liquidity.[93] Contingent commitments, those depending on an event or based on over the counter (OTC) derivative instruments, are a particular source of liquidity risk; however, firms have indicated that these risks pale in comparison to the liquidity risks of cash or near cash instruments and securities.[94] The paper stresses the need for high-level management of liquidity risks at the senior management and board of directors' level.[95] Since Barings Bank, one should hope that senior management is more attuned to the issues.

Generally, there are three kinds of risk exposures that firms monitor: (1) target liquidity ratios; (2) currency, interest rate, and derivatives exposure; and (3) value at risk (VAR) and market exposure.[96] For target exposure, firms might use barometers of acceptable exposure or liquidation potential in which a firm determines how it would fare in the first 14 days of a stress scenario or a maximum cumulative outflow, which measures how much liquidity goes out the door.[97] These last two methodologies are nearly identical. Forex and derivatives exposure targets maturity mismatches. Time bands will vary from overnight to nine weeks and will frequently employ cash cushions of over 100 percent to allocate to these activities.[98] Of course, that's not very informative because the current market value might not be an indication of the embedded risk. VAR involves a model to determine the maximum expected loss on a portfolio over a given period of time frequently with reference to the volatility of the corporate bond spread. (Liquidity at risk models are in the offing.)[99]

The IOSCO paper admits that many firms have no strategy for dealing with liquidity risks. Typically, these are part of a universal banking group.[100] But the paper is chock-full of ideas about corporate division of responsibilities.[101] It also argues for limit setting, which is enshrined in banking law,[102] and credit diversification—having several sources of funds. Insofar as the paper argues for matching maturity bands, this issue is dealt with by regulatory capital. In the category of creditor diversification, firms are counseled to limit the amount of commercial paper (of the securities firm) held by one investor.[103] Firms also tend to keep abreast of currency mismatches and adopt leverage ratios based on multiples of shareholder's equity as a percentage of gross and net leverage.[104] Firms also use various stress tests and scenario formulations that break away from historical correlations and include off-balance sheet items and making tests at least twice a year.[105] Many firms believe that stressful market conditions are adequately dealt with through the use of haircuts on collateral.[106] Intragroup liquidity transfers may be discouraged by a

100 percent risk weighting in some jurisdictions, but, in general, there are few substantial limitations explaining why securities affiliates of universal banks or financial conglomerates rely on parent companies rather than make their own assessments.[107]

In the accompanying survey, firms provided different definitions of liquidity, including the value of unencumbered assets after haircuts plus revolving credit lines or the value of securities that can be pledged plus the unused portion of revolving credit. But most firms stressed a more immediate definition such as the ability to generate cash or cash equivalents to meet obligations or the ability of a firm to survive in a difficult market condition without balance sheet liquidation.[108] Most firms manage liquidity at the central level to take into account both time differences and regulatory structure; however, firms with a holding company or parent company structure manage liquidity at a central level.[109] This suggests the regulatory structure currently in place,[110] which just considers the securities firm as a stand-alone entity, is unrealistic. The corporate structure to manage liquidity risk differs from firm to firm; in one firm, including a treasurer, in another, it is a senior managing director, but most firms employ a committee structure.[111] There are a great variety of management structures to manage relations with funding sources. Certain firms articulate elaborate goals about the management of liquidity risk: one firm states that integration of unsecured funding strategies and the stabilization of liquidity are necessary to maintaining investment grade rating, and another firm states that it intends to be able to fund its business for another 12 months without resorting to additional funding sources.[112] One firm outlines a general asset diversification, which tends to ensure liquidity: 9 percent government, money markets, cash; 12 percent derivatives; 16 percent resale agreements; 32 percent borrowed securities; 16 percent segregated cash and receivables; and 11 percent equities, corporate bonds, and municipals.[113] Certainly, there is nothing intuitive about this model. It is a rule of thumb. It suggests that the formulation is far more specific than the leverage ratio of 5 percent of total equity that the U.S. CFTC determines causes an early warning.[114] But the formulation suggests that capital allocation models, even internal risk based models, would enhance capital requirements. Naturally, the Capital Adequacy Directive (CAD) for securities firms[115] is far more precise than the CFTC, but both are perhaps more oriented toward long-term capital, which is only distantly correlated to liquidity. In order to secure liquidity, firms that are not part of conglomerates monitor the rollover of short- and long-term debt. Other firms limit reliance by diversification of types of debt.[116] Using a support ratio of unused capacity to total borrowing capacity, the ratio for firms varied from 0 to 100 percent; and the liquidity ratio of the potential unused pledge value of securities and other liquid assets to short-term debt and long-term debt due short-term varied from 70 percent to 510 percent.[117] While many firms do not apply haircuts to assets in general in assessing a liquidity position, all firms apply haircuts to customer assets to protect against bad debt.[118] In the catchall, whether or not there were additional issues that had not been asked, two firms stated their reliance on customer assets and retail deposits as potential areas of weakness.[119] This highlights the problem that, even where investor funds are segregated by law, there is a risk of improper use of customers' funds in a crunch.[120]

The report "Hedge Funds and Other Highly Leveraged Institutions"[121] in the wake of the collapse of Long Term Capital Management (LTCM)[122] concentrates on monitoring the exposure of securities firms to hedge funds through counterparty risk assessment. In a rare moment of true candor, causing one to remark that what is unique is to be truly valued, the paper declares that highly leveraged institutions (HLIs) are structured in such a way as not to trigger the disclosure requirements imposed on public companies.[123] The only source of information about HLIs is provided to counterparties in transactions.[124] There are several ways in which a regulated securities firm may interact with a HLI that will create credit risk: first and foremost as a counterparty, but also as a clearing or settlement facility, as a prime broker, or as a short- or long-term lender.[125] Here the report continues with all the usual provisos about specific attention to sublimits and new products, correlation between credit risk and market risk, and the correlation between the firm's proprietary position and market position. Unfortunately, this is hortatory language. No one has any intention of enacting any of this.

Then there is the category of legal risk. Here the issues are the jurisdiction of incorporation and operation, legal capacity to enter into agreement, legal limits, relationship between group members and legal remedies; many concepts of financial law may not be tested in some jurisdictions.[126] The report is chock-full of recommendations about what highly leveraged organizations (HLOs) should disclose and even offers some helpful tips about what securities firms should do; however it is truly startling that four years after LTCM there are not international standards on exposure to credit and legal risk to HLOs in terms of disclosure and capital charges for this category, as well as exposure limits and correlation requirements with proprietary positions. I assume most securities regulators keep their money in bank deposits.

More generalized credit risk is the subject of another IOSCO paper.[127] Securities firms are subject to counterparty risk in the form of bridge loans, margins, repurchase agreements, and clearing and settlement risks, and most frequently determine if the collateral on hand is sufficient and must assess the risk of default through credit ratings, credit rating migration, and both public and private default statistics.[128] The credit risk is broken down here into the probability of default, which hinges on the aforementioned and is a concept that has certainly been beaten into the reader by now, and recovery rate, the proportion of the market value that is expected to be recovered if the counterparty defaults.[129] In my view, this is a singularly useless concept since nothing is as unascertainable as the recoverable portion, particularly of a derivative instrument once a counterparty has defaulted, given a given market's tendency to develop into a feeding frenzy once the games have been taken together with unforeseeable cross contagions.[130] We are not talking about leased office buildings as collateral. Different kinds of contracts tend to accumulate or disburse credit over time, and the total credit exposure may differ from the sum of credit exposures.[131] Market and credit risks are frequently interchangeable given the likelihood that they will run in tandem, and while, as stated above, the growth of derivatives has increased risk, the securitization of credit risk has made it market tradable.[132] There follows in the report a long diatribe on derivatives and how difficult they are to measure, the salient features of which are that in the 1980s firms used to equate a swap with offsetting a bond purchase of the same maturity but this overstated the risk on the swap since the swap only involves mutual coupon payments, not an exchange of principal payments, which overstates the risk of a swap.[133] At this juncture there follows the formulation: individual mark to market position > netting of mark to market positions > collateral > current exposure net of collateral > potential future exposure > stress test > stressed potential future exposure > monitoring process.[134] Whether we include backtesting in stress testing or recovery expectations in collateral or any number of other tests, eventually there is an endgame. In the first part of this chapter, the complex IRB tests of the new G-10 accord were given ample consideration. Early under this heading, stylized balance sheets were discussed. In chapter 4, a cross section of actual banks are considered in their treatment of loan categories. Ultimately, it's endgame or instinct. Despite all the mathematical pretensions, there is no magic formula. "Mirror on mirror mirrored is all the show."

However, the document continues on for another eight pages entitled "Advice to Firms." This considers bilateral and multilateral netting arrangements, netting by novation (analogous to securitization issues here) and is really straight legal advice. These subjects are covered under payments and settlement systems in chapter 3. One can imagine this author's opinion as to what such free legal advice offered by securities regulators is worth.

The much-touted IOSCO paper "Objectives and Principles of Securities Regulation"[135] can fairly well be summarized as saying it's good when securities markets are good and fair and everything goes well and everyone's fair. However, it might also be helpful as a checklist if you are setting up a securities regulator in Outer Mongolia or if you are a law professor in search of a topic for an international law review article or a politician looking for a platform to which no one can object.

By contrast, the International Standards for Enhanced Disclosure[136] rivals the Basel Capital Adequacy framework in terms of its wide acceptance and usage. The international disclosure standards come with one major qualification and several minor ones—they do not address the issue of which bodies of accounting or auditing principles may be followed by the issuer in preparation of its financial statements. They also do not address business combinations, tender offers, going private, or certain interested party transactions, and do not apply to collective investment schemes or startups with no history of operation. Nor do they address insider-trading laws, requirements to disclose material developments, or antifraud prohibitions. They also do not discuss suitability, particularly size type, such as asset size imposed by stock markets.[137]

The directors, senior management, advisors, and auditors must be set forth.[138] For all offerings, the time period for which the offering will remain open must be specified definitively; there must be timetables for paying up securities, due dates, methods of payment, and full treatment of preemption rights. The company shall provide five years of the most recent financial data, or less if the company has been in existence for less time, though not for less than three years and in the same currency as the financial statement. Interim financial data may be submitted, and if unaudited, must state the fact. The data should include, at a minimum, net sales or operating revenue; income (loss) from operations; income (loss) from continuing operations; net income (loss); net income (loss) per share; total asset; net assets; capital stock (excluding long-term debt and redeemable preferred stock); number of shares as adjusted to reflect changes in capital; and dividends declared per share in both the currency of the financial statements and the host country currency, including the formula used for adjustments and diluted income per share. Such amounts must be determined in accordance with the body of accounting principles used in preparing the financial statements.[139] The exchange rate between the reporting currency and the host country currency should be disclosed as of the last practicable date and the highest and lowest level for each of the previous six months and for the five most recent years.[140]

A statement of capitalization and indebtedness (distinguishing between guaranteed and unguaranteed, secured and unsecured indebtedness) must be included as of a date no earlier than 60 days prior to the statement showing the company's actual capitalization adjusted to reflect the sale of new securities. Indebtedness should also include indirect and contingent liabilities.[141] (Query as to whether a statement prepared in accordance with Generally Accepted Accounting Standards [GAAP] and the 97/3[142] rule of Enron renown would comply with this section.) The estimated net amount of the proceeds of an offer must be broken down into each principal amount of intended use in order of priority and the amount and sources of other funds must be stated, and if no purposes are intended for the funds raised, the company must disclose the purpose of the offering. If assets are to be acquired from affiliates, this must be disclosed.[143] Industry specific risk factors, including country of operation; absence of profitable operations in recent periods; possible absence of a liquid trading market for the securities; pending expiration of patents, trademarks, or other contracts; and dependence on limited customers or suppliers must also be disclosed.[144]

A section entitled "History and Development of the Company" involves all the legal information about the company including mergers, consolidation of significant subsidiaries, acquisitions and disposals of assets, material changes in types of products produced, expenditures and divestitures and any takeover offers by third parties, terms, and conditions.[145] In "Operation and Financial Review and Prospects"[146] IOSCO has attempted something akin to the SEC's management discussion and analysis[147] wrapped together with a forecast of future trends.[148] Given the international nature of the standard, inflation is a key concern,[149] as is foreign currency fluctuation[150] and government fiscal and monetary policy[151] and the extent to which these policies are hedged.[152]

Liquidity and cash flow are separately addressed, and the specific restrictions on a subsidiary's ability to transfer funds to the company in the form of loans or cash dividends must be disclosed,[153] as well as information on a company level of borrowings, on the types of instruments used, on the maturity profile of debt, currency, and interest rate structure. A discussion of treasury policy and the extent to which borrowings are at fixed rate is also required, as is one about the use of financial instruments for hedging purposes.[154]

Information concerning the company's material commitment to capital expenditures, research and development information, and trend information must also be disclosed.[155]

In the arena of directors, senior management, and employees, extensive disclosure is required, although the definition of person covered will vary from country to country.[156] Information about compensation, including in-kind benefit, must be included.[157] However, there is an important exemption in the event individual disclosure is not required by home country rules. The standard itself covers all contingent compensation. Information about major shareholders, defined as over-5-percent owners, must be provided to the extent known.[158] Information must be provided about major shareholder and related party transactions and whether such transactions are fair to the company.[159]

Part 8 is wait and see since IOSCO is working on developing standards here on international accounting and auditing. However, balance sheet, income statement, changes arising either from changes in equity other than those arising from capital transactions, or all changes in equity, cash flow statement, related notes, notes analyzing changes in each caption of shareholders' equity must all be audited by an independent auditor.[160]

The last year of each financial statement must not be older than 15 months at the date of the public offering, and no older than 12 months at the time the document is filed (unless the host country permits otherwise).[161] This is patently ridiculous. Sometimes, you wonder why IOSCO goes to the trouble. Well, I suppose someone is paying them. How hard is it to get an auditor. No one says he or she has to be sober or competent. Many of the companies listed can't be practicably sued in host countries since they don't have any other assets. The least an investor deserves is an up-to-date audited financial statement. If the issuer is in Outer Mongolia, then he can just fly in an auditor from Inner Mongolia on a Cessna. The rest of the document contains boilerplate securities offering language about the offering, sale, and distribution of securities,[162] which streamlines more cumbersome processes under municipal law and stock exchange rules.

In 2000, the SEC issued a concept release on international disclosure requirements and intimated its intent to work with the International Accounting Standards Board (IASB), which had worked with IOSCO to reconcile GAAP and International Accounting Standards Committee (IASC).[163] IOSCO identified 30 core principles and 150 other concerns about reconciliation of international reporting requirements for cross-border issues. The International Accounting Standards Committee completed its work in 2000.[164] In general, foreign issuers seeking a U.S. listing must submit a Form 20F statement. The IASC document recommends standards that are to be supplemented by reconciliation statements.

According to Professor Hal Scott of Harvard Law School, Optimum Standard Issuance (OSI) should allow an issuer to issue internationally using one set of disclosure documents in primary securities offerings.[165] He cites the growth of foreign issuers from 78 in 1990 to 529 in 1998, representing over $146 billion in market capitalization. The issuer nationality approach, in contrast, argues that a lower standard of disclosure may suffice for a country such as Germany where financial institutions have monitoring roles. And if private standards informed public standards, disclosure might differ between debt and equity or big and small companies.[166]

The new international disclosure regime adopted by the SEC in September 1999[167] was trumpeted by the SEC as enabling the IOSCO standards to be considered “an international passport.”[168] But one New York law firm commented that it is a passport that entails expensive U.S. visa requirements.[169] Scott comments that standardization has not been forthcoming in enforcement or accounting rules. He says that U.S. adoption of International Accounting Standards 8 would require agreement on a governance structure for updating and interpreting rules.[170] There are several proposals for extending multijurisdictional disclosure regimes, such as the U.S.-Canada mutual recognition—Multi-Jurisdiction Disclosure System (MJDS).[171] These proposals generally suggest that the place of incorporation or the nationality of the issuer would determine the disclosure regime. The EU provides the penultimate example of mutual recognition. According to a study by the Treasury in 1998,[172] despite minimal additional requirements to list in other member states, issues of translation and income tax restatements have kept the number of cross-border issuers low; the 1999 and 2000 Deutche Telekom offerings appear to be the only European-wide distribution.[173] The U.K. Treasury suggests that issuers may prefer to list in one member state and have issuers purchase and trade the security in that member state. In chapter 1, I suggested that the maze of conduct of business rules in the United Kingdom, for instance, as well as the lack of harmonized accounting standards, impede the creation of a single European market for securities.

In proposals by U.S. academics, enforcement would generally have to be the responsibility of the home country rather than the host country, and the private right of action would require equity holders to litigate in the home country, unlike the situation in the EU. Scott proposes the establishment of an offshore free zone that would abide by a minimum disclosure regime. Such offerings would currently run afoul of Rule 144(a)[174] and Regulation S.[175] He says that investors have different expectations of securities purchased offshore in terms of the enforcement and disclosure regimes applicable, and U.S. investors ought to be able to participate in a foreign primary offering. He even allows that directed selling efforts could take place in the United States with the proviso that they be subject to the antifraud provisions of Rule 10b-5. (He allows for direct purchase but not resale in the United States until the current 40-day waiting period under Reg. S has tolled.) While Scott's proposal appears to be the most balanced approach for easing requirements for cross-border issuers, it is unlikely to be considered in the current climate. Yet, it causes one to reconsider the basis of securities regulation. As a practical matter, there has been widespread abuse of Reg. S, and the ubiquity of the Internet[176] makes international offers more common whether or not they run afoul of U.S. regulations.

Under Part 2, titled "Disclosure Issues Outside the Scope of the Standards," there is a thread that is really about liability for omissions and misleading statements. Section 1 is titled "Materiality" and is listed by country. Under the European Union (EU), Article 4 of the Listing Particular is mentioned, which, although it doesn't contain the word materiality, seems to have a fondness for the word "particular,"[177] and everything depends on the particular nature of the issuer, which would enable the investor and their investment advisors "to make an informed assessment . . . [of the] securities." Under U.S. law, materiality is the big bear. The question of what defines materiality under U.S. law is an admixture of law and fact. An omitted fact is material, according to the Supreme Court, if "there is a substantial likelihood that a reasonable shareholder would consider it important in deciding how to vote."[178] It does not require proof of a substantial likelihood that the disclosure of the omitted fact would have caused the reasonable investor to change his vote. Put another way, there must have been a substantial likelihood that the disclosure of the omitted fact would have been viewed by the reasonable investor as having significantly altered the total mix of information made available.[179]

This is a very silly standard considering that materiality ultimately has to do with liability. This is highlighted with respect to the current bugbear projections and forward-looking statements. The EU perspective is all over the map, with the minimum requirements being stated in the Listing Particulars Directive[180] and other standards being diverse.[181] In the United States, the issue is explosive.[182] However, here we have reached an impasse, at least insofar as international issuers are concerned. These are issuers who are highly unlikely, in most instances, and certainly in the case of initial public offerings, to be successfully sued in London or New York. Yet, there is a definite advantage in having them make forward-looking statements. The issue can be rectified under the complex definition of scienter required by U.S. courts,[183] so that all securities can be subject to one standard, but that certainly would leave little standing of the total mix standard enunciated by the Supremes.

THE IASB

The IASB situated in London has 14 member countries and was reconstituted in 2001. A publication prepared by Ernst and Young illuminates the subtle distinctions between GAAP and International Accounting Standards. Accountancy evolved in tandem with the Law Merchant as practiced in the British Empire and as a necessary corollary or even a precondition of international mercantilism, but in the twentieth century, it received its greatest infusion of new conceptual frameworks from the development of tax law in the United States, formulated by legal minds forever mindful of Mr. Justice Learned Hand's dictum distinguishing between tax avoidance and tax evasion. Since the permanent institution of the income tax in 1913, tax law has grown into a mass specialization for lawyers and accountants. The evolution of GAAP is discussed in chapter 5.

Differences between GAAP and IASB standards abound, and they are hardly de minimis. In a survey of 32 companies, the results were literally all over the board. There was simply no correlation between accounting under GAAP and under IASB standards.[184] Four companies were excluded from the chart because their income deviated by more than 100 percent. Five companies had income more than 40 percent lower or higher under GAAP. Deferred taxation, intangible assets, tangible fixed assets, pension and other post-retirement benefits, and equity-based compensation plans and goodwill followed by capital instruments and debt headed the list of irreconcilable differences.[185] International Accounting Standards 8 requires disclosure of any change in accounting standards and the reasons for the change. GAAP waffles in this regard. Certain changes require complete restatement such as first in first out (fifo) and long-term construction contracts; however, in general, companies have been able to change accounting methods without notice, with a catch-up adjustment disclosed between extraordinary items and net income.

Insofar as tangible fixed assets are concerned, we are speaking principally about leasing and the treatment of real property or intellectual property, which, for the purposes of this discussion, we will consider to be derivative of property law and regulation. In Anglo-Saxon law, property is unique, and GAAP is derivative of the common law. Ernst and Young's treatise is silent about tangible assets, but the Internal Revenue code speaks volumes, as does applicable case law. Remedies, particularly specific performance, can literally not be accounted for. Thus, we read, in the Ernst and Young treatise, "Under

U.S. GAAP, there are no specific rules for accounting for investment property."[186] Perhaps in public corporate accounting there are no specific rules for investment property, and we should query why this is so. In general, investment property is depreciated over its useful life, and real estate investors would be dismayed to find out they were not conforming to Generally Accepted Accounting Principles.

Ernst and Young provide examples of comparisons between GAAP and International Accounting Standards standards. The first is Swisscom in which Swisscom enters into cross-border leases to recognize gains although under U.S. accounting standards the gains would be offset by the losses since the gains and losses offset one another over the terms of the leases; the derecognition of financial assets may occur only when they are financially isolated from the transferor in case of bankruptcy.[187] The interest of a parent in a subsidiary is reduced when the parent sells shares in the subsidiary. GAAP offers specific rules while International Accounting Standards rules are general.[188]

Under both GAAP and International Accounting Standards, there is a rebuttable presumption that the equity method of accounting be employed to those investments where an investor possesses significant influence, defined as 20 percent or more. U.S. GAAP recognizes two types of special purpose vehicles based on the criteria set out in Emerging Issues Task Force (EITF) 90–15. (This is the notorious 97/3 rule of Enron renown.) Qualifying special purpose entities (SPEs) should not be consolidated if they meet the criteria set out in Financial Accounting Standard (FAS) 140.[189] It is likely that International Accounting Standards will require more SPEs to be consolidated than GAAP, as SIC-12 (Interpretation by the Standing Interpretations Committee) applies to SPEs in general while the requirements under U.S. GAAP deal with specific categories of SPEs.[190]

In fact, FAS 125 Accounting for Transfers and Servicing of Financial Assets and Extinguishments of Liabilities focuses on control and the financial nature of the assets. In October 2000, the Financial Accounting Standards Board (FASB) issued FAS 140 to replace FAS 125. The purpose of FAS 140, set forth in the footnote,[191] is clearly to separate the entity from the transferor. If the reader hearkens back to the discussion of securitization, he or she will recall the principal purpose of the notion of securitization is to make the transferor remote from the ultimate SPE. This, in fact, was accomplished in Enron. By contrast, International Accounting Standards rules on contingent liabilities provide a catchall that would have detected the spread of Enronitis in Raptors et al. and would have acted as effectively as a roach motel. International Accounting Standards 37 defines a contingent liability as arising from past events confirmed only by the occurrence or nonoccurrence of uncertain events not wholly within the control of the entity or a present obligation arising from past events that is not recognized because it is not probable that an outflow of resources embodying economic benefits will be required.[192] The IASB standard embodied in standard 5 speaks only about a probable situation or one that can be reasonably estimated.[193] It can't be so difficult to define a contingent liability if you wish to.

Certain other examples from the Ernst and Young survey of 32 companies reconciling International Accounting Standards accounting to GAAP under Form 20F as required by the SEC[194] help clarify the most common distinctions between International Accounting Standards 8 and GAAP standards. (Unless otherwise noted all transactions are for the year 1999.) Very significant differences include the treatment of research in progress; thus, when Hoechst Aktiengesellschaft (1998) made two acquisitions in 1996 and 1997, it was required to expense DM 25 million and DM 493 million, whereas under International Accounting Standards 8 these costs could have been allocated as part of the purchase price, capitalized as goodwill and amortized over their expected useful life.[195] Likewise, Sulzer Medica Ltd amortized $132 million in connection with an acquisition under International Accounting Standards 22, which was required to be expensed under U.S. GAAP.[196] Beijing Yamaha Petrochemical Company revalued its property, land, and equipment. Under U.S. GAAP no such reevaluation is allowed and depreciation is based on cost.[197] In accordance with International Accounting Standards 36 "Impairment of Assets," which requires an assessment of a recoverable amount when assets might be impaired, OAO Rostelecom believed that the Russian economic crisis of 1998 posed such an indication. Because the sum of future undiscounted cash flow was in excess of carrying cost, the asset was not deemed impaired under GAAP, but International Accounting Standards 36 calls for a discounted cash flow assessment; in this case 20 percent was deemed appropriate.[198] Hoechst Aktiengesellschaft (1998) did not capitalize interest on constructed assets as it is not required under International Accounting Standards 23. Total capitalized interest equaled almost DM 900 million. Once again Hoechst was required to reconcile to U.S. GAAP, this time at a considerable loss. Inventories are valued much higher under International Accounting Standards than under GAAP. Hoechst, in this instance, ended with valuations that were lower by DM 30 million for 1998 and DM 11 million for 1997.[199] The U.S. economy grew by 5.1 percent in the first quarter of the year 2002; 3.5 percent of the growth was attributed to the sale of inventories.[200] In other words, if International Accounting Standards inventory accounting had applied, the U.S. growth rate would have been about 2 percent.

On May 5, 2002, the International Accounting Standards 8 proposed changes in International Accounting Standards that were significant.[201] Under the proposed change to International Accounting Standards 1, liabilities that are due to be settled within 12 months must be classified as current, other than those subject to a grace period, which must be listed as current liabilities; all loans in breach must be classified as current; reasons for nondisclosure must be more than impractical, but require undue cost and effort; management must explain changes in accounting method; they must prohibit extraordinary items;

and they have to discuss significant expected future events that have the most significant impact on the business and must disclose in the summary of accounting policies the measurement basis used in preparing financial statements and the other accounting standards used that are relevant. The revision to International Accounting Standards 1 also requires that all material items be aggregated by category, and reclassification of items is only permitted if a similar classification would lead to undue expense; and where this is the case, the reclassification must be explained. New rules standardize the number of shares and classes, holdings of options and entity control, and the cumulative effect of changes in net accounting as well as the amounts of capital distributions to and transactions with owners.[202] In respect to accounting standards, this standard is beyond the most recent proposal of the SEC regarding disclosure of accounting methods, and it tracks other changes in SEC regulations that curiously supplant FASB rules.

Under revisions to International Accounting Standard 2, last in first out (lifo) (the preferred method for carrying inventory in the United States) is no longer an allowed method of accounting; "fifo" or average weighted cost is the proper method; reversals of write downs are made mandatory; the carrying cost of inventories, accounting method used, and the carrying amount of inventories pledged as collateral must be reported.[203] International Accounting Standards 8 requires restatement of past periods if there has been a change of accounting method, unless this involves an undue cost; requires a full certification by management of the financial statement; and eliminates the allowed alternative, which allowed changes in accounting to be recorded as profit or loss in the current period and provided comparative information for prior periods. The net effect had been for the change of accounting to be reflected in retained earnings.[204] This standard is slightly more onerous than U.S. standards in that it seems to require comparative information in more situations. In other changes under International Accounting Standard 10, companies that declare dividends after the balance sheet date do not need to recognize these as liabilities; International Accounting Standard 15, regarding the effect of changing prices, is temporarily repealed pending an international agreement; exchanges of plants and equipment and intangible assets should be at fair market value; and subjecting estimations of assets' fair market value will now require a discussion of how such value is determined by an active market with reference to observable prices on arm's length terms or other valuation techniques.[205] Leases are now to be broken down into land and building (naturally land can't be depreciated), and initial costs in entering into leases may be capitalized.[206] Functional currency is the currency in which an entity principally operates, but reporting currency can be different, though both must be translated at closing costs of transactions and in the same manner as foreign operations in general. Capitalization of exchange differentials is no longer permitted.[207] Related party disclosures become more stringent (such as amount of transaction) but there is no requirement that management compensation and expenses be disclosed.[208] Minority shareholder interests should be separated from parent's interest in the consolidated returns, and investments in subsidiaries are to be carried at cost except to the extent accounted for as financial instruments.[209] Associate interests are not to be considered joint ventures if the investment is accounted for at fair value.[210] Obligations that can be settled in cash or shares are to be included in ordinary shares for computation of dilutions per share.[211] Property held under an operating lease may be termed investment property if the lessee used the fair value rather than cost model and if the lease is considered a finance lease. The choice between cost model and fair value mode of accounting for investment property is maintained in order to allow less advanced property markets to develop appraisal capacities.[212] International Accounting Standard 8 deals with ongoing improvement projects involving leases, financial instruments, and business combinations.[213]

The U.K. Accounting Standards Board (ASB) adopted six new accounting standards, Financial Reporting Exposure Drafts (FREDs) 23 to 28: reporting foreign currency (except for the recycling of translation difference of profits and losses from consolidating foreign entities); related party disclosures (but retaining the FRED provision to name the controlling party); eliminating "lifo"; eliminating earnings per share from the balance sheet (except retaining the provision that employee stock ownership plan [ESOP] shares held in trust are to be included as assets in the balance sheet); events after the balance sheet, based on International Accounting Standard 8; and proposed to adopt two International Accounting Standards standards on long-term contracts; and tentative changes to the revaluation of tangible fixed assets at fair value (replacing the British Value to business model). It did not adopt changes to consolidated reporting and reporting of associates, or changes on accounting methods or lease accounting,[214] concluding that there was a long row to hoe before 2005. Clearly, the ASB approach is convergence, and possibly toward commonality, rather than toward harmonization.

OFFSHORE FINANCIAL CENTERS (BIS, IMF, AND OECD)

Offshore financial centers (OFC) had banking assets, including bonds and notes, of $4.8 trillion dollars in 1997;[215] OFC bank assets as a share of total cross-border assets stood at 52.4 percent. About 85 percent of offshore financial assets are bank assets.[216] Typically, OFCs are free of reserve requirements and exchange controls and generally include minimum regulatory requirements. Many OFCs are located within the border of countries and include London, the largest,[217] and U.S. international banking facilities and the Japanese offshore market. Offshore facilities are typically carried out through offshore branches, which are legally nearly indistinguishable from the parent.[218] A combination of ease of incorporation and adequate legal frameworks, which safeguard deposits, are some of the legitimate reasons for OFCs.[219] But a high level of bank secrecy and the possibility of tax avoidance or evasion are other reasons for such centers, which also tend toward increasing the possibility of effective money laundering.[220] Typically, OFCs engage in three types of transactions: eurocurrency loans and deposits, eurobonds, and OTC transactions[221] (which one would presume includes hedge fund investments). The underwriting of eurobonds is an important business of OFCs, and, as of 1997, $746.1 billion of money market instruments including notes and bonds were issued at OFCs.[222] Naturally, OFCs include offshore assets of the United States, the United Kingdom, and Japan, as well as assets of Barbados and similar countries; money laundering does not necessarily require the use of OFCs as is evident in the episodes involving the Bank of New York and Citibank.[223] Yet, it is safe to assume that most of the proceeds of ill-gotten gains end up in OFCs, particularly those that are not offshore venues of highly regulated countries like the United States and the United Kingdom.

In 1992, BIS G-10 issued the Minimum Standards for Banks,[224] which was followed by a report by a working group composed of OFC regulators that included 29 recommendations.[225] However, these reports are principally aimed at enabling OFCs to get information about parent companies. And the report does not adequately address affiliated institutions.[226] Offshore banks are more likely to be profitable (because of a lighter regulatory burden) and more liquid;[227] however, they are more likely to be highly leveraged and therefore less solvent.[228] This exploitation of the risk reward tradeoff is likely to result in greater financial instability. The downloading of funds to parents accentuates derivative instrument mismatches, foreign currency risks, and other risks; the uploading of funds to offshore banking centers may hide bad loans and other risky exposures of the banking group.[229]

The free flow of capital offshore can lead to volatility in onshore economies. In Thailand in 1993, offshore flows led to increased real estate leverage and, by 1995, two-thirds of foreign inflows were intermediated by foreign branches. By 1996, the Thai supervisors introduced a 7 percent reserve requirement on foreign borrowing.[230] In Malaysia, a review of offshore branches revealed large losses that had not been previously recognized at one bank and, in Korea, regulations at onshore banks meant that *chaebols* tapped external sources through offshore facilities, which created problems in loan portfolios that were not detected because of weaknesses in consolidated supervision.[231] In Argentina, during the 1995 financial crisis, depositors at OFCs and shell banks (booking facilities) in Uruguay and the Cayman Islands suffered $3 to $4 billion in losses; by exploiting prudential arbitrage, onshore banks were able to avoid domestic capital adequacy requirements, provisioning, credit portfolio diversification, and disclosure requirements.[232] These are only the documented evidence of volatility caused by OFCs. The full impact of OFCs on the 1998 Asian crisis can only be conjectured upon. The role of OFCs in equity movements in the United States in the last few years and particularly the role of OFC hedge funds[233] are not fully understood.

Other issues are raised by OFCs that are not associated with specific onshore markets and may be considered truly offshore. A good example of such OFCs is those in the Caribbean basin. In the late 1990s, concerns over money laundering and tax evasion led to concerted efforts by the international community, and this focus became more intensified after September 11, 2001, as officials attempted to locate the source of terrorist funds. Two international forums are the Financial Stability Forum (FSF) (of the BIS) and the Financial Action Taskforce (FATF). In April 1990, the FATF had issued a report including 40 recommendations, including (1) the criminalization of money laundering; (2) increased international coordination in investigation, prosecution, and extradition, and exchange of suspicious information; and (3) existence of supervisory policies including know your customer.[234] Twenty-six nonmember countries were evaluated by the FATF on such criteria as loopholes in financial regulation, regulatory obstacles to cooperation such as secrecy provisions, and inadequate resources for dealing with money laundering or general lack of provisions for reporting suspicious transactions. Of the 15 noncomplying countries and territories, at least 10 were from the English-speaking West Indies.[235] In the Bahamas, for instance, the ownership of anonymous accounts and bearer shares was banned as were anonymous international business companies that issue bonds and bearer shares,[236] and in the Caymans, the authorities ordered 62 shell banks to open offices and keep records.[237]

After the events of September 11, the United States enacted the USA Patriot Act,[238] which, despite its ostensible purpose, involves the regulation of money laundering in general. The extraterritorial reach of the act is part of the objective of the act: "To deter and punish terrorist acts around the world."[239] The Federal District Courts are given jurisdiction over enforcement of foreign financial institutions with respect to money laundering violations when foreign financial institutions maintain an account at a U.S. financial institution even if a transaction occurs outside the United States, and the act empowers the secretary of the Treasury and the attorney general to issue a summons or subpoena to any foreign bank that maintains a correspondent account in the United States, requesting the institution to produce records even if held abroad. The secretary of the Treasury is also empowered to impose extensive additional reporting requirements on classes of international transactions, jurisdictions, or accounts including (1) recording the identity and legal parties of all signatories and those whose transactions are routed through it; (2) reporting the identity and legal parties of all beneficial owners; (3) under certain conditions, banks are required to ascertain the ownership structure of foreign financial institutions; and (4) any account of any foreign bank is subject to forfeiture without a tracing requirement. Broker-dealers are required to submit suspicious activity reports (SSIs) and nonbank financial institutions may not maintain an account for a foreign shell bank.[240] The Patriot Act also amends relevant definitions to include within the scope of its jurisdiction the underground banking system by including anyone engaged "in an informal money system" and any "network of persons engaged in facilitating the transfer of money domestically or internationally outside of conventional banking facilities."[241] The act also requires that the identity of all customers opening an account be ascertained according to minimum standards to be specified by the U.S. Treasury and relaxes the rules about bank-sharing of information pertinent to money laundering among themselves and with enforcement agencies.[242] The importance of anti–money laundering provisions has been highlighted by terrorism.

Despite criticisms of the USA Patriot Act that it allows the "security anti-terrorist tail [to] proverbially wag and skew the overall global financial system,"[243] efforts at containing money laundering were remarkably inefficacious prior to the passage of the act. Prof. Barry Rider points to the use of nontraditional underground banking systems by terrorist groups.[244] In the context of money laundering proceeds from illegal drug transactions and fraud in the United Kingdom, Prof. Rider "guesstimates," "The amount of money actually taken away from criminals was, and is, laughable by comparison. Some have put the figure as low as .0001 percent of the estimated amount subject to the relevant orders."[245] In contrast with the United States, the United Kingdom passed the Anti-Terrorism, Crime, and Security Act 2001, which is limited to countering the threat of international terrorism.

THE IMF AND THE IBRD

The International Monetary Fund and the International Bank for Reconstruction and Development (IBRD) are part of the tripartite Bretton Woods Agreement, which included the General Agreement on Tariffs and Trade (GATT), recently ratified after 50 years and now called the World Trade Organization (WTO), which, although it includes the General Agreement on Trade in Services including financial services, is beyond the ken of this tome, being the ultimate in international make-believe. The International Monetary Fund, and, to a lesser extent, the World Bank, is often considered the work of John Maynard Keynes, but it is really the brainchild of one Henry Dexter White. Keynes's brief was apparently to assert commonwealth trade preference and a bilateral Anglo-American hegemony. He didn't really do very well. He also devised a system that didn't stress conditionality but rather market discipline.[246] Most revealing is the fact that, expressed in today's dollars, Keynes's system was far larger than the amount of money currently dedicated to IMF resources.[247] Of course, that is comparing apples and oranges; the IBRD is also in the business as discussed below; and who could foresee the private bank readiness to lend. Until 1979, Britain had exchange controls. There are many who believe once Article 2 of the fund was eviscerated and exchange rates were allowed to float, a direct consequence of the failure of the United States to support gold at $35 dollars per ounce as per letter agreement, the raison d'être of the IMF was lost. As discussed in chapter 1, the IMF found a new raison d'être in the less developed countries (LDC) crisis of the early 1980s, and it found one again in the late 1990s with the Asia crisis, the Brazil, and Russia crises. One might suppose the IMF gives good value. After all, the Pacific dragons are chugging along as if nothing happened and Russia has an export surplus of about $20 billion a year. All's well that ends well, right? With about $43 billion Special Drawing Rights (SDR) in credit outstanding and an additional $25 billion SDR in standby arrangements[248] (at about 1.2 SDR to the dollar), this is a cheap resolution to an expensive problem, and Asian economies have reformed in the process. Isn't that what the newspapers say? In reality, the situation is far more complex.

Before proceeding with this inquiry, I would like to call attention to the expertise of IMF employees as exemplified by an article on Latin American lending entitled "Is Latin America Different?"[249] This article is about as insightful as the economic projection made by the IMF in the same journal—*The World Economic Outlook.* "Why then do Latin American Governments not adjust the composition of their debt toward domestic denominated currency-denominated debt? This could be done by issuing external debt denominated in national currency. However, for reasons that are not entirely clear yet to economists, historically only a handful of mature economies have been able to do so."[250] What if these guys had to get a real job? Well, maybe it's better that they don't. Judging by Merton Miller's tidal effect at Long-Term Capital Management, a few more economists in the real world and even Warren Buffet would be strapped for bus fare.

But let's run the scenario. Put yourself in the position of the local Citibank officer. It's Friday afternoon in the capital of a Latin American country, and a borrower comes in and wants to borrow a cool 20 billion in escudos. You go blank for a minute. Then you remember it's the national currency. You've forgotten since you pay for everything in dollars. Well, you figure he's been reading an IMF article. You're in seventh heaven. If it all goes right, you'll be doing the rumba for the next 10 years. You get on the horn to your man in New York, but he doesn't have any escudos, and none of his friends have got that much. They're all trying to unload the odd lot, but that's all. The only one who's got that kind of escudos is your borrower's uncle, El Presidente, and he can print as many as he wants. But somehow that's not kosher. You're glum for a moment, then your buddy calls you back. He tells you the wonderful thing about derivatives is that you don't need all those escudos. You give him dollars and if the escudo goes down against the dollar, he'll pay the difference; a counterparty can pay the difference. That's great, you say. How much will it cost? Oh, he says, about half as much as the loan. You think. No problem. My borrower's really into this. But then your buddy can't find a counterparty the bank will accept. What creditworthy counterparty will guarantee that kind of risk? Naturally, your borrower tells you if escudos go up in value you've made out like a bandit, but nobody expects that. Then why do banks lend to Latin American countries at all? The answer here is that they make a lot of money doing it. David Rockefeller offered an insight when he said the petrodollars were coming in so rapidly they had to do something with them.[251] Investing in treasuries is boring and not always that profitable. Banks have short-term deposits and they look for short-term profits. They look to international organizations to pick up the slack. However, the IMF is supposedly performing a monitoring role as well as a lending role. How then did it not forewarn the marketplace about an international crisis when 60 percent of the loans in Asia had a maturity of less than one year?[252] Each and every member of the IMF executive team deserves a model fiddle replicating Nero's fiddle for fiddling while the international monetary system burned.

Before turning our attention to the crackerjack team at the helm of the World Bank, let's consider what the World Bank does. It gives aid to a wide variety of clients in a wide variety of programs, for basket-case countries as well as market-oriented countries, which it aids through the International Finance Corporation (IFC). With approximately $160 billion in loans outstanding and only a few billion in paid-in capital,[253] it is potentially a source of instability. The U.S. Treasury is committed to an additional $7 billion in commitments out of a total of $33 billion. Recently, a great proportion of these have been dedicated to structural adjustment loans, doing exactly what the IMF does, particularly in Asia and Eastern Europe.

Unlike the do-nothing IMF, the World Bank has been busy—installing a special filtration system in the executive suite at a cost of $7 million in order to enable the important executives to smoke, an action of which this author heartily approves. Luckily, McKinsey and company were on hand to negotiate structural reforms in Asia. No one, not even know-nothing bankers, would leave it to the IMF or the World Bank. However, the World Bank recently underwent a structural imperative in which it devoted $437 million to "refuelling." I wonder if they have an aircraft carrier in the building in Washington or whether they bought an expensive cigarette lighter. There is also a pipeline expenditure. Perhaps this is under the building, or is it merely to justify the cost of the giant lighter?[254] All of this is intended to improve the 60/40 administrative/disbursements split. If these people had been running a charity anywhere in the civilized world, they'd all be in jail. James Wolfensohn, the president of the World Bank, was once an investment banker. He must have gone native.

One could continue with the ceaseless badinage; but, why not let P. J. O'Rourke finish the job:

> Then there is the aforementioned World Bank, financed by wealthy nations such as the U.S. and Japan, and other wealthy nations. Its purpose is to loan money to underdeveloped areas, and I can't understand why it won't loan money to me, since in

many areas I'm as underdeveloped as it gets. The World Bank charges interest rates like your dad does when you borrow a twenty. Thirty three percent of the projects funded by the World Bank are considered a failure by the bank itself. The World Bank operates on the same business principles as a Reagan era savings and loan. And apparently on the same moral principles—because villigation was just fine with the World Bank; in fact, it had already prepared something on that order in the reams of busybody economic advice with which international organizations pester the globe. How would we like it if the Organization of African Unity told us to get out of our suburbs and move downtown?

The World Bank loaned Tanzania oodles of money. Further oodles were loaned by other kindly aid agencies. Tanzanians now have a total foreign debt equal to almost two years worth of everything produced in the country. Tanzania is $7.4 billion in hock. The money will be repaid . . . when Rush Limbaugh becomes secretary general of the U.N. But don't worry, the International Monetary Fund is on the case . . . good farmland sells for . . . $1650 an acre. Since there are more than 29 million Tanzanians, $20 billion [the total amount received in aid] would have bought each family a larger-than-average farm plot, and everybody could have gone back to doing what they were doing before ujamaa (villigation) was thought of. One more reason that Tanzania is poor is that we've paid them to be." (P. J. O'Rourke, *Eat the Rich*, Grove/Atlantic, Inc., 1998).

The political quid quo pro for the boost in the IMF quota increase by the U.S. Congress in the Asia crisis was the creation of a panel of outside experts,[255] the International Financial Institutions Advisory Commission, to deliver a report on reforming the IMF and the World Bank (The Meltzer Report). The Meltzer Report called for the restriction of the IMF role to countries that prequalified and the downsizing and reorganization of multilateral development banks including the elimination of the private arm of the World Bank—the IFC. Under the Meltzer Report, the IMF would not be authorized to negotiate policy reform.[256] The U.S. Treasury, in a response to the Meltzer Report, argued for stricter conditionality, loaning money at high prices to encourage rapid repayment.[257]

While the U.S. view that the IMF should limit its role by adopting a stricter view of conditionality is undoubtedly correct in my opinion, it has been unfortunately bundled in finance theory in the Lerrick Meltzer Proposal,[258] which calls for the IMF to guarantee private sector debt with a put instrument upon the event of a default, so that the IMF would use its resources to set a floor at 85 percent of its estimate of the long-run value of the debt. Under the proposal, the sovereign would make three simultaneous announcements: (1) a moratorium on the debt, (2) a plan to restructure within three months, and (3) an announcement that the IMF had agreed to establish a floor.[259] Just as one was about to cede the floor to Milton Friedman and his acolytes, this proposal convinces one that the IMF is not the worst possible case scenario. To suppose that these guesstimates can be scientifically made is nothing short of lunacy, and while a short-term role for the IMF is essential, any plan is subject to revision, as any lawyer who has worked on any loan, even a home mortgage, understands. The IMF easily demonstrates the fallacy of the proposal. By invoking the language of law viz. a trustee who would receive irrevocable instructions about the collateralized loan obligation of the IMF. As the trustee surrenders the bonds to the IMF and the member for repayment, the member would agree to retire its obligation to the IMF on a fixed schedule and dedicate one-half of all new borrowings to early redemption.[260] While my heart does not go out to irresponsible debtor nations, sticking them in a procrustean bed is no answer either.

IMF conditionality is also assailed from a different quarter. Joseph Stiglitz, former chief economist of the World Bank, Nobel Laureate, and former chief of former President Clinton's Council of Economic Advisors, fires a broadside at IMF "market fundamentalism" while sparing the World Bank in his book *Globalization and Its Discontents*. His critique begins by citing the IMF demands for financial market liberalization in Ethiopia; despite "sound macroeconomic framework,"[261] the IMF suspended Ethiopia Structural Adjustment facility. According to Stiglitz, "The obvious problem with the IMF's logic is that it implies no poor country can ever spend money on anything it gets aid for. If Sweden, say, gives money to Ethiopia to build schools, this logic dictates that Ethiopia should put the money into its reserves."[262]

Stiglitz also alleges that East Asian countries had been successful as the result of industrial policy, high savings rates, and good investment strategies. "The countries had been successful not only in spite of the fact they had not followed most of the dictates of the Washington Consensus, but because they had not."[263] As a consequence of the Asia crisis, gross domestic product (GDP) in Indonesia fell 13.1 percent, in Korea by 6.7 percent, and in Thailand by 10.8 percent, and three years after the crisis, Indonesia's GDP was still 7.5 percent below what it had been before the crisis.[264] According to Stiglitz, Asian leaders blamed the hot money that came along with capital liberalization as the source of the problem.[265] He cites Malaysia's decision not to risk the IMF's wrath, keep interest rates low, and stem capital flow as contributing to its relatively shallow downturn.[266] The IMF provided a total of $95 billion to stabilize East Asian currencies in the belief that this money would sustain the exchange rate. As a byproduct of this tact, foreign bank loans could be repaid.[267] Stiglitz also offers another insight into the consequences of financial market liberalization: Thailand had imposed strict limits on investment in real estate, but the IMF contended that this interfered with the efficient allocation of capital by the market. The real estate bubble was naturally a leading cause and byproduct of the financial market crisis.

Stiglitz is also quite convincing in his analysis of the Russian ruble crisis in 1998. Throughout the 1990s, billions of dollars that the IMF loaned Russia showed up in Cypriot and Swiss bank accounts days after the loans were made; the IMF would contend that these were not their dollars, which caused Stiglitz to observe, "The remark demonstrated either a remarkable lack of understanding or a level of disingenuousness that rivaled Geraschenko's [Chairman of the Central Bank of Russia] or both."[268] He also covers the familiar ground that privatization in Russia turned over state enterprises to their former managers. In one instance, government assets were turned over to private banks in exchange for short-term funds, and soon the government defaulted; after the charade of an auction, the oligopoly, who were owners of the banks, made off with the assets for a fraction of their value.[269]

Stiglitz's thesis is that countries that do not follow IMF prescriptions or follow them loosely such as Hungary and Poland in Eastern Europe as opposed to the Czech Republic, and China, which has capital controls and other restraints of the free movement of capital, Malaysia, and even Korea have faired better than those countries that take their lead from IMF market fundamentalism; he adduces much evidence in support of this thesis. He says that Russia, which was excluded from international lending markets after its IMF default, had returned to the market in 2001. He tenders the possibility that many countries are better off eschewing international capital markets and the IMF; he also intimates that the IMF's program of conditionality should be modified to allow for less Draconian methods of structural readjustment. Insofar as he criticizes the IMF mania for currency convertibility, he is hearkening back to the original mandate of the IMF, which existed to support fixed exchange rates. But fiscal restraint, if not financial liberalization, has always been the hallmark of IMF structural adjustment programs.

But the bent of *Globalization and Its Discontents* does not explain why Korea, even if not a star pupil of the IMF, followed most of its prescriptions in 1997. In 1997, the Korean finance minister's plan for economic reform failed.[270] Between December 1 and 6, Korea agreed to a $55 billion rescue package, in exchange for which Korea agreed to reduce the current account deficit, introduce freer trade, reduce growth to 2.5 percent, and reduce the budget deficit to 1 percent. Enhanced supervision of credit institutions and general financial liberalization was to be introduced. Once the center-left politician Kim Dae Jung agreed to abide by the terms of the IMF agreement, a tranche of $3 billion was released at the end of December and another tranche of $10 billion was released in January. Korea announced that restrictions of foreign investment and ownership would be lifted, and, suspiciously, Korea was able to induce foreign banks to rollover loans the next day. At the end of January, Korea agreed to an interest rate of about 2.5 percent over sixth month Libor for approximately $22.5 billion in foreign bank loans; and in February, legislation was passed that allowed foreign companies to mount takeover bids, which is expected to force the large *Chaebols* to restructure. In March, legislation was passed allowing foreigners to own land. In April, Korea made a debut on the international capital markets, made possible in part as the result of a $30 billion balance of payments surplus. In May, the IMF agreed to allow Korea to expand its budget deficit to 1.7 percent of GDP to fund unemployment claims. At the same time, Moody's downgraded 19 Korean banks; and *Chaebols* announced plans to sell $30 billion in assets to foreign investors. In

June, the government released a death list of 55 companies to be targeted for liquidation. Only in June did Korea demur from market fundamentalism in closing only 5 small banks of 22 total.

Despite Prof. Stiglitz's assertion that Korea did not follow IMF prescriptions that closely, Korea appears to be a poster child for IMF conditionality. It has abided by almost all the free market prescriptions imposed by the IMF and the international financial community. Of course, Korea was an uneasy patient, in the end hampered mostly by contagion from other Asian countries and short-term bank loans.

China presents a more complicated scenario. Only in April 2002 did China formally begin participation in the IMF's Data Dissemination Program.[271] There is, as of yet, no IMF Country Report for China. Officially, China grew at a rate of 7.3 percent in 2001,[272] but one economist questions whether China grew at all in the last four years.[273] Officially, China's four major banks reported sales of RMB 124.5 billion assets (about $15 billion); and about RMB 80 billion were allocated to support the bankruptcy of state-owned enterprises.[274] Information disclosure "has been emphasized" by the China Securities Regulatory Commission, the Ministry of Finance has tightened accounting rules, and a Code of Conduct for Listed Companies appeared in 2002.[275] A fiscal stimulus package of RMB 150 billion (1.5 percent of GDP) was enacted this year following similar packages enacted since 1998. The stock of credit to enterprises fell RMB 711 in the first quarter of 2001,[276] suggesting a credit crunch of substantial proportions. But the most important and trustworthy figures emanating from China are the balance of payment surplus of $47 billion and the foreign direct investment figures, also $47 billion (including Hong Kong).[277] As of March 2002, China had nearly $230 billion in international reserves and had a little over $50 billion in liabilities to foreign banks.[278] This is the bulwark of China's financial strength. It has veered away from IMF domination, but it has done so with an inherently conservative policy of accumulating international (mostly dollar) reserves, which portend ill for the structural integrity of the international monetary system, since the U.S. debt is monetized by Asian countries such as Japan and China (and China's dependent Hong Kong) in order to preserve the export driven economy of such countries. These issues will be considered again in the context of Japan and in the conclusion.

The head of China's central bank admitted that 25 to 35 percent of loans by banks are not being repaid.[279] On May 9, 2002, Standard and Poors (S&P) estimated that the situation might be twice that bad, with 50 percent of loans nonperforming, dwarfing the gigantic problems of the Japanese banking system.[280] Beginning in 1999, the government attempted to relieve banks of bad loans amounting to $170 billion and repackaging and reselling them. The governor of the Chinese Central Bank said that new more stringent rules will put the percentage at 30 percent. By comparison, the highest estimate for Japan puts the percentage of bad loans at 15 percent.[281] Moody's rates the big four Chinese banks at Baa, three notches above investment grade, while Standard and Poors rates the banks BB+, four grades lower, a notch below investment grade.[282] Like Japan, China has not discovered a mechanism for allocating credit between good and bad investments; or it is intent on gaining foreign exchange reserves through export at the expense of its domestic industries and allows the banking sector to teeter on the brink rather than write off loans that will vastly increase government debt, slow foreign investment, and lead to a marked depreciation of the currency unless there is a sale of dollar reserves.

Kenneth Rogoff, chief economist of the IMF, mindful of comments made by Stiglitz about former chief economist Irving Fisher, who Stiglitz suggests toed Robert Rubin's party line and was rewarded with a job at Citibank, felt the need for a spirited attack on Stiglitz's book:

> Let's look at Stiglitzian prescriptions for helping a distressed emerging market debtor, the ideas you put forth as superior to existing practice. Governments typically come to the IMF for financial assistance when they are having trouble finding buyers for their debt and when the value of their money is falling. The Stiglitzian prescription is to raise the profile of fiscal deficits, that is, to issue *more* debt and to print *more* money. You seem to believe that if a distressed government issues more currency, its citizens will suddenly think it more valuable. You seem to believe that when investors are no longer willing to hold a government's debt, all that needs to be done is to increase the supply and it will sell like hot cakes. We at the IMF—no, make that we on the Planet Earth—have considerable experience suggesting otherwise. We earthlings have found that when a country in fiscal distress tries to escape by printing more money, inflation rises, often uncontrollably. Uncontrolled inflation strangles growth, hurting the entire populace, but especially the indigent. The laws of economics may be different in your part of the gamma quadrant, but around here we find that when an almost bankrupt government fails to credibly constrain the time profile of its fiscal deficits, things generally get worse instead of better.[283]

The kind of invective used here ignores parts of Stiglitz's argument. While Stiglitz clearly overstates the case in regard to Korea, he is quite correct that IMF lending to Russia, and the privatization programs that resulted, served only to promote the interests of the oligarchs and represented a very poor usage of IMF assets. The experiences of Poland and Hungary in their more gradualist approach, compared to the Czech Republic, and the experience of Malaysia compared to Thailand and Indonesia make one consider what the primary mission of the IMF is. It may be that only the two extremes, of strict conditionality and the suspension of convertibility, are appropriate remedies for countries facing structurally problematic external debt. Furthermore, the IMF's role of promoting market liberalization, as in causing the restrictions to be lifted on real estate lending in Thailand, and its failure to issue warnings about the preponderance of short-term bank debt make one question whether it is, on balance, a hindrance to the smooth functioning of the international economy. Its failure to warn about the preponderance of short-term bank loans in the composition of loans to Pacific Rim countries causes one to conclude that the IMF staff live for the adrenaline rush created by international crises. Certainly, the IMF does not subscribe to the adage that an ounce of prevention is worth a pound of cure.

Whether or not there are any situations that merit IMF lending while monetary policy is eased—the prescription employed by the United States and other First World economies at the onset of a domestic financial crisis, is not altogether clear. It is not altogether consonant with White's plan for the IMF as conceived at Bretton Woods.[284] On the other hand, the Articles of Agreement as originally conceived were not intended to support convertible exchange rates. And the objective of maintaining currency convertibility and promoting financial market liberalization at every turn is not only an expression of market fundamentalism. It evidences the fact that the IMF has become a toady of international banks and seeks to make such banks whole, which only serves to promote moral hazard. But the international banks per se are not the only clientele served by the IMF. For example, the United States was interested in containing the Asia crisis, thus preserving the capital base of international banks (U.S. banks were not even the primary beneficiaries) and allowing financial markets to continue their giddy upward spiral. The speed and breadth of recovery in the economies of debtor nations is low on the IMF's agenda.

Ultimately, the World Bank should be phased out as a lending institution and serve solely as a source for information gathering to enable private lenders to underwrite below market rate loans supported by a fund remote from lending decisions. The IMF serves a more central purpose, perhaps. But one that should not be abused. The greatest problem posed by both the IMF and the World Bank is the incompetence of their lending officers and executive staffs. Appointment often results from political favor and insulates the lucky recipient from the quiddities of the job market. The procurement of staff should follow the process of hiring in the banking industry with some preference given to international experience. Country of origin should play no part in the hiring process. The current staff of the IMF and the World Bank should be summarily fired (except for economists who are by and large competent but should be subject to tenure-like processes). The cost of firing the staff would be minimal compared to the cost of paying for their continued mistakes. However, if they cannot be fired they should be paid in nonconvertible currency. (Both the IMF and the World Bank are chock-full of the stuff.)

Meanwhile, the Asia crisis? Or the Latin American crisis. Argentina has defaulted, but what about Brazil? The United States supported Brazil's application to the IMF for a $30 billion loan. Brazil's $264 billion external debt is twice the size of Argentina's, and American banks, such as J.P. Morgan Chase and Citibank, in general, have double the exposure. There is considerable U.S. investment in Brazil, including GM Plants. Shares in J.P. Morgan and Citibank jumped 6 percent once the news of the package was released.[285] Thus, there is an indirect effect on European and Asian banks. Paul Krugman, who is skeptical on the future of Brazil, notes that Fleet Bank and Citibank alone have close to $20 billion in loans to Brazil.[286] The fiscal cost of bank recapitalization has been estimated at 26.5 percent of GDP in Korea, 56.3 percent in Indonesia, and 32 percent in Thailand.[287] The cost in Argentina has not yet been estimated. Some of this money was borrowed from the IMF and the IBRD. The rest was put on the proverbial credit card, and we shall wait for the other shoe to fall.

Equally importantly, the role of these institutions must be rethought ab initio. They must no longer serve as the alter ego of the corporate world or the failed conscience of an unjust world financial system. The late Yale economist Robert Triffin lectured interminably on how LDCs were required to keep reserves in dollars that far outbalanced loans from international multilateral agencies.[288] Witness China. It has $19 billion in loans from the World Bank and $140 billion in dollar reserves that it is now throwing at traders and losing rapidly in a hopeless effort to support the yuan. The conclusion will demonstrate the vital role that such institutions, particularly a reconstituted International Monetary Fund, must play in a new world order to redress the structural imbalances in current accounts.

THE NEW BASEL CAPITAL ACCORD, DEVELOPMENTS 2003: OBSURANTIST BANKING REGULATION

The third consultative document of the BIS Committee on Banking Supervision was issued in July 2003.[289] This document combines general rules on consolidation with ever more precise rules on securitization, increased reliance on external rating agencies, and absurd mathematical prescriptive formulas, which will ensure that capital adequacy ultimately becomes the province of the priesthood of banking regulators and compliance and risk management experts while the directors and even the management of banks are increasingly in the dark as to the nature of regulatory capital. Furthermore, the disclosure provisions of the New Capital Accord become increasingly meaningless to the market.

The consultative document begins by touting the principle of consolidation of all financial activities of groups, whether regulated or unregulated, wherever possible, except for minority interests where control is not present.[290] Part 2 of the document considers the first pillar of banking supervision, the minimum capital requirements, and provides for transition for the present accord.[291]

Claims in the regular retail portfolio of a bank which meet certain conditions are risk-weighted at 75 percent and residential property which is occupied by the borrower or rented is risk-weighted 35 percent.[292] The consultative document also allows extremely generous provisions for past due loans,[293] and specific criteria are provided for external credit assessments.[294] How important these criteria are in the oligopolistic structure of the credit rating business[295] remains to be seen.

This consultative document also addresses the fact that financial institutions use a number of devices to mitigate risk which previous banking supervision documents have failed to account for, including collateralization by deposits, third party guarantees, or credit derivatives.[296] But these very precise indicia are subject to qualitative internal risk management systems.[297] Counterparty risk for repo transactions is minimized because qualifying transactions require that the counterparty be a "core market Participant."[298] Banks are permitted to use a VAR model as an alternative to standard or own estimate haircuts.[299] Here, however, the nomenclature becomes positively bewildering with green, yellow, and red zones to define exceptions.

Part 3 defines the internal risk-based approach to credit risk, regardless of all the references to the same in Part 2, the standard approach. This part appears to contain definitions of classes of assets such as project finance, object finance, income producing real estate, high volatility commercial real estate, retail exposures, qualifying revolving retail exposures, and equity exposures.[300] The internal risk-based approach is further subdivided into the foundation and the advanced approach.[301]

The remainder of the discussion of the first pillar can only be of interest to bank regulators and compliance officers; and, herein lies the rub. While well-intentioned banking regulators who have spent their entire careers in banking regulation, particularly U.S. regulators who drive the process,[302] hammer out details with specialized bank risk managers who have limited interaction with bank management who may actually be pulling the strings at an Olympian distance, the nature of regulatory capital becomes increasingly meaningless. Meanwhile, Japanese banks, if deferred tax benefits are excluded, have less than 2 percent of tier-one regulatory capital.[303] It is almost inconceivable how the framers of the New Capital Accord can imagine that the disclosure provisions discussed in the consultative document can have any meaning in the context of their rarefied babble. The wholesale removal of capital adequacy from the public debate, through less than subtle attempts at obscurantism, reflect a view on the part of regulators that capital adequacy is the province of advanced and specialized econometricians. The inherent lack of transparency is a godsend to international banks that are loathe to have their capital adequacy provisioning accessible to the public. After all, the presumption is that any international bank has oodles of capital unless market rumors specify otherwise. The United States has announced that only the 10 largest banks will be subject to the new accord. But these banks control 99 percent of international assets.[304]

The Securitization Framework, however, is more precise management of securitization risk than previously discussed.[305] A synthetic securitization is defined as containing at least two distinct tranches with different credit risks. Synthetic securitizations have independent requirements.[306] For all securitizations, three categories of residual risk are defined: clean up call; credit enhancement risk; and early amortization.[307] Two other definitional terms are excess spread—the cushion and implicit support.[308] If securitizations meet specific criteria, they are eligible for external credit assessments and subject to the risk weighting for the investment grade. These are divided into long- and short-term holdings.

Section V of Part I considers operational risk. Here again are three methodologies: the basic indicator approach, where banks hold a specific percentage of capital against operational risk; the standardized approach, where bank activities are divided into eight business lines; and the advanced measurement approach, under which the bank's internal risk-based measurement system will govern. Section 6 specifies which assets may be held in the trading book as opposed to the bank book. Generally, these are assets which are traded by trading desks. Risk is determined by marking to market, marking to model, or independent price verification. Banks must also take account of counterparty risk for OTC instruments, repos, and other transactions in the trading book.[309] Counterparty risk is considered "specific risk" and commensurate with treatment of risk in the banking book under the 1996 market risk amendment.[310] There is also an add-on factor to cover future exposure.[311]

Part 3 considers the supervisory review process. This part is essentially a rehash of what has come before,[312] stressing the importance of what can only be described as intangibles, a process for overall risk in the context of a bank's risk profile, excess holding of capital over minimum levels, and early intervention by regulators. Certain specific risks to be addressed by regulators include interest rate risk in the banking book, stress tests under the IRB approach, securitization risks, and credit concentration risk.[313]

Part 4 considers the third pillar—market discipline, which includes disclosure. Disclosure should be semi-annual, and banks must strike a balance between safeguarding proprietary information and the public's right to know. Pillar 3 applies at the top level of the banking group. Perhaps the most important element of the disclosure requirement is that part of the qualitative disclosure differentiates between regulatory disclosure and disclosure for accounting purposes, particularly in distinguishing between consolidation for accounting and regulatory purposes.[314] It is unclear how the appendices on disclosure differ from securities disclosure regimes in the more advanced securities markets such as the United Kingdom and the United States. Perhaps most important of all is the 15 percent of tier-one capital limitation on innovative instruments.[315]

In August 2003, the Committee on Banking Supervision released its paper on principles for banking supervisors for cross-border issues.[316] This document notes that the New Accord will not change the legal responsibilities of national supervisors or their regulatory responsibilities. This principle reiterates the fact that the New Accord is not a legal document but a set of principles to be implemented nationally. The home country supervisor is responsible for the supervision of a banking group on a consolidated basis, and the home country supervisor in the event of a conflict will have the final say, subject to host country legal requirements and other factors governing the regulation of subsidiaries. Supervisors should avoid performing redundant work or uncoordinated approval and validation work to minimize the regulatory burden. Plans should be developed well in advance of the implementation date, which is currently scheduled for 2006.

On January 15, 2004, the Committee on Banking Supervision published an update on Basel II.[317] The Committee agreed to simplify the treatment of securitization related exposures. Banks will be allowed to drive risk weights for unrated commercial paper conduits subject by mapping their internal risk assessment formulas to external credit ratings. A less complex formula will be used for unrated securitizations in general. Also, originators and investors in securitizations will be treated identically. Some other complexities in the treatment of securitizations will be eradicated by stressing the concept of seniority in tranches and lowering the risk weighting for these tranches. The Committee also agreed to refine the rules on recognizing credit risk mitigation techniques and will undertake a review of counterparty credit risk in coordination with IOSCO. The Committee has also demonstrated willingness to increase flexibility under Pillar 2, moving away from a system of automatic add-ons.[318]

NOTES

1. James Baker, *The Bank for International Settlements Evolution and Evaluation.* Westport, CT: Quorum Books, 2002.
2. Bank for International Settlement, "Profile" (March 2002).
3. *Ibid.*
4. Bank for International Settlements, "The New Basel Capital Accord: A Consultative Document" (May 31, 2001).
5. *Ibid.*, p. 1.
6. *Ibid.*, p. 2.
7. *Ibid.*, pp. 2–3.
8. *Ibid.*, p. 3.
9. *Ibid.*, p. 4.
10. *Ibid.*, p. 7. All claims are based on the bank's general capital requirement of 8 percent. The 150 percent or 12 percent risk weighted category is new.
11. *Ibid.*, par. 34.
12. Federal Reserve Board, Federal Deposit Insurance Corporation, Options Clearing Corporation, and Office of Thrift Supervision, "Joint Press Release: Agencies Issue Final Rule Lowering Risk Weighting for Claims on Securities Firms" (April 9, 2002).
13. *Op. cit.*, par. 35.
14. *Ibid.*
15. *Ibid.*, par. 42–44.

16. *Ibid.*, Chapter 2, pp. 45–60.
17. *Ibid.*, SubChapter B. Credit Risk under the Standardized Approach.
18. *Ibid.*
19. *Ibid.*, III The IRB Approach.
20. *Ibid.*, 3 Adoption of Element of the Advanced Approach.
21. *Ibid.*, par. 193.
22. *Ibid.*, par. 232–34.
23. *Ibid.*, 2 Minimum Requirements for Corporate Exposure ii Criteria to Ensure Meaningful Differentiation of Risk.
24. *Ibid.*, C par. 255.
25. *Ibid.*
26. *Ibid.*, 3C.
27. *Ibid.*, 3E.
28. *Ibid.*, Minimum Requirements for EAD Exposure, par. 379.
29. *Ibid.*, 2 Minimum Requirements for Retail Exposures, par. 444–47.
30. *Ibid.*, par. 450. Banks must also have an internal definition of default for each category subject to objective criteria, 90 days past due, forgiveness of indebtedness, or a declaration of bankruptcy. Par. 466.
31. *Ibid.*, D Rules for Sovereign Debt, II Inputs to Risk Weighted Function.
32. *Ibid.*, E.
33. *Ibid.*, F Calculation of IRB Granularity Adjustment to Capital.
34. *See* chapter 1, "The FSA before the Financial Services and Markets Act."
35. IV Asset Securitisation, 1 The Treatment of Explicit Risks Associated with Asset Securitisation under the Standard Approach.
36. *Ibid.*
37. *Ibid.*, 2 The IRB Hybrid Approach.
38. *Ibid.*, 3 Treatment of Implicit and Residual Risks Arising from Securitisation.
39. *Ibid.*, V Operational Risk.
40. *Ibid.*
41. *Ibid.*, 3, 556.
42. *Ibid.*, VI Trading Book Issues.
43. 12 C.F.R. Section 225 Appendix E: Implementation of Amendment to the Basel Capital Adequacy Accord, January 1996.
44. IV Market Discipline C Disclosures The Structure of Capital.
45. *Ibid.*
46. *Ibid.*, 1 Credit Risk in the Banking Book, I) quantitative.
47. *Ibid.*, 3 Interest Rate Risk in the Banking Book 4 Operational Risks.
48. *Ibid.*, E Disclosures: Capital Adequacy.
49. Bank for International Settlements, "The Standardised Approach to Credit Risk," consultative document (May 31, 2001).
50. Bank for International Settlements, consultative document (May 31, 2001).
51. Bank for International Settlements, "The Internal Ratings Based Approach," consultative document (May 31, 2001).
52. Bank for International Settlements, "Principles for the Management and Supervision of Interest Rate Risk," consultative document (May 31, 2001).
53. *Ibid.*, par. 84.
54. *Ibid.*, Annex 1.
55. *Ibid.*, B Simulation Approaches.

56. *See* chapter 4.
57. Financial Services Authority, Davies, speech (2000).
58. Basel Committee on Banking Supervision, International Organization of Securities Commissions, and International Organization of Insurance Supervisors, "Risk Management Practices and Regulatory Practices: A Cross-Sectoral Comparison" (November 2001).
59. *Ibid.*, 3, p. 4.
60. *Ibid.*, p. 5.
61. *Ibid.*, p. 4.
62. *Ibid.*, II Risk Management Securities Sector p. 12.
63. *See infra* 94.
64. *Op. cit.*
65. *See* chapter 3, "Deregulations: The Commodities Futures Modernization Act."
66. Cross-Sectoral Comparison, *supra* note 58, Part III time frames, p. 31.
67. *Ibid.*
68. *Ibid.*, pp. 38–39.
69. *See* chapter 1, note 171, and chapter 3, "Net Capital Rules."
70. *See infra* notes 73–74. *See also* chapter 3, "Net Capital Rules."
71. *See* "The Capital Adequacy Directive" and chapter 3, "Net Capital Rules."
72. *See* chapter 1, note 132, and accompanying text.
73. Cross-Sectoral Comparison, *supra* note 58, p. 53.
74. *Ibid.*, p. 41.
75. *Ibid.*, pp. 60–64. These range from total deduction to full consolidation and along the way include risk weighting and several other approaches; under each of the approaches the solo risk weighting applies to the subsidiary, so the only question is the parent. In some cases, double gearing would be allowed. In my view, this should be permissible on a case-by-case basis. In the United States, banks cannot own securities firms, so the only combination where the subject is at issue is a bank/insurance combination, and it is not allowed.
76. *See* chapter 4, Gramm-Leach-Bliley.
77. Cross-Sectoral Comparison, *supra* note 58, Annex 2, p. 77.
78. Bank for International Settlements, International Organization of Securities Commissions, and International Association of Insurance Supervisors, "Intra Group Transactions and Exposures Principles" (Basel: December 1999).
79. *See* chapter 4, "Gramm-Leach-Bliley. . . ."
80. *See* chapter 7, "The *Keiretsu*."
81. Phone interview with General Counsel, 1992.
82. *See infra* note 58.
83. Bank for International Settlements, International Organization of Securities Commissions, and International Association of Insurance Supervisors, "Cross-Sectoral Comparison: Core Principles" (November 2001).
84. *Ibid.*, 5 par. 31.
85. *Ibid.*, c) par. 51–52.
86. *Ibid.*, par. 53.
87. *Ibid.*, 64 and Section 6 c.
88. *See* chapter 3, notes 101–8, and accompanying text.
89. *See* chapter 6, "The EU Proposed Directive. . . ."
90. International Organization of Securities Commissions, "Sound Practices for

Managing Liquidity Risk as Securities Firms" (May 2002). Operational risk is defined as loss resulting from the failure of internal systems, including individuals and infrastructure, p. 1.

91. *Ibid.*, par. 10.
92. *Ibid.*, par. 11.
93. *Ibid.*, par. 12. In practical terms, repo agreements are the best source of liquidity. *See* chapter 3, note 43.
94. *Ibid.*, par. 21–22.
95. *Ibid.*, B. par. 31–37.
96. *Ibid.*, par. 39.
97. *Ibid.*, par. 41–43.
98. *Ibid.*, par. 44–45.
99. *Ibid.*, par. 46–49.
100. *Ibid.*, par. 55.
101. *Ibid.*, sections D and E.
102. *See* note 21 and accompanying text.
103. *Op. cit.*, par. 71.
104. *Ibid.*, par. 73.
105. *Ibid.*, par. 75–79.
106. *Ibid.*, par. 86–90.
107. *See* chapter 1, "Consolidated Supervision," and chapter 3, notes 132–33 and accompanying text.
108. *Op. cit.*, Annex 1 Questionnaire, Question 1.
109. *Ibid.*, Question 2.
110. *See infra* notes 75 and 76.
111. *Op. cit.*, Question 3.
112. *Ibid.*, iii.
113. *Ibid.*, III 1.
114. *See* chapter 3, note 125.
115. *See* chapter 1, "Capital Adequacy Directive for Securities Firms and Credit Institutions."
116. IOSCO "Sound Practices for Liquidity Risk," *supra* note 90 Annex 1 III 3.
117. *Ibid.*, 7, the end of firm's last fiscal year's ratios.
118. *Ibid.*, 17.
119. *Ibid.*, VI, 4.
120. *See generally*, chapter 3, "Net Capital Rules."
121. International Organization of Securities Commissions, Report by the Technical Committee, "Hedge Funds and Other Highly Leveraged Institutions" (November 1999).
122. *See* chapter 4, "The International Debt Crisis. . . ."
123. *Op. cit.*, par. 14.
124. *Ibid.*, par. 19.
125. *Ibid.*, par. 28.
126. *Ibid.*, par. 43–48.
127. International Organization of Securities Commissions, Report by the Technical Committee, "The Management of Credit Risk by Securities Firms and Recommendations to Firms and Regulators" (May 2000).
128. *Ibid.*, Introduction and 1A.

129. *Ibid.*, 1A.
130. *See* chapter 4, "The International Debt Crisis. . . ."
131. *Ibid.*, B.
132. *Ibid.*, C.
133. *Ibid.*, D.
134. *Ibid.*, E.
135. International Organization of Securities Commissions (IOSCO), "Objectives and Principles of Securities Regulation," IOSCO Report, updated with references to work done by IOSCO since September 1998 (February 2002).
136. International Organization of Securities Commissions, "International Disclosure Standards for Cross-Border Offerings and Initial Public Listing by Foreign Issuers" (September 1998).
137. *Ibid.*, Introduction.
138. *Ibid.*, I "Identity of Directors, Senior Management, and Auditors."
139. *Ibid.*, II "Offer Statistics and Expected Timetable III Key Information A Selected Financial Data."
140. *Ibid.*
141. *Ibid.*, B Capitalization and Indebtedness.
142. *See* chapter 4, note 71.
143. IOSCO Disclosure Standards, *supra* note 136.
144. *Ibid.*, D.
145. *Ibid.*, IV Information on the Company.
146. *Ibid.*, V.
147. *See* chapter 4, note 141, and accompanying text.
148. *See infra* notes 181–84.
149. IOSCO "Disclosure Standards" *supra* note 136, V2.
150. *Ibid.*, 3.
151. *Ibid.*, 4.
152. *Ibid.*, 3. The discussion is only about hedging currency, but in reality government policy may be hedged.
153. *Ibid.*, B Liquidity and Capital Resources.
154. *Ibid.*, 2.
155. *Ibid.*, C and D.
156. *Ibid.*, Directors, Senior Management, and Employees.
157. *Ibid.*, B.
158. *Ibid.*, VI Major Shareholders.
159. *Ibid.*, VII Major Shareholders and Related Party Transactions.
160. *Ibid.*, VIII Consolidated Financial Statements and Other Information.
161. *Ibid.*, 4. If the document is older than nine months, it should contain interim financial statements, including a balance sheet showing changes in equity, which may be condensed but must contain major line items (5) and B. disclose significant changes.
162. IX The Offer and Listing.
163. Securities and Exchange Commission (SEC), Division of Corporate Finance, "International Reporting and Disclosure Issues" (May 31, 2001).
164. International Accounting Standards Committee, "IASC 2000 Standards" (2000).
165. Hal Scott, "The Internationalization of Public Primary Securities Markets," *Law and Contemporary Problems* (summer 2000): p. 71.
166. *Ibid.*, at 99–100.

167. *Supra* note 163.

168. International Disclosure release, *supra* note 136.

169. Comment of Sullivan and Cromwell to Jonathon Katz, cited in "The Internationalization of Primary Securities Markets," *supra* note 160, at 78.

170. Michael Peel, "Accord Puts Common World Standards Back on Track," *Financial Times*, Nov. 19, 1999, at 14, and Lucinda Kemeny, "Global Watchdog under Threat," *Accounting Age*, October 7, 1999, at 7, cited in "The Internationalization of Public Securities Markets," *supra* note 165, at 79.

171. These include proposals that issuers follow national laws of countries that have sufficient disclosure regimes; nationality and place of incorporation are proposed as a means of determining which law would govern. *See generally*, "The Internationalization of Public Primary Securities Markets," *supra* note 168.

172. United Kingdom, H. M. Treasury, "Public Offers of Securities" (1998).

173. *Ibid.*

174. Rule 144(a)—Section 230.144A Private Resale to Institutions Fed. Sec. L. Rep. (CCH) 84,523 (May 5, 1990).

175. Reg. S—Offshore Offers and Sales, Securities Act Release No. 6779 (1987–88 Transfer Binder Fed. Sec. L. Rep. [CCH] Sec. 84,242 [June 10, 1988]).

176. The Securities and Exchange Commission has issued an interpretation as to when advertising over the Internet would not be considered an offering within the United States. The issuer must employ efforts reasonably designed to avoid targeting U.S. persons; however, when the issuer is domestic and the securities are unregistered (in the United States) public securities, more restrictive provisions apply such as employing a password system and requiring persons to certify that they are not U.S. nationals (SEC, "Statement of the Commission Regarding the Use of Internet Web Sites to Offer Securities, Solicit Securities Transactions, or Advertise Investment Services Onshore," 63 Federal Register 14,806 [Mar. 27, 1998]).

177. *See* chapter 1, note 85 and accompanying text.

178. *TSC Industries v. Northway Inc.* 426 US, 438, 499 (1976).

179. *Ibid.*

180. *See* chapter 1, note 85 and accompanying text.

181. *The European Union*—The Listing Particulars Directive (Schedule A paragraphs 7.1 and 7.2) requires a company to give

> General information on the trend of the issuer's business since the end of the financial year to which the last published annual accounts relate, in particular:
>
> - the most significant recent trends in production, sales and stocks and the state of the order book, and
> - recent trends in costs and selling prices.
>
> Information on the issuer's prospects for at least the current financial year.

Other information on projections and forward looking information is neither mandatory or forbidden under the directive. The following (European Union) EU countries have additional requirements:

> *Belgium and Germany*—It should be indicated if this information has been audited by the auditors.
>
> *France*—If the company makes a projection, a limited review must be conducted by the auditor or a negative statement must be given.

Luxembourg—Companies that are not able to present annual accounts for the three consecutive years preceding the official application for listing will have to complete their application for listing with forecasts established for three years. Forecasts, in this case, mean any indications relating to the activities into which the company has engaged or is intending to engage, to the viability of the company's business, its commercial potentials, and any other evaluation as to the evolution of their financial results. Such forecasts must be set up by an independent expert or consultant or be submitted to an independent expert or consultant in the case they have been set up by the company itself. The prospectus must mention in all cases that these forecasts do not bind the company with respect to future results and that these forecasts are included in the prospectus solely for information purposes. Companies that need such a waiver of the requirements for three years' annual accounts must publish quarterly financial statements for the period for which the waiver has been granted initially, i.e., at least until publication of the annual reports of the third year, and the prospectus will have to mention that the quarterly reports will be available at the place mentioned. Companies that do not need waivers of the requirement for three years' annual accounts and who make a forecast would need to submit that forecast to an independent expert or consultant and the prospectus will have to mention that these forecasts do not bind the company with respect to future results and that these forecasts are included in the prospectus solely for information purposes.

Spain—Projections applicable to the current fiscal year in which the prospectus is filed are regulated in "Annex A" of the Ministerial Order of July 12, 1993, and in the Ministerial Order of June 19, 1997. This regulation requires projections for a maximum of two financial or fiscal years; the information must be reviewed by an independent expert, whose report must be included in the prospectus. (Listing Standards, *Ibid.* Part IIB).

The United Kingdom—Profit forecasts in listing particulars generally have to be reported on by an issuers' sponsors and auditors or reporting accountants. However, where the laws or regulation in the country where an overseas company has its primary listing require a statement to be included in listing particulars as to the future prospects of the company, which constitutes a profit forecast, the London Stock Exchange will allow its inclusion without the need for it to have been reported on, provided that the issuer confirms to the exchange in writing that the statement has been properly compiled on a basis consistent with the accounting policies normally adopted by the company and has been made after due and careful inquiry.

Where new companies do not have an adequate trading record (such as scientific research–based companies and companies undertaking major capital projects) they may be required to include an estimate of future funding and profit and dividend projections that will need to be reported on. This authority is subject to the U.K. Listing Authority now under the jurisdiction of the FSA. Special rules apply under the Amendment to the Listing Particulars. *See* chapter 1, note 1.

182. The inclusion of forward-looking information that has a reasonable basis in filed documents is encouraged by the SEC. A statement of the SEC's position is set forth in Item 10(b) of Regulation S-K. There is a statutory safe harbor for forward-looking statements made by certain reporting issuers and specified persons that is set forth in Section 27A of the Securities Act of 1933 and Section 21E of the Securities Exchange Act of 1934. This safe harbor permits greater flexibility to those who make use of the statutory protections; a safe harbor for issuers who make oral forward-looking statements also is provided. In addition, in Rule 175 under the Securities Act of 1933, there is a regulatory safe harbor for forward-looking statements by issuers or outside reviewers retained by issuers made in documents filed with the SEC. This safe harbor generally provides that such statements will not be deemed to be fraudulent statements unless the statements were made or reaffirmed without a reasonable basis or were disclosed other than in good faith. *See* chapter 4.

183. *See also* chapter 4, note 12 and also notes 4–6.

184. Ernst and Young, *IAS/US GAAP Comparison* (International Accounting Standards Committee, 2000) citing cross reference of a list of 32 companies preparing financial statements under International Accounting Standards (IAS) to a list of foreign filers on the New York Stock Exchange and the National Association of Dealers Automated Quotations (NASDAQ) and file form 20F, with two exceptions relating to the year 1999.

185. *Ibid.*, table 3, p. 621.

186. *Ibid.*, p. 257.

187. *Ibid.*, p. 623. *See also* Ernst and Young Chapter 2 Section 2.3.3.

188. *Ibid.*, p. 625.

189. Financial Accounting Standards Board, Emerging Issues Task Force, 90–15 Appendix (D)(2). *See also*, *IAS-GAAP Comparison*, *supra* note 184, at 109.

190. *Op. cit.*, pp. 104, 626.

191. *Ibid.*, pp. 109–10, *see also* FASB Standard No. 140.

192. *Ibid.*, p. 404.

193. *Ibid.*, p. 405.

194. *See supra* notes 164–65 and accompanying text.

195. *Op. cit.*, p. 631 Extract 7.

196. *Ibid.*, p. 632 Extract 8.

197. *Ibid.*, p. 637 Extract 13.

198. *Ibid.*, p. 638 Extract 14.

199. *Ibid.*, p. 643 Extract 19.

200. "Why Not So Alluring," *The Economist*, May 30, 2002. Additional differences include treatment of currency when the currency is not in the parent company's own currency. Here Generally Accepted Accounting Principles (GAAP) is more stringent, requiring market reporting; in regard to deferred tax, once again GAAP is more stringent. Options are also treated more stringently under GAAP. On the whole GAAP appear more stringent; yet actual results for the 32 companies do not bear this out. Perhaps this is because GAAP is more lax on consolidated accounting rules and interest expense.

201. International Accounting Standards Board, "Proposal for Improving International Accounting Standards" (May 5, 2002).

202. *Ibid.*, Exposure Draft, Revised IAS 1.

203. *Ibid.*, Exposure Draft, Revised IAS 2.

204. *Ibid.*, Exposure Draft, Revised IAS 8.

205. *Ibid.*, Exposure Draft, Revised IAS 16.

206. *Ibid.*, Exposure Draft, Revised IAS 17.

207. *Ibid.*, Exposure Draft, Revised IAS 21.

208. *Ibid.*, Exposure Draft, Revised IAS 24.

209. *Ibid.*, Exposure Draft, Revised IAS 27.

210. *Ibid.*, Exposure Draft, Revised IAS 28.

211. *Ibid.*, Exposure Draft, Revised IAS 33.

212. *Ibid.*, Exposure Draft, Revised IAS 40.

213. *Ibid.*, Invitation to Comment.

214. Accounting Standards Board, Inside Track 31, "Six Proposals for Steps toward International Convergence" (April 2002).

215. Luca Errico and Alberto Musalem, "Offshore Banking Centers: An Analysis

of Micro- and Macro-Prudential Issues," International Monetary Fund, Monetary and Exchange Affairs Department, IMF Working Paper no. WP/99/5 (1999), p. 10.

216. *Ibid.*, p. 5.

217. *Ibid.*, p. 12.

218. *Ibid.*, p. 13.

219. *Ibid.*, p. 9.

220. *Ibid.*, p. 10.

221. *Ibid.*

222. *Ibid.*, p. 14.

223. *See* U.S. General Accounting Office, "Private Banking: Raoul Salinas, Citibank, and Alleged Money-Laundering," GAO/OSSI-99-1 (October 1998).

224. Bank for International Settlements, Committee for Banking Supervision, "Minimum Standards for the Supervision of International Banking Groups and Their Cross-Border Establishments" (1992).

225. "The Supervision of Cross-Border Banking," report by a working group of the Group of Offshore Banking Supervisors and the Basel Committee on Banking Supervision (October 1996). The report aimed to improve supervisors' access to banks and banking records and delineated the responsibilities between home and host country regulators. Powers include the ability to carry out regular onsite inspections and offshore monitoring, funding, large exposures, and deposit concentrations. As in the context of the Second Banking Directive, the principal issue posed is often liquidity and several countries insist on parent guarantee of liquidity.

226. *Ibid.*, p. 26. The United States and EU have different rules requiring consolidation. In the United States, consolidation is required if there is majority interest under Generally Accepted Accounting Principles (otherwise the amount is deducted from capital). In the EU, under International Accounting Standards, the measure is "effective control." The report does not address "parallel owned" banks, banks with the same ownership.

227. *Ibid.*, pp. 27–28.

228. *Ibid.*, p. 29.

229. *Ibid.*, p. 33.

230. *Ibid.*, p. 35.

231. *Ibid.*, p. 36.

232. *Ibid.*

233. *See* note 122 and accompanying text.

234. Financial Action Taskforce on Money Laundering at <http://www.oecd.org/fatf/> (June 2000 with updates to September 2001); and International Monetary Fund and International Bank for Reconstruction and Development, "Enhancing Contributions to Moneylaundering: Policy Paper" (April 26, 2001) Annex II. In June 2001, the Bahamas and the Cayman Islands were removed from the list.

235. *Ibid.*

236. Esther Suss, Orel Williams, and Chandima Mendis, "Caribbean Offshore Financial Centers: Past, Present, and Possibilities for the Future," International Monetary Fund Working Paper no. WP 02/88 (May 2002).

237. *Ibid.*

238. "Uniting and Strengthening America by Providing the Appropriate Tools Required to Interrupt and Obstruct Terrorism Act," Short Title "International Terrorism and Money Laundering Act of 2001," Pub. Law no. 105–56 (2001).

239. USA Patriot Act "Preamble."

240. *Ibid. See* Joseph J. Norton and Heba Shams, "Money-Laundering and Terrorist Financing: Post September 11 Responses—Let Us Take a Step Back and Take a Deep Breath," *International Lawyer* 36 (spring 2002): p. 103n. Sections 311, 312, 313, and 319 (b) deal with the relationship between the United States and foreign jurisdictions. Under Section 326 "know your customer" obligations of the act, under subsequent Treasury regulations, financial institutions are required to consult the list of suspected terrorists and organizations provided by "any list of any Government Agency." *See* "Money-Laundering and Terrorist Financing," *Ibid.* at 121.

241. *Ibid.*, Sec. 359.

242. *Ibid.*, Sec. 358.

243. "Money-Laundering and Terrorist Financing," *supra* note 240, at 123.

244. Barry Rider, "Shutting the Stable Door," *Company Lawyer* 22, no. 10 (2001): p. 289.

245. *Ibid.*

246. James Broughton, "Why White, Not Keynes, Inventing the Post-War Monetary System," IMF Working Paper WP/02/52 (March 2002).

247. *Ibid.*, pp. 17–18.

248. International Bank for Reconstruction and Development, Annual Report, Schedule 3 (April 30, 2001).

249. International Monetary Fund, World Economic Outlook, Chapter 2, Three Essays on How Financial Activity Affect Real Activity, "What's Different about Latin America" (May 2002).

250. *Ibid.*

251. David Rockefeller: Memoirs, "Surviving OPEC (recycling Petrodollars)" (Random House, 2002), p. 285.

252. *See* chapter 4, note 177.

253. International Bank for Reconstruction and Development, Annual Report (2001).

254. Structural Improvement Initiative 1997.

255. Fred Bergsten, Ito Takatoshi, and Marcus Noland, *No More Bashing* (Institute for International Economics, 2001).

256. International Financial Institutions Advisory Commission, Report (Washington, D.C.: 2000).

257. U.S. Treasury, "Response to the Report of the International Financial Institution Advisory Commission" (2000).

258. Blueprint for a Lender of Last Resort (Unpublished October 2001). Cited in International Monetary Fund, "Involving the Private Sector in the Resolution of Financial Crises: A Staff Note on the Lerrick Meltzer Proposal" (April 10, 2002).

259. *Ibid.*

260. *Ibid.*

261. Joseph Stiglitz, *Globalization and Its Discontents* (Penguin Allen Lane, 2002).

262. *Ibid.*, p. 28.

263. *Ibid.*, p. 91.

264. *Ibid.*, p. 97.

265. *Ibid.*, p. 91.

266. *Ibid.*, p. 93.

267. *Ibid.*, p. 95.

268. *Ibid.*, p. 150.

269. *Ibid.*, p. 159.
270. "Asia in Crisis," *Financial Times*, Guide Korea: May 1997 to July 1998.
271. International Monetary Fund, "China Formally Begins Participation in the IMF's General Data Dissemination System," news brief 02/36 (April 19, 2002).
272. World Bank, Country Survey Economic Update (April 9, 2002).
273. *Financial Times*, *supra* note 270.
274. *Op. cit.*, Box 1.
275. *Ibid.*
276. *Ibid.*, p. 3.
277. *Ibid.*, pp. 6–7.
278. Joint Bank for International Settlements, International Monetary Fund, Organizations of Economic Cooperation and Development, World Bank Statistics on External Debt (Updated May 31, 2002).
279. Keith Bradsher, "More Worry over Loans by Big Banks in China," *New York Times*, May 10, 2002.
280. *See* chapter 7, notes 124–28.
281. *Ibid.* This may be the official estimate, but, as in the instance of China, private estimates run much higher.
282. *Ibid.*
283. International Monetary Fund, Kenneth Rogoff, "Open Letter to Joe Stiglitz."
284. *See supra* note 247 and accompanying text.
285. Edmund Andrews, "IMF Loan to Brazil Also Shields U.S. Interest," *New York Times*, Business Desk, August 9, 2002.
286. Paul Krugman, "The Lost Continent," *New York Times*, Editorial Desk, August 9, 2002.
287. Mark Stone, "Large Scale Post Crisis Corporate Sector Restructuring," International Monetary Fund Discussion Paper PDP 00/7 (July 2000).
288. Foreign loans of U.S. banks went from $14 billion in 1970 to $405 billion at the end of 1982 (Robert Triffin, "The Paper Exchange Standard: 1971–19??," in *International Monetary Cooperation: Essays in Honor of Henry C. Wallach*, Princeton Essays in International Finance No. 69, 70, 81 [1987]).
289. Bank for International Settlements, Committee on Banking Supervision, third consultative document, part I, "Scope of Application."
290. *Ibid.*, part 2, "The First Pillar: Minimum Capital Requirements." For banks using the internal risk-based approach or the advanced measurement approach for operational risk, the floor is 90 percent the first year of implementation and 80 percent the second year of what the requirement would have been under the original accord.
291. *Ibid.*, par. 44–45.
292. *Ibid.*, par. 48, depending on specific provision, can be anywhere from 50 percent to 150 percent with discretion if extensive provisions are made. Certain higher risk categories either BB or B claims on sovereigns or corporates are weighted at 150 percent plus (*ibid.*, par. 52–53).
293. *Ibid.*, par. 60 et seq.
294. *Op. cit.*, B. "The Standardized Approach—Credit Derivatives." The use of such devices is subject to "legal certainty" (*ibid.*, par. 88 et seq.). Haircuts on repo style transactions are detailed, subject to master netting agreements. Alternatively banks may use VAR models (*ibid.*, par. 106–9). Eligible collateral is defined (*ibid.*, par. 116). Treatment for pools of credit risk mitigants and first to second to default credit deriv-

atives are considered in par. 174–79. Standard supervisory haircuts are given in 122–23. However, financial institutions may calculate haircuts based on internal estimates subject to supervisor's permission (*ibid.*, par. 125).

295. Short-term assessments are deemed to be issue specific (*ibid.*, par. 73).

296. *Ibid.*, par. 134–36.

297. *Ibid.*, par. 142.

298. *Ibid.*, par. 149 et seq.

299. *Ibid.*, Part III.

300. *Ibid.*, 2.

301. *See* chapter 2, "The New Capital Adequacy Accord."

302. *Ibid.*

303. *See* chapter 7, "Recent Developments 2003."

304. "Evolving Capital Standards for Banks: The New Capital Accord," Federal Reserve Bulletin (September 2003), pp. 395, 400–401.

305. Consultative document *supra* note 289 at 5.17.

306. *Ibid.*, chapter 2, IV, "Securitization Framework."

307. *Ibid.*, iii, par. 510 et seq.

308. *Ibid.*, V.

309. *See* notes 64–65, 120–121 and accompanying text.

310. *Op cit.* 4, 675 et seq. *See also* note 43.

311. Where the add-on is a first to default, the credit rating will be determined by the lowest credit rating in the basket. For a second to default position, the credit rating will be determined by the second lowest credit rating (*ibid.*, 676).

312. *See* "The New Capital Adequacy Accord."

313. *Op cit.*

314. *Ibid.*, par. 771, "Qualitative Disclosure."

315. Annex 1, based on an agreement of October, 1998.

316. Bank for International Settlements, Committee on Banking Supervision, "High Level Principles for Cross-Border Implementation of the New Accord" (August, 2003).

317. Bank for International Settlements, Press Release, "Continued Progress toward Basel II" (January 15, 2003).

318. *Ibid.*

CHAPTER 3

Payment and Settlement Systems, Futures, and Intermarket Systemic Risk

This chapter will review the relevant material issued by the international community on payment and settlement clearance systems through 2003; and then will proceed to discuss failures that have occurred in the United States in 1987 and 1991 and how such potential shortcomings have been rectified. The Recommendations on Payment and Settlement Systems issued by the Committee on Payment and Settlement Systems (CPSS) of the G-10 countries and the Core Principles for Securities Settlement Systems were issued by a task force comprised of the International Organization of Securities Commissions (IOSCO) and the CPSS and are applicable to all countries and do not specify the mechanisms that are embedded in highly complex systems such as Euroclear (a European securities settlement system) or Clearing House Interbank Payment System (CHIPS) (the U.S. payment system); consequently, they are really core principles. In the final section, the particular needs of U.S. payments and securities settlement systems will be considered, with particular emphasis on intermarket risk, between securities, futures, and derivative markets.

PAYMENT SYSTEMS

The Core Principles

The Core Principles for Systemically Important Payment Systems is, by its own admission, a blueprint for all countries.[1] While the Core Principles build on the Lamfullusy Report of 1990,[2] which established netting principles, they insist that there has been much progress made in real-time gross settlement systems. While applicable to all countries, a credit debit system is preferable to those that use checks. The report identifies five kinds of risks to which payment systems are prone: (1) credit risk, (2) liquidity risk, (3) legal risk, (4) operational risk, and (5) systemic risk.[3] The legal risk may derive from contract law, case law, insolvency law or jurisdictional issues in the case of cross-border payments, or specific rules governing payment systems. Systems should provide same-day settlement, preferably during the day, but at the end of the day as a minimal requirement. In systems where multilateral netting is used, real-time settlement is preferable. Core Principle number 5 insists that, at the least, in a system in which netting is involved, the system should be able to withstand the failure of the largest debtor using netting. Core Principle number 6 is that assets should have little or no credit or liquidity risk and preferably should take the form of a credit or debit or an account at the Central Bank. The procedure should provide for maximum access allowing safety and allow orderly withdrawal from the system either at the Central Bank or participant's request, and the terms of entry should be publicly disclosed (Principle 9). Where the payment system is not directly owned by the Central Bank, the Central Bank should monitor compliance with the core principles.[4]

Insolvency law is particularly important in that some countries have zero hour rules that can void a transaction ab initio. This situation can be contended with by collateralization of the limits of a participant's trade, provided that the collateral is perfected as a security interest.[5] It is essential that final settlement be defined as a term of art. The European Union (EU) Directive, for instance, contends with this issue, and exempts all netting contracts in a payment system from national insolvency law.[6] In the United States, all 50 states have adopted Section 4A (103 and 104) of the Uniform Commercial Code, which defines funds transfer. However, it should be noted that the funds are paid when withdrawn, and if not, withdrawn on midnight of the same day when the receiving bank learns of the transfer. Thus, the Fedwire system is not automatically protected from insolvency although there is an express exemption from the automatic stay contained in Section 362 of the Bankruptcy Code for margin and settlement payments.[7] Under the Federal Deposit Insurance Corporation Improvement Act of 1991 (FDICIA), bilateral netting, pursuant to contractual provisions, of any obligations of financial institutions or members of any clearing organization (including broker-dealers and futures commission merchants) is exempt from "any other provision of law."[8] Notwithstanding Bankruptcy Code provisions exempting gross obligations from any stay by a bankruptcy court, it was necessary to determine whether obligations such as margin or settlement obligations were contemporaneous with the transaction. FDICIA, by looking toward net obligations, should render the obligations of financial institutions to clearing corporations less ambiguous and further establish bilateral netting between financial institutions (particularly in the foreign exchange domain). Circumstances exist under which financial institutions may enforce contracts, notwithstanding the automatic stay and other restrictions under the Bankruptcy Code, such as rights of set-off and security interests.[9] However, cross-margining agreements and solvency arrangements do not protect clearing corporations with risks posed by off-exchange markets.[10]

In general, market participants rely on bank credit for liquidity. Banks located in Chicago rely on New York money center banks to determine the creditworthiness of clearing organization participants. As a practical matter New York money center banks, which are few in number, will take the lead in initiating credit. Thus, it was fairly simple for Chairman Greenspan to arrange for the access of credit by informally contacting New York money center banks.[11]

A Bank for International Settlements (BIS) report takes issue with the benefit to be derived from delivery versus payment.[12] The BIS report distinguishes between credit risk, which can be alleviated by delivery versus payment, and liquidity risk, which is likely to be increased despite the fact that credit risk would no longer exist. The report also draws an analogy between currency clearing systems and securities clearing systems and determines that, because of their direct effect on national payment systems, liquidity and credit risks are inherently greater in currency clearing systems than security clearing systems.[13] The BIS report notes a distinction between foreign exchange netting systems, which may require limits to credit exposure, and maximum fund transfers.[14] However, the report concludes that such credit standards are not necessarily appropriate to securities markets. In this connection, it is valuable to note that the Fedwire system provides for gross payments and finality, while the National Securities Clearing Corporation and Depository Trust Corporation provide for netting and unwinding.[15]

Recent attention to bank settlement systems has focused on currency risk, principally because it is by definition incapable of being addressed by a domestic clearing and settlement system.[16] Herstaat Risk has been at the forefront of concern over an international clearing and settlement system.[17] The complex structure of settling currency transactions drastically reduces the ability of dealers to control the timing of the settlements of the different legs of their currency contracts. One potential incentive could be created if central banks encouraged the establishment of a market-based system for daylight credit.[18] Furthermore, the use of bilateral and multilateral netting would significantly reduce risks between specific institutions. The questions of multilateral netting arrangements have been addressed by the G-10 BIS forum.[19]

The United States

The Federal Reserve Banks (FRBs) posit net debits and credits to depository institutions' accounts since there is a mismatch between debits and credits during the day (daylight overdrafts). In 1985, the FRB developed a Payment System Risk (PSR) policy for daylight overdrafts, which began as a net debit cap system for each depository institution.[20] From 1986 to 1993 the value of daylight overdrafts grew at an annual rate of 13 percent. In 1994, the FRB began charging daylight overdraft fees and in 1995 daylight overdrafts fell from $125 billion to $80 billion. The fee was initially assessed at 24 basis points and rose to 36 basis points in 1996.[21] Fedwire is a continuous gross settlement system using a delivery versus payment system, meaning that when an institution initiates a transfer, it authorizes the system to block its account. Clearing House Interbank Payment System, a privately owned and operated bank clearing system, is ancillary to Fedwire and usually involves interbank payment.

In 2000, the FRB conducted a review of its payment system policies and sought comment on proposed changes, reacting, in the first instance, to the perceived need to provide greater liquidity to certain money-centered banks by allowing them to post collateral if they wished to exceed their net debit caps. The FRB report noted that certain initiatives such as CHIPS intraday finality (new CHIPS), the Continuous Linked Settlement (CLS) bank, and federal-reserve-processed credit transactions exacerbated liquidity concerns.[22] Institutions would have to have self-assessed net debit caps in order to avail themselves of this option. The FRB also requested comment on other proposals, including increasing the amount of capital required for assessing net debit caps for foreign branches and agencies to ensure greater liquidity and modifying rules for electronic check presentment to allow for greater usage of these instruments, and sought comment about maintaining its current $50 million government securities transfer limit, implementing differential pricing for collateralized and uncollateralized daylight overdrafts, and rejecting payments for same day finality, which would cause an institution to exceed the sum of both.[23] It is, naturally, the last two of these proposals that are most likely to lead the discerning observer to be noncommittal on the question of whether or not the FRB has properly priced risk.

The Fedwire system processed more than $2.4 trillion in checks, government securities transactions, funds transfers, cash deposits and withdrawals, and other transactions in 2000. Only $13 billion in overnight overdrafts were recorded (this number is unavailable for 2001, in which case it would be much higher as the result of September 11). Although Fedwire processed 175 times more checks and other transactions than Fedwire funds and securities transfers, transfers represent 95 percent of the total value of transactions.[24] The Depository Trust and Clearing Corporation (DTCC) activity has grown from $280 billion in 1999 to $420 billion in 2000,[25] and accounts for a significant part of the increase of daylight overdrafts (of an overall 35 percent increase from 1995 to 2000, the funds sector has increased 110 percent).[26] However, 98 percent of daylight overdrafts constitute less than 50 percent of risk-based capital; the vast majority of depository institutions pay less than $1,000 per year in fees.[27]

September 11

September 11 shows the payment system in crisis. The primary vehicles used by the FRB were short-term open market operations, the discount window and swap facilities with the Bank of England, the Bank of Canada, and the European Central Bank.[28] On September 11 and September 21, daylight overdrafts were 32 percent and 36 percent higher, respectively, despite a drop of aggregate payment to $1.8 trillion per day ($1 trillion less than the average of a year earlier).[29] Overnight overdrafts increased from $9 million a year earlier, for instance, to $4 billion on September 12, and discount window loans rose from $200 million to $45 billion. When markets began to function better, open market operations increased from $25 billion to $100 billion.[30] Naturally, the largest users of daylight credit are depository institutions with assets of $200 billion or more,[31] the money-center banks. These banks with the PSR haircuts could find that their access to credit would be severely limited under a full collateralization policy, or they would be required to pay significant fees.[32]

SECURITIES SETTLEMENT SYSTEMS (SSS)

In November 2001, the BIS and IOSCO issued their joint recommendations for securities settlement systems.[33] The report describes the principal aspects of the legal framework for an SSS as enforceability of transactions; insolvency protection of assets, particularly in the instance of the insolvency of a custodian; immobilization or dematerialization of assets (paperless book entry transactions); netting arrangements; securities lending arrangements including repurchase arrangements; finality of settlement arrangements; arrangements for achieving delivery versus payment; default rules; and rules for achieving liquidation of collateral or assets pledged.[34] Participants must have a high degree of certainty regarding their rights in the system, including their rights in security, and preferences thereto, vis-à-vis a nonparticipant, their rights in the event of the default of another participant or a component of the system or a customer from another jurisdiction.[35] The legal framework for the system must have reference to the domicile, principal place of business, and place of incorporation of each component of the system: the securities firm, intermediary, customer and customer's bank; the interaction between these laws and the laws governing the operation of the SSS must be given consideration.[36] When a system crosses borders, participants should be aware of the conflict of laws, e.g., systems that require stock transfers to be entered in a domestic registry do not allow private contractual arrangements to circumvent this public policy.[37] Currently a dialogue is underway on harmonizing international law in the Hague Conference of Private International Law relating to the promulgation of a Convention on the Laws Applicable to Proprietary Rights in Indirectly Held Securities.[38]

Trade confirmation should occur no later than T + 1, preferably T + 0. Increasingly, trade confirmation is becoming automated.[39] Settlement cycles should be no longer than T + 3 and shorter if possible. Government bonds are frequently settled in T + 0 and in some equity markets are considering T + 1.[40] The costs and benefits of a central counterparty (CCP) that interposes itself between the buyer and seller should be evaluated.[41] Most CCPs require members to post collateral. Frequently, credit risk is enhanced by insurance, and liquidity is maintained by means of bank credit lines.[42] Securities lending is encouraged to finance securities portfolios, provide liquidity to the market, and to provide a means of curing a securities transaction that has already failed.[43] Once initiated, securities lending imposes risks that require marking these borrowings to market daily and employing master legal agreements.[44] The general nature of the report is highlighted when it refers to markets that do not allow repurchase of securities for short selling.[45] An issue not addressed by this report or reports of IOSCO in general is the nature of complex securities markets in particular. Some of these issues are covered in chapter 4. But there are a host of others, including self front running, price discovery in different markets, and other issues arising from market fragmentation or the sophistication of the participants.

The report recommends that securities be dematerialized or immobilized whenever possible and title transferred by means of Central Securities Depositories (CSDs). To promote this policy, global notes that represent the whole issue should be encouraged.[46] The settlement of securities should be on a delivery versus payment basis (DVP) so that there is no risk that the securities are delivered and payment not received. DVP can be achieved through gross or net settlement, and settlement can be throughout the day, at intervals, or at the end of the day.[47] DVP is something of a misnomer. As discussed above in the context of payment systems, it requires that securities be blocked, not transferred, before payment is received. Intraday or real-time settlement is essential for parties conducting repurchase agreements, since end of the day settlement and next day settlement entails substantial risk. It is also essential for Central Securities Depositories linkages. The report recommends that unilateral revocation of unsettled transfer instructions late in the day not be permitted.[48]

Central Securities Depositories need to address the possibility of a participant's default, and the recommendation is that the Central Securities Depositories be able to step in and perform in the event that the largest participant in the system fails. But the failure of the largest participant could lead to multiple defaults, so that each market participant's responsibilities in the event of multiple defaults should be set forth. In general, the best approach is a combination of credit limits and collateral requirements.[49] All credit extensions are fully collateralized, and the Central Securities Depositories applies haircuts to collateral to account for market volatility.[50] (Just like the FRB under the PSR.) In a particularly pointed addition, the report notes, if a central bank grants credit in its own currency to market participants, such credit is unlimited.[51] Under FDICIA, the FRB may, with the approval of the Treasury, act as a lender of last resort to securities firms.[52] The method of payment, if it does not involve a central bank, must utilize a bank that poses as little settlement risk as possible; otherwise, the failure of the bank can involve the failure of the CSD. In some instances, the CSDs have organized themselves as limited purpose banks available to market participants.[53] This section highlights the interrelationship between the payment system and the securities settlement system.

Operational reliability identifies the risks of operational controls or information systems going haywire, either as a result of human error or technical malfunction. There should always be adequate back-up and contingency plans to allow for timely recovery of operations.[54]

Protection of clients' assets is, of course, one of the hallmarks of all securities regulation systems.[55] Where a custodian, even a CSD, holds customers' assets in a segregated account, customers' assets are not safe if there are not sufficient assets to satisfy all customers. Frequently, there are additional compensation schemes. Additionally, the legal framework must prioritize claims in bankruptcy so that clients' funds and assets can be moved to an unfrozen account. Cross-border holdings involve several layers of custodians. The global custodian should ensure that each subcustodian has appropriate legal measures in place. In addition to insolvency, the global custodian should ensure that the subcustodian who holds the actual security is appropriately insured against fraud or that legal provisions exist to safeguard the customer.[56]

There must be fairly open access to CSDs and CCPs; otherwise, there is the danger of concentrating risk in a small group. However, the group granted access must have sufficient financial resources and awareness of the legal risks and responsibilities. The criteria should be transparent and publicly disclosed. Some jurisdictions find it useful to allow the authorities to establish the criteria.[57]

Currently, there are internationally recognized securities messaging systems and internationally recognized securities numbering procedures that are gaining acceptance, particularly in cross-border transactions.[58] Disclosure about the risks of CSDs and CCPs is another issue emphasized. These are to be contained in the CPSS/IOSCO disclosure recommendations. The regulatory framework and the division of responsibility between the central bank that has the responsibility for payment systems and the securities regulator should be delineated and disclosed. The report mentions, but does not specifically endorse, a cooperative agreement.[59]

The final recommendation is that the Central Securities Depositories that establish cross-border links should design and operate such links to reduce risks. There are five manners in which settlement of cross-border securities transactions can occur: (1) where the nonresident counterparty establishes direct links through membership in the Central Securities Depositories where the settlement occurs; (2) through local agent, where the nonresident counterparty (this means the securities firm) employs a local agent and defines the services contractually; (3) through a global custodian, who provides the nonresident counterparty with subcustodians in multiple markets; (4) International Central Securities Depositories, such as Euroclear and Clearstream, originally intended to deal in eurobonds, which now deal in a wider range of instruments and currencies (look for one in your favorite instrument or security); (5) links between Central Securities Depositories. In all events, cross-border transactions compound problems, exposing counterparties to multiple custodians, conflicts of law, weak links, where provisional credit may result in failure to settle and where a system that allows for overdrafts or debit balances is exposed to additional risks from systems,[60] particularly from other markets that make no such provisions.

SECURITIES AND DERIVATIVE SETTLEMENT SYSTEMS IN CRISIS: INTERMARKET SYSTEMIC RISK

Since the New York Stock Exchange (NYSE) was closed on September 11, and for several days thereafter, there were no claims on the DTCC, and, therefore neither it nor Fedwire was placed under stress; nor were the derivative markets—the Chicago Board of Trade (CBOT), where options are traded, or the Chicago Mercantile Exchange (CME), where futures are traded—operating at full throttle; so, the events of September 11 do not provide a framework to measure payment and securities systems under stress. And we must have recourse to earlier events that, although they do not capture the complexities of exchanges at the millennium, do provide examples of securities markets that remained open during near meltdowns.

The Single Regulator

After the 1987 market break, a presidential task force (the Brady Commission) was charged with investigating the break. The Brady Commission concluded that the prospect of clearing house failures reduced the willingness of lenders to finance market participation, leading to a crisis competence that raised the specter of full-scale financial breakdown. To reduce the possibility of financial gridlock and attendant risk to the financial system, the task force recommended that clearing for stock options and stock index futures be unified through a single mechanism.[61] In its study of the market break the Brady Commission concluded that securities and derivative markets composed one market. While the implications of this unified market theory are not immediately clear, current administrative and legislative initiatives are intent on establishing effective intermarket regulation.[62] The principal regulatory changes since the 1987 market break have been instituted at the exchange level.

The SEC and the Commodities Futures Trading Corporation (CFTC) came to different conclusions regarding jurisdiction over derivative instruments. Pursuant to the Shad Johnson accord in 1982, the SEC has jurisdiction over all options, while the CFTC has jurisdiction over all futures contracts.[63] After the October 1987 market collapse, a SEC report came to the conclusion that futures market volatility was largely responsible for the abrupt drop in the underlying securities markets, and that the function of market makers was undermined by the workings of the futures market, which left no time for the market maker mechanism to function.[64]

In spite of the failure of portfolio insurance in 1987, a continuous process of indexation by institutional investors is underway.[65] Transactions in stock index futures are an ideal way to change the balance between debt and equity. A holder of a portfolio of common stocks may, by selling index futures contracts, achieve the functional equivalent of selling off stock and investing the proceeds in Treasury bills or some equivalent instrument. Buying futures contracts when stocks are already owned in portfolio is equivalent to margining that portfolio and selling short-term debt instruments and investing the proceeds in stocks.[66]

A growing sentiment exists that consolidation of the CFTC and the SEC is required to coordinate the actions being taken by stock exchanges, futures exchanges, and options exchanges to reduce market volatility. In this regard the SEC would be the likely candidate.[67] The need for centralized regulation of financial markets prompted Congress to grant the FRB participation in the process of regulating margin requirements on financial and stock index futures,[68] but there appears to be very little feeling among regulators that the FRB has any interest or ability to regulate margin requirements on futures.[69] While it has held the power to regulate stock margin requirements since the Securities and Exchange Act, margins have remained the same since the early 1970s.

Intermarket Risk

Following the 1987 market break, a plethora of reports were issued regarding clearance and settlement systems.[70] The reports are varied in their specific recommendations.

Because clearance and settlements of futures already occur intraday rather than over a several day period, issues in securities clearance and payment systems differ from those in futures settlement systems.

The Bachmann Task Force on clearance and settlement reform in the U.S. securities markets concentrated on the current clearance and settlement system with a view toward strengthening the safety and soundness of the clearing system.[71] The task force noted that shortening the settlement period would reduce risk where time equals risk. The view that time equals risk is one reason that margins on Standard and Poors (S&P) 500 futures are so much lower than those on stock equities. For example, the Working Group on Financial Markets concluded, on the basis of historical volatility in the period from June 1, 1984, to October 2, 1987, that the maintenance margin providing protection against 99 percent of price movement is 2.32 percent for the S&P 500 index and 7.88 percent for the typical stock, assuming protection is required for the one-day settlement period in futures and the five-day settlement period in stocks.[72]

The Bachmann Task Force concluded that the dual equities and futures market participants, having losses in one market, might be unable to meet obligations in other markets and both clearing organizations may cease to act for the participant in question. An agreement between the Options Clearing Corporation (OCC) and the National Securities Clearing Corporation provides each clearing corporation with funds equal to any margins collected at the other clearing corporation, if the dual member becomes insolvent and the clearing corporation suffers a loss as a result of liquidating the member's transactions.[73] These arrangements, which involve member insolvency, are to be distinguished from cross-margining agreements, discussed below, where the same margin account is used for separate positions.

Under a cross-margining agreement between the OCC and the CME, OCC members may reduce costs by cross-margining securities futures positions against offsetting option positions.[74]

The OCC and the CME have jointly developed an intercreditor agreement to share control over collateral positions held by common participants in special cross-margin accounts. Participants must agree to grant OCC liens on futures positions maintained at the CME and to grant the CME tier on options positions maintained at the OCC. This arrangement has significantly reduced overall margins requirements. For example, in the market break on October 13, 1989, one firm reduced its margin requirements by approximately 54.2 percent from what would have been required without cross-margining.[75]

Circuit breakers are temporary trading halts in various kinds of trading practices and include price limits for indexes, restrictions on program trading, and index arbitrage. The current integration of circuit breakers between the NYSE and the CME has been staged with due consideration to the interrelationship between the two markets.[76] In addition to these integrated circuit breakers that first occur at 100 point movement in the Dow Jones Industrial Average (Dow), NYSE Rule 80A restricts institutional program trading and index arbitrage by providing for collars that restrict trading program orders on the electronic superdot order routing system whenever there is a movement of 50 Dow points. The paradox revolving around Rule 80A is that it actually acts to disconnect the futures market from the underlying market by severing the arbitrage link between them whenever the price level moves to cause a trading halt in index arbitrage.[77]

The evidence on the efficacy of circuit breakers in practice is uneven at best. Studies of the use of circuit breakers in the market break of October 13, 1989, call into question the impact of circuit breakers in general. One study by the SEC's Office of Economic Analysis found more price dispersion, when circuit breakers were in place, on October 13, 1989, than on October 16, 1987, another Friday on which the market fell by about 60 points with no circuit breakers in place. Consequently, the study concludes that circuit breakers may have impaired, rather than aided, price discovery on October 13.[78]

It follows that the best rationale for circuit breakers is not that they make markets more efficient but rather that they provide breathing spaces where markets have become technically incompetent to deal with the volume and direction of orders. Whether they accomplish the added feat of aiding price discovery in the short term is really inconsequential, compared to the damage that can occur in their absence, when clearing systems are simply overwhelmed.

Currently, NYSE rules calling for restrictions on index arbitrage trading on S&P contracts are imposed when the Dow Jones Industrial Average moves up or down from the previous day's close by 180 points.[79]

Deregulation: The Commodities Futures Modernization Act

On April 21, 1998, Brooksley Born, head of the CFTC at the time, was told by Robert Rubin that she had no right to pursue her plan to determine whether more regulation was needed for over the counter (OTC) derivatives. In May, the CFTC issued a study raising the issue of OTC derivatives regulation. In July, Alan Greenspan told the House Banking Committee that Ms. Born was trying to pick a fight with capital markets: "If somebody says to me, 'I'm contemplating punching you in the nose,' I don't presume that is a neutral statement." Even after the failure of Long Term Capital Management (LTCM), Congress passed a six-month moratorium on regulation of derivatives, which lasted until Ms. Born's term expired. Then, it passed the Financial Modernization Act, which allowed most OTC derivatives to escape legislation.[80]

Enron used derivatives to mask balance sheet problems. This has prompted a loss of $200 billion in the market capitalization of energy companies between the last quarter of 2001 and the last quarter of 2002.[81]

The Commodities Futures Modernization Act of 2000 (CFMA),[82] resulting from the deregulatory zeal of the 106th Congress, which also promulgated Gramm-Leach-Bliley,[83] allowed the trading of narrow-based securities futures contracts and phased in options on securities futures contracts.[84] The CFMA also established a joint regulatory framework for security future products by the CFTC and the SEC.[85] The CFMA and the Exchange Act as amended specify a number of standards and conditions, termed "listings standards," which must be met for security futures products to be listed on a recognized exchange.[86]

Under the CFMA, contracts for sale of a commodity for delivery on a future date and options on such contracts and options on commodities can be cleared only through a derivatives clearing organization (DCO), unless the commodities are excluded or exempted under the act or cleared under a securities clearing system.[87] However, the import of the CFMA is to allow firms that have adhered to 14 core principles outlined under the CFMA to register as DCOs. Under the CFMA, the term "DCO" includes organizations that perform settlement or netting of contracts executed by participants of a DCO.[88] The Core Principles include financial resources, public disclosures, risk management including collection of collateral, default rules that involve the priority of customer claims, the financial resources to perform the central counterparty function, and system safeguard, which involves testing of hardware functions.

The regulation of commodities under the Commodities and Exchange Act[89] has evolved considerably over the past two decades, and two kinds of transactions have been identified: future and forward contracts. Traditionally, the view was that forward contracts that did not rely on the possible delivery of goods were exempted; however, in *Transnor Ltd. v. BP North America Petroleum*,[90] the court held that a forward contract for Brent Crude was subjected to CFTC jurisdiction since "The 15-day Brent Crude Market has . . . assumed aspects of the futures market while retaining elements of the forward market." The court held that the agreements included aspects of speculation, and investment and speculative houses were involved in the market, and the interest of these market participants did not parallel the interest of elevator operators or farmers. Furthermore, although there is no contractual means to satisfy the contract other than through delivery, such terms as have been available have enabled market participants to create "an essentially paper market."[91]

However the CFTC, noting that the contracts have no right of offset, and the parties to the contract may have to take delivery, concluded that, "The specific delivery obligations that impose substantial economic risks of a commercial nature known to the participants . . . are within the scope of section 2(a)1 exclusion from the SEC Commission's regulatory jurisdiction."[92] In July 1995, however, the futures-forward decision was tested again in a CFTC enforcement action.[93] Here, the CFTC determined that, in practice, the evident intent of the parties was to speculate on the price of the underlying commodity, in part because a future price or pricing formula allowed for settlement versus delivery.

The Commodities Futures Modernization Act responds to the uncertainty by providing broad exclusions and exemptions from the Commodities Exchange Act (CEA).[94] The act creates the category of eligible market participant, predicated generally on eligible swap participant, based on certain factors.[95] Excluded commodities include interest rate swaps, currencies, securities, indices, credit measures, and other indices with no cash market. Exempt commodities include all excluded commodities as well as bandwidth, metals, and energy products.[96] Transactions in exempt commodities by eligible market participants are subject to antimanipulation but not antifraud provisions.[97]

After Enron, several bills were designed to repeal the exemptions and exclusions. The Feinstein Bill would repeal the exclusion for energy derivative transactions and other commodities currently excluded, including interest rate swaps.[98] Another bill would merge the CFTC and the SEC into a new agency having jurisdiction over securities and commodities.[99] The Federal Energy Regulatory Commission (FERC) and the CFTC have jurisdiction over different types of power and natural gas contracts. Under the Federal Power Act, any rate that is "unjust and unreasonable" is unlawful.[100] Unlike the CFTC, which does not generally have jurisdiction over spot transactions, FERC has jurisdiction over physically settled transactions, defined by FERC as transactions entered into within 24 hours of delivery.[101] FERC has traditionally taken the view that it does not have jurisdiction over financially settled contracts,[102] but it has jurisdiction to investigate the cash price of a commodity.[103] In February 2002, FERC began its Western Markets Manipulation Investigation into Enron and other manipulation in the Western oil markets.[104] The current investigations will determine how CFTC and FERC jurisdiction will meld, and whether there are separate criteria for market manipulation.

Net Capital Rules

The purpose of the net capital rule has been to promote liquidity and to require that broker-dealers maintain specified amounts of net capital in relationship to aggregate indebtedness of customer-related receivables under the customer protection rule and proprietary positions.[105] The functional purpose of the rule is to ensure that a broker-dealer can liquidate without the need for a formal proceeding if it falls below minimum net capital rules.[106] Under the basic method of the rule, the broker-dealer must maintain net capital in excess of the greater of a specified minimum, or 6⅔ percent of its aggregate indebtedness.[107] Most major securities firms use the alternate method discussed below. A broker-dealer must also maintain capital of 2 percent of its customer-related receivables.[108]

Section 15(c)(3) of the Securities and Exchange Act of 1934 prescribes rules that safeguard the acceptance and use of customer securities and the carrying and use of customers' deposits or credit balances.[109] Under 15(c)(3), the commission adopted the Customer Protection Rule 15(c)(3–3): broker-dealers in computing net capital must make additional adjustments to net worth relating to unrealized profits and losses,[110] subordinated liabilities,[111] contractual commitments,[112] collateralized liabilities,[113] options,[114] commodities, commodities futures,[115] and stock index futures.[116]

Under the catchall provision, the rule treats unsecured receivables, and securities for which there is no ready market, as being subject to a 100 percent risk weighting. The SEC also applies 100 percent deduction to any proprietary position if a broker-dealer cannot demonstrate that a ready market exists for the securities.[117] Obviously, these custom-made financial instruments can be diverted to unregulated affiliates. Even proprietary positions that require broker-dealer status can be traded in other markets, particularly London.[118]

The CFTC, which regulates futures commissions merchants (FCM), relies solely on segregation of customers' accounts to determine FCM capital. Unlike the SEC's capital rules, which derive from the net debit of customers' accounts,[119] the CFTC requires complete segregation of customers' accounts[120] and requires that FCMs hold 4 percent of customers' money as net capital.[121] The CFTC's jurisdiction over net capital rules extends to broker-dealers to the extent that they hold hedged or covered positions.[122]

The haircuts required for broker-dealers on equities are substantially higher than are those required under the Capital Adequacy Directive (CAD) of the EU.[123] However, an unhedged long or short position of the S&P 500 index under the CAD may attract a 10 percent weighting (8 percent + 2 percent). If a hedged position were held, the CAD would apply a weight of 2 percent maximum (together with possible additional capital requirements by member states to ensure that the index moves with the underlying securities), that, in sum, may be far lower than the 6.67 percent minimum that U.S. net capital requirements would apply.[124]

Unlike U.S. capital rules, the CAD deals only with proprietary positions of broker-dealers. Rules regarding the segregation of customer funds are conduct of business rules and are consequently considered the prerogative of the individual member states, although there is a 2 percent specific risk capital requirement on gross positions. Another contrast between the United States and the EU is that underwriting may be capitalized with 45-day subordinated debt in selected circumstances, and, in all cases, original maturity of one year debt as opposed to debt with an original maturity of two years minimum in the EU,[125] but U.S. regulators require haircuts on securities that are the subject of an underwriting unlike the CAD.[126]

Securities houses are regulated only for those activities within a broker-dealer's status. The holding companies of broker-dealers are largely unregulated, although the Market Reform Act of 1990 enables the SEC to obtain information about the holding company and the upstreaming of funds.[127] One corporation that owns broker-dealers has over 200 separate entities and three holding companies within its organizations, and another broker-dealer has over 400 subsidiaries and 300 affiliates.[128] The Bachmann report notes that market disturbances in unregulated affiliates, particularly those engaged in forex, interest rate swaps, currency forward, and futures transactions, are likely to have a spillover effect on regulated entities, broker-dealers, and futures commission merchants.[129] Consequently, liquidity and solvency concerns increase for the conglomerate, trading activity in the securities and derivative markets may also be subject to spillover effect. This absence of consolidation is a big advantage that firms enjoy over EU counterparts.

To bolster the capital required of firms with large dealer operations, SEC adopted an amendment prohibiting the broker-dealer from making withdrawals of net capital if, after these withdrawals, the broker-dealer net capital would be less than 25 percent of the firm's haircut on its securities position.[130] The SEC believes that if a firm were to reach this level, regulatory authorities would be able to increase surveillance and take appropriate action, including requiring the firm to liquidate securities positions.[131] Pursuant to this amendment, the SEC may also restrict, for a 24-day period, withdrawals of capital based on the insecure financial position of a broker-dealer.

The risk assessment of holding companies[132] consisting primarily of requirements for affiliates of broker-dealers, is novel to the security regulatory system but is an exception to the concept of form supervision (as opposed to consolidated supervision). The SEC has adopted rules requiring reporting for holding companies that are "material associated persons" of broker-dealers.[133] Among the important activities conducted by securities houses that are not regulated by the SEC are all forms of futures and futures index trading, which are regulated by the CFTC, and interest rate swaps, currency swaps, and bridge loans, which are frequently conducted in unregulated subsidiaries.[134]

The reporting systems of the CFTC seem almost instantaneous when compared with the gathering of data by the SEC. It could be said that to the extent that futures markets provide a vehicle for smoothing the timing of distribution of dividends and creating cash flow certainties, they are efficient; but, like any insurance scheme, if used for unintended purposes, they become inefficient. Futures markets have certainly drawn capital from the equities market, but their existence has also enabled increased institutional investor participation in equities that proceeded largely through indexing.[135]

CBOT and the CME adopted a risk-based capital requirement for their members in 1998, and in 2000, the National Futures Association followed suit. As of the end of 2000, this resulted in an increase of net capital of $849 million for the 190 FCMs registered. The CFTC requirement is that 4 percent of the amount required to be segregated be set aside as net capital. The risk-based capital requirement is 8 percent of customer and 4 percent of noncustomer risk maintenance margin based requirements, based on open contracts on U.S. and foreign markets.[136] The CFTC net capital rules penalize FCMs whose customers hold excess margins since that enlarges segregated customer funds on which CFTC rules are based.[137]

If the CFTC eliminated its net capital rules, the net effect would have been a decrease of only $34 million.[138] The report recommends that the CFTC eliminate its net capital rules and adopt the exchanges' risk-based capital rules.[139] Generally, firms have far more than the minimum required capital. For example, J.P. Morgan Future Ltd. had approximately $379 million of regulatory capital when it required $220 million. Merrill Lynch Futures Inc. had $384 million in regulatory capital when it required about $296 million.[140] Dual registered broker-dealer/FCMs such as Merrill and DLJ had about seven times the required adjusted net capital.[141]

In August 2002, the SEC and the CFTC, under authority delegated by the FRB under Regulation T, established margin requirements for unhedged security and securities index futures positions so that they are in line with exchange-traded options. The rules allow exchanges to set lower margins for strategy-based offset positions.[142]

STOCK INDEX FUTURES AND MARKET VOLATILITY

Nowadays, real time gross settlements systems are hybrid systems in which payments are held in a queue, netted continuously, and eventually returned if there is not sufficient liquidity in a last cleanup round.[143] Determination of when final settlement occurs is essential, and another term of art is prompt net settlement.[144] In multilateral net settlement systems, a pool of collateral or lines of credit are necessary for participants, in which case the legal control of the collateral and the terms of the agreement must be considered. Naturally, telecommunications are essential, as the committee remarks, but the growth of backup facilities and Telcom Hotels and storage facilities internationally has made this a moot point in G-10 countries and, increasingly, around the globe. Systems like those in the United States, which are owned by a cooperative of money center banks, must make special efforts to see the views of a variety of participants.[145] In Australia, Canada, and the euro area, the central bank has been given clear authority to oversee the payment system.[146]

Appropriate intermarket regulation ought to be directed at stemming systemic risk. A priority is the consolidated regulation of securities holding companies to the extent that these companies engage in related unregulated securities, derivatives, and forex business.

However, as indicated in chapter 2 under the IOSCO section dealing with containing systemic risk from securities markets, the aim is that securities firms have ample funds to protect segregated clients' funds, and holding-company regulation is merely supplemental. Yet, in all instances, holding companies should be a source of strength. It would also be advisable if there were a consolidated capital requirement for securities and futures markets. The new margin requirements for unhedged positions are a movement in this direction; all entities should be assessed for over the counter risk for trading in unregulated affiliates in derivative instruments, especially with regard to hedge fund counterparty risk.

In October 2003, the SEC proposed a voluntary alternative method for computing net capital which would lead the way to consolidated supervision for those firms taking advantage of the rule.[147] To take advantage of the rule, a broker deal must have an entity-wide internal risk management system and must consent to group-wide supervision at the holding company level. A company under the rule must maintain tentative net capital of $1 billion and net capital of $500 million and could apply for exemption from other SEC net capital rules. A broker deal could use its proprietary VAR model to calculate risk. The proposed rule makes explicit reference to the EU consolidated supervision directive,[148] and the SEC speculates that the proposed rule would minimize duplicative regulatory burdens. Firms would also have the advantage of eliminating separate systems to determine regulatory net capital. The risks to be monitored would include market, credit and legal risk. The VAR model would need to specify 10-day movements to a 99% confidence level. The SEC would be required to authorize the VAR model which would have to be the same used to report risk to senior management and be reviewed by a public accounting firm.[149] Firms would need to assess a capital charge by counterparty.[150] The specifics of the proposed rules take into account the new Basel Capital Adequacy Accord, and operational risk must be consistent with the Accord.[151] In all respects, the proposed rule moves U.S. net capital rules for securities firms in the direction of the new Basel Capital Adequacy Accord and the EU Directive on consolidated supervision of conglomerates.

NOTES

1. Bank for International Settlements (BIS), Committee for Payment and Settlement Systems, "Core Principles for Systemically Important Payment Systems" (January 2001).

2. Bank for International Settlements, Lamfallusy Report (1990).

3. *Op. cit.*, Section 3

4. *Ibid.*, Section 4 Responsibilities of the Central Bank.

5. *Ibid.*

6. *Ibid.*, and 98/26/EEC O.J. Eur. Comm. L.166 11/06/98, p. 45.

7. Section 362 also provides protection for margin and settlement payment and provides protection from Title 11 (Section 201 of Title 11 U.S. Code [as amended 1011]). Separate legislation enacted in 1989 extends similar protections to counterparties dealing with most U.S. bank and thrift institutions. *See* § I1 of the Fern Deposit Insurance Act, 12 U.S.C. § 1821, as amended by § 212 of the Financial Institutions Reform, Recovery, and Enforcement Act of 1989. Section 362 also allows nonbankrupt parties to terminate swap agreements, allowing the filing of a bankruptcy petition, and to use collateral held. (101st Cong. 2nd Sess., H.R. 4612, An Act to Amend Title 11 of the United States Code I regarding Swap Agreements and Forward Contracts [1990]. Sections 1€32, 105, 106.) Additional provisions allow counterparties to enforce netting agreements for a broad range of forward rate agreements and to net out or offset positions. A broad range of forward contracts are exempt from automatic stay, antitermination, and preference provisions (Sections 211, 202, 203, and 204).

8. Federal Deposit Insurance Corporation Improvement Act of 1991 (FDICIA) § 402 Definitions, § 403 Bilateral Netting, § 404 Clearing Organization Netting, § 405 Pre-Emption.

9. The Bankruptcy Code currently excepts from the automatic stay of § 36 the right of certain financial institutions and intermediaries to set-off claims, nut debts, and property for margin and settlement payments subject to the rights of Securities Investor Protection Corporation. *See* Bankruptcy Code, § 352B(6) serf. Currently the only authority that a broker-dealer may rely upon for margin calls made after the petition is filed are statements from the House Report of 1984 Amendments to the Bankruptcy Code. Section 555 could permit a liquidation of the securities account,

subject to certain questions, that is, whether a security contract exists after the securities are settled in the account, and whether the broker-dealer has a right to liquidate positions as a result of the bankruptcy. The rights to make settlement payments and margin calls are covered under § 546E of the Bankruptcy Code and are defined in § 741(5), § 761(15). Uncertainty about what constitutes a settlement payment may signal need to clarify existing law (*see*, for example, *Bevill Bresler and Schulman, AC Management Corp. v. Spencer Savings and Loan Assoc.*, 878 F.2d 742 [3d Cir. 1989]). Report of the Bachmann Task Force on Clearance and Settlement Reform in the U.S. Securities Markets, Securities and Exchange Commission, Release No. 34-30802, 57 Fed. Reg. 17812 (June 22, 1992).

10. The Bachmann Task Force also considered daily mark-to-market securities in the National Securities Clearing Corporation (NSCC) system but felt that it would require constant bookkeeping and a complex payment system. Twenty-one percent of retail purchase trades are settled by check delivered through the mail, and only 20 percent of these trades measured in dollar value arrive on or before T plus 3, thus without requiring management accounts, it is necessary to implement an electronic payment system as a payment option for securities customers. Negotiations are already underway to use the Automated Clearing House, an electronic payment system used by over 22,000 banks, thrifts, and other financial institutions on behalf of corporations and individuals for securities transactions. For institutional trades, it may be necessary to create an interactive system for affirmation of trades (*ibid.*, at 19).

It is also very helpful, in shortening the settlement cycle, to reduce the use of physical certificates. The number of certificates provided to investors and participants through the Depository Trust Corporation dropped from 16 million certificates annually in 1980 to 6 million certificates in 1990 (*ibid.*, at 20). However, the U.S. Working Committee of the Group of 30 clearance and settlement project and the Bachmann Committee recommend that settlement among financial intermediaries and their institutional clients occur in a book entry form and have made a series of proposed rule changes that would enable the implementation of this recommendation (*ibid.*, at 21).

11. *Ibid.*, at 17.

12. Bank for International Settlements, Delivery versus Payment in Security Settlement Systems: Report prepared by the Committee on Payment and Settlement Systems of the Central Banks of the Group of Ten Countries (Basel: September 1992).

13. The report also speaks to the advantages of same-day payments by showing the association of next-day payments with the creditworthiness of the guarantor (either the settlement bank or the clearing system).

14. *Op. cit.*, p. 33, citing 0–10 and Bank for International Settlements, Report on Multi-Lateral Netting (1990).

15. *Cf.* BIS Delivery versus Payment, *supra* note 12, at A20 and A22–24.

16. "Herstaat Risks" refer to the 1974 failure of the Herstaat Bank because of currency speculation. This failure disrupted the eurodollar interbank market for several months.

17. *See* "Large Value Payment Systems: What Have We Learned?" (Remarks of Wayne Angel, Board of Governors, Federal Reserve System at the 12th Payment System International Conference, London, England, October 7, 1992).

18. *Ibid.*, at 15.

19. Delivery versus Payment, *supra* note 12, citing Report on Multi-Lateral Netting, *supra* note 14.

20. Board of Governors of the Federal Reserve System, Division of Payment

Operations, Stacy Coleman, "The Evolution of the Federal Reserve's Intraday Credit Policies," Federal Reserve Bulletin (February 2002), p. 67.

21. *Ibid.*, p. 67. The fee was originally intended to rise to 46 basis points but the success of the program made this unnecessary.

22. *Ibid.*, pp. 72–73.

23. 66 Fed. Reg. 30193 et seq. (June 15, 2001). *See generally, op. cit.* In December 2001, the board adopted the interim policy and upped the capital requirement for foreign branches and agencies from 10 percent to as much as 35 percent and adopted a modified posting time for ECP. 66 Fed. Reg. 34419 (December 10, 2001).

24. *Op. cit.* p. 74.

25. *Ibid.*, p. 79.

26. *Ibid.*, p. 78.

27. *Ibid.*, p. 80.

28. *Ibid.*, p. 81.

29. *Ibid.*

30. *Ibid.*, p. 82.

31. *Ibid.*, p. 83.

32. *Ibid.*, p. 84.

33. Bank for International Settlements and International Organization of Securities Commissions, Committee on Payment and Settlement Systems, Technical Committee of the International Organization of Securities Commissions, "Recommendations for Securities Settlement Systems" (November 2001).

34. *Ibid.*, 3.4.

35. *Ibid.*, 3.5.

36. *Ibid.*, 3.6.

37. *Ibid.*, 3.7.

38. *Ibid.*, 3.8.

39. *Ibid.*, 3.10–3.12.

40. *Ibid.*, 3.13–3.16.

41. *Ibid.*, 3.17.

42. *Ibid.*, 3.20–3.22.

43. *Ibid.*, 3.23.

44. *Ibid.*, 3.26.

45. *Ibid.*, 3.24.

46. *Ibid.*

47. *Ibid.*, 3.32–3.33.

48. *Ibid.*, 3.38–3.41.

49. *Ibid.*, 3.42–3.46.

50. *Ibid.*, 3.46.

51. *Ibid.*

52. Pub. Law. 102-232 (December 19, 1991) (12 U.S.C. Section 1811) section 141 requiring a two-thirds majority of the Federal Reserve Board and a joint determination of the secretary of the Treasury (in consultation with the president).

53. *Op. cit.*, 3.47–3.51.

54. *Ibid.*, 3.53–3.59.

55. *See* chapter 1, notes 268–69.

56. *Op. cit.* 3.60 to 3.64.

57. *Ibid.*, 3.68–3.71.

58. *Ibid.*, 3.78–3.80.

59. *Ibid.*, 3.64–3.87.

60. *Ibid.*, Annex 4.

61. *See generally*, Report of the Presidential Task Force on Market Mechanism, January 12, 1988 (hereinafter Brady Report).

62. Hearing before the Subcommittee on Telecommunications and Finance, the Committee on Energy and Commerce, House of Representatives, 101st Cong. 1st Sess. on H.R. 1609, A Bill to Amend The Securities Exchange Act of 1934 7 Provide Additional Authorities to Prevent Disruptions to the Nation's Security Market; Testimony of William J. Brodsky, President Chief Executive Officer, Chicago Mercantile Exchange, p. 1581. Arrangements have been instituted at the New York Stock Exchange (NYSE) and the Chicago Mercantile Exchange (CME) for cross-margining systems between the CME and the Options Clearing Corporation (OCC). (A system has been developed through the Intermarket Surveillance Group to police frontrunning and self-frontrunning ["Testimony of Gerald Bearne," *ibid.*, at 59].) One of the means by which frontrunning or similar strategies may be achieved is by means of exchange of physicals where futures are sold and securities are purchased. This strategy is usually executed in London in order to avoid NYSE restrictions and to avoid disturbing the U.S. market. This strategy demonstrates the need for greater international regulatory control (Memorandum to Chairman Ruder from Ketchum, Richard G. Director, Division of Market Regulation, *ibid.*, at 239).

63. Allen Shick, "A Review and Analysis of the Changing Financial Environment and the Need for Regulatory Realignment," *Bus. Law* 44 (November 1988, pp. 43, 45).

64. *See* Brady Report, *supra* note 61; *see also* Division of Market Regulation, SEC, role of index related trading in the market decline on September 11 and 12, 1986.

65. Carolyn Brancato, "Institutional Investors and Capital Markets: 1991 Update," Institutional Investor Project, Columbia, Columbia University School of Center for Law and Economic Studies (September 1991).

66. For example, in 1984 the one way commission cost of selling 100 Standard & Poors (S&P) 500 future contracts was approximately $1,250 where the cost of selling the same amount of underlying stock would have been $17,000. (3, *supra* note 63, at 51, citing H. Stoll and R. Whaley, "Expiration Day Effect of Index Options and Futures," p. 1, included in background material for Roundtable on Index Arbitrage, July 9, 1986 [SEC].)

67. Schick, *supra* note 63, at 64.

68. Future Trading Practices Act, 106 Stat. 3590; Pub. Law 102-546; Title 5, 501 amending 7 U.S.C. § 2a; any contract market in a stock index future shall file any change in the level of margin on the contract with the Federal Reserve Board (FRB). The FRB may request that levels be set to preserve the financial integrity of the contract market or its clearing system or to prevent systemic risk.

69. Board of Governors of the Federal Reserve System, A Review and Evaluation of Federal Margin Regulations, A Study by the Staff (1989); *see also* Paul Kupiee, "Initial Margin Requirement and Stock Returns Volatility; Another Look," Federal Reserve Board, Finance and Economic Discussion, Series no. 53 (1989); and Mark Warshawsky, "The Adequacy and Consistency of Margin Requirements in the Markets for Stocks and Derivative Products," Federal Reserve Board, Staff Study no. 158 (1989).

70. In addition to the studies cited in *supra* notes 1 and 3, Interim Report of the Working Group on Financial Markets submitted to the President of the United States,

May 1988; J. R. Kessler, "Study on Improvements in the Settlement of Cross-Border Securities Transactions in the European Economic Community," "Study for the Commission of the European Community," Directorate Generale XV, Financial Institutions and Company Law (July 1988); Clearance and Settlement Systems in the World Securities Market—Report of the Group of 30, New York and London, March 1989.

71. Bachman report, *supra* note 10.

72. *See* Working Group on Financial Markets, *supra* note 10. *See also*, Board of Governors of the Federal Reserve System, "A Review and Evaluation of Federal Margin Regulations," Staff Study (Washington, D.C.: 1984).

73. Bachmann, *supra* note 10, at 27812.

74. "One Chicago, Options Clearing Corp., and Chicago Mercantile Exchange Inc. Sign Clearinghouse Agreement," OCC Press Release, April 30, 2002.

75. Commodities Futures Trading Corporation, Division of Economic Analysis, Report on Stack Index Futures and Cash Market Activity during October 1989, May 1990.

76. "Market Volatility and Investor Confidence: Report of the Board of Directors of the New York Exchange" (June 7, 1990), p. 4.

Stage 1	*Stage 2*	*Stage 3*	*Stage 4*
12 S&P pts.	24 S&P pts.	36 S&P pts.	48 S&P pts.
100 Dow pts.	200 Dow pts.	300 Dow pts.	400 Dow pts.
Duration			
60 mins.	90 min.	120 mins.	150 mins. (*Ibid.*)

77. Merton Miller, *Financial Innovation and Market Volatility* (Cambridge, Blackwell 1991).

78. *Ibid.*, at 245. (In the period immediately after the crash of 1987, the main emphasis of those calling for better regulation was on the danger to the safety and integrity of the entire payment system imposed by the massive flows of cash margin funds. The force of this argument may have been undercut by the fact that the financial system managed to survive despite the biggest one-day move in U.S. stock market price history. Several functional disabilities were apparent. The first was that the quotations for stock prices were running 60 to 90 minutes behind [*ibid.*], which led to the illusion of a discount on the futures market and purveyed misinformation to the stock market. With many halts on the NYSE on the morning of October 20, it was feared that all trading in New York might come to an end, leaving the CME to face the flood of sell orders alone. With no offsetting arbitrage buying demand, the CME floor traders would have had little hope of unwinding the long positions they had assumed on the way down, and no way of absorbing more of the selling wave from New York. Prices might have collapsed, thus threatening the solvency of the clearing firms. The CME closed that Exchange at 12:15, local time.)

79. These restrictions will be lifted when the Dow Jones Industrial Average (DJIA) trades within 90 points of its previous close. Under Rule 180B, Trading Halts are in three levels and triggered by 950, 1,900, and 2,850 points. The "collars" of 80(A) act

to reduce the volume of trade substantially. "New Rule 80A 'collars' and 80B 'circuit breakers' for third quarter 2002: Effective July 31 through Sept. 30, 2002," NYSE Information Memo, 02-27 (July 1, 2002), "New Rule 80A collars and Rule 80B circuit breakers Levels for Four Quarter 2002," setting the collars at 160 points and removing them at 80 points up or down from the previous day's close, and triggers of 800, 1,650, and 2,450 points, NYSE Information Memo 02-44 (October 1, 2002).

80. Jacob Schlesinger, "The Deregulator: Did Washington Set the Stage for Current Business Turmoil?" *Wall Street Journal*, October 17, 2002, p. 1, A-12.

81. *Ibid.*

82. Pub. Law 106-554, 114 Stat. 2763, December 21, 2000.

83. *See* chapter 4, "Gramm-Leach-Bliley. . . ."

84. *Op. cit.*, section 251 (a) The term "security futures product" is defined in section 1(a)32 of the Commodities Exchange Act (CEA) and 3(a)56 of the Exchange Act to mean "any put, call, straddle or privilege on any security future." The term "security future" is defined in 1(a)31 of the CEA and 3(a)55 of the Exchange Act to include futures contracts on narrow based securities indexes and individual securities. The Commodities Futures Modernization Act of 2000 (CFMA) also provides that options on securities futures contracts can be traded beginning in 2003. *See* Commodities Futures Trading Corporation (CFTC), "Listing Standards and Conditions for Trading Security Futures Products" 17 C.F.R. Part 41 (November 1, 2001).

85. *Ibid.*

86. Section 2(a)1d of the CFMA and 6(h) of the Securities and Exchange Act of 1934 as amended. The subject stock must be a common stock registered under Section 12 or such other equity as the CFTC and the Securities and Exchange Commission (SEC) deem appropriate. The contract market or registered derivative transaction execution facility must file with the SEC under Section 19(b) of the Securities and Exchange Act.

87. CFMA, *supra* note 82 Appendix E adding section 5b of the Commodities Exchange Act.

88. *Ibid.*, sec. 1(a); *see* CFTC, "A New Regulatory Framework for Clearing Organizations," 17 CFR part 39 (August 29, 2001).

89. 7 U.S.C.A. par.1 et seq.

90. 738 F. Supp. 1472 (S.D.N.Y. 1990).

91. *Ibid.*, at 1492–93.

92. Exemption for Certain Contracts Involving Energy Products, 58 Fed. Reg. 21286-02 (April 20, 1993). The order was limited to commercial participants, contracts for the sale of crude oil, and bilateral contracts subject to negotiation.

93. *In the Matter of MG Refining and Marketing, Inc. and MG Futures Inc.* CFTC Docket no. 95-14 (1995).

94. *See generally*, Committee on Regulation of Futures and Derivative Instruments, "The Aftermath of Enron: More Regulation or Continued Deregulation" (American Bar Association, annual meeting, Aug. 9–13, 2002).

95. 17 C.F.R part 35. Financial institutions, insurance companies, and other entities having assets over $5 or $10 million depending on the category of exclusion.

96. Agricultural products are not specifically defined.

97. CFMA, *supra* note 82, Section 2(h)(3). 2(g) further defines "exempt commodities." The act also creates "derivative transaction execution facilities," which is subject to both commodity and participant limitations, which are further defined as those which the CFTC determines are highly unlikely to be subject to manipulation; and

the Exempt Board of Trade, which is an unregulated market, subject only to CFTC antifraud and antimanipulation provisions.

98. S.1951, 107th Congress, (2002). This bill would also create a new exemption based on nonagricultural commodities, between European Commercial Papers (ECPs) subject only to antifraud and antimanipulation, repeal the exemption for electronic trading facilities, and require dealer trading facilities to comply with CFTC net capital rules.

99. H.R. 4038 107th Cong. (2002).

100. FPA Section 205 (a), 16 U.S.C.A. 824d (2001).

101. *San Diego Gas and Electric Co. v. Sellers of Energy and Ancillary Services into Markets Operated by the California Independent System Operator and the California Power Exchange*, 95 F.E.R.C. Par. 62545; *see also* The Aftermath of Enron, p. 19.

102. *See* e.g., Annual Charges under the Omnibus Budget Reconciliation Act of 1986, CNG Power Services et. al. 87 F.E.R.C par. 61047.

103. 17 C.F.R.11.2 (2001).

104. "Fact-Finding Investigation of Potential Manipulation of Electric and Natural Gas Prices," 98 F.E.R.C. par. 61, 165.

105. Steven Molinari and Nelson S. Kibler, "Broker Dealers' Financial Responsibility under the Uniform Net Capital Rule—A Case for Liquidity," *George J.* 72 (1983), p. 1; and Michael Jamroz, "The Net Capital Rule," *Bus. Law* 47 (May 1992), p. 863.

106. The net capital rule promotes orderly self liquidation of broker-dealers and reduces the likelihood that the failed broker-dealer would have to be liquid pursuant to the Securities Investor Protection Act of 1988 (15 U.S.C. §§ 78aaa-7811). Recently the SEC has proposed rules for raising the minimum capital to $250,000 because of the $250 million in customer property self-liquidations in 1987 and 1 percent. One firm held $70 million of customer securities although it only had $61,000 net capital. Proposed Rule Securities and Exchange Commission 17 C.F.R. Part 2 Release No. 34-272249, 54 Fed. Reg. 40395 (October 1989).

107. Or $25,000, 17 C.F.R. § 240, 156-1(a). There is also an "early warning" level which requires that, if net capital falls below a certain level or if it discovers a material internal control inadequacy, the broker dealer must file a notice with the SEC (17 C.F.R. 240, 7a–11).

108. 17 C.F.R. § 20.15(c)(3j-l(f)) (1991) defining the computation of custom receivables is at *ibid.* 156-3(a). The broker-dealers are also required to deduct from their net uncertain percentages, known as "haircuts," of the market value of securities and commodities positions. The rule takes into account the holding in unrelated long and short positions in securities.

109. 17 C.F.R. § 15(c)(3). The first part of the rule deals with customer securities and requires broker-dealers to have physical possession or control of all fully paid and excess margin securities carried for the accounts of customers. The broker-dealer must make a daily account to show that it is complying with this section of the rule. *Ibid.*, 15c-3c.

The second part of the rule deals with customers' funds and requires broker-dealers to make a weekly computation of the form for debt of reserve requirements (156-3a). If the credit exceeds the debits, the broker-dealer must deposit the excess by the morning of the second business day following computerization in a special bank account for the exclusive benefit of customers. *Ibid.*, 15(c)(3-3el).

110. *Ibid.*, 15(c)(3)-1(c)(2)(i).

111. *Ibid.*, 15(c)(3)-1(d).

112. *Ibid.*, 15(c)(3)-1(c)(2)(viii).

113. *Ibid.*, 15(c)(3)-1(c)(2)(xiii).

114. *Ibid.*, 15(c)(3)-1(a). In 1985 the SEC issued a no-action letter that allowed broker-dealers who were not options market makers to compute deductions based on the market value of the option rather than on the underlying security, with a maximum deduction of 50 percent of the market value of the option. Deductions depend upon whether the broker-dealer is a market maker.

115. *Ibid.*, 15(c)(3)-1(b).

116. The CFTC net-capital rule can be found at 17 C.F.R. § 1.17 (1991). If the broker-dealer is a clearing member, the broker-dealer must deduct the margin requirement of the applicable clearing organization. If the broker-dealer is a member of a self-regulatory organization, the broker-dealer must deduct 150 percent of the maintenance marginal requirement.

117. 17 C.F.R. § 240.15(c)(3)-1(c)(2)(vii) (1991).

118. Securities commissions represented about 34 percent of broker-dealer revenues in 1980, but this figure dropped to about 17 percent by 1990. Meanwhile, the proportion of broker-dealer revenues derived from other sources, such as interest income or fees from handling mergers, increased from about 31 percent to 47 percent. Government Accounting Office, "Securities Firms: Assessing the Need to Regulate Additional Financial Activities" (April 1992), at 39.

119. Rule 15(c)(3), *supra* note 54.

120. This segregation broke down in the market break of 1989 according to the CFTC Report.

121. 17 C.F.R. § 1.17(a)(i)(B).

122. 17 C.F.R. § 1.17(c)(5)(x). The word "cover" is used in a manner fundamentally equivalent to "hedge," as defined at 17 C.F.R. § 1.17.J(I). The definition of "covered" or "hedged" is unclear because positions shift rapidly. The SEC issued a no-action letter to the NYSE stating that in the event a position is determined not to be covered in the future by the CFTC, the net capital requirement for a basket or an index will be no less than 5 percent. Letter from Michael A. Macchiaroli, Assistant Director, Division of Market Regulation, SEC, to David Marcus, Executive Vice-President, Regulatory Services Group, New York Stock Exchange, Inn (February 17, 1986).

123. *See* chapter 1, "The Capital Adequacy Directive."

124. *See* chapter 1, note 227. For example, the S&P futures contract of 6/22/92 was $210,000 and the margin requirement was 5.87 percent (interview with staff of CFTC), which equated $12,320. Under the Capital Adequacy Directive (CAD) this would attract a weighting of $21,000 for an unhedged position, but a hedged position would only require $4,200 capital. *See supra* note 122.

125. 17 C.F.R. § 240,156-1(d)(11)(5). Temporary and Revolving Subordination Agreements. The 45-day term is available three times a year for firms that maintain 120 percent more of the minimum requirement. The exemption on which broker-dealers rely more is allowing them to enter into subordination agreements for less than one year, but net capital must be 200 percent of the minimum requirement. *See also* chapter 1, "The Capital Adequacy Directive for Securities Firms . . . ," and accompanying text.

126. It is questionable whether U.S. capital rules alone would have been sufficient to prevent a market meltdown had not the FRB urged banks to lend to securities firms and thus keep liquidity in the security system during 1987. Their ability to do so was augmented by the fact that, at the time, securities activities were not conducted in

bank affiliates as they currently are in Section 20 subsidiaries of bank holding companies. Furthermore, several broker-dealers might have failed had they not had sufficiently strong parents, including Shearson Lehman, which is a subsidiary of American Express, and Prudential Bache, which is a subsidiary of Prudential Insurance. (For example, American Express provided an additional $750 million capital to Shearson Lehman Brothers Holdings Inc and its broker-dealer to offset the $966 million loss incurred by these entities in 1990, following major restructuring expenses and decreased operating revenues. Following similar difficulties in 1991 the Prudential Insurance Company of America provided $200 million in capital to the holding company of its broker-dealer, now called Prudential Securities Inc., and purchased several million dollars in bridge loans from an affiliate of the broker-dealer. Finally, General Electric purchased $750 million of high yield bonds and bridge loans from Kidder, Peabody and Co. Inc., and Credit Suisse contributed $300 million in capital to, and purchased a $250 million bridge loan from, the First Boston Corporation's immediate holding company. Information about the First Boston Corporation 1990 earnings was not publicly available ("Securities Firms: Assessing the Need to Regulate Additional Activities," p. 43).

127. *See supra* notes 76 and 77, and accompanying text.

128. "Securities Firms: Assessing the Need to Regulate Additional Financial Activities," *Supra* note 118, at 31.

129. Bachmann Report, *supra* note 10.

130. 17 C.F.R. § 240.15(c)(3)-I(e)(2) (1991).

131. Net Capital Rule Exchange Act Release No. 28,347, Fed. Sec. L. Rel (CCH) 84,618, at 81,014 (August 15, 1990). *See also* Jamroz, *supra* note 47, at 895, 896, for an account of the Drexel case.

132. 17(h)(1) Risk Assessment for Holding Companies, added by Act of October 16, 1990 (Market Reform Act), § 4(a) Pub. Law. 101-432,104 Stat, at 963; 17(h), Additional Information; 17(h)(3) Associated Person Subject to Banking Regulation; 17(h)(4) Exemption; 17(h)(5) Authority to Limit Disclosure.

133. The rules require the following disclosure: (1) organizational chart; (2) risk management policies; (3) pending legal proceedings; (4) off-balance sheet items; (5) aggregate securities and commodities positions; (6) financial instruments; (7) bridge loans; (8) funding sources; and (9) real estate holdings. Regulation 244-170) Requirement to Maintain and Preserve Information (57 Fed. Reg. 321591); Regulation 240.17(h)-2T Reporting Requirement of Risk Assessment. Section 240.17(h)-IJ (57 Fed. Reg. 32159).

134. The leverage ratio (which is the ratio of tc liabilities to total equities) for all registered broker-dealers increased from 13 to 1 in 1984 to 18 to 1 in 1990. Among the 13 largest U.S. broker-dealers studied in a Government Accounting Office Report: "Securities Firms: Assessing the Need to Regulate Additional Activities" *supra* note 118, the leverage ratio was 17 to 1. (*Ibid.*, at 41.) According to this Government Accounting Rep based on SEC sources, U.S. securities firms had excess capital (i.e., tl capital in excess of that required) averaging 6 to 12 times required. This statistic indicates that net capital rules do not account for the risks of doing business; and that for securities firms capital rules, unlike bank capital adequacy ratios, are far below the real level necessary in the course of business.

135. Of the total assets under management in 1990, 11.6 percent were in indexed equity funds, up from 9.3 percent in 1986. As of September 30, 1990, the largest 15 pension funds with investments in indexed equities had invested a total of $1,416 billion in all types of equities, or 41.3 percent of their total assets. Of this, $89 billion

was explicitly invested in indexed equities. Indexed equities, therefore, accounted for a dollar weighted average of 62.0 percent of all equities in these funds and 25.6 percent of their total assets, *ibid.*, at 13. (One obvious advantage of the futures market is that it provides regulatory competition between the SEC and the CFTC. The question of whether derivative markets [options and futures] divert funds from underlying markets is one that has been raised by regulators. [This paragraph is drawn from interviews with regulators from the Securities Investment Board, members of the U.S. Government Accounting Office, and former economists at the Securities and Exchange Commission.] Pursuant to the Market Reform Act, I SEC has proposed rules that would implement a large trader reporting system under the authority of § 13H of the Securities and Exchange of 1934, adopted as part of the Market Reform Act of 1990. Rule 13H would establish an efficient, activity-based reporting system for gathering information about large traders and their trading activity. [Securities and Exchange Act Release no. 29593 56 Fed. Reg. 42550 (August 14, 1991).] The SEC was arguably spurred to do so by superior CFTC data.)

136. CFTC, Division of Trading and Markets, "Review of SRO Risk-Based Capital Requirements and Comparison to the Commission's Net Minimum Capital Rules" (April 2001), p. 6.

137. *Ibid.*, p. 13. The risk-based requirements were higher for 49 firms and lower for 29. One hundred and twelve firms were unaffected.

138. *Ibid.*

139. *Ibid.*

140. *Ibid.*, Exhibit F.

141. *Ibid.*

142. 67 Fed. Reg. 53145-53180 (August 14, 2002) 17 C.F.R. part 41; 17 C.F.R. 242. The CFMA supra note 82 adds subsection 2 to Section 7(c) of the Exchange Act, which directs the FRB to establish initial and maintenance margins for securities futures. CFMA Section 7(c)(2)(b) allows the FRB to delegate rulemaking authority to the CFTC and the SEC jointly.

143. *Ibid.*, Core Principle Three, Box B; Examples include Euro Access Frankfurt, Paris Net Settlement System, and the Proposed New CHIPS system in the United States.

144. In Canada, a central bank guarantee in a netting system assures final settlement.

145. *Ibid.*, 7.10.13.

146. *Ibid.*, Section 8 "The Central Bank should ensure that the system complies with core principles," Box 21.

147. SEC, Proposed Rule "Alternate Net Capital Requirements for Broker Dealers that are Part of a Consolidated Supervise Entity," SEC Release no. 34-48690 (October 24, 2003).

148. *See* Chapter 6, "EU Consolidated Supervision Directive."

149. A one-year period of observation is required as well as calculation of capital charges for three bands over 18 months. For certain positions, scenario analysis would be appropriate.

150. Account is to be taken of large exposure to single counterparties. Credit risk weight of counterparties would be based on annual probability of default and would require a credit charge from 2% to 230% and higher if a counterparty has defaulted.

151. *See* Chapter 2 "New Capital Accord," which includes capital shareholder equity and excludes, inter alia, goodwill and deferred tax assets.

CHAPTER 4

The Deteriorating Integrity of the U.S. Financial System

There is a story about a pig with three legs. A tourist is visiting France, and he sees a pig with three legs. He asks the farmer why the pig has three legs. The farmer says, "But, Monsieur, this is not any ordinary pig. This pig saved my daughter from drowning, and he drove away a gang of bullies that followed my son home from school." But the tourist is perplexed, "But why does the pig have three legs?" "But monsieur," the farmer says, "A pig like this you do not eat all at once." There have been several crises that the U.S. economy has sustained since it fell off the gold standard in 1971, none perhaps so serious as the hyperinflation that eventually resulted. But the economy and the capital markets always came back. It is a truism that owning equity in the long term is better than owning debt. Financial deregulation, until recently, seemed to proceed producing few exogenous shocks. If the Savings and Loan (S&L) crisis was a mess, it was cleaned up efficiently and quickly by enacting the Federal Deposit Insurance Corporation Improvement Act of 1991 (FDICIA) and the Resolution Trust Corporation, and wasn't the Federal Savings and Loan Insurance Corp. (FSLIC) bankrupt for years anyway? If the United States ran big budget deficits, Clinton's election enabled higher tax rates, and victory in the Cold War led to a declining military budget. Then we had a period of sustained growth unequal to any in American history. The National Association of Dealers Automated Quotations (NASDAQ) emerged out of nowhere to rise to over 5,000. Banks were now in every business imaginable, and consumer spending could solve any problem when cautious business executives stopped increasing capital spending. Led by the enthusiasm of boosters, Congress passed Gramm-Leach-Bliley (GLB), which only reinforced what regulators had already done in allowing banks to form whatever ungodly business combinations they chose. There was a crisis in Asia that almost ended the party, but that was all resolved by International Monetary Fund (IMF) lending initiated by the United States. Japan has amassed a budget deficit of 130 percent of gross domestic product (GDP). The problem with those Asians is that they didn't have Generally Accepted Accounting Principles (GAAP). Congress, which shared in the largesse of the era, responded not only with GLB, but enacted the Private Securities Litigation Act, which protected all those providential chief executive officers (CEOs) in such sectors as energy and telecom from annoying shareholders.

In September 1996, Lawrence Lindsey, on the Board of Governors of the Federal Reserve Board (FRB), was concerned about rising stock prices. Mr. Lindsey fretted that the economy had developed a gambler's curse. While acknowledging that bursting the bubble might have unpleasant consequences, he said, "I think it is far better that we do so while the bubble still resembles surface froth."[1] The FRB did not end up raising interest rates that day or at the subsequent meeting. The stock market did react to Greenspan's "irrational exuberance" speech, but, although he talked of another more forceful speech, none ever materialized. Instead, several years later he embraced the new economy paradigm.[2] The FRB did raise interest rates once in 1997 and several times in 1999 and 2000. But the FRB never targeted the stock market, and these rate hikes were explained in terms of taming inflation. Mr. Lindsey, now an economic advisor to President Bush, says that it is too early to tell whether the FRB should have raised interest rates earlier: "Economic historians will be debating this issue for decades to come."[3]

This chapter will seek to show that a probusiness judiciary, compliant and uninformed regulators, and grateful legislators have all eaten part of the pig. Now the external debt of the United States may have more severe consequences than the budget deficit ever did and the current account is as large as any annual budget deficit. This is the result of consumer debt and negative savings, resulting from a society bent on spending its way out of recession time and time again, not only through the good offices of the federal government but by mortgaging the future to foreign holders of U.S. debt. "Securities" will consider the regulation of securities by the Securities and Exchange Commission (SEC) in the decade leading up to Enron and after Enron. Within that section, "Securities Litigation Anyone?" is concerned with the allocation of securities in initial public offerings (IPOs) to favored customers of investment banks that fuelled NASDAQ and the bubble economy, and the role of analysts in pumping up the bubble while receiving bonuses, in some cases, based on sales directly from corporate finance departments despite the Chinese wall between investment banks and broker-dealers. "The SEC under Chairman Levitt . . ." covers Arthur Levitt's tenure as SEC chairman in 1993–2001 and balances his achievements against the formidable obstacles of interest group pressure. "Accounting for the SEC," the crux of the matter, will recount SEC initiatives in reaction to Enron, particularly in accounting regulation, a responsibility that it has delegated to the Financial Accounting Standards Board (FASB) for 70 years. "Disclosure in the United States since Basic and SEC Initiatives" will consider judicial standards for material disclosure. "Banking" involves banking regulation. "The International Debt Crisis of 1998 . . ." will tell the tale of the Asia crisis, the fall of Long-Term Capital Management (LTCM), and the role of the New York Fed in unwinding its positions, and "Gramm-Leach-Bliley . . ." discusses the Gramm-Leach-Bliley Act, which repealed the Glass Steagall Act and allowed for the creation of bank holding companies, enabling financial conglomerates to acquire banks. "Enron and Beyond" concerns Enron-related conflicts of interest on the part of banks. "The Composition of Banks and Finance Company Assets" considers the current state of U.S. banking assets, including equity linked mortgage, consumer debt, and exposure to commercial real estate. "Macroeconomic Consequences" will consider the macroeconomic effects of expanded securities markets in the United States, deteriorating banking assets, the current account deficit, and the negative savings rate.

SECURITIES

Securities Litigation Anyone?

In 1995, Congress enacted the Private Securities Litigation Reform Act (PSLRA), which created requirements for a lead plaintiff to have the choice of attorney in class action suits, limited accountant and auditor liability, and created a safe harbor for forward-looking earnings forecasts. A representative plaintiff must sign an affidavit that he is not being given any consideration for serving as a representative plaintiff. He is required to file a notice of the suit, and the lead plaintiff, the plaintiff with the greatest pecuniary interest or the plaintiff who initiated the suit, is then entitled to choose the attorney.[4] The consequences of this act have been to create a complex system of court appointment of attorney. Professor James Cox says that, by changing the requirements for class action suits, Congress determined that "being a defendant in a class action suit was no more than legalized bad luck."[5] Currently, the approach is to create a sealed bid auction among lawyers to determine who would best represent the class.[6]

Despite these obstacles, defendants have been able to predominate in a number of actions, but there are additional chilling effects of the PSLRA. The act requires that, in alleging that the defendant made an omission or a false statement, that he or she did so "in a particular state of mind."[7] There is an additional hurdle of loss causation[8] and mandatory sanctions if a court makes a finding that civil procedure has not been followed.[9] Loss causation limits the liability of "aiders and abettors" to the depreciation in value directly resulting from the false or misleading statement or material omission.[10] One odd quality of the PSLRA is that in the safe harbor provisions for forward-looking projections and in those provisions governing liability, an individual is liable only if someone "knowingly committed a violation of the securities law."[11] In *In re Comshare*, the Court interpreted the PSLRA as altering, not the ultimate requirement of scienter, but the pleading that the plaintiff had to make in order to get past the initial bar to state a cause of action.[12] Yet, it seems clear that the Court meant to recalculate the balance of justice in favor of the securities defendant.

Meanwhile the malfeasance of broker-dealers on Wall Street has brought about a whole new kind of securities law violations that have resulted in both private and government actions. Credit Suisse First Boston made a $100 million settlement with the government for its alleged kickback schemes in which it made favorable allocations of hot IPOs to favorite clients in exchange for tie-ins and other fee business.[13] The SEC releases in this area can only be described as insufficient. In January 2000, the SEC gave a notice of proposed rule change to the National Association of Dealers (NASD) rules "relating to trading in 'hot equity'" offerings.[14] This proposal has languished as of the time of this writing, long after such offerings have become a moot point. In August 2000, the legal staff of the Division of Market Regulation issued an opinion that tie-in arrangements for purchases in the aftermarket violate securities law and Regulation M in particular.[15] Sometimes these kickbacks were straight commission on future sales, as much as one dollar for every three in profit, or may have been laddering, which is the allocation of shares at wholesale prices in return for a commitment to buy in the open market. This would represent straightforward market manipulation. Nearly 250 lawsuits have taken aim at the way securities offerings were conducted. According to Michael Perino, a law professor at St. John's, "This is a very different kind of allegation. In the class action involving an IPO, the allegation involves some sort of misrepresentation or omission of information. The allegations here go to the IPO process itself." Despite the PSLRA, the number of class action lawsuits doubled in 2001.[16] Christopher Lovell of Lovell and Stuart won a $1 billion award in 1998 when he accused the seven major investment banks of colluding in NASDAQ stock price fixing, and he is now in the process of a suit involving the IPO market.[17]

Elliot Spitzer, the attorney general of New York, brought suit against Merill Lynch alleging that the firm was pumping its clients' stocks. On May 21, 2002, Spitzer reached an unprecedented agreement with Merill in which Merill agreed to the following: 1) to sever the link between compensation of brokerage and analysts and investment banking; 2) to prohibit investment banking input into analyst compensation and to create a new investment review committee; 3) establish an independent monitor for this agreement to be chosen by the attorney general; 4) disclose in Merill research reports whether it has received or is entitled to receive any compensation from any client; 5) upon the discontinuation of coverage of a company, issue a statement to that effect; 6) pay a $100 million fine; and 7) issue a statement of contrition.[18] Nonetheless, the people who commit malfeasance continue to work in the securities industry.

Despite the limitation of the PSLRA, shareholders and lawyers continue to bring forth worthwhile claims, and the attorney general of New York has taken action. The SEC will be unlikely to rock the boat. Yet, the settlement that Spitzer achieved demonstrates the necessity of the separation of investment banking and brokerage since the supposed Chinese wall is exactly that—a porous wall. What is of interest here is that the NASDAQ appears to have attained its apex through the willful violation of the securities laws. The money lost cannot be recovered. More importantly, the damage that the bubble did cannot be repaired.

The SEC under Chairman Levitt 1993–2001

Arthur Levitt's tenure as SEC chairman was, surprisingly, characterized by a great many successes and pitched battles with the securities and accounting industry. Although his tenure is best remembered for lost battles, expensing options, separating auditing and consulting, and codes of conduct for analysts, Levitt had many successes including ensuring more independent trustees at FASB; ending collusion by NASD market makers to maintain spreads and interfering with the small order execution system (this resulted in the censure of the NASD and three years' probation); improvements in the automated quote system, including the switch to decimals, which limited front running and similar less-than-best execution practices; some improvement in FASB standards, ensuring the relative independence of the FASB; and the promulgation of Regulation FD (Fair Disclosure).[19]

Levitt recounts how he did not have the political leverage to end conflicts of interest between brokers and investors by producing a broker compensation best practices code. But there has since been considerable backsliding.[20] During Levitt's tenure, the SEC brought enforcement actions against highly reputable mutual funds, including Van Kempen, which involved a situation in which investors were not told that this incubator fund had made most of its profits on capital of less than $400,000, and most of the profit came from return on investment in 31 hot IPO funds.[21] Levitt has many other peeves against the mutual fund industry, including soft dollar arrangements, other fees including distribution and marketing, and tax traps where investors are paying more capital gains from high turnover and redemptions. In the spring of 2000, Levitt tried to convince the stock exchanges that they needed new rules on conflict of interest for brokers and analysts.[22] By March 2000, analysts' optimism was resulting in 92 buy recommendations for every sell recommendation.[23]

Regulation FD, which ended privileged disclosure to analysts by requiring disclosure of material facts, especially earnings, to be public, was passed despite the strenuous objections of the Securities Industry Association (SIA). According to Levitt, prior to the enactment of Regulation FD, "The result was an unhealthy form of barter in which some companies gave away information in return for favorable ratings."[24] In the fourth quarter of 2000, 96 percent more companies provided pre-announcements of whether they would hit their target.

Levitt's battle with the industry over stock options is now legendary and is considered in detail in the following chapter.[25] FASB, which had initiated the expensing of options proposition, was in the process of requiring market value accounting for derivatives. Once again, a lobby group called the Financial Executives International proposed reductions in FASB's size, limiting existing standards to a time limit, and establishing a separate group to set FASB's agenda.[26] The SEC succeeded in getting a 50/50 split of the number of trustees who represented the public interest, and FASB promulgated its rule on market value of derivatives. Levitt writes in *Taking on the Street*, "But I was shocked when I saw how auditors behaved in these dustups. They failed to rally to the cause of investors, and instead supported the demands of their corporate clients. They had become advocates. I would forever look upon the accounting profession differently after this episode."[27] In 1995, Senator Gramm sought his committee's approval for a 25 percent reduction in the SEC budget. From 1995 to 1997, the SEC's budget remained constant for inflation while initial public offerings increased by a factor of 12. In 1997, Levitt noted that the funding was below that of the sport fish restoration program.[28]

In 1997, an anonymous letter arrived at the SEC office in Miami alleging conflicts of interests in the Tampa office of Coopers and Lybrand. (In the meantime, Coopers merged with Price Waterhouse to form PriceWaterhouse-Coopers.) The investigation uncovered over 8,000 violations of auditor independence rules, instances in which auditors owned stock in companies that they were auditing.[29] In response to proposed SEC auditor independence standards, Anderson CEO Bob Grafton said, "Arthur, if you go ahead with this, it will be war." Senator Phil Gramm threatened an appropriations rider that would bar the SEC from enforcing the rule. Eventually, a compromise was struck in which no auditor could perform more than 40 percent of internal audit services. A standard was also maintained under which auditors would violate the independence rule if in the opinion of a reasonable investor the auditor performed services that made it impossible for the auditor to act without bias. Specific precluded services included actuarial or appraisal services, giving investment advice, or owning stock.[30]

During Levitt's tenure, the SEC and the NYSE and NASD added significant requirements to the audit committee's composition and responsibilities. In 1998, Levitt had called attention to the audit committee's role in fighting financial fraud. In particular, he was concerned about the qualifications of audit committee members.[31] In response to Levitt's challenge, the NYSE and the NASD created a blue-ribbon panel that recommended 10 guidelines that would enable audit committees to function more effectively, including independence, financial literacy, and written rules and guidelines.[32] Specifically, the blue-ribbon panel asked the NYSE and the NASD to define independence, require that each member of an audit committee be financially literate, and require audit committees to draft a charter and to disclose it in their proxy statements.[33] The final recommendation was that the audit committee charter should reflect the fact that the outside auditor is responsible to the audit committee.[34] In response, the NASD and the NYSE adopted independence standards[35] that have since been superseded.[36]

These rules had little impact on Enron. Its audit committee had been praised for its stellar credentials by *Chief Executive* magazine.[37] With Wendy Gramm, former CFTC Commissioner, and the Chair of the Audit Committee, Robert Jaedicke, an accounting professor at Stanford Business School, as members, the audit committee fit the definition of financial literacy but not independence. One member was paid fees for consulting and other members were employed by universities to which Enron gave large grants. These conflicts did not violate the new independence requirements as of 1999;[38] but they do violate 2002 independence requirements.[39] Enron's audit committee had conducted a review of the off-balance sheet partnerships in February 2000 and met for one hour before each board meeting.[40] Jaedicke, testifying before a House Committee, said, "We do not manage the company. We do not do the auditing. We are not detectives."[41] Also, the in-house counsel, Robert Mintz, grew concerned about the off-balance sheet partnerships and retained Fried Frank Shriver and Jacobsen to review them and was advised that Enron should stop the partnerships.[42] These facts make one wonder whether the many changes wrought by Sarbanes-Oxley will alter the current practices of audit committees. While the CEO certification requirements might make a difference,[43] liability for members of the audit committee will evolve only through case law. Generally, directors' duty of care is met when directors act in good faith, in a manner which is in the best interest of the corporation, and have a level of care that "a person in a like position would reasonably believe appropriate under similar circumstances."[44] Generally, inside directors have been held to a higher standard of care,[45] and some courts have held audit committees to this higher standard of care because of their special positions.[46]

The SEC adopted three staff bulletins defining materiality in the same terms as *TSC v. Northway*[47] and *Basic v. Levinson*[48] rather than a quantitative standard and adopted standards on revenue recognition.[49] The SEC also adopted amendments to rule 10–01 of Regulation S-X to require review of 10Q by the outside auditor and required that a copy of the outside auditor's report be included in the 10Q.[50] Finally, the SEC provided for two safe harbors, which stated that the audit report and related disclosures would not be considered "soliciting material."[51]

Between 1997 and 2000, 700 companies restated their earnings. Only three companies had restated their earnings in 1981. Levitt says, "It wasn't just a case of a few bad apples, either. Blue-chip companies with sterling reputations were manipulating their numbers in ways that were downright misleading."[52] Following a speech by Levitt at NYU entitled "The Numbers Game," the

American Institute of Certified Public Accountants (AICPA) and the Big Five Accounting Firms went along with a new body called the Independence Standards Board, the chairman of which was Harvey Pitt, who represented the accounting industry. Levitt had intended that the body restrict consulting services by auditors, but Pitt and the accounting industry backpedaled, delivering a white paper, written by Pitt, that advocated the expansion of consulting services as a means of improving the quality of audits.[53]

The SEC took the lead in the numbers game by issuing Staff Accounting Bulletin 101, which was issued to clarify when companies could record revenue on their books, which provoked an enormous outcry from Silicon Valley and lawmakers. Another battle involved the pooling of interests, which did not require firms to capitalize goodwill, the excess paid for acquisitions over market. Another compromise was reached that ended the pooling of interests but only required that the companies deduct goodwill when assets became impaired.[54] AOL expected to boost profit by as much as $6.8 billion because it was no longer required to capitalize goodwill. The Bank of America, which generated $12 billion in goodwill, could boost profit by as much as $600 million per year.[55]

By 2001, the Enforcement Division was involved in numerous high-profile cases involving accounting fraud—Waste Management and Sunbeam topping the list. But other companies like Lucent, Motorola, and Cisco were legally able to take big bath restructuring charges perfectly legally by providing minimal disclosure.[56] Motorola provided vendor financing of $1.7 billion to Turkey's wireless carrier to finance a sale to Turkey's telecom company Telsor. In March 2001, it referred to "one customer in Turkey" who was responsible for $1.7 billion of $2.8 billion in long-term financing receivables. Cisco took a $2.8 write-down on inventory in 2001 and, by burying the excess inventory charge, it claimed that it had achieved a $230 million profit. This subject will be revisited in the context of Sarbanes-Oxley Section 906(a) and (b), provisions that provide for criminal penalties for improper certification of financial reporting requirements, and SEC civil enforcement actions initiated by the Levitt-era SEC will be examined to determine which kinds of incomplete financial disclosure is proscribed by the act.[57] But it should be noted that many forms of inaccurate financial reporting are perfectly legal under GAAP. Some of these will be discussed in detail in chapter 6, "Reform."

The use of pro forma earnings distorts the purposes of GAAP, even if, in general, these might be more reliable measures of stock market performance than GAAP.[58] The Levitt tenure did not involve any regulation of pro forma earnings; nor did it do much to stop allotments of IPOs.[59] While the IPO issue still languishes, analyst conflicts of interest have been addressed by subsequent SEC rules and Sarbanes-Oxley; pro forma earnings were the subject of an enforcement action in 2002, and the SEC has issued a release on the subject.[60]

However, the foregoing illustrates the problem of overcoming interest group pressure. The small accounting industry made $14.5 million in contributions in the 2000 election cycle, ranking it above the defense industry.[61] More importantly, the securities industry gave $39 million in soft money during the same election cycle and $53 million in contributions to individual candidates.[62] Whether Levitt was an effective infighter and achieved the maximum benefit for the investor or whether he invested valuable regulatory goodwill in losing battles such as expensing options and separating auditing and consulting is an open question to be settled by history. Had Levitt focused only on best execution and reform of accounting standards alone, he might have been able to achieve this limited agenda. That the expensing of options and the separation of auditing and accounting are yet to be achieved in the post-Sarbanes-Oxley era underscores the difficulty of the regulatory agenda that he chose.

Accounting for the SEC

In 2002 business as usual was changed forever by the Enron collapse and the subsequent Global Crossings filing. The SEC has been concerned about financial disclosure for some time. Former Commissioner Hunt cited the accounting staff reminder that statements designed to be misleading in financial disclosure might be actionable.[63] He cited recent changes to proposed listing rules issued jointly by the NASD, the American Stock Exchange, and the New York Stock Exchange requiring that three members of the auditing committee be financially literate and that one have training in accounting.[64]

When Enron exploded like a supernova on public consciousness, the SEC responded in April 2002, issuing a proposed rule for disclosure of certain management transactions, including loans to officers and directors, and requiring timely reporting,[65] and another proposed rule issued on the same day for accelerating reporting dates.[66] The pièce de résistance, however, was issued on May 10, 2002,[67] entitled "Changes in Critical Accounting Methods." The term "critical accounting method" is a term of art under FASB methodology, rule number 8. The basic thrust of this final release is that it relies on restatement of critical accounting methods and disclosure thereof to notify the public and analysts of material changes in the accounting processes of reporting firms. This also requires a retrospective restatement.

However, this change places the onus on the accounting profession, which has, through its lobbying efforts under the direction of then lobbyist Pitt, enacted the Private Litigation Securities Act of 1995 limiting liability for accounting firms. Pitt, in a statement before the Senate Committee on Banking, Housing, and Urban Affairs, insisted that investors have won large awards in Cendant. He points to rules on off-balance sheet reporting (items to be included in management discussion and analysis) issued in a proposed release dated December 12, 2002, in fact, the work of the accounting firms themselves.[68] He also announced the formation of a public accountability board to serve under the SEC, but he believed that the responsibility for financial accounting should remain in the private sector, presumably under auspices of this new board, the FASB, and the Emerging Issues Task Force (EITF). These are the people that brought us the 97/3 rule that enabled Enron, had it cared to follow the letter of the law, not to consolidate the Raptors partnerships or to account for the unfunded swaps.

There is an 804-page book on hedging rules for tax and accounting purposes;[69] yet, Enron can make a $200 million loan from Citibank disguised as an unpaid interest rate swap. This shows up nowhere on Enron's balance sheet. Currently, the Financial Accounting Standards Board is in the process of changing rules regarding such unfunded swaps. FASB amended its treatment of derivative hedges requiring unfunded swaps to be accounted for as two component parts—a swap with nil value and a loan.[70]

Then there are those partnerships with names like Chewco and Raptors that are off-balance sheet under the 97/3 rule, which means that as long as the owner of the Special Purpose Entity (SPE) risks 3[71] percent of the capital, it is the owner of the corporation, even if there is some provision causing the original seller, in this case Enron, to end up with the liabilities. There are some good reasons for this in the context of private corporations. The result of such transactions not appearing on the balance sheet of public corporations in a 10K or any other document filed with SEC amounted to over $2 billion for Enron and resulted in a loss of over $90 billion in market capitalization. The Worldcom price tag has been raised to up to $7.1 billion of inflated earnings,[72] and least one ex-official of Worldcom has pleaded guilty to inflating earnings by over $5 billion.[73]

In the Change of Critical Accounting Method Proposed Rule, the SEC asked the issuer to ask itself whether a change in accounting method would have a material impact on the financial statement, in which case the accounting method must be disclosed. Under the first part of the proposal, a company that adopts an accounting method that required it to make estimates about events that were highly uncertain would have to reveal its accounting method if another accounting method would yield materially different results. Under the second part of the proposal, a company that initially adopted an accounting standard with a material impact would have to explain what circumstances gave rise to its adoption of the accounting method.[74] Obviously this is a model of clarity that will obviate the need for reporting off-balance sheet financing. The proposal, according to the release, is intended to make financial statements more transparent. Also, the proposal does not require disclosure of a new accounting method, "where the company must make its best judgment as to how to apply the new accounting method in the absence of interpretive guidance."[75] The SEC also "may revisit other circumstances where the company may exercise discretion of its accounting policies under GAAP at a later date."[76]

The SEC then goes on to say that it would require disclosure of critical accounting estimates and any known trend, circumstances, events, or uncertainties that are reasonably likely to occur and materially affect the methodology of accounting.[77] How can an uncertainty be reasonably likely to occur unless it is death, taxes, or bureaucratic bungling?

For each critical accounting estimate, a company would have to explain "the sensitivity of [each estimate] to financial results by each change in critical accounting method."[78] Shouldn't it be the other way around? Second, the company would have to explain its historical changes in method for the past three years. Part of what the SEC appears to be getting at, since, at one juncture, it uses the example of an over the counter (OTC) derivative, is that it doesn't want to regulate haircuts on financial instruments for nonsecurities firms.[79]

The next section is entitled "Quantitative Approaches to Sensitivity." (Personally, it never worked for me.) A company could assume it changed the material assumptions in its accounting method or it changed its accounting method. A company may determine the amount of change it assumes. "Reasonably possible" means, we are told, "that the possibility of an event occurring is more than remote but less than likely."[80] Obviously, the SEC is trying not to assume the negative scenario used to determine interest rate risk as a shock scenario of a 200 basis point change in interest rates.[81] Then, the company would use the upper and lower range (is that 1st and 99th percentile as under the new G-10 accord?). The proposal asks whether item 306 of Regulation S-K should be amended to determine whether the audit committee has discussed the changes with its auditors or senior management, or, whether, presumably, senior management[82] is playing hooky.

Companies would have to disclose segment information to the extent that not to do so would amount to an "incomplete or misleading picture."[83] The three examples given as to how the critical accounting release would work in practice involve the price of copper, product returns, and plant and equipment. This is deceptively simple compared to real accounting issues. But all of this is in the context of Rule 175 and Rule 3b-6, which provide safe harbors for forward-looking statements.[84] This proposed rule was never enacted. Despite awkward phrasing, disclosure of critical accounting policy changes is essential to investors and analysts. The accounting industry lobby was clearly victorious here. Although the SEC may have attempted to circumvent FASB at this early post-Enron date, the disappearance of this proposed rule is mysterious. Obviously, the SEC Office of Chief Accountant did not have sufficient resources to support its stance, demonstrating the limitations of SEC rulemaking on accounting issues.

Frequently, the text of the petition or interpretive rule cited above[85] footnotes the Emerging Issues Task Force. Since the task force is the forum that interprets FASB rules, it takes precedence over the interpretive rule in a general context, or does it? The problem here is that we are far away from the law per se. Congress had no problem amending the Securities and Exchange

Acts in order to promulgate the Private Securities Litigation Act[86] and would eventually enact the Sarbanes-Oxley Act discussed in chapter 6; but, Mr. Pitt was quite correct in pointing out in his testimony that the SEC has the right to set rules for financial accounting.[87] Curiously enough, these sections specifically set forth the right of the SEC to promulgate rules on consolidated accounting, a task that they never seem to have taken up.

There was little support for Mr. Pitt's ideas for a public accounting board under the auspices of the private sector that would supersede the POB (the Public Oversight Board, which was dissolved at the behest of its members when the FASB refused to fund it). Testifying before Congress, Alauna Peters says that, "The change [in the accounting profession] has to be radical and immediate."[88] She continues, "Based on my observation, it is critical for the power of any new self regulatory agency to be based in legislation . . . and should not be affiliated with or responsible to any accounting firm or the AICPA."[89] She made mention of the Petition for Interpretive Release, stating that the agreement reached between the SEC, the Big Four, and the AICPA one week before public disclosure of the deal and notice to the POB was the proximate cause that led the members of the POB to disband.[90] Charles Bowsher, the chairman of the POB, recounted how the Securities Practice Committee (SECPCS) of the AICPA funded the POB, and on May 3, 2000, withdrew funding, declaring that the POB should no longer conduct general audits of accounting firms. Mr. Bowsher proposed a statutory basis for a self-regulatory organization.[91] The mot juste was delivered by Sarah Teslik of the Council of Institutional Investors: "If fifth graders picked their teachers, fifth graders would get As."[92]

One of the defenders of the FASB status quo before the Senate Committee investigating the Enron debacle was, not surprisingly, the chairman of FASB, Mr. Jenkins, who stated that, although all the transactions in Enron may have been accounted for at fair market value at the date of the transaction, they contained embedded liability and "quantitative sensitivity."[93] He added that a company was already required to disclose in a footnote the fair value of its commitments, guarantees, and long-term obligations. His best defense of the FASB status quo was the Powers Report,[94] which acknowledged that Enron understated its obligations. As a consequence of the failure to consolidate, Enron indicated it had overstated its income by approximately $500 million and understated its liabilities by $2 billion.

The Chewco and LJM1 restatement reduced net income by nearly $500 million over four reporting years (principally in the last three years) and reduced shareholder equity by nearly $2.2 billion and increased debt by $2.7 billion.[95] For the Chewco Partnership, $11.4 million in equity was required, but the money was advanced by Barclay Bank and secured by pledges of collateral characterized as reserves.[96] The existence of the cash collateral was fatal to the 3 percent requirement since the $6.6 million could not be both collateral and equity.[97] Wilmer Cutler and Pickering, which prepared the report for Enron's Board of Directors, seemed to be obsessed with understanding the motivation for the failure to fund the 3 percent, almost in the same way as a criminal lawyer is fascinated by a particularly complex murder. Although Enron ultimately decided to give up the ghost on LJM1, it may not have done so if Chewco had not failed. The Powers Report is ambivalent about the legality of the Special Purpose Vehicle used in that partnership.[98] In the LJM1 deals, the report says, "There are plausible, more innocent explanations of some of the repurchases, but a sufficient basis remains for further examination." Thus, the report is not conclusive about the LJM1 partnerships. In the Talon's partnership (which was linked to the LJM1 deal), Enron purchased a put on its own shares from Talon that would not be creditworthy if the Enron shares fell below a certain strike price[99] (the put was leveraged). The point of this entire discussion is that there are no means of discrediting a sham transaction. Without an administrative or legal appellate process, when accounting practices comply with the letter of FASB rules, there can be no punishment. In fact, there can be no liability for false or misleading statements under the securities law.

Although Mr. Jenkins does not specifically mention it, unfunded swaps, energy derivatives deregulated under the Financial Modernization Act of 2000,[100] as well as the put option on Enron shares, accounted for a great deal of Enron's downside. FASB has been hard at work on a new standard for accounting for financial derivatives. Yet this report is curiously absent from his testimony.

Under Chairman Pitt, the SEC delved into the question of pro forma earnings. These announcements tend to ignore restructurings and loan losses. In January 2002, the SEC reached a settlement with Trump Casinos.[101] Trump Casinos et al. recorded a one-time profit from termination of a lease of $17.2 million. In its pro forma release, Trump Casinos et al. failed to disclose this one-time gain and attributed its overall profit of $14 million to operational improvements. The SEC release also states that Trump et al., in this misleading pro forma statement, violated 10b and 10b-5 of the Securities and Exchange Act by knowingly or recklessly issuing the pro forma release.[102] Already, in December 2001, in the aftermath of Enron, the SEC issued a "Cautionary Advice Regarding the Use of 'Pro-Forma' Financial Information in Earnings Releases."[103] The SEC declared that "pro forma" earnings results are subject to the antifraud provisions of the Securities and Exchange Acts. Companies are required to disclose the "controlling principles" that govern the release of financial information. For example, if certain transactions are omitted in the calculation, these one-time charges must be applied to comparable periods. Companies are further admonished to pay attention to the materiality of the omissions. The SEC commends the pro forma earnings guidelines of the Financial Investors International and the National Investor Relations Institute.[104] These rules will be superseded by SEC rules issued pursuant to Sarbanes-Oxley.

In a release on 8K filings, the SEC created a catch-all that essentially increased disclosure requirements to cover, among other matters, related party disclosures and contingent liability disclosures à la Enron and 97/3.[105] In general, the proposed release proposes the shortening of the filing deadline, depending on the nature of the triggering event, from 5 or 15 days to 2 days for events that trigger disclosure under 8K. The current events that trigger disclosure include a change in control, a disposal or acquisition of a substantial amount of assets, a company's bankruptcy or receivership, a change of certifying accountant, the resignation of a director, and a change in the company's fiscal year.[106] This release adds 11 items that would have to be reported in an 8K filing, thereby revolutionizing 8K filings.

A company would have to disclose any material agreement entered into which is not made in the ordinary course of business. This would include any letter of intent entered into and all material terms of the agreements[107] and the obvious converse, termination of an agreement not in the ordinary course of business;[108] and termination or reduction of business with a customer when such business equals 10 percent or more of revenues for the fiscal year.[109] Bankruptcy or receivership would need to be reported,[110] which is straightforward, and creation of a direct or contingent liability that is material to the registrant.[111] A loan entered into by an affiliate would be covered under this section. The discussion specifies materiality. Examples include registered sales of debt securities, guarantees, bank loans or credit facilities, keepwell agreements, and obligations to purchase assets. The next item to be disclosed is events triggering a material, direct, or contingent obligation.[112] This section will only be triggered by notification in writing of the triggering event. Another item to be reported under 8K is exit activities including write-offs and restructuring charges.[113] The obligation to report will come to fruition when a company definitely commits to a course of action that will incur a material write-off or restructuring charge under GAAP. The section requires an estimation of future cash expenditures that may go beyond GAAP requirements. Companies will be required to report changes in ratings from any rating agencies.[114] Naturally, this information is publicly available and will not have much impact. The same is true for notice of delisting or failure to satisfy listing requirements.[115] Unregistered sales of equities that have to be reported elsewhere will now have to be reported in a more timely fashion under 8K,[116] and material modifications to rights of securities holders have been moved back to 8K.[117] A new item allows a board to make a decision of nonreliance on previously audited financial statements.[118] Previously, the burden was on a director to proffer a letter about a resignation that involved disagreement with the management. This is now an affirmative corporate responsibility in any instance where the director leaves as the result of a disagreement.[119] Reporting is also required when a company appoints a new officer or director.[120] Under the proposal, companies would also be obliged to report amendments to the articles of incorporation or bylaws and changes to the fiscal year under 8K.[121]

Companies also have to disclose any event that would "materially limit" employees and participants in a stock option plan from acquiring or disposing of their assets, other than a blackout period.[122] Under this proposal, the SEC requested comment on whether there should be notice of waivers of companies' codes of ethics,[123] self-imposed or exchange-imposed, and whether changes of critical accounting methods discussed above[124] should be disclosed in the 8K form.[125] Disclosure requirements now require foreign issuers to file their forms electronically with Electronic Data Gathering Analysis and Retrieval (EDGAR). EDGAR filings are required, generally, for annual reports and certain other situations, including tender offers.[126]

Disclosure in the United States since Basic and SEC Initiatives

These reforms of ongoing disclosure, which reappear in Sarbanes-Oxley and are discussed in chapter 6, "Reform," must be understood in the context of case law. *Basic v. Levinson* held that "no corporate developments" statements in the course of merger talks were materially misleading and violated 10b-5.[127] This case affirmed the "total mix" standards of *TSC v. Northway.*[128] The case also confirmed that the materiality of a contingent event depended on "a balancing of both the indicated probability that an event would occur and the anticipated magnitude of the event in the light of the totality of company activity."[129] Several other cases distinguished between merger talks that were not material and those that were.[130] The duty not to mislead has been extended to interviews.[131] In *Virginia Bankshares Inc. v. Sandberg*[132] statements to the effect that a merger would produce a high value and "fair" price were misleading even if the language was opinion and conclusory: "Such conclusory terms in the commercial context are reasonably understood to rest on a factual basis that justifies them as accurate."[133] Disclosure in publicity materials that substantially misstated the prospects for a new disk drive resulted in a $100 million verdict against Apple Computer,[134] and overstating the demand for a product in the case of *Convergeant* was held to be misleading;[135] and in *In re Seagate*[136] defendants made severally partially curative statements that, taken as a whole, were adjudged to be misleading. *In Re Gap Litigation*[137] begins a line of cases that focus on management discussion and analysis (MD&A) disclosure. Plaintiffs contended that Gap had made inadequate disclosure regarding cost, but the court held that Gap had made adequate disclosure of inventory. The court found that Gap's destiny statement was mere "puffing," which was not relevant. However, in *Engelhard,*[138] the court contrasted the company's internal memos with its public disclosures. In *In the matter of Caterpillar Inc.,*[139] the SEC made clear that it intends to enforce the MD&A disclosure requirements where the magnitude of a Brazilian subsidiary mandated a specific discussion. In *Salant,*[140] the commission found that Salant had a duty to disclose its liquidity problems in its MD&A. This case is a borderline financial reporting case, but, in this instance, the financial position vis-à-vis liquidity must be disclosed in the MD&A.[141] The *Bank of Boston*[142] case was decided entirely on grounds of deficient MD&A disclosure and involved the Bank of Boston's failure to disclose that reserves on real estate would have to be increased. In *Weil v. Dominion Resources Inc.*,[143] the court held that the simple failure to disclose management misconduct does not amount to material omissions.[144] Another issue in disclosure is raised by Regulation FD, which forbids making selective disclosures to analysts without public disclosure.

In a separate release for a proposed rule, Certification of Disclosure of Companies Quarterly and Annual Reports,[145] the SEC proposed that companies' chief financial officers and principal executive officers would certify in an annual report that (1) he or she has read the report; (2) to the best of his or her knowledge the information contained in the report is true in all important respects to the end of the period covered in the report; and (3) the report contains all the information that he or she is aware of and that he or she believes is important to a reasonable investor as of the end of the reporting period. The report will also contain a statement that information is "important to the reasonable investor" if (1) there is a substantial likelihood that the reasonable investor would view the information as significantly altering the total mix of the report or (2) the report would be misleading to the reasonable investor if the information were omitted from the report.[146] This language deliberately traces the language of *TSC Industries Inc. v. Northway Inc.*[147] and *Basic Inc. v. Levinson.*[148] Under *Basic*, materiality of a contingent or speculative event will depend upon balancing the probability that an event will occur and the anticipated magnitude of the event in light of the totality of the company.[149] Elsewhere, I have criticized the *TSC v. Northway* standard in that it does not qualify the materiality of the omission.[150] The standards of *Basic* are more exacting, but these relate to forward-looking events that are now governed, to the extent disclosed in the appropriate section, by the safe harbor of the Private Securities Litigation Reform Act.[151] However, this release has been superseded by more precise principles in Sarbanes-Oxley.

In these releases, the SEC was trying to cling to the notion that disclosure is the hallmark of the securities laws. However, as much as many of these disclosures are welcome, if belatedly, proper accounting requires more than disclosure. Such proposals and other issues relating to reform of securities disclosure practices will be discussed in chapter 6, "The Sarbanes-Oxley Act. . . ."

BANKING

Gramm-Leach-Bliley:[152] Banking on a Change

Ironically, it was the Supreme Court, in a series of decisions that led the way to Federal Reserve Orders, that paved the way for GLB. I suppose the

Supreme Court does not live in a vacuum; it is entitled to take judicial notice of the *Wall Street Journal* in the same way that Abraham Lincoln asked the court to take judicial notice of the moon being full in a murder trial (a classic in evidence for U.S. law students). But it is odd that it was only in 1990, after nearly 60 years of Glass Steagall, that the incidental to banking language in Glass Steagall was interpreted to allow banks to underwrite securities, first eligible types, then ineligible types.[153] As time passed, the Federal Reserve became more liberal and increased the gross revenue of banks for securities ineligible activities from 5 percent to 10 percent to 25 percent of gross revenue of all securities activities.[154] Within three years, the Federal Reserve Board had followed up with an order allowing the merger of Travelers Insurance and Citibank.[155] Consequently, Professor Jonathon Macey is quite correct when he asserts, "Glass Steagall was already a dead letter when [GLB] was passed. All the act did was formalize the death."[156]

The material legislation is contained in Title 1 of the act, entitled, "Facilitating Affiliations between Banks, Securities Firms, and Insurance Companies." Section 101 repeals sections 20 and 32 of Glass Steagall, but significant impediments remain. Section 103 of the GLB amends the Bank Holding Company Act[157] by creating a new beast called a financial holding company, which can engage in any activity related to finance, and outside the United States, a financial holding company can acquire any assets of a financial institution whether or not related to finance.[158] All the relevant case law is codified here with respect to bank eligible activities. All this was enacted despite the profitability of banks, in the range of 15 to 18 percent, but the rationale is justified because financial service holding companies actually serve to bolster bank capital that has rapidly deteriorated.[159] Foreign banks' branches are put on a par with U.S. banks and have rights to branch, without special requirement, through a bank holding company.[160] However, commentators still manage to gripe about U.S. leverage ratios that remain in place[161] despite the new G-10 accord.

Title 2 of the act gives the FRB complete control over determining which activities are incidental to banking, thereby eclipsing the authority of the OCC and the OTC.[162] Blatantly absent from GLB is any regulatory oversight of intragroup exposures.[163] The GLB authorizes banks that are state member banks and certain other banks[164] to maintain financial subsidiaries that may underwrite and deal in securities, sell insurance, and serve as a travel agency.[165] Financial subsidiaries must not exceed 45 percent of the bank's total assets or $50 billion. Intraday extensions of credit and other issues involving arm's length terms between affiliates are covered.[166]

The FRB issued a proposed Regulation W, which extends the scope of sections 23A and B of the Federal Reserve Act, which governs loans between banks and their affiliates. In general, banks are required to adequately collateralize all loans and to extend credit only on market terms. Also, Section 23A limits the exposure to each affiliate to 10 percent of bank's capital. As proposed, Regulation W applies to all banks, although the Federal Reserve Act applies only to state member banks. The rule includes (1) quantitative restrictions with individual affiliates and affiliates in the aggregate, (2) collateral requirements for extension of credit to an affiliate (intangibles are not acceptable as collateral), (3) the prohibition on the purchase of low-quality loans from an affiliate, (4) the requirement that all transactions be consistent with "safety and soundness" principles, and (5) the attribution rule, which specifies that any funds used for the benefit of an affiliate will be considered to have been lent directly to the affiliate.[167] In October 2001, the FRB approved J.P. Morgan Chase's application to allow the bank to provide certain indemnities and certain extensions of credit made by the bank for its securities affiliate J.P. Morgan for its securities lending operations.[168]

The International Debt Crisis of 1998 and the Failure of LTCM

The United States intervened in this crisis by using its role in the International Monetary Fund to bail out Asian economies, Brazil, and Russia; the New York Fed was involved in unwinding the positions of LTCM in order to avert the systemic risk of a global financial crisis that would have had repercussions not only internationally but within the United States itself. The situation was new insofar as LTCM was not a bank. As the deputy governor of the Bank of Japan said in a speech to the Bank for International Settlements, we tend to think of the central bank as the lender of last resort (LLR) for banks, whereas financial crises can begin in a nonbank financial institution; yet he admitted that, with regard to the 1998 financial crisis, the position of the Bank of Japan was to remain aloof even as Japanese banks themselves were under siege.[169] According to many sources, the Russian LTCM crisis, unlike the crisis in Asia and Mexico, had spillover effects internationally and was associated with risk aversion in the United States. It was, in the view of market participants, "the worst crisis in recent memory."[170] One component of the crisis that differentiated it from other crises was that the instruments affected were tradable securities rather than bank loans. During this period, the spread between both sovereign debt in emerging markets and traditional corporate bonds, on the one hand, and liquid Treasury securities, on the other, increased dramatically. Even the spread between the 29-year U.S. Treasury bond and the 30-year bond reached dramatic levels. It is now known that LTCM lost more than 55 percent of its end-of-December capital. With assets still at $126 billion, the leverage ratio had increased from 28 to 55 to 1. The New York Fed felt compelled to act, and, on September 23, it urged or required 14 banks to participate in a bailout. What defines this event as contagion is that countries with no particular trading activities with the United States or Asia reacted similarly.[171] Most economists studying contagion see it as unanticipated shocks, a global mood of investor dissatisfaction transmitted across national boundaries.[172] Within a short period, the Board of Governors reacted by cutting interest rates three times between September 29 and November19.[173]

Here we are again back at 23 Wall Street in the panic of 1907, when J.P. Morgan sat around a table and told everyone what they owed to end the panic. The New York Fed, at its inception, was run by Benjamin Strong, a close disciple of Morgan (who had been J.P.'s auditor during the panic of 1907) and had far more power than the Board of Governors.[174] It was only during the Roosevelt administration that power shifted to the Board of Governors. In fact, a huff had developed between the Board of Governors and the New York Fed, with the New York Fed pleading with the Board of Governors to raise interest rates in the spring and summer of 1929.[175] With the New Deal, power had passed to the Board of Governors. But in 1998, a cabal of New York bigwigs had encouraged and succeeded in getting the New York Fed to organize a bailout. And all the Board of Governors could do was follow suit. What had happened is that LTCM was playing with tricky derivatives based on thin spreads between sovereign debt instruments. And where had it gotten this capital from? The money had come from New York money center banks. And how? Merton Miller was a principal of the firm, and he was known as a genius. So the firm just signed for $120 billion. Merton Miller was known for the Miller Modigliani theorem, that a firm's performance was not affected by its debt to equity ratio. He was one of those brilliant young economists with their mathematical machines.[176] LTCM tolled the death knell of finance theory for everyone except the central bankers who continue to practice it. When banks lend to unregulated entities such as LTCM, a hedge fund and, consequently, not a qualified securities firm, they are required to hold 8 or 12 percent of capital. What should have contained banks was the single exposure to one borrower limitation.

My own narrative of how LTCM and the Russian market collapse created the worst disaster in memory is one of constant bailouts: first of Mexico, then of Asia, and then of Russia once again. It is also the case that of the $380 billion in external indebtedness of Asian countries effected at year end 1997, 60 percent had a maturity of less than one year, and the decision to borrow short-term is ascribed to the borrowers, based on their assumption that the exchange rate would remain in a tight band and they could roll over their loans.[177] Were I a banker, these are not the kind of borrowers to whom I would lend $380 billion. I suppose that's the banking business. But the moral hazard associated with international lending in the 1990s began with Mexico. The moral hazard associated with LTCM began with finance theory. More importantly, the fragility of the U.S. banking system, and consequently the world financial system, was revealed.

Enron and Beyond

Banks have been hit by Enron and related corporate scandals principally arising out of their having made loans that were disguised as unfunded swaps and for their transactions involving off-balance sheet entities. J.P. Morgan, Chase, Citigroup, Credit Suisse, Canadian Imperial Bank of Commerce, Barclays, and Deutchebank were all implicated. Interestingly, the complaint, filed by the leading plaintiff class action attorneys, Milberg Weiss Bershad, Hynes and Lerach, linked all the alleged wrongdoings, including violations of 10(b) and 20(a) to the repeal by Gramm-Leach-Bliley[178] of the Glass Steagall Act's restrictions on the combination of commercial and investment banking.[179] In *J.P. Morgan Chase v. Liberty Mutual Insurance*,[180] J.P. Morgan Chase brought suit on behalf of two offshore ostensibly independent entities that had entered into gas and crude oil futures to compel 11 sureties to honor surety bonds guaranteeing the obligation of the sureties to perform (ironically the plaintiffs included two insurance subsidiaries of Citibank). The judge who affirmed "the absolute and unconditional obligation of the sureties to perform" denied the motion for summary judgment because the defendants had shown that arrangements "appear to have been nothing but a disguised loan—or at least to have sufficient indicia thereof that the Court could not possibly grant summary judgment to the plaintiffs."[181] J.P. Morgan subsequently amended the complaint to assert that the insurers were aware that the transactions were loans and had fraudulently concealed their doubts about the enforceability of the sureties.[182] There were rumors that New York District Attorney Robert Morgenthau was considering investigating transactions for violation of New York State's Martin Act.[183] Meanwhile, several banks have filed actions against J.P. Morgan and Citibank. Unicredito Italiano's suit alleges that Citibank and Morgan negligently and fraudulently misrepresented Enron's financial condition, thus inducing Unicredito to fund its share of a loan participation agreement of which Citibank and Morgan were lead banks. The complaint emphasizes the multifaceted relation of these two banks with Enron, and specifically notes the role played by them in helping Enron create off-balance sheet entities that were used to fraudulently conceal Enron's deteriorating financial condition.[184] The Dutch Bank Rabobank filed suit in New York State Supreme Court against Royal Bank of Canada.[185] Rabobank imputes knowledge of Enron's true financial condition through three employees. These three employees were charged with fraud in a federal criminal complaint based on a scheme to defraud their former employee Nat West. The Unicredito Italiano complaint terms Enron, Citibank's and Morgan's "client, partner, and borrower."[186]

While no banks have incurred any liability thus far, when banks begin to eat their own kind, there is cause for alarm. The specific allegation that the repeal of Glass Steagall was responsible for the fiasco may hit closer to the mark than any other prose written by Milberg Weiss. It may be that banks acting as investment banks and taking on more roles than would be prudent were in part responsible for Enron's collapse. But Citibank and J.P. Morgan Chase have been criticized for the expansion of their investment banking activities. There are current probes into Salomon Bros., a Citibank subsidiary, and J.P. Morgan's expansion into venture capital in its acquisition of Hambrecht Quist is, in part, responsible for its staying the course in the Telcom sector, which contributed substantially to the dramatic fall in its market capitalization (from $100 billion to $40 billion as of September 2002).[187] The *Financial Times* concludes about CEO Bill Harisson, "His vision of creating a universal bank dominant in syndicated lending, debt underwriting, trading, derivatives, private equity, and asset management is now in jeopardy."[188] J.P. Morgan offered a rather dubious defense to the reporters: "In its defense, J.P. Morgan says it does not lend money to gain investment banking business any more than its competitors."[189] But, the current situation puts J.P. Morgan in the ironic position of justifying the reenactment of Glass-Steagall-type legislation, even though J.P. Morgan and Company was split down the middle by the original Glass Steagall Act despite lack of evidence that its investment banking arm contributed to the Wall Street crash.[190]

The Composition of Banks and Finance Company Assets

In the early 1990s banks held a great deal of U.S. treasuries and made profits on the spread between long-term treasuries and interest rate deposits. With the shrinking of the U.S. budget deficit, the composition of bank assets has changed considerably. Consumer and industrial loans have increased sharply, but the composition of this asset is definitely declining as highly rated borrowers have increasingly fled to the securities markets. While mortgage-backed securities and consumer lending increased sharply in the mid-1990s, they fell considerably afterward, no doubt reflecting the trend toward securitization, but rose by 8 percent in 2000, reflecting perhaps the greater difficulties faced in securitizing credit card receivables; yet only 10 percent of banks reported tightening their standards for credit card debt.[191] Banks are supposed to have originated 40 percent of credit card securitizations.[192] Home equity loans jumped 24 percent in 2000.[193] Exposure to commercial real estate has grown at more than 10 percent annually since the mid-1990s.[194] It is a truism to say that the quality of the assets on balance sheets has declined precipitously, given the shift out of treasuries to agencies paper and the growth of commercial real estate lending. Supposedly, banks tightened their lending standards in the latter part of 2000 and while commercial and industrial loans rose only by 2 percent, yet they unloaded high-risk loans that they reported, under the flexibility allotted them, as amounting to only 6 percent of the consumer and industrial (C&I) category.[195]

Altogether, commercial banks have over $6 trillion in assets,[196] dwarfing the assets of finance companies, which total about $1.1 trillion.[197] Yet, finance companies grew almost 50 percent from 1996 to 2000.[198] They had cumulatively owned and securitized approximately $431 billion of consumer loans, which makes consumer loans in the present portfolio of banks and the cumulative portfolio of insurance companies about $900 billion. Add another

$100 billion or so for bank-originated securitizations and the total is about an even trillion. To paraphrase Everett Dirksen, or rather to update his remarks, a trillion here and a trillion there, and soon you're talking about real money. Finance companies had also owned or securitized about $180 billion of mortgages. Certainly, many, if not most, of these must be equity or second mortgages.

How banks rate their own assets provides insight into the internal rating systems espoused by the new G-10 accord.[199] Although the accord has not been formally implemented with the exception of the 1996 Amendment on Market Risk,[200] U.S. banks, at least, have begun to orient themselves to the terminology of the accord. Consequently, the probability of default (PD) and the expected loss (EL) and grades of corporate loans are already incorporated into the vernacular of most U.S. banks.[201]

From the household side of the equation, Americans have continuously decreased their savings to the point where they are now net debtors. Not surprisingly, banks have chosen to grade their loans as point in time rather than through the cycle, i.e., assessing the current condition of the loan rather than how the loan would perform under stress, which is how rating agencies evaluate loans.[202] The PD and the probability of default on a particular loan (LIED)[203] are supposed to be factored together to produce the EL. Yet, only about 40 percent of banks have a two-dimensional approach, although banks would probably dispute this, claiming that the individual exposure is factored in. Forty-eight of the 50 largest banks have watch lists that correspond to regulatory standards for problem loans,[204] but on all other loans labeled "pass" by regulators, the number of grades varies from two to the low twenties.[205] Most banks do not rate retail loans unless they securitize them.[206] Relationship managers rather than the credit staff appraise small and medium-size loans, generally since they are considered to be in a better position.[207] Even at large banks, unwritten and cultural considerations about loans seem to predominate.[208] A loan review staff has final determination over assets and tends to examine only a sample of loans in each category.[209] Mapping, using external credit information about bond default rates, can be useful, but since banks use a current status rather than through the cycle approach, mapping can result in overestimating the PD in an upturn and underestimating it in a downturn.[210] Banks have also tended to underestimate the risks associated with corporate bonds. However, in the rated categories (by external rating agencies), and likely to be reflected in the commercial and industrial category (about half of overall bank assets),[211] the largest banks, at year end 1997, had 45 percent of assets that were rated BB or worse, regional banks 60 percent and small banks (with under $25 billion in assets) 75 percent.[212] Certainly, this will have only deteriorated in the current financial market.

In my judgment, the quality of assets of commercial banks, let alone other categories of banks, is appalling. The mixture of loans, consumer, second-rate corporate, and commercial real estate is the result of disintermediation. Although bank profitability has been high in the last few years, banks, as stand-alone units, when compared with A or better rated commercial firms, are really junk status. The new G-10 accord, in its complex variations, other than by standardizing classes of loans and requiring reporting of retail banking exposures, will do little to ameliorate the situation that is the result of macroeconomic forces and financial deregulation. More appalling than the situation of banks is the status of household savings in America, which contributes directly to bank profitability and the quality of assets, but has also caused the influx of foreign capital to rise to unsustainable rates.

MACROECONOMIC CONSEQUENCES

The External Debt of the United States and Its Possible Consequences

In 2000, the current account deficit was approximately $460 billion.[213] It was slightly less in 2001 at $400 billion. The last few years represent the highest ever in absolute terms and as a percent of GDP (or certainly since 1914). In 1986, it approached 3 percent of GDP until it fell to 0 in 1991.[214] The current account, simply stated, is the amount we spend over the amount we save and includes goods and services and interest and other income flows from portfolio investment. This amount is ultimately offset by income from foreign direct and portfolio investment (268 payments—159 receipts).[215] That is the interest on external debt that represents the net return on capital from investment income.

The amount of the trade deficit is offset by net capital flows from foreign sources to the United States, which have risen. The overall U.S. net investment position has fallen from about $0 in 1995 to $1.5 trillion in 2001 and nearing $2.8 trillion by year end 2003.[216] The nature of foreign direct investment has changed from being composed principally of U.S. treasuries to being composed of a mixture of debt and equity. Transactions in U.S. equity securities accounted for by foreigners have risen from less than 1 percent to 20 percent in less than a decade.[217] At the same time cross-border lending by U.S. banks fell 50 percent. The staff of the Division of International Finance at the FRB concludes, on the first page of its article, that "cross border transactions in securities are now great enough to significantly affect national [U.S.] markets and to significantly affect the health of the international financial system."[218] In the period of 1994 to 2000, China's position increased fivefold while Luxembourg's increased 20 percent. The increase in Luxembourg's position, in which it held more securities in the United States than its GDP, reflects the problem with offshore banking centers. We do not know the nationality of the actual holder of the debt, given custodial accounts and the complexity of booking entries. Canada and the European countries held more equity than debt in 2000, while the Asian countries and the offshore

Caribbean facilities held more debt than equity.[219] Nominally, residents of Japan and the United Kingdom have consistently led other countries with total assets nearing approximately $500 billion each. Canada and other European countries account for another $300 billion while the unknown category accounts for about the same, and the rest of the world an even trillion. Net foreign acquisitions of U.S. securities were $461 billion in 2000 and were higher for 2001.[220] The overwhelming percentage of portfolio investment is debt rather than equity, but the composition of this debt has shifted substantially from treasuries to independent agencies such as Federal National Mortgage Association (Fannie Mae) and Government National Mortgage Association (Ginnie Mac) and corporate bonds.[221] One would also assume that asset securitization, particularly of consumer debt and equity linked bonds, accounts for a sizeable proportion of these securities.[222] Consequently, one is inclined to agree that international transmissions of news are more than ever likely to affect the performance of U.S. capital markets and directly affect the price of debt instruments.

Household Savings Rates and the Consequences for the U.S. Economy

The U.S. savings rate is negative. Despite slowing economic activity in 2001, household debt increased 7¾ percent and now totals (including mortgage indebtedness) $7.2 trillion, double the amount in 1991 at the beginning of the U.S. economic expansion.[223] Home mortgage debt, including equity-linked mortgages, rose 98 percent in this period and accounts for 70 percent of indebtedness. (Other consumer debt also doubled, although this might be slightly overstated, because of greater use of credit cards, which, even if paid when due, reflect indebtedness.) Home equity lending was up 142 percent to $619 billion for the same period; the good news is that households had $47.1 trillion in assets.[224] The composition of household assets has changed. In 1991, households had 15 percent of their assets in corporate equity and now hold 27 percent of their assets in corporate equity (down from 36 percent in 2000),[225] and 52 percent versus 44 percent of corporate equity is held indirectly. (About 40 percent of the total is held in retirement accounts.) The market value of owner-occupied homes has risen by $4.6 trillion to $11.3 trillion (about 55 percent of it equity, $5.7 trillion), compared to a market value of $12.8 trillion in directly and indirectly held equities. Naturally, a great deal of equities are concentrated in a smaller percentage of the population than home ownership. Householders were net sellers of equity, selling a net $1.6 trillion in equity, although their overall percentage of equity increased as a result of capital gains on equities held; pension funds were also net sellers, while mutual funds were net purchasers of $900 billion in equities.[226]

This is the story of negative savings of households, the erosion of bank balance sheets, and the enormous deterioration of the net debtor position of the United States. Obviously, households have come to rely on equity appreciation in order to fulfill their lifestyles. The corporate sector has embarked on a net investment program and replaced equity with debt. Householders rely on the appreciation of their homes to ensure their financial position. In the event that the housing market depreciates, large withdrawals from the equity market, particularly the mutual fund sector, are assured. Conversely, it seems intuitive that any major correction in the market will lead to reduced consumption. Corporations are vulnerable to rises in interest rate. The shortage of domestic savings makes the United States very vulnerable to the appetite of international investors for U.S. equities. This appetite cannot be sustainable. While the United States might offer better prospects for investment than other places, it is vulnerable to interest rate and exchange rate shocks. The first will cause foreign investors to flee to treasuries; the second will cause foreign investors to demand higher interest rates for U.S. investment, and then to flee to treasuries. It seems that, from whichever angle one regards the problem of negative net savings of households and the extraordinary and unsustainable capital flows to the United States, the system is almost certain to contract.

CONCLUSION

The deteriorating quality of banking assets is equally worrisome. While the complete prohibition of bank securities affiliation has not withstood the test of time and no longer makes sense, since securities underwriting has proved the safer activity as the result of disintermediation, I would only allow banks to own securities firms if they did so through a financial holding company and deducted the capital of the securities firm from bank capital to avoid double leverage (in all jurisdictions bank capital is deducted from securities firms capital since it is not immediately available).[227]

More importantly, capital has been diverted from home equity, withdrawn in the form of consumer credit card debt or equity linked mortgages. Banks should be made to reassess their consumer debt portfolios, including equity-linked mortgages. Ultimately, tighter standards will result in decreased banking profitability but increased banking safety and soundness. Banks have had a good ride. Now it is time for them to engage in prudent lending.

However, these changes in prudential supervision and accounting standards will not exist in a vacuum. We cannot support the external debt. Although Fred Bergsten is quite correct when he says that one and a half trillion dollars is not an excessive amount of external debt for the United States,[228] the debt is growing at over $400 billion a year. It is the amplitude of growth that cannot be supported. In order to save, private consumption must be reduced and that will inevitably mean GDP reduction. Only a broad middle-class tax cut, coupled with limitations on equity linked mortgages and consumer debt, may lead to a soft landing. Increasingly, this is unlikely without a large-scale devaluation of the dollar and a precipitous growth in exports. To understand the cause of U.S. trade and current account deficit, it is necessary to be familiar with the political economy of Japan and other Asian countries that rely on trade surpluses.

On July 31, 2002, President Bush signed into law the Sarbanes-Oxley Act, which created the most far-reaching changes in corporate governance and regulation of the accounting profession since the New Deal. This legislation is the subject of chapter 6, which will also consider possible future reform.

NOTES

1. Jacob Schlesinger, "The Deregulator: Did Washington Set the Stage for Current Business Turmoil?" *Wall Street Journal*, October 17, 2002, p. 1, A-12.

2. Federal Reserve Board (FRB), "Structural Changes in the New Economy" (Remarks by Chairman Alan Greenspan before the National Governors Assoc., July 11, 2000).

3. *Ibid.*

4. Private Securities Litigation Act, Section 101, amending the Securities Act of 1933, adding Section 27.

5. The Eighth Annual Abraham Pomerantz Lecture, "The Social Meaning of Shareholder Suits," *Brooklyn Law Review* 65 (1999), p. 3.

6. Jill Fisch, "Lawyers on the Auction Block: Evaluating the Selection of Class Counsel by Auction," *Columbia Law Review* 102 (2002), p. 650.

7. Private Securities Litigation Act Section 101 b 2 Required State of Mind.

8. *Ibid.*, 3(c)2.

9. *Ibid.*, c 4.

10. *Ibid.*, Section 105, amending Section 12 of the Securities Act of 1933 (15 U.S.C. 77l).

11. *Ibid.*, Title II Reduction of Coercive Settlement Section 201 Proportionate Liability amending Section 21D of the Securities and Exchange Act of 1934, (g)2B. Under Section 10(B), reckless conduct shall not be construed to constitute a knowing commission of a violation of the securities law.

12. 183 F.3d 542 (1999).

13. *New York Times*, December 12, 2001.

14. Securities and Exchange Commission (SEC), "Notice of Proposed Rule Change to NASD Rules Relating to 'Hot Equity' Offerings," Release no. 34-42325 (January 10, 2000).

15. SEC, Division of Market Regulation, Staff Legal Bulletin no. 10, "Prohibited Solicitations and 'Tie in' Agreements for 'After-Market' Purchases" (Aug. 25, 2000). The release states that such agreements and solicitations violated rule 101 and 102 of Regulation M (17 C.F.R. 242 Rule 101 and 102) and may violate antifraud and anti-manipulation provisions of the securities laws generally.

16. *Ibid.*

17. Diana Heinriches, "Investing It, a Question of Fees," *New York Times*, Sept. 13, 1998, Section 3, p. 7.

18. "Spitzer, Merrill Lynch Reach Unprecedented Agreement to Reform Invest-

ment Practices" (Press Office of the Attorney General State of New York, May 21, 2002).

19. SEC, "Selective Disclosure and Insider Trading," Final Rule, SEC Release no. 33-7881, 34-43154 (effective October 23, 2000). Regulation FD does not establish a duty of disclosure under 10b-5 or give rise to a private right of action. A "knowing or reckless" conduct standard applies, ensuring that liability will arise only when an issuer or its personnel "knows" or "is reckless in not knowing" that the disclosure is both material and nonpublic. This regulation can only be enforced by the SEC and does not give rise to a private right of action.

20. Arthur Levitt with Paula Dwyer, *Take on the Street: What Wall Street and Corporate America Don't Want You to Know/What You Can Do to Fight Back* (Pantheon Books, 2002), p. 28; rules in 2001 required brokers to disclose, each quarter, where they send orders and whether they receive a rebate.

21. *Ibid.*, p. 45.

22. *Ibid.*, p. 67.

23. *Ibid.*, p. 73.

24. *Ibid.*, pp. 94–95.

25. *See* chapter 5, "Lobbying. . . ."

26. *Op. cit.* pp. 112–13.

27. *Ibid.*, p. 115.

28. Jacob Schlesinger, "The Deregulator: Did Washington Set the Stage for Current Business Turmoil?" *Wall Street Journal*, October 17, 2002, p. 1, A-12.

29. *Op. cit.*, p. 1.

30. SEC, "Final Rule: Revision of the Commission's Auditor Independence Requirements," SEC Release no. 33-7919, 34-43602 (Feb. 5, 2001).

31. Arthur Levitt, "The Numbers Game" (Remarks before the NYU Center for Law and Business, September 28, 1998).

32. Report and Recommendations of the Blue Ribbon Committee on Improving the Effectiveness of Corporate Audit Committees (1999). *See generally*, ABA, Section of Business Law, "The Post-Enron Role of Audit Committees" (Paper presented by the Committee on Criminal Laws at an annual meeting, August 9–13, 2002).

33. *Ibid.*, pp. 27–28.

34. *Ibid.*, pp. 29–31.

35. 240 C.F.R. Section 14(a)(101) (1999).

36. *See* chapter 6, notes 3 and 4. The National Association of Dealers Automated Quotations (NASDAQ) rule also required a formal charter. The New York Stock Exchange relegated financial judgment to the business judgment of the board. *See also* chapter 8, notes 2 and 3.

37. Carrie Johnson, "After Enron, A New Focus on Board," *Washington Post*, March 8, 2002, at E1.

38. *Supra* note 30.

39. *See* chapter 6, notes 58 to 62, and accompanying text.

40. Reed Abelson, "Enron's Many Strands: Boardroom Reactions; Trying Not to Be the Next Enron," *New York Times*, Jan. 26, 2002, at E1.

41. *Ibid.*

42. Richard A. Oppel, Jr., "Enron's Many Strands: Early Warnings; Lawyer at Enron Warned Officials of Dubious Deals," *New York Times*, Feb. 7, 2002, at A1.

43. *See* chapter 6, "Certification and Economic Crime. . . ."

44. Model Business Corporation Act, Section 8.30; however, courts have held inside directors to a higher standard of care because of their position.

45. *Feit v. Leasco Leasing and Data Processing Equip. Corp.*, 332 F. Supp. 544 (E.D.N.Y. 1971).

46. *Tischler v. Baltimore Bank Corp.*, 801 F. Supp. 1493 (D.Md 1992) and *In re* Am International, Incorporate Securities Litigation, 606 F. Supp. 600 (S.D.N.Y. 1985).

47. *Infra* note 147.

48. *Infra* note 148.

49. "Materiality," SAB no. 99; 64 Fed. Reg. 45150 (1999); "Restructuring and Impairment Charges," SAB no. 100; 64 Fed. Reg. 64291 (1999) and "Revenue Recognition in Financial Statements," SAB no. 101; 64 Fed. Reg. 1122290 (1999).

50. 17 C.F.R. § 229.10 (2001). The Securities and Exchange Commission also amended Item 302(a) of Regulation S-K to require certain financial data for the past two-year period. (17 C.F.R. § 228.302[a].) New Item 306 of Regulation S-K (17 C.F.R. 306 [2001]) and Item 7(d) of Schedule 14(a) (240 C.F.R. § 14[a]) would also require the company to include a report by an outside auditor. Companies were also required to disclose whether auditors were independent (17 C.F.R. § 228.306[a][3] and 229.306[a][3]).

51. Under Item 306(a) of Regulation S-K or 7(e)(3) of 14(a), and these disclosures would be subject to limited liability under Regulation 14(a) or (c) (SEC, Final Rule, "Audit Committee Disclosure," 64 Fed. Reg. 73389 [1999]).

52. *Take on the Street, supra* note 20, p. 117.

53. *Ibid.*, p. 119.

54. *Ibid.*, p. 122; *See* chapter 5, note 149, and accompanying text.

55. *Ibid.*, p. 170.

56. *Ibid.*, pp. 160–74.

57. *See* chapter 6, "Certification and Economic Crime. . . ."

58. *See* chapter 5, notes 215 to 218, and accompanying text.

59. *See supra* notes 13, 14, 21, and 22.

60. *See infra* notes 101 to 103.

61. *Take on the Street, supra* note 20, p. 131, citing a study by the Center for Responsive Politics.

62. *Ibid.*, p. 247, citing a study by the Center for Responsive Politics.

63. Speech by Commissioner Hunt before the 31st Annual Meeting of the Institute on Securities Regulation, November 4, 1999, citing Staff Accounting Bulletin no. 99 (SAB 99).

64. *Ibid.*

65. SEC, Release no. 33-8090, "Proposed Rules for Disclosure of Certain Management Transactions" (April 12, 2002), amending Form 8K and adding disclosure on a current basis of certain management transactions including loans of money to a corporate officer or director.

66. SEC, Release no. 33-8009, "Proposed Rules for Accelerating Periodic Reports Filing Dates and Access to Web Information."

67. *See infra* note 74.

68. *Supra* note 4.

69. Financial Accounting Standard Board Rulebook.

70. Exposure Draft, Amendment of Statement 133 on Derivative Instruments and

Hedging Activities (May 1, 2001) replacing par. 6b. *See also* Tentative Guidance (May 6, 2002).

71. "Ex Official of Worldcom Pleads Guilty to Fraud," *New York Times*, August 9, 2002.

72. "$7.1B in Errors," *CNN/Money*, August 9, 2002.

73. *Op. cit.*

74. SEC, Proposed Release no. 33-8098 "Disclosure in Management Discussion and Analysis about Critical Accounting Methods" (May 10, 2002).

75. *Ibid.*, B. *See* footnote 40 of the proposal and accompanying text.

76. *Ibid.*

77. *Ibid.*, C.

78. *Ibid.*, 3 and 4.

79. *See* chapter 3, note 123, and accompanying text.

80. *Ibid.*

81. *See* chapter 2, notes 53 to 56.

82. "Critical Accounting Methods," *supra* note 74, Section 5: Requests for Comment between Senior Management and the Audit Committee.

83. *Ibid.*, 6 Disclosure Relating to Segments.

84. *Ibid.*, K. Application of Safe Harbors to Forward Looking Information.

85. *See* note 103.

86. *See supra* note 4 and accompanying text.

87. Pitt cites Section 7B of the Securities Act and Section 13 of the Securities and Exchange Act.

88. Testimony of Alauna Peter before the Senate Committee on Banking, Housing, and Urban Affairs (March 20, 2002).

89. *Ibid.*

90. *Ibid.*

91. Testimony of Charles Bowsher before the Senate Committee on Banking, Housing, and Urban Affairs (March 20, 2002).

92. Testimony of Sarah Teslik before the Senate Committee on Banking, Housing, and Urban Affairs.

93. Testimony of Financial Accounting Standards Board Chairman Jenkins before the Senate Committee on Banking, Housing, and Urban Affairs (March 20, 2002).

94. Report of Investigation by the Special Investigative Committee of the Board of Directors of Enron Corp., William Powers, chair, Raymond Troubh, Herbert Winokur, Wilmer Cutler Pickering counsel (February 1, 2002), at 3.

95. *Ibid.*, at 3.

96. *Ibid.*, at 49–50.

97. *Ibid.*, at 52.

98. *Ibid.*

99. *Ibid.*, at 103–4.

100. *See* chapter 3, notes 82–86, and accompanying text.

101. SEC, "In the matter of Trump Casinos and Resorts, Inc.," Accounting and Auditing Release no. 1499, Administrative Proceeding File no. 3-10680 (Jan. 16, 2002).

102. *Ibid.*

103. SEC, Release nos. 33-8039; 34-45124 (January 22, 2001).

104. NIRI/FEI Guidelines.

105. SEC, Proposed Rule, "Additional 8K Disclosure Requirements and Acceleration of Filing Date," Release no. 33-8106; 34-46084, File no. S7, 22-02.

106. *Ibid.*

107. *Ibid.*, item 101.

108. *Ibid.*, item 102.

109. *Ibid.*, item 103.

110. *Ibid.*, item 202.

111. *Ibid.*, item 203.

112. *Ibid.*, item 204.

113. *Ibid.*, item 205.

114. *Ibid.*, item 301.

115. *Ibid.*, item 302.

116. *Ibid.*, item 303.

117. *Ibid.*, item 304.

118. *Ibid.*, item 402. There is a minor amendment regarding change of certifying accountant item 401; minor changes to Changes in Control of Registrant item 501.

119. *Ibid.*, item 502.

120. *Ibid.*, item 502 c and d.

121. *Ibid.*, item 503.

122. *Ibid.*, item 504.

123. *Ibid.*, Questions regarding waivers of corporate codes of conduct.

124. *See supra* note 74.

125. *Ibid.*, Questions regarding critical accounting method.

126. SEC, Final Rule, "EDGAR Filing for Foreign Issuers," Securities Act Release no. 33-8099, Exchange Act 34-45922 (May 14, 2002).

127. *Infra* note 148.

128. *Infra* note 147.

129. *SEC v. Texas Gulf*, 401 F.2d 833 (1968).

130. *See Taylor v. First Union Corp. of South Carolina*, 875 2d 240 (cert. denied 489 US 1080), *Hartford Fire Insurance v. Federated*, 723 F. Supp. 976 (S.D.N.Y. 1989) in which bondholders were not informed about merger talks that would make their bonds riskier. But *see In re* Columbia, 724 F. Supp. 237 (S.D.N.Y. 1990).

131. *Buxbaum v. Deutche Bank A. G.* The chief executive officer (CEO) denied talks of a takeover in an interview. Fed. Sec. L. Rep. (CCH) Par. 90969 (S.D.N.Y. 2000).

132. 501 U.S. 1083 (1991), 111 South Court 2749 (1991).

133. *Ibid.*

134. *Ibid.*, and 886 F.2d 1109 (9th Cir. 1989).

135. 948 F.2d 507 (9th Cir. 1991).

136. Fed. Sec. L. Rep. (CCH) 94502 (N.D. Cal. 1989).

137. Fed. Sec. L. Rep. (CCH) 94742 (N.D. Ca. 1988) affirm. 935 F.2d 1470 (9th Cir. 1991).

138. 704 F. Supp. 1296 (D.N.J. 1989).

139. SEC, Exchange Act release no. 30532 (March 31, 1992). *See also*, *In re* Shared Medical Systems Corporation Exchange Act, SEC Release no. 33632 (Feb. 17, 1994).

140. SEC, Exchange Act Release no. 34046 (May 12, 1994).

141. *See also*, America West, Exchange Act Release no. 340407 (May 12, 1994).

142. SEC, Exchange Act Release no. 34-36877 (Feb. 26, 1996).

143. Fed. Sec. L. Rep. (CCH) Par. 98714 (N.D. Va.).

144. *Greenstone v. Cambes Corporation* Fed. Sec. L. Rep. 96904 (D. Mass.). In *Anderson v. Abbot Laboratories*, Fed. Sec. L. Rep. (CCH) 91340 (N.D. Illinois 2001). The failure of a pharmaceutical company to report an FDA investigation was ruled non-material.

145. SEC, Release no. 34-46079 S7-21-02.

146. *Ibid.*

147. *TSC v. Northway*, 426 U.S. 228 at 449.

148. *Basic v. Levinson* 485 U.S. 224 (1988).

149. *Ibid.*, at 239.

150. *See* chapter 2, notes 179–180, and accompanying text.

151. *See supra* note 4 and accompanying text.

152. Pub. Law no. 106-102, Nov. 12, 1999, 113 Stat. 1338 (1999) codified in scattered sections of 12,15,16,18, U.S.C.A.

153. *J.P. Morgan and Co., Inc., Chase Manhattan Corp., Bankers Trust New York Corp., Citicorp, and Securities Pacific Corp.* (75 Fed. Reserve Bull. 192 [March 1989]). These prudential prohibitions were in addition to other prohibitions contained in an earlier FRB order allowing banks to underwrite a narrow range of eligible securities (*Citicorp/Morgan/Bankers Trust*, 73 Fed. Reserve Bull. at 485), and preclude the holding company or any affiliate from purchasing eligible securities from the subsidiary during the underwriting and for 60 days thereafter (*J.P. Morgan, supra* note 184, at 202). The *J.P. Morgan* decision changes this to 30 days (*Ibid.*, at 208), and prevents banks from lending to issuers to enhance the creditworthiness of securities underwritten by underwriting subsidiaries. (Note that under *Bankers Trust 1*, [Bankers Trust 1, 408 U.S. 134 (1984)] commercial paper is a security [it has always been treated as such in Europe] and is also subject to Section 5 of the Securities and Exchange Act, despite particular exemptions under the act.) The application of § 5 (registration requirements) of the Securities Exchange Act has been known to result in U.S. persons being excluded from investment opportunities. (*See* The Division of Market Regulatory Securities and Exchange, Commission Summary of Internationalization Roundtable on February 17, 1987, p. 21. *See also*, "Note, Moving Away from Section 5," *U. Pa. J. Int. Bus. L.* 102 [1988], p. 225.)

154. Revenue Limit on Bank-Ineligible Activities of Subsidiaries of Bank Holding Companies Engaged in Underwriting and Dealing in Securities, 61 Fed. Reg. 68750, 68752 (Dec. 30, 1996).

155. Traveler's Group, Inc./Citibank, Inc. "Order Approving Formation of a Bank Holding Company and Notices to Engage in Nonbanking Activities" (under Section 3 of the Bank Holding Company Act of 1956 [12 U.S.C. 1842]) (Sept. 23, 1998).

156. Jonathon Macey, "The Business of Banking: Before and After Gramm-Leach-Bliley," *Journal of Corporation Law* (summer 2000): p. 690.

157. Specifically Section 4 of the Bank Holding Company Act of 1956, 12 U.S.C.A. 1843.

158. GLB Title I, section 4.

159. *See* "Enron and Beyond" (this chapter).

160. *Op. cit.*

161. *See* chapter 2, note 43.

162. *Ibid.*, Title 2.

163. *See* chapter 2, notes 78–79, chapter 3, notes 132–133, and chapter 6, "The EU Proposed Directive. . . ."

164. The Options Clearing Corporation (OCC) has authorized its member banks to have financial subsidiaries also.

165. GLB, *infra* note 152 Section 121; the specific requirements are set forth in 12 C.F.R. 208.71.

166. *Ibid.*, GLB, 12 U.S.C. § 24a(a)(6). There are additional limitations including acting as a principal in insurance underwriting with certain exceptions and issuing annuities or dealing in real estate development or investment with certain exceptions. Banks must be "well managed" as determined with reference to specific examination ratings. If a bank is one of the 100 largest banks, it must have one class of debt securities issued that is investment grade recognized by one of the three national statistical rating agencies (*see* chapter 6, "The Role of Rating Agencies" and accompanying text). The second 50 of the 100 largest banks can meet these rules or equivalent rules established jointly by the FRB and the Treasury. These rules do not apply unless the financial subsidiary engages in any of the newly authorized activities. Under the rule in 12 CFR 208.71., banks must deconsolidate capital ratios and deduct the equity investment in the subsidiary for capital adequacy purposes (deducting 50 percent from tier one and tier two capital and 100 capital from tier one capital for purposes of leverage ratios). Under this rule, financial subsidiaries are considered affiliates for purposes of Section 23(A) and (B) of the Federal Reserve Act. Banks may not engage in activities that are complementary to banking under the Bank Holding Company Act Section 4(k)(1), unless the secretary of the Treasury determines that such activities are permissible for financial subsidiaries.

167. 12 C.F.R. Part 250.243,244,245. Final Rules clarifying indirect credit extensions that may benefit affiliates and extending an exemption to securities that have a readily identifiable and public market and prohibitions on the purchase of poor quality assets from affiliates are covered in 12 C.F.R. Part 250. Provisions applying the interim and final rules to nonstate member banks are self-executing through existing prior legislation. A final Regulation W will be issued by the FRB around November 2002.

168. For example, FRB, Letter to J.P. Morgan Chase for exemption from 23A of the Federal Reserve Act, 12 U.S.C. 371c (October 31, 2001), for certain indemnities and certain extensions of credit to J.P. Morgan Securities Inc. in connection with its securities lending.

169. Bank for International Settlements, Committee on the Global Financial System, Speech of Yatacha Yamaguchi at the Third Joint Central Bank Research Conference on Risk Measurement and Systemic Risk (March 7, 2002).

170. "International Contagion, Spillover Effects of the Russia and LTCM Crisis," prepared by Mardi Duney, Rene Fry, Brenda Gonzalez-Hermosillo, and Vance Martin Vance (Presented at the Bank for International Settlements, the Committee on the Global Financial System, March 7, 2002).

171. *Ibid.*

172. For example, G. L. Kaminsky and S. L. Shmuckler, "What Triggers Market Jitters: A Chronicle of the Asia Crisis," *Journal of International Money and Finance* 18, no. 4: pp. 537–60. They make no distinction between anticipated and unanticipated events. The centerpiece of their argument is that the biggest mood swings occur on days of no news.

173. *Op. cit.*, p. 11.

174. *House of Morgan*, cited in the introduction, note 4, pp. 181–82, 244.
175. *Ibid.*, p. 313.
176. For an excellent overview of Finance Theory, *see* Peter Bernstein, *Capital Ideas: The Improbable Origins of Modern Wall Street* (New York: Free Press, 1992).
177. Bank for International Settlements, "Report of the Working Group on Strengthening Financial Systems," sec. 2.2.3 (October 1998).
178. *See* "Gramm-Leach-Bliley . . ." (this chapter).
179. Consolidated Complaints for Violation of Securities Laws at Par. 643, *Mark Newby et al. v. Enron Corp. et al.* (Civil Action H-01-3624). *See also* American Bar Association, Committee on Banking Law, "After Enron: How Many Roles Can Banks Play?" p. 5.
180. 189 F. Supp. 2d 24 (S.D.N.Y. 2002).
181. *Ibid.*
182. "Chase Counters Accusers in Disguised-Loan Case—Insurers Were Not Deceived, Bank Says," *New York Times*, July 2, 2002, p. C2.
183. "J.P. Morgan, Citigroup Face Fresh Scrutiny in Work with Enron," *Wall Street Journal*, July 2, 2002, p. C1.
184. *Unicredito Italiano v. J. P Morgan Chase, Inc. and Citigroup* (D. Delaware, C.A. no. 02-104).
185. *Cooperative Centrale Raifessan-Boerenleen Bank B.V. v. Royal Bank of Canada* and Does 1–20.
186. *Op. cit.*, par. 65.
187. *See generally*, "J.P. Morgan Plunge Reflects Fears over Strategy," *Financial Times*, September 19, 2002, p. 27.
188. Lisa Saigal, Gary Silverman, and Charles Petzlik, "Harrison in Line of Fire as his Vision Crumbles," *Financial Times*, September 19, 2002, p. 27.
189. *Ibid.*
190. *See* introduction, note 4, and accompanying text.
191. Federal Reserve Bank, Division of Monetary Affairs, "Profits and Balance Sheet of Commercial Banks in 2000," Federal Reserve Bulletin (June 2001), p. 367.
192. *Ibid.*, p. 373.
193. *Ibid.*
194. *Ibid.*
195. *Ibid.*, p. 371, FRB Survey of Terms of Business Lending.
196. *Ibid.*, p. 368.
197. FRB, Division of Research and Statistics, "Survey of Finance Companies," Federal Reserve Bulletin (January 2002), p. 1.
198. *Ibid.*
199. *See* chapter 2, "The Committee on Banking and Supervisory Practices."
200. *See* chapter 2, note 43, and accompanying text.
201. Federal Reserve Board, Division of Banking Supervision and Regulation, "Credit Risk Rating at Large U.S. Banks," Federal Reserve Bulletin (November 1998), p. 897.
202. *Ibid.*, p. 898, about a quarter of banks have a one year horizon, one quarter have a longer horizon, and half have no specific time period at all.
203. *See* chapter 2, notes 22, 29, 33, 38, 41–42, and accompanying text.
204. "Credit Risk Rating at Large U.S. Banks," *supra* note 201, p. 901. Other Assets Especially Mentioned (OAEM) Substandard, doubtful and loss. Some omit the loss category.

205. *Ibid.*, p. 902. Among the 25 largest banks, 36 percent assign half or more of their loans to a single risk grade.
206. *Ibid.*
207. *Ibid.*, p. 904.
208. *Ibid.*, p. 907.
209. *Ibid.*, p. 908.
210. *Ibid.*, p. 914.
211. About $3.5 trillion.
212. *Op. cit.*, p. 917.
213. William Helkie, "Use of International Transactions in 2001," Federal Reserve Bulletin (May 2002), p. 235.
214. *Ibid.*, p. 236, chart, Sources: Department of Commerce and Bureau of Economic Analysis.
215. *Ibid.*, p. 243, chart 7, Source: Bureau of Economic Analysis.
216. *Ibid.*, p. 244. The net portfolio position is about negative $1.8 trillion, the difference being accounted for by the surplus position in U.S. foreign direct investment.
217. Division of International Finance, Federal Reserve Board, "The U.S. System for Measuring Cross Border Positions and Securities: A Primer with Discussion of Recent Developments," Federal Reserve Bulletin (October 2001), p. 634.
218. *Ibid.*
219. *Ibid.*, p. 637.
220. *Ibid.*, Sources: Treasury International Capital (TIC) reporting system and Bureau of Economic Analysis.
221. *Ibid.* In 2000, $280 billion in debt compared to $180 billion in equity, but historically, between 1995–99, $204 billion compared to $63 billion.
222. *See* note 191 *supra.*
223. "The U.S. Accounts and Their Uses," Federal Reserve Bulletin (July 2001), pp. 431, 434.
224. *Ibid.*, p. 436.
225. *Ibid.*
226. *Ibid.*
227. *See* chapter 2, notes 74–75, and accompanying text.
228. *No More Bashing*, cited in chapter 7, note 2.

CHAPTER 5

Through the Looking Glass: Corporate Governance and Financial Reporting

CORPORATE GOVERNANCE

In the context of headline news, shareholder activism was particularly successful in 2002. As of June, shareholders have won 76 proxy fights versus 70 times for all of the previous year.[1] The president of Marsico Capital, which manages $12 billion, has been writing companies about overgenerous options. Chris Davis, who oversees $30 billion in investment, assembled a group of money managers, including Warren Buffet, who collectively control 10 percent of stock market capitalization and pressured blue chip companies such as General Mills and SCB Communications, which, the group believes, give away too much shareholder wealth to corporate executives.[2] Disney was convinced to separate auditing and consulting functions (not required by Sarbanes-Oxley) and, at Bank of America, a resolution to slash golden parachutes garnered over 50 percent of the vote. But the impact of institutional investor activism ought not to be overstated because of the free rider problem. Without more concentrated ownership of shares, it is unlikely to lead to systematic changes in corporate governance although entrenched management is in for a slightly bumpier ride.[3]

Professor Jack Coffee identifies the trade-off in corporate governance between the characteristic of liquidity, which provides investors with a ready exit option, and the characteristic of monitoring, which provides investors with a voice in the corporate management. Professor Coffee has phrased the debate about U.S. institutional investor participation in corporate governance as "liquidity versus control."[4] It is his contention that shareholders in such countries as Japan and Germany forego liquidity for control, that it is difficult, if not impossible, to unite the two, and that the choice between liquidity and control is simply a specific application of the choice between "exit and voice."[5] It is perfectly correct for legal scholars to be wary of applying the Japanese institutional investor model to the U.S. scenario. Participants in an organization may either voice their views or exit from the organization. In the corporate governance arena, shareholders may voice their views through participation, either through proxy solicitation or through election to the board of directors, or, they may simply exit by selling their shares.[6]

The gains from shareholder voice are somewhat limited.[7] To enumerate a partial list: shareholders may monitor compensation to officers, limit expansion of the business, decide on a dividend payment policy to the extent of earnings, and determine in general which part of the business should be wound up. Even this agenda might be considered excessive to incumbent management.[8] Shareholders are most able to affect process and present structural proposals, rescinding or weakening poison pills, opting out of any takeover statutes, changing the state of incorporation and the related law, and determining the level of management compensation.[9] In the language of contract theory, shareholders can help resolve conflicts between management and shareholders by resuming or exercising residual power. Such residual power becomes more important given the evolution of antitakeover statutes throughout the United States.[10]

Another terminology is proximity and objectivity. In systems like those of the Netherlands and Germany, there is a finely textured relationship between monitoring management by large shareholders and autonomous supervisory boards of directors.[11] The proximity-objectivity model specifies that monitoring is best performed if the monitor is both well informed and objective. However, objectivity might require that distance be maintained between the monitor and the management; proximity may allow the monitor to be well informed, but close and thus intrusive.[12] Boards, once in place for a while, begin to identify with management,[13] regardless of their nominative independent status. All management has to do is present information in a way slightly slanted to its perspective. In a setting where monitors are not sure about their ability, no monitor is likely to condition its intervention decision based on the privately observed quality of the project.[14]

In Japan, as discussed in chapter 7, the *keiretsu* is the dominant form of monitoring. Corporate governance systems vary in the degree of protection they afford to various claimants. The U.S. system affords a great degree of protection (comparatively) to small stakes equity claimants, while the German system affords strong protection for fixed claimants. Other systems like those in Russia and Italy may afford little protection to any claimants.[15] In the United States, the market for corporate control substitutes for monitors so that monitoring is often ex post rather than ex ante.[16] However, this mechanism might be ineffective in a market where prices make hostile acquisitions untenable.

Free-rider problems resulting from the dispersion of ownership may be insurmountable. The separation of ownership and management has been described as the agency problem. The view that U.S. corporations are categorized by separation of ownership and control was firmly established by Berle and Means in 1932.[17] Whether the separation of control is a consequence of the economic and technical forces that shaped U.S. capitalism or an adaptation to political forces that limit the scales and powers of financial institutions is still being debated.[18]

In 1992, the Securities and Exchange Commission (SEC) relaxed rules on proxy solicitation, making it easier for shareholders to communicate with one another. All shareholders who have no special relationship with the company are exempted from proxy requirements. Shareholders who own more than $5 million in stock must notify the SEC but do not require permission.[19] CalPERS's chief executive officer (CEO) Dale Hanson caused a stir when he wrote a letter to the chairman of GM asking him to explain the procedure for replacing CEO Roger Smith. The institutional activists have attacked greenmail, poison pills, golden parachutes, and crown jewel sales. When Pennsylvania passed an antitakeover statute in 1990, institutional investors sent letters to companies to ask them to opt out of the protection afforded and 60 percent of companies obliged under threat of sellouts.[20] Since TIAA-CREF indexes 80 percent of its funds, it has longer holding periods for stock, thus causing it to be viewed favorably by companies as patient capital.[21] In 1993, the Institute of International Investors published a list of underperforming companies.[22] TIAA-CREF reported in 1994 that it issued 18 proposals but successfully negotiated away 14 of them before they were put to a shareholder vote.[23]

Margaret Blair, a senior fellow at the Brookings Institute, stated in her 1995 book that she had serious reservations about part of the corporate governance reform agenda, including proposals to give large shareholders greater access to directors and encouraging them to communicate with other shareholders without informing all shareholders. She believes that the great strength of the U.S. capital market is the protection it affords small shareholders, which should not be undermined.[24] The Private Securities Litigation Reform Act (PSLRA)[25] already advantages major shareholders. She also believes that, if control tilts too far in the direction of the shareholder, other stakeholders would be disadvantaged. In firms where human capital is particularly important, including high-tech and service sector firms, "employees (and sometimes other stakeholders) have as much claim to being owners of the corporation as do shareholders."[26] Blair advocates the concentration of employee stock ownership plans (ESOPs) in company shares. If the results of studies include profit sharing, the results are quite clear that employee ownership increases productivity. Although the Department of Labor affords particular rights to a trustee of a plan to override voting if he or she considers it in the best interest of the beneficiaries as shareholders only, labor unions as of 1994 had become shareholder activists, submitting 71 governance-related shareholder proposals at more than 50 companies (coming from pension fund trustees and individual union members).[27]

In studies of employee stock ownership incentive plans, there is no evidence that such a mechanism is unstable or a temporary ownership structure. Firms with 20 percent or greater stock ownership (5 out of 27 were defense contractors) are generally less capital intensive than other publicly traded companies.[28] Both market managers and analysts would benefit from improvements in assessing the rate of return on investment in human resources. A problem is that the private sector understands the downside of disclosure. Such information is part of a larger agenda underway to measure intangible assets.[29] However, if returns to knowledge workers continue to increase, wage inequality will eventually result in an institutional response to income differential.

However, the dominant form of ownership in the United States remains dispersed ownership, and this status quo results in large measure from legal considerations. Legal restraints limit the active role or stance that institutional investors can take in the running of a company, and current law militates against large block holding by institutional investors. Under Section 13(d) and related SEC rules pursuant to the Williams Act, a 5 percent stake triggers disclosure requirements. That can be onerous.[30] Furthermore, owning a 10 percent stake can trigger short-swing profit forfeitures under Section 16(b) of the Securities and Exchange Act of 1934 and related rules.[31] Section 16(b) currently requires that any gain by any officer, director, or 10 percent beneficial holder of any class of equity securities of a reporting company, resulting from a purchase of securities that occurs within six months of any earlier purchase or sale, must be disgorged to the corporation.[32] The SEC has indicated that if investors form a voting group that requires disclosure under the Williams Act, such a group will be deemed to be subject to Section 16(b) if it collectively controls 10 percent or more of a class of equity securities.[33] One obstacle to institutional investor participation in corporate management is liability under insider trading rules. Aside from Section 16(b) liability for short-swing profits, any institutional investor that has its nominee serving as a corporate director will have access to inside information, which could create liability under the SEC rule.[34] In the mid-1980s, the U.S. Department of Labor warned Employee Retirement Income Security Act (ERISA) fiduciaries that participation in corporate governance was not optional,[35] and Department of Labor rulings required pension plan trustees to monitor "the activities of the investment manager" to whom voting discretion is delegated.[36] As discussed above, the best way to make institutional investors active is to restrict portfolio diversification, and a diversified portfolio may be achieved with as few as 15 or 20 stocks.[37] An obstacle is created by ERISA, which mandates diversification under Section 1104A "so as to minimize the risk of large losses," unless it is clearly prudent not to do so.[38] Furthermore, incentive compensation contracts are strictly forbidden for investment advisors registered under the Investment Advisors Act of 1940.[39] A controlling shareholder is liable for securities law violations committed by controlled corporations unless an affirmative defense can be established.[40] Obviously, any entity attempting to exercise control would lose some of its ability to trade securities. Consequently, there is an inherent trade-off between control and liquidity. Minor clarifications for a Section 16(b) indexed investor who buys for the long term but recurrently needs to adjust his portfolio would not solve the problem posed to an institutional investor who would actually seek a measure of control. In Germany and Great Britain, where substantial limitations on bank ownership of equity securities have not existed, financial institutions still have not exceeded the 5 percent level of ownership.[41] However, in Japan, banks own considerably more.[42] Although bank-holding companies in the United States are entitled to hold up to 5 percent of their assets in equity securities, banks have made little use of these powers.[43]

Banks and open-end mutual funds, which must stand ready to redeem securities on a daily basis, have very thin equity and are thus unwilling to actively invest in equities for long-term holding.[44] Banks and insurance companies are the institutions least willing to oppose corporate management.[45] Private pension funds are subject to a related form of pressure in that corporate management can and does instruct the professional investment management firms on matters usually including voting in a proxy contest.[46] Money managers are also reluctant to be labeled activist shareholders, lest institutional activism trigger political repercussions.[47]

Yet certain institutional investors have successfully played the activist card. Steel Partners has been involved in two successful proxy fights. In both Liquid Audio, acting in concert with another institutional investor,[48] and in United Industrial Board,[49] it has succeeded in electing dissident directors to the board. However, in both these instances, these institutional directors can best be described as transitory since they are attempting to influence the sale of the company, and have made a takeover offer for Liquid Audio. They had the support of Institutional Investor Services, a proxy advisory service. The Packard family unsuccessfully attempted to fend off an acquisition of Compaq by Hewlitt Packard, and the stakes of the proxy fight ran to $100 million.[50] A billionaire investor is involved in his second proxy fight to install dissident directors at Computer Associates.[51] While substantial reforms in 1992 facilitated the process of communication among outside shareholders,[52] evidence suggests that proxy fights have been most successful in the market for corporate control and less so in resolving other corporate issues.[53] Thus, only in the instance of companies facing acquisition have dissident shareholders had some success in electing directors. In most instances, the agency problem is not mitigated by institutional investor activists and these investors cannot become broadly successful as a class until the various limitations on large block holding discussed above[54] are eliminated. Thus, Professor Coffee's characterization of institutional investors as "resembling spectators at the Roman Colliseum content with bread and circuses, unwilling to organize for political reform as long as the gain continues"[55] remains a fair assessment today.

CORPORATE GOVERNANCE AND FINANCIAL REPORTING

Because financial accounting provides financiers with the primary source of independent verification about the performance of managers, one commentator has concluded, "Thus it is clear that corporate governance and financial accounting are inexorably linked."[56] However, only 3 percent of the papers referenced in a general survey of accounting articles concern corporate governance.[57] Chief among these areas is the usefulness of financial accounting in predicting takeover targets.[58] Other issues in the general survey include executive compensation and stock market performance, golden parachutes, and executive and board compensation. Consequently, an article in the *Journal of Accounting and Economics* concludes there is a dearth of research published in accounting journals on the role of financial accounting in corporate governance.[59] However, a newly developing methodology surveys such questions as how financial reporting correlates with the nature and extent of the corporate governing mechanisms. Recent research focuses on the quality of financial disclosure and the cost of capital,[60] quality of audits,[61] and the board of directors/audit committee quality[62] and the determinants and effects of earnings management[63] and manipulation of earnings.[64] Another area is performance pricing in lending, but there is also a dearth of research in this area.[65] Since financial reporting is the primary mechanism through which public companies communicate with shareholders, lawsuits under 10b-5 frequently allege a material misstatement or omission in the financial statement. There is some research on the relation of accounting and shareholder litigation and management acts to mitigate this cost.[66] Preliminary research suggests that in addition to predicting takeovers, financial accounting information is a good predictor of institutional investor activism and proxy fights.[67]

Under agency theory, the separation of ownership and control involves an inherent conflict. Corporate control mechanisms are the means by which managers are disciplined to act in the investors' interest. These mechanisms involve both internal mechanisms, such as managerial incentive plans and director monitoring, as well as external mechanisms such as debt-holder monitoring, the securities laws, competition in the product market, and the market for corporate control. Financial accounting produces direct input into monitoring by contributing significantly to the determination of the share price.[68] Not surprisingly, literature in finance and economics documents substantial cross-border differences in the degree of protection afforded investors against expropriation by corporate insiders from laws and their enforcement.[69] Furthermore, the depth and liquidity of the stock market are highly correlated with the existence of legal protection of minority shareholders.[70] The financial accounting regime is an important determinant that is measured by an index, based on 90 items, developed for each country by the Center for Financial Analysis and Research.[71] Earnings and the cash portion of compensation paid to executives have become increasingly less important in determining total executive compensation. Share price is the principal determinant.[72] Evidence suggests that accounting information has become less important in determining CEO compensation in recent years, particularly as the cash portion of compensation shrinks.[73] Other determinants of CEO compensation are product market competition. In those industries in which there is higher product substitutability, peer group comparisons are more appropriate at creating opportunities for more precise comparison.[74] This might help explain the tendency of corporations to diversify in other businesses, creating corporate conglomerates, or to obfuscate the nature of their business by complex financial transactions, as in the case of Enron, and by endless acquisitions within one industry, as in the instance of Worldcom.

In the last 15 years, a considerable amount of evidence has documented the prevalence of managerial behavior that does not benefit the investor. The best survey of the literature is an article published in 1997 in the *Journal of Finance* by Andrei Shlieffer, Professor of Economics at Harvard, and Robert Vishny of the University of Chicago, entitled simply "Survey of Corporate Governance."[75] The poor history of diversification and its negative impact on shareholder wealth has been documented.[76] In general, optimistic viewpoints of the corporate governance system are provided by law professors such as Romano[77] and Easterbrook and Fischer,[78] while Michael Jensen, a business school professor at Harvard, believes it to be a deeply flawed system[79] that should be replaced by a move toward more highly leveraged organizations, similar to that accomplished by leveraged buyout (LBO). Jensen argues that free cash flow causes managers to choose to reinvest rather than return the money to the investors. Jensen uses the example of the oil industry in the mid-1980s when oil producers spent $20 per barrel to explore for new oil reserves when the market price of oil was $6 per barrel.[80] Mark Roe, a professor at Harvard Law School, sees the virtues of the Japanese and German systems.[81]

The question of why investors give their money to corporations without receiving sufficient control rights in exchange centers on excessive investor optimism.[82] As of 1997, evidence already pointed to poor long-term performance of initial public offerings (IPOs) and to earning manipulation during issues.[83] Since managers can time the granting of options to periods before good news is announced and delay such options during periods of bad news, incentive compensation poses an issue of self-dealing and is looked at askance by courts; thus, corporations have generally kept down incentive-based performance (although, naturally, the higher the stock price, the better the remuneration).

However, most investors suppose that they gain rights, the most important of which is the right to vote on mergers, liquidations, and the elections of boards of directors.[84] In general, a disastrous performance is required before boards of directors will act to remove incumbent management. Because the investment of shareholders is sunk, investors have fewer protections than other stakeholders.[85] Large shareholders naturally receive greater protection from the problem of agency. Such shareholders can oust management though proxy fights or a takeover. In the United States and the United Kingdom, and increasingly elsewhere, the hostile takeover, the market for corporate control, addresses corporate governance problems. When large shareholders are banks and other financial institutions, they can be soft on management because their desire is to get more business. This situation is suggested by the German and Japanese model where banks garner economic rents for monitoring in the form of above-market interest rates.[86]

Recent years have seen a flood of research on debt as the means of solving agency problems. If the borrower defaults on any covenant, the lender gets additional rights. In a later generation of papers, beginning in the 1990s, the incomplete contract methodology leads to the characterization of debt as an instrument that takes control only when the going gets bad.[87] The analysis of equity investment cannot explain how firms manage to raise equity in countries where there is virtually no protection of investors. The best hypothesis suggests that reputation for good performance is the principal lightening rod of investment in these countries.[88]

Consistent with the evidence that large investors reduce agency costs, the available evidence suggests that LBOs are an efficient mechanism for maximizing shareholder value.[89] Shlieffer and Vishny state, "Our analysis leads us to conclude that both legal protection of investors and some form of concentrated ownership are essential elements of a good corporate governance system." They lump Germany, Japan, and the United States together as having successful corporate governance systems while viewing Italy as having a weak one. The flaw in Schleiffer's survey article, aside from its dismissive stance of institutional investor activism, is that it fails to address the tradeoff between liquidity and control posed by Professor John Coffee in 1991 and restated by Professor Jon Macey as "objectivity versus proximity." The optimum system should have both legal protections and investor control.

Financial accounting, according to Bushman, et al., can enable managers and shareholders to distinguish between good and bad investments, and can be a source of information about investment opportunities for other firms (as in the market for corporate control); as a source of governance control, financial accounting, in the estimation of Bushman, et al., is a better measure of executive compensation than share price. Finally, better financial disclosure can reduce firms' liquidity risk. If investors are convinced of the quality of financial disclosure, firms can undertake long-term (illiquid), high-return investments.[90] However, one is not necessarily convinced that financial accounting rather than hype led to the greatest illiquid investment craze of all times in the 1990s. But, mutatis mutandis, in other contexts, good financial disclosure will reduce an unnecessary emphasis on liquidity.

Naturally, there is a positive correlation between countries with a high demand for external financing and GDP growth,[91] and a similar high correlation between research and development (R&D) expenditure and GDP growth in countries with a high demand for external financing.[92] But there are so many other factors impacting on the demand for external financing. This demand is low in countries with low GDPs, for instance; the emphasis on legal and accounting regimes is itself highly correlated with the degree of industrial development. A more useful approach may be garnered by comparing similar industrialized countries. Yet, the premises derived offer opportunities for future research. In particular, Bushman, et al., state, "It would be interesting to explain the extent to which these differences can be explained by inter-industry differences in the information conveyed by U.S. GAAP [Generally Accepted Accounting Principles] due, for example, to high-tech versus low tech, maturity of the industry and the importance of intangible assets or investment in R&D." Indeed it would.

FINANCIAL REPORTING AND CORPORATE GOVERNANCE

Financial Reporting: The Evolution of U.S. Accounting

In the United States, the American Association of Public Accountants (AAPA) was organized in 1886 by a few elite U.S. practitioners in alliance with British Accountants. A rival organization, the New York State Society of Certified Public Accountants, competed with the AAPA for leadership.[93] In 1896, the New York legislature passed a law that required the licensing of accountants, appointing a three-person board to administer testing and limiting applicants to American citizens and those intending to become American citizens.[94] The New York State Board of Examiners for Certified Public Accountants came into existence, and the pass rate for the exam was about a third, dropping to a low of 2 percent in 1916.[95] Illinois quickly followed suit and reciprocity provisions were enacted.[96]

The practice of accountancy developed along with the Interstate Commerce Commission (ICC), particularly as a consequence of the Hepburn Act of 1906, and had important implications for the accounting profession and informed the regulatory process. Uniform accounts played a central role in evaluating rate equity. Cost of service was rejected as a means of setting rates since accountants were unable to agree on a formulation. Eventually, the ICC formulated a system for determining railroads' financial break-even point.[97] Although accountants failed to achieve a place in regulating insurance or railroads, they did achieve a place as advisors to executive agencies.[98] The role of accountants in the debate over federal income tax was a high-water mark in the development of the profession. In a move presaging the enormous influence of the accounting lobby in the last decade of the twentieth century, the AAPA organized the Committee on Federal Legislation.[99] Its success in influencing the government to accept accrual accounting allowed capital-intensive industries to reduce their liabilities by deducting substantial charges for depreciation.[100] In 1916, the American Institute of Accountants (AIA) emerged to supersede the AAPA.[101] Instead of membership on a state basis, there were only two classes of members and the ruling council was no longer chosen by state delegation, eliminating the need to build a broad consensus.[102] In 1921, the Internal Revenue Service (IRS) began issuing revenue regulations, and confrontations between taxpayers and the IRS led to demands for an oversight board. Consequently, the AIA successfully pressed for the Board of Tax Appeal, whose members were chosen by the president rather than the secretary of the Treasury. In the 1920s, bankers, who had earlier pressed for regulation of accountants by the Federal Reserve Board (FRB) and the Federal Trade Commission (FTC), once again became critical of the AIA for their practice of certifying pro forma statements.[103]

In *Ultramares Corporation v. Touche*, Benjamin Cardozo as chief judge of the New York Court of Appeals delivered an opinion ruling that, although the plaintiffs had been unable to prove their specific charges, the conduct of the defendant had constituted constructive fraud and thus opened the door to third party liability.[104] As a consequence of the crash of 1929, the New York Stock Exchange (NYSE) agreed to work with the AIA in the development of standards for financial reporting.[105] The FTC also began to issue rules prohibiting client relationships that might destroy auditor independence.[106] The AIA organized the opposition to the undistributed earnings tax and succeeded in watering down Treasury Secretary Morgenthau's proposal.[107]

By 1936, the SEC commissioner and chief accountant were making critical comments about the work of practitioners. Finally, in 1938, the AIA issued "A Statement of Accounting Principles" and assigned the Committee on Accounting Procedure the task of promulgating accounting standards.[108] Incorporating a former chief accountant of the SEC and a longtime critic of the AIA helped restore AIA credibility; the SEC chief accountant established the policy of conditionally accepting the guidance of the AIA's statement of position pronouncements.[109] The falsification of financial records at McKesson Robbins caused the AIA to issue its "Statements on Auditing Procedure" in 1939 and to broaden its code of ethics to mirror SEC requirements.[110] The SEC did not recommend that it exercise its right to issue detailed accounting regulations; its acceptance of the AIA was in part the result of the AIA's success in establishing itself as the legitimate national representative of the accounting profession. In the view of one commentator, the gradual emergence of compromise between competing elites—in the New Deal context, business and government and the diverse elements within the accounting profession—resulted in compromise because no single faction could concentrate sufficient power to dominate. In the development of the AIA, social values were essential determinants in shaping the outlook of its leaders.[111]

Taxation and Financial Reporting

The impact of tax accounting on financial accounting should not be understated. For instance, according to one commentator, federal income tax regulations have been a major obstacle to depreciating reporting. Despite the admonition of the Committee on Accounting Procedure of the AIA in the 1960s that "sound financial accounting procedures do not necessarily coincide with the rules which govern what shall be included in 'gross income' or allowed as a deduction therefrom in arriving at taxable net income,"[112] this commentator concludes, "The tax tail wags the accounting dog."[113] Changes in reporting procedure frequently followed changes in tax regulation. For instance, in 1962, the fact that Big Steel's net income fell well below that of 1961 was really the result of tax changes that permitted steel-making equipment to be deducted over 18 rather than 25 years. The Accounting Principles Board, in the estimation of the commentator, seems to have relinquished responsibility for determining sound accounting principles to the Internal Revenue Service.[114] The concern over tax considerations reflects an era when corporate taxes were much higher and the emphasis on quarterly reports significantly less. However, this history is essential in explaining the derivation of contemporary accounting concepts. Distortion from depreciation is far simpler to understand than that from goodwill, for instance.

Beginning in the 1960s in earnest, lobbying began in such areas as accounting for investment tax credit, business combinations and goodwill, restructuring of troubled debt, oil and gas exploration, marketable securities, and employee stock options.[115] The United Kingdom has witnessed lobbying in connection with research and development, deferred taxes, and goodwill.[116]

In 1958, a managing partner of Arthur Anderson concluded, "Even though accounting progress from 1900 to 1930 was great, it was not sufficient to prevent the financial misrepresentations that accumulated and burst in the 1929–1932 crash."[117] To illustrate the differences employed by companies, he used oil companies as an example: some companies use accelerated depreciation at double the normal rates for both book and tax purposes while others claim accelerated depreciation for tax purposes and straight line for financial reporting. Among these, some properly accounted for deferred tax; others did not. Some companies charged intangible drilling costs to expense; others did not. Some provided for deferred tax while others did not. Some companies recognized that they did not own the land and did not include it for accounting purposes. Others disregarded the legal consequences and considered royalty payments to be a means of financing. In 1954, the issue of deferred tax recognition for companies that used accelerated depreciation but provided lesser amounts on the financial book resulted in new legislation requiring recognition of deferred taxes (if material).[118] But the new law contained an exception of which the Anderson partner (from the good old days) said, "Here again we have a failure in professional responsibility by the committee members who assented to its issuance."[119] This is another example of how taxation has affected book accounting.

The largest body of tax research in accounting examines the coordination of taxes and other factors in business decisions and focuses on the interaction of financial reporting and tax factors; thus, many choices in accounting, financing, marketing, production, and other business functions involve weighing the tax incentives for lower taxable income against the financial reporting incentives to increase book income.[120] The question of whether firms choose last in first out (lifo) because it minimizes the present value of the firm's tax liabilities or avoid "lifo" because it lowers reported earnings is addressed in a 1998 article that reviews the literature and determines that tax savings dominate earnings management when firms choose "lifo."[121] The Tax Act of 1986 reduced the benefits of qualifying incentive stock options.[122] There is some evidence that tax considerations abound in the termination of defined benefit plans that are overfunded.[123] The Tax Reform Act of 1986 and its gradual lowering of rates in the years following enabled managers to plan to shift earnings to future periods. Shifting to avoid taxes was coordinated with earnings management to cover debt covenant violation costs. Many firms also took advantage of net operating loss carrybacks to years before the rates fell. Additional studies found that the alternative minimum tax,[124] in the context of mandated accrual basis reporting, caused firms to defer income, disadvantaging their book position, in order to benefit from lower taxes.[125] The provision in the 1993 tax law that allowed amortization of goodwill resulted in an increase in the probability of a transaction structured to obtain an increased basis for goodwill; a significant increase in the purchase price premium is also detected.[126]

Lobbying: The Expensing of Options

The ne plus ultra of political lobbying in the accounting rules was caused by the furor over the expensing of stock options in the United States. U.S. accounting rules resulted in a zero compensation expense for stock options under APB (Accounting Practices Board) 25, issued in 1972.[127] The Financial Accounting Standards Board (FASB) had made known its intent to require the expensing of stock options, and Congress reacted vehemently. The public furor in Silicon Valley resulted in a Silicon Valley stock option rally. By April 1994, Ed Markey, the Chair of the Energy and Commerce Committee in the House, which had jurisdiction over the SEC, addressed a letter to the SEC chairman asking when the economic consequences of FASB regulation would be considered.[128] In May 1994, Senator Lieberman offered his opposition as an amendment to another bill, and Senator Boxer said, "If we need to legislate accounting rules, I am not going to walk away from that fight."[129] Senator Levin, the only senator who supported FASB's action, read into the record a letter from Warren Buffet, "If options aren't a form of compensation, what are they? If compensation isn't an expense, what is it? And, if expenses shouldn't go into the calculation of earnings, where should they go?"[130] A resolution against FASB was passed 88 to 9. There was also a resolution to the effect that FASB independence shouldn't be compromised that passed 94 to 2.[131] Well, consistency is the hobgoblin of small minds. In October 1995, FASB issued FAS (Financial Accounting Standard) 123 in which it expressed a preference that options be expensed, but firms applying APB 25 (naturally the vast majority), and thus showing a zero compensation expense, were required to disclose "the pro forma net income and, if earnings per share is presented, the pro forma earnings per share as if the fair value based accounting method in this Statement had been used to account for stock-based compensation."[132]

Intangible and Nonfinancial Drivers

The impact of accounting standards on share price has been a subject of considerable research. FASB denies that financial accounting is intended to directly value equity: "Information may help those who desire to estimate the value of a business enterprise, but financial accounting is not designed to measure directly the value of an enterprise."[133] FASB includes among its potential users of information both investors and creditors.[134] Alternative uses, for creditors in particular, include measuring liquidity[135] (greatly enhanced by the cash flow statements).[136] However, any use of financial accounting data is subject to verification, which is principally the process of preventing misrepresentation.[137] Market-value accounting values individual assets, not the firm, and not all assets are valued at market; thus the balance sheet provides an input to equity, not a valuation of equity.[138] Goodwill, for instance, represents the difference between market value and the net asset value of a firm, but, absent patents, copyrights, and so on, the value of goodwill can only be realized by the sale of the entire firm. Debt contracts likely exclude goodwill and other intangibles from the balance sheet because these cannot be realized in liquidation.[139] By 1900, many U.S. industrial firms had higher par value than net asset value because of goodwill, but by the 1920s many of these firms had been able to write off goodwill without impairing the right to pay dividends[140] (presumably limited by debt covenants). In a study in the 1930s, there were considerable write-ups of investments and property plant and equipment but few write-ups of goodwill since debt covenants tended to exclude intangibles.[141] Regulation limited write-ups so that the practice of revaluing assets was virtually extinct by 1940.[142] Apparently, several founding commissioners of the SEC were associated with the FTC, which had made attempts to regulate accountants,[143] and they argued that the write-up of assets was largely responsible for the crash of 1929, although subsequent empirical research suggests that the argument was flawed.[144] The SEC did not lift the ban until the 1970s, and few firms took advantage of the liberalization. The SEC used the registration process to effect these bans,[145] one of the very few instances of its direct involvement in accounting standards.

In the new economy paradigm, intangible assets such as R&D, brand names, and human capital become increasingly important. Economic growth is no longer driven by factories, machines, office buildings, or mineral resources, but by human and intellectual capital and reputational assets. Microsoft, for instance, had only $1.9 billion in property and equipment yet had a stock market capitalization of $328 billion in September 2000.[146] In August 2000, Disney had a market capitalization of $117 billion. Company books recorded $11.3 billion in tangible assets, but after accounting for intangible assets, the market placed a value of $83 billion on the company. The general tendency of financial accounting has historically been to err on the side of conservatism. According to the FASB, "Historically, managers, investors, and accountants have generally preferred that possible errors in measurement be in the direction of understatement of net income and assets . . . [This] convention of conservatism . . . was once commonly expressed in the admonition to 'anticipate no profits but anticipate all losses.'"[147]

The argument is that investment in intangibles, including R&D, should be capitalized rather than expensed as an ordinary business expense. This treatment is afforded purchased goodwill under the purchase method in the event that one company buys another. In the last few years, firms have securitized cash flows from intangibles, specifically patents.[148] After lobbying by new economy companies such as Cisco, the new accounting rules do not require a company to write down intangibles purchased unless the acquired goodwill becomes impaired.[149] The Brookings Task Force introduced the idea that intangibles can be divided into human capital and structural capital, and human capital walks out the door every night, so what is left of intangibles is structural capital.[150] There are several assets that cannot be separated out and sold, according to the taskforce, including R&D in progress, business secrets, reputational capital, proprietary management systems, and business processes.[151] The value derived from an intangible might not bear any relationship to the cost; therefore, a methodology should be developed to assess value.[152] The taskforce determined that the accounting treatment of R&D focused on the wrong problem. What investors want is information about intangible assets, and this discussion could be presented in the management discussion and analysis section of financial reports.[153] Much of the discussion of intangibles has been formulated as a question of value drivers—those factors that influence the future of a firm and are not quantifiable in historic profits. FASB 131 establishes the regular review by a firm's CEO on identifying reportable segments. Such information, the taskforce suggests, might be included in this section in a footnote.[154] The taskforce believes that a stronger safe harbor than one allowed under the PSLRA would encourage firms to experiment with disclosure.[155] Yet, it is hard to see how the current standard, requiring scienter construed by courts in interpreting the PSLRA safe harbor,[156] could be more advantageous to business.

In the *GAAP Gap: Corporate Disclosure in the Internet Age*,[157] Robert Litan, a senior fellow in economics at the Brookings Institution, and Peter Wallison set forth the case that GAAP does not take into account factors like market share or give significant attention to factors other than financial information, and, in general, most important disclosures are not in financial statements, which are staggered information, but rather more timely information. They argue that the gap between market and book value demonstrates the increasing irrelevance of GAAP and that the timing of financial statements does not keep pace with the age of the Internet, which should be utilized to provide more timely financial disclosure. On the issue of the revaluation of intangibles, they urge that the SEC inaugurate a period of experimentation.[158] The book to market value was at one to one for corporate assets until 1983, shot up to 3 to 1 in the early 1990s, and eventually rose to 6 to 1.[159] They do not doubt that markets have been "irrationally exuberant"[160] but doubt that it has been so for 17 years and attribute the discrepancy to the increasing importance of intangibles including employee training, R&D, and building customer bases.[161] The greater importance of intangibles is, in their view, evidenced by the total factor productivity (TFP) growth, which is based on increases in knowledge rather than additional inputs.[162] The growth in TFP, as many economists have noted, may not be permanent and may self-referentially reflect a bubble, but the issue of intangible value has certainly never been appropriately addressed.

Given the panoply of data that is important to investors, Litan and Wallison recommend increased timely disclosure of economic data including data regarding market share and competitors' businesses. More broadly, they suggest that disclosure must be forward looking, and that the data should be accessible through extra markup computer language (XML), which allows the collection of various sets of data resulting in information that is user driven rather than issuer driven. Here, one encounters a semiotic conundrum about the nature of financial information. Consider Worldcom. About $9 billion of expenses were capitalized rather than expensed, and there were no analysts following this huge company who were savvy enough to catch this understatement of simple expenses when the figure of $17 billion, which Worldcom paid for leasing lines, included at least $2 billion in improper capitalized expenses.[163] (The total revenues were over $90 billion.) The obfuscation, even though the expenditure was in no way as opaque as the financial dealings of Enron, was equally resistant to analysts' skills. To view corporate balance sheets and income statements as data sets that can be extracted by users is at best only a partial elaboration of the nature of financial information. The self-proclaimed thesis of the *GAAP Gap* is that the new economy has created the "need for a new system of corporate disclosure." One is tempted to suggest that an accounting system ought not to reflect market prices where market price is a result of a very short-lived bubble. But intangibles have become increasingly important even though they have always been important. There is an odd tendency to collapse the technology issue in corporate disclosure: the new economy high-tech companies, where intangibles are essential to determining value, and the pervasiveness of the Internet as enabling a user-driven corporate disclosure system. With the benefit of hindsight, one might suppose that the issue of the revaluation of intangibles is overblown and, had intangibles reflected market valuations, the accounting profession would have been blamed for the National Association of Dealers Automated Quotations (NASDAQ) bubble. However, the issue of the revaluation of intangibles remains significant, although it is a balance sheet rather than an income statement issue. While the authors recommend that cost-based accounting be abandoned, they also are skeptical of a top-down approach that mandates a one-size-fits-all approach.[164] However, the gathering storm that surrounds corporate disclosure does not particularly auger a subjective corporate disclosure standard. To state that "the current standard-setting system is fundamentally antithetical to the culture and possibilities of the Internet"[165] seems to overstate the transforming possibilities of the Internet.

In the instance of AOL, which capitalized its customer acquisition cost from 1994 to 1997, Litan and Wallison conclude that the better, more accurate presentation would have been to allow the capitalization of expenses, but expensing would have been a better idea if AOL had turned out a failure. But financial reporting obviously cannot be providential. That capitalization might have provided a more accurate representation of the true state of affairs given future share price and the matching of income and expenses, even if these occur in different periods (a goal that would have been better achieved through capitalization), may stress a less important purpose of financial accounting. Expensing consumer acquisition costs is, in my view, more appropriate, since income is diminished and may not be recuperated. However, if these items were one-off expenses, then capitalization may have been more appropriate. Noting that conventional accounting is based on transactions, they note the case of Xerox, which exploited its patent but did not account for the loss of goodwill resulting from the poor quality of service. The quality of suppliers and contractual relationships are not reflected in conventional accounting.[166]

In a Pepsico conference call involving 30 questions, only 5 of 30 questions concerned financial reporting issues, of which 3 were for more specific segment reporting. In an Exxon conference call, only 6 of 40 questions involved financial statements.[167] The American Institute of Certified Public Accountants (AICPA) produced a report in 1990 in which it suggested such kinds of disclosure as the number of patents per year, the reject rate for products, and customer order backlog comparisons.[168] In 1998, FASB initiated a study of nonfinancial disclosure, and the food industry working group identified six value drivers—sales growth, margin enhancement, product innovation, product quality, brand effectiveness, and articulation of financial and operational strategies, and each category involved several subcategories.[169] In fact, many of these categories are disclosed under management discussion and analysis, a part of the SEC disclosure regime that has recently been expanded.[170] However, effective disclosure is still an elusive goal.

One set of proposals explicitly states that all measures should be quantitative, standardized to facilitate comparisons, and relevant to increases and decreases of value.[171] The Swedish company Skandia included its version of value drivers in its 1994 and 1995 annual report including funds assets/employee, market share, customers lost, administrative expenses/managed assets, cost of administrative errors, and competence development costs per employee. In 2000, the AICPA Committee on Assurance Services noted that accountants were well suited to deliver opinions on the quality of systems for designing effective means of evaluation of nonfinancial issues in business performance.[172] This is similar to the proposal of the U.K. Steering Committee on Company Law.[173]

In 2000, Amazon.com issued its acquisition costs per customer. This was a much-sought-after measurement by analysts and the company's stock shot up six points, but the company did not segment these into product line customers or reveal the average revenue from customers who signed up each month.[174] The behavior of the market in this instance seems to add fodder to Keynes's characterization of the stock market as a beauty contest in which the average man picks the winner. Stressing the democratizing potential of the Internet allowing investors to utilize extensible binding language (XBL) and XML technology places too much faith in both technology and investors. Disclosing disaggregated data may finesse liability that arises from disclosing aggregated data, but such data in the wrong hands—those of anyone who is not highly sophisticated—is likely to do more harm than good.

Fulsome disclosure can lower the cost of capital, and the correlation between greater disclosure and share price is equally self-evident;[175] however, greater disclosure has not been forthcoming, probably because few corporations wish to lead the pack. Recent developments have somewhat increased nonfinancial disclosure, but recent events have shown the relevance of financial reporting. However, the observations of Litan and Wallison, like those of the Brookings Task Force,[176] ought not to be brushed aside. And FASB should initiate a project on nonfinancial disclosure and ultimately enunciate an objective standard.

R&D tax credits are considered a fair way to tilt the balance of investment in favor of intangibles, which are disadvantaged under financial accounting principles. However, in my opinion, very limited investments in R&D that can be determined to be nonrecurring, and campaigns to build brand awareness or develop patents should be capitalized subject to a value, rather than a cost approach, since, unlike the situation with tangibles, cost bears very little relation to value. Yet, underlying all of this is the question of the relation of a financial statement, particularly an income statement, to the true and fair position of the company.

FINANCIAL REPORTING: CONCEPTUAL ISSUES

The purpose of financial disclosure is not necessarily to promote efficient markets through the allocation of resources. Regulators may be concerned with the welfare of financially unsophisticated investors.[177] In the estimation of one writer, this would imply that the object of disclosure is to redistribute wealth rather than promote financial efficiency, since investors could and do engage the services of intermediaries.[178] In my view, this is a false dichotomy.

Voluntary disclosure may be motivated by several considerations. Disclosure tends to increase six months before an offering,[179] and analyst coverage of firms with more disclosure tends to increase.[180] There is also an increase in analyst coverage in firms that make conference calls.[181] Conference calls and the Internet are becoming progressively more important as channels for investor communication.[182] Meanwhile the correlation between earnings and stock market performance has deteriorated over time.[183] This is partly explained by an increase in innovation, which raises the importance of nonfinancial disclosure.[184] However, the instance cited—the wireless communications business—is now inapposite. The perilous performance of Vodaphone and Worldcom indicate that whatever perceived value nonfinancial information could determine was far less important than the relatively unimpressive earnings.

Innovations in organizational form such as closely coordinated supply chains and strategic alliances have increased efficiency while, at the same time, creating interdependencies that involve implicit contracts and thereby challenge the current accounting standards that largely ignore them. Coca-Cola, for example, has outsourced its low-margin bottling activities and boosted earnings, but it is susceptible to the complex web of relationships with bottlers who have become increasingly less profitable. Current accounting standards generally ignore these relationships.[185] But their very existence assails the notion of entity reporting.

Demands for the globalization of financial reporting standards raise several questions, including whether, given the disparities in the development of financial reporting infrastructure, it is desirable. What economic forces will determine the speed of convergence? What will be the political consequences of convergence? And, in the absence of convergence, will information be enhanced by global accounting standards?[186] The experience in the European Union (EU), which has adopted the convergence approach under International Accounting Standards (IAS) standards,[187] will provide an excellent format to test these questions. The process of convergence of banking capital adequacy standards[188] already provides significant empirical results on the merits and demerits of convergence, as does the experience of accounting convergence in the EU, which began in 1979 with the Fourth Directive on

Company Law.[189] These could provide the basis for a hypothesis on benefits and liabilities of convergence in future research.

In FASB's tenure, conservatism in financial accounts has increased substantially until fairly recently.[190] Firms are interested in having bad news reflected in financial statements before good news is unveiled. (These results are from 1967–93 and become less significant toward the end of the period.) Once again, tax considerations are paramount; according to one commentator, "Overall, the evidence suggests the existence of implicit pressure to conform tax accounting methods to those used for financial reporting purposes and to conform reported accounting income to tax income."[191]

One view is that there is no guidance for how to determine earnings as distinct from cash flow because earnings are booked in periods other than that in which they are earned, and the recognition of earnings varies according to each firm's cash flow and investment cycle. Furthermore, GAAP rarely makes a distinction between one-time gains and relatively permanent income streams.[192] This assertion is not entirely helpful. The example given is transitory versus permanent increase in sales. However, it would take a clairvoyant to determine this, even though there are instances in which a separation can be made. In general, the extent to which accounting earnings measure future cash flows is likely to be less for higher growth, higher risk firms.

An opposing view determines that value relevance literature has produced results. Pension cash flows are inherently less risky than other cash flows; other studies predict that management discretion reduces reliability, the reliability of fair value estimates of bank loans and nonfinancial intangible assets, and find that fair value estimates of intangibles (not disclosed under GAAP) are highly correlated with share price.[193] Additionally, economic rents (resulting from intangibles) can be estimated.[194] An asset, despite its lack of liquidation value, may be a valuable asset of the firm.

The principal purpose of fundamental analysis in valuation is to determine mispriced securities. As described by Graham and Dodd in *Security Analysis* in 1934,[195] rewards from fundamental analysis would diminish in an efficient market; a switch of accounting methods without a change in cash flow would not affect prices. Choice between disclosure in footnotes and balance sheet would have no impact.[196] But positive accounting theory predicts that the use of accounting numbers affects a firm's accounting choice. While the efficient market hypothesis inaugurated capital markets research in the 1960s, theories of inefficient markets are catalysts for financial market research today.[197] Many advocate changes in GAAP because GAAP has a low correlation with share price.[198] For reasons of disclosure liability, GAAP is oriented toward historical information, while securities' prices reflect future expectations.

There are several reasons why earnings would not reflect price. Because price is comprised of expectations of future cash flow, which, under the efficient market hypothesis, are instantaneously reflected, the matching of income and expense of historical earnings reflect price changes with a lag. The deficient GAAP hypothesis is self-explanatory. Frequently, it focuses on the capitalization versus expensing of R&D. The revival of interest in fundamental analysis is rooted in evidence of market inefficiency and the fact that it may take years for prices to reflect fundamental value. As we have seen, firm owners and analysts have incentives to issue rosy forecasts.[199] However, as one study asserts, long-term horizon forecast is problematic.[200] No kidding. Return predictability tests determine whether indicators other than earnings are better predictors of long-term prices. The most common theme is that markets overreact to announcements, which represents investor's naïve fixation on certain numbers.[201]

The extent to which codetermination in supervisory boards in Germany affects stock prices has led to the hypothesis that diverse stockholders would face a labor-dominated board or a weak board; therefore, stock remains in large blocks and fluidity comes from blocks changing hands, and capital markets are thin. Thus, selling out in an IPO, for instance, would reduce the value of the block's position and result in a substantial discount. In addition to limiting liquidity, this fact also limits access to equity capital.[202]

Historic cash flows are reported as a means of describing the reporting entities' capacity to generate cash flows. In the United States, this was followed by two FASB Concept Statements in 1980 and 1984.[203] In 1987, FASB produced a requirement for a cash flow statement.[204] The FASB standard stated that, generally, gross cash flow is more relevant than information about the net amount of cash received and payments, except where the turnover is quick, the amounts large, and the maturation short, or where the entity is holding or disbursing cash on behalf of its clients (such as banks and securities firms).[205]

Among the criticisms leveled, an operating cash deficit does not mean that a company is losing resources since it might be financing the buildup of stocks.[206] One author gives the example of Royal Dutch Shell in 1975 to 1981, which had an immense resource base and had no problem borrowing from the market.[207] Another author expresses the importance of interacting cash flows from different segments; even here, a degree of discretion is allocated to management.[208] Cash flow may be most useful in determining liquidity but long-term value is best determined with reference to profit statements.[209] Here there is an analogy to securities firms that are always valued at liquidation value.[210] In bankruptcy terminology, cash flow accounting ignores going concern value.

In the United Kingdom, fund statement reporting was revised twice,[211] and, in 1990, the ASB followed the FASB and produced a prescription for cash flow accounting in an ASB standard.[212] In the ASB 1991 statement, it was determined that cash flow had an advantage over traditional working capital because working capital can obscure liquidity while cash flow is a normal feature of business and not a term of art; cash flow is a direct input into business valuation, and a fund statement is largely based on the difference between two balance sheets without providing new data; and cash flow statements may include information not disclosed in a flow of funds statement.[213] But cash flow accounting is not a panacea. Criticizing both cash flow statements and statements of value, one author concluded that these measures tend to usurp rather than supplant the measure of profits and put little emphasis on an interrelated position statement.[214]

Earnings under GAAP are less closely correlated with price and long-term performance than Wall Street earnings reports. These earnings reports typically disregard certain expenses under GAAP that the Street judges to be nonrecurring in order to determine earnings that are correlated with cash flow. The differences between GAAP and the Street have grown exponentially since the early 1990s. Tracking services, such as First Call and Zaks, are increasingly discarding more charges from the definition of earnings, thereby increasing net profit.[215] The value relevance literature has documented a decline in the association between GAAP earnings and stock prices.[216] Examples of GAAP earnings charges left out of pro forma earnings include restructuring charges, write-downs and impairments, research and development costs, merger and stock purchase costs, mandatory stock compensation expense, goodwill amortization, and certain results of subsidiaries.[217] Beginning in 1990, there is a sharp divergence between GAAP and pro forma earnings. Eighty-three percent of firms discussed GAAP only in 1988, while only 28 percent discussed GAAP only in 1997; while only 18 percent discussed both in 1988, 70 percent discussed both in 1997.[218]

In recent years, the discrepancy in earnings has been so large that average Street earnings yields rises per annum were 3 percent compared with 1½ percent for GAAP earnings, net of extraordinary earnings. Even though accrual amounts are added to losses, most other nonrecurring expenses are never recovered.[219] According to Bradshaw and Sloan, the shift in emphasis from income statement to balance sheet encapsulated in Financial Accounting Standard Board concepts and standards is partially responsible.[220] Because of these and other charges that are irrelevant in predicting cash flow, Bradshaw and Sloan suggest that the SEC and the accounting profession work together to formulate standardized measurements, "a more reliable and unbiased alternative to Street earnings."[221] But the real issue is the necessity of standardizing the measure that investors use. The natural proclivity of management and analysts is often to pump IPOs and other investment banking clients' issues to increase earnings. In general, it is in the public interest for the SEC to regulate these announcements, a duty in which it has thus far proved derelict.

NOTES

1. Cover story, quoting Patrick McGurn, vice-president of Institutional Investor Services, *Business Week*, June 24, 2002.

2. *Ibid.*

3. *Ibid.*

4. John Coffee, "Liquidity versus Control: The Institutional Investor as Corporate Monitor," *Columbia L. Rev.* 91 (1991): pp. 1277, 1300–1302.

5. Albert Hirschman, *Exit Voice and Loyalty: Responses to Decline in Firms' Organizations and States* (1970).

6. *Ibid.*

7. Robert Monks and Nel Minnow, *Power and Accountability* (1991), at 256.

8. *See* "Business Round Table Corporate Governance and American Competitiveness," *Bus. Law* 26 (1990): p. 241.

9. Bernard Black, "Agents Watching Agents: The Promise and Limits of Shareholder Voice," *UCLA L. Rev.* 39 (1992): pp. 811, 831–34.

10. *See* J. Grundfest, "The Subordination of American Capital," *J. Financial Econ.* 27 (1990): p. 89.

11. Andrew Boot and Jonathon Macey, "Objectivity, Proximity, and Adaptability in Corporate Governance," Center for Economic Policy Research Discussion Paper no. 2257 (1999).

12. *Ibid.*, p. 13.

13. *Ibid.*, p. 14.

14. *Ibid.*, p. 21.

15. *Ibid.*, p. 2.

16. *Ibid.*, p. 4.

17. Adolph Berle and Gardiner Means, *The Modern Corporation and Private Property* (Business Enterprise Reprint series 1982, reprint of 1933 edition).

18. Mark Roe, "A Political Theory of American Corporate Finance," *Columbia L. Rev.* 91: p. 10; Mark Roe, "Political and Legal Restraints on Ownership and Control of Public Companies," *supra* note 59.

19. Securities and Exchange Commission (SEC), "Regulatory Reform of Communication among Shareholders, Fact Sheet" (October 15, 1992).

20. Margaret Blair, *Ownership and Control Rethinking Corporate Governance* (Brooking Institute, 1995), p. 166.

21. *Ibid.*, p. 167.

22. *Ibid.*, p. 169.

23. *Ibid.*, p. 171.

24. *Ibid.*

25. *See* chapter 4, note 4.

26. *Op. cit.*, p. 239.

27. *Ibid.*, p. 317.

28. Margaret Blair, Douglas Kruse, and Douglas Blasi, "Employee Ownership: An Unstable Form or a Stabilizing Force," in Margaret Blair and Thomas Kochan, *The New Relationship: Human Capital in the American Corporation* (Brookings, 2000).

29. *Ibid.*, introduction, p. 19.

30. 15 U.S.C. 4, 78M(d) (1988), Rule 13(d)l to 13(d)7, 17 C.F.R. §§ 240.13(4)1 to 13(d)7.

31. 17 U.S.C. § 78P-D (1988), Rule 16A1 to 161311, 17 C.F.R. H 240.16A, 1–16E.11.

32. Securities and Exchange Act of 1934, § 168, 15 U.S.C. § 78 P(B) (1988).

33. *See* SEC Rule 16A(l) 17 C.F.R. § 240, Rule 16A-1A (1991).

34. As pension funds and mutual funds switch to the index strategy, a question arises as to what the purpose of monitoring would be for an index investor. Both Coffee, *supra* note 4, at 1340 and Monks and Minnow, *Power and Accountability*, *supra* note 7, believe that an indexed fund is a permanent shareholder and is consequently well positioned to behave as a corporate monitor. However, the great degree of diversification that indexation involves means that the benefits to be derived from corporate monitoring are small in such an instance.

35. *Ibid.*, at 1353.

36. "Labor Department Opinion Letter on Proxy Voting," 17 Pens. Rep. (BNA no. 5, January 23, 1990, pp. 244–46), cited in Coffee, *supra* note 4, at 1353–54, footnotes 299, 302.

37. James Dodd Loreie, James Dodd, and Mary Hamilton Kempton, *The Stock Market: Theories in Evidence* (2d ed., 1985), p. 85; Richard Brealey and Stuart Meyers, *Principles of Corporate Finance* (3d ed., 1988), p. 156, cited in Coffee, *supra* note 4, at 1355.

38. 29 U.S.C. § 1104A(1)C (1988).

39. Coffee, *supra* note 4, at 1363, citing investment Advisor Act of 1940, V 205(a)(1), 15 U.S.C. § 80-b-5(a)(1) (1988); also, citing Tamar Frankel, 2 The Regulation of Money Managers 285–300 (IV78); Harvey Bines, The Law of Investment Management, § 503 (1978).

40. Securities Act of 1933, § 15, 15 U.S.C. § 770 (1988); Securities and Exchange Act of 1934, § 20, 15 U.S.C. § 78T (1988). This rule is partly mitigated by Rule 144, which permits an affiliate to sell up to the greater of 1 percent of a class or the average weekly trade by a security every three months. Securities Act Rule 144(e) 17 C.F.R. § 230.144(c) (1991).

41. Coffee, *supra* note 4, at 1314.

42. Stephen Prowse, "Institutional Investment Patterns and Corporate Financial Behavior in the United States and Japan," *J. Fin. Econ.* 27 (1990): p. 43. *See also* M. Jenson and W. Meckling, "Theory of the Firm: Managerial Behavior, Agency Costs, and Ownership Structure," *J. Fin. Econ.* 3 (1976): p. 30.

43. For example, Citicorp, the largest U.S. banking institution, with total assets of over $200 billion, holds only about $1 billion in equities as of 1990. (Coffee, *supra* note 4, at 1315.)

44. *Ibid.*, at 1319. (The proportion of equity capital to total assets has steadily fallen from 60 percent in the early nineteenth century, to 20 percent at the turn of this century, to below 10 percent since the early 1950s, to under 5 percent since the mid-1970s.)

45. James Brickley, Ronald Lees, and Clifford Smith, "Ownership Structure and Voting on Anti-Takeover Amendments," *Journal of Financial Economics* 20 (1988): pp. 267, 276.

46. "Pension Forum: Taking the Offensive," *Institutional Investor* 101 (December 1987); *see also*, Black, *supra* note 9, at 882–85.

47. As of 1990, one-third of all equity investments held by institutional funds are indexed to a standard index such as Standard & Poors. (Coffee, *supra* note 4, at 1339, citing David Walker, "The Increasing Role of Pension Plans in the Capital Markets or in Corporate Governance Matters," in *Institutional Investing: The Challenges and*

Responsibilities of the Twenty-First Century [Arnold W. Sametz, ed., 1991].) The New York Stock Exchange has reported that analysts estimate between $200 and $300 billion, or 30 percent of institutional assets, are held in portfolios that replicate a market index. New York Stock Exchange Press Release (June 12, 1990), cited in Coffee, *supra* note 4, at 1339.

48. "MM Companies: Its Directors Defeat Liquid Audio Nominees," *Dow Jones Business News*, October 3, 2002.

49. "Steel Partners Nominee Kassan Named to United Industrial Board," October 4, 2002.

50. "Costs Mount in Proxy Fight," *C-NET News.com*, March 13, 2002.

51. "Wyley Launches New Bid to Topple CA Management," *Computer World*, June 27, 2002.

52. There have been several developments since 1992 in proxy solicitation, particularly to do with electronic media, and a release to make it easier for issuers to communicate with shareholders. *See generally*, Craig Nordlund, "The Proxy Solicitation Process: Developments in Shareholder Communication," PLI, Preparation of Annual Disclosure Documents (January/February 2002).

53. *See* Stephen Choi, "Proxy Issue Proposals: Testing the Outcome of the 1992 SEC Reforms," *Journal of Law, Economics, and Organization* 16 (2000): p. 233.

54. *See supra* note 30–39.

55. Coffee, *supra* note 4, at 1317–18. Compare Keynes, *supra* note 104, cited in quote on pp. 166–67.

56. Richard Sloan, "Financial Accounting and Corporate Governance," *Journal of Accounting and Economics* 32 (December 2001): p. 337.

57. *Ibid.*, p. 339.

58. K. Palepu, "Predicting Takeover Targets: A Methodological and Empirical Analysis," *Journal of Accounting and Economics* 8 (1986): pp. 3–36.

59. *Op. cit.*, p. 340.

60. C. Botosan, "Disclosure Levels and the Cost of Capital," *The Accounting Review* 72 (1997): p. 323.

61. C. Becker, M. De Fond, J. Jaimabalvo, and K. R. Subramanyam, "The Effect of Audit Quality on Earnings Management," *Contemporary Accounting Research* 15 (1998): p. 1; and J. Francis, E. Maydew, and H. Sparks, "The Role of Big Six Auditors in the Credible Reporting of Accruals," *Auditing: A Journal of Theory and Practice* (1998), cited in Sloan, *supra* note 56, at 340.

62. J. Carcello and T. Neal, "Audit Committee Quality and Auditor Reporting," working paper, University of Tennessee; K. Peasnall, P. Pope, and S. Young, "Board Monitoring, Earnings Management, Do Outside Directors Influence Abnormal Accruals?" working paper, Lancaster University, cited in Sloan, *supra* note 56, at 342.

63. S. Rangan, "Earnings Management and the Determinants of Seasoned Equity Offerings," *Journal of Financial Economics* 51 (1998): p. 101; S. Teoh, T. Wong, and I. Welch, "Earnings Manipulation and the Underperformance of Seasoned Equity Offerings," *Journal of Financial Economics* 51 (1998): p. 63.

64. P. Deechow, R. Sloan, and A. Sweeney, "Causes and Consequences of Earnings Manipulation," *Contemporary Accounting Research* 13 (1996): p. 1, cited in Sloan, *supra* note 56 at 342.

65. Sloan, *supra* note 56, at 343.

66. *See*, e.g., Skinner, "Why Firms Voluntarily Disclose Bad News," *Journal of Accounting Research* 32 (1994): p. 38.

67. *Op. cit.*

68. Robert Bushman and Abbie Smith, "Financial Accounting Information and Corporate Governance," *Journal of Accounting and Economics* 32 (2001): p. 237.

69. R. La Porta, F. Lopez-De-Silanes, and R. Vishny, "Legal Determinants of External Capital," *Journal of Finance* 52, no. 3: pp. 1131–50.

70. *Ibid.*

71. R. La Porta, F. Lopez-De-Silanes, and R. Vishny, "Law and Finance," *Journal of Political Economy* (1998): pp. 1113–55.

72. Robert Bushman, E. Engel, J. Millioron, and A. Smith, "An Empirical Investigation of Trends in the Absolute and Relative Use of Earnings in Determining Cash CEO Compensation," working paper, University of Chicago, cited in Bushman, *supra* note 68, at 256.

73. *Ibid.*, cited in Bushman, *supra* note 68 at 283.

74. M. DeFond and C. Park, "The Effect of Competition on CEO Turnover," *Journal of Accounting and Economics* 27 (1999): pp. 35–56.

75. Andrei Schlieffer and Robert Vishny, "A Survey of Corporate Governance," *Journal of Finance* 52 (1997): p. 737.

76. *See*, e.g., Robert Comment and G. William Schwert, "Poison or Placebo? Evidence of the Deterrent and Wealth Effects of Modern Anti-Takeover Measures"; *see also* Steven Kaplan and Michael Weisbach, "The Success of Acquisition: Evidence from Divestitures," *Journal of Finance* 47 (1992): p. 107.

77. Roberta Romano, *The Genius of American Corporate Law* (American Enterprise Institute, 1993).

78. Frank Easterbrook and Daniel Fischel, *The Economic Structure of Corporate Law* (Harvard University Press, 1991).

79. Michael Jensen, "Active Investors, LBO's, and the Privatization of Bankruptcy," *Journal of Applied Corporate Finance* 21: p. 35; and Michael Jensen, "The Modern Industrial Corporation, Exit, and the Failures of the Internal Control Systems," *Journal of Finance* 48 (1993): p. 48.

80. Michael Jensen, "Agency Costs of Free Cash Flow, Corporate Finance, and Takeovers," *American Economic Review* 76 (1986): p. 323.

81. Mark Roe, *Strong Managers, Weak Owners: The Political Roots of American Corporate Governance* (Princeton University Press, 1993). Roe particularly demonstrates the limitations placed on financial institutions in the corporate governance arena.

82. "A Survey of Corporate Governance," *supra* note 75, p. 748.

83. *Ibid.*, p. 750.

84. Henry Manne, "Mergers and the Market for Corporate Control," *Journal of Political Economy* 75 (1965): p. 110.

85. *Op. cit.*, p. 752.

86. *Ibid.*, pp. 759–61. *See also* chapter 1, notes 26–27, and chapter 7, notes 25–26.

87. *Ibid.*, p. 762.

88. *Ibid.*, p. 766.

89. *Ibid.*

90. Bushman 2001, *supra* note 68 at 292–96.

91. Rajan and Singales, "Financial Dependence and Growth," *American Economic Review* 88 (1998): pp. 559–86.
92. W. Carlin and C. Mayer, "Finance, Investment, and Growth," working paper, University of Chicago, cited in Bushman 2001, *supra* note 68.
93. Paul Miranti, *Accountancy Comes of Age: The Development of an American Profession, 1886–1940* (Chapel Hill: University of North Carolina Press, 1990), p. 33.
94. *Ibid.*, p. 57.
95. *Ibid.*, p. 58.
96. *Ibid.*, pp. 61–62.
97. *Ibid.*, pp. 89–90.
98. *Ibid.*, p. 94.
99. *Ibid.*, p. 97.
100. *Ibid.*, p. 96.
101. *Ibid.*, p. 103.
102. *Ibid.*, p. 115.
103. *Ibid.*, p. 139.
104. *Ibid.*, p. 140.
105. *Ibid.*, p. 142.
106. *Ibid.*, p. 153.
107. *Ibid.*, pp. 164–66.
108. *Ibid.*, p. 174.
109. *Ibid.*, p. 175.
110. *Ibid.*, p. 176.
111. *Ibid.*, pp. 190–91.
112. American Institute of CPAs, Accounting Terminology Bulletin no. 1, p. 76.
113. Allan Drebin, "Cash-Flowitis': Malady or Syndrome?" in Thomas Lee, ed., *Cash Flow Reporting: A Recent History of Accounting Practice* (Garland Publishing, 1993), p. 43.
114. *Ibid.*, p. 49.
115. *See* Maurice Moonitz, "Some Reflections on the Investment Credit Experience," *Journal of Accounting Research* (spring 1966): pp. 47–61; Robert Van Riper, *Setting Standards for Financial Reporting: FASB and the Struggle for Control of a Critical Process* (Quorum Books, 1994).
116. Tony Hope and Rob Grey, "Power and Policy Making: The Development of an R&D Standard"; Tony Hope and John Briggs, "Accounting Policymaking—Some Lessons from the Deferred Taxation Debate"; and Christopher Nobes, "A Political History of Goodwill in the U.K.: An Illustration of Cyclical Standards Setting," *Abacus* (September 1992): pp. 142–49.
117. Leonard Spaceck, "Can We Define Generally Accepted Accounting Principles," in *Cash Flow Reporting, supra* note 113, p. 60.
118. *Ibid.*, p. 45, citing ARB 44 but it does not apply to utilities.
119. *Ibid.*, p. 46.
120. D. Schackelford and T. Shevlin, "Empirical Tax Research in Accounting," *Journal of Accounting and Economics* 32 (2001): p. 321.
121. N. Jenkins and M. Pincus, "LIFO Versus FIFO: Updating What We Have Learned," working paper, University of Iowa, cited in "Empirical Research," *supra* note 120, at 329.

122. *Op. cit.*, at pp. 330–31.
123. *Ibid.*, p. 332.
124. *Ibid.*, p. 333.
125. *Ibid.*, p. 338.
126. *Ibid.*, p. 347.
127. Stephen Zeff, "Playing the Congressional Card on Employee Stock Options: A Fearful Escalation in the Impact of the Economic Consequences Lobbying on Standards Setting," pp. 177–78, in T. E. Cooke and C. W. Nobes, *The Development of Accounting in an International Context: A Festschrift in Honour of R. H. Parker* (1997).
128. *Ibid.*, p. 184.
129. *Ibid.*, p. 185.
130. *Ibid.*, citing Congressional Record Senate S5035, 5040.
131. *Ibid.*, p. 186.
132. FAS 123, paragraph 45.
133. SFAC no. 1, par. 41.
134. *Ibid.*, par. 30 and 35.
135. *Ibid.*, par. 49.
136. *See generally, Cash Flow Reporting, supra* note 113.
137. R. W. Holthausen and R. L. Watts, "The Relevance of Value-Relevance Literature for Financial Accounting Standard Setting," *Journal of Accounting and Economics* 31 (2001): pp. 3, 28.
138. *Ibid.*, p. 32.
139. *Ibid.*, p. 33.
140. *Ibid.*, p. 34.
141. S. Fabricant, "Reevaluations of Fixed Assets 1925–1934" (National Bureau of Economic Research, 1936) and J. Yang, *Goodwill and Other Intangibles* (New York: Ronald Press, 1927), cited in Holthausen and Watts, *supra* note 137 at 35.
142. R. G. Walker, "The SEC's Ban on Upward Asset Reevaluations and the Disclosure of Values," *Abacus* 28 (1992): pp. 3–35, cited in Holthausen and Watts, *supra* note 137 at 35.
143. *Op. cit.*
144. *Ibid.*
145. Holthausen and Watts, *supra* note 137, at 35.
146. "Unseen Wealth: Report of the Brooking Task Force on Intangibles," Margaret Blair and Steven Wallman, co-chairs.
147. Financial Accounting Standards Board, "Qualitative Characteristics of Accounting Information," Statement of Financial Accounting Concepts 2, par. 91–93 (1980).
148. One of the first issues was a $100 billion bond offering by Dow Chemicals in 1994. In 1999, Formula 1 issued a $1.4 billion contract backed by its intellectual property rights in contracts including staging and advertising. "Unseen Wealth," *supra* note 146 at 107. *See also* Clark Eustace, "Intellectual Property and the Capital Markets," working paper (City University Business School, May 2000).
149. "Unseen Wealth," *supra* note 146, at 40.
150. *Ibid.*
151. *Ibid.*, p. 54.
152. *Ibid.*, p. 63.

153. *Ibid.*, p. 67.
154. *Ibid.*, p. 69.
155. *Ibid.*, p. 70.
156. *See* chapter 4, note 11, and accompanying text.
157. Robert Litan and Peter Wallison, *The GAAP Gap: Corporate Disclosure in the Internet Age* (American Enterprise Institution Brookings Joint Center for Regulatory Studies, 2000).
158. *Ibid.*, p. 5.
159. *Ibid.*
160. Robert Schiller, *Irrational Exuberance* (Princeton University Press, 2000).
161. *Op. cit.*, p. 6.
162. *Ibid.*
163. Amey Stone, "How Everyone Missed Worldcom," *Business Week*, July 3, 2002.
164. *Op. cit.*, p. 12.
165. *Ibid.*, p. 24.
166. *Ibid.*, p. 34.
167. *Ibid.*, p. 37.
168. *Ibid.*, p. 38.
169. *Ibid.*, p. 41.
170. *See* chapter 4, "Accounting for the SEC."
171. *See generally*, Baruch Lev, *Intangibles: Management Measurement and Reporting* (Brookings, 2001).
172. *The GAAP Gap*, *supra* note 157, at 65.
173. *See* chapter 1, note 373, and accompanying text.
174. *Op. cit.*, at 58–59.
175. *Ibid.*
176. "Unseen Wealth," *supra* note 146.
177. W. Beaver, *Financial Reporting: An Accounting Revolution* (Prentice Hall, 1998).
178. P. M. Healy and K. G. Palepu, "Information Asymmetry, Corporate Disclosure, and the Capital Markets," *Journal of Accounting and Economics* 31 (2001): p. 405.
179. *See* working paper by Lang and Lunholm, University of Michigan, cited in Healey, *op. cit.*, at 421.
180. *Ibid.*, p. 416.
181. J. Francis and L. Soffer, "The Relative Informativeness of Analysts Stock Recommendations and Earnings Forecast Revisions," *Journal of Accounting Research* 35 (1997): p. 192.
182. *Op. cit.*
183. J. Chang, "The Decline in Value Relevance of Earnings and Book Values," working paper, University of Pennsylvania, cited in Healey, *supra* note 178.
184. *Ibid.*, and E. Amir and B. Lang, "Value-Relevance of Nonfinancial Information: The Wireless Communications Industry," *Journal of Accounting and Finance* 22 (1996): p. 3.
185. *Ibid.*, p. 433.
186. *Ibid.*, p. 434.
187. *See* chapter 1, note 454.
188. *See* chapter 1, "The EU Single Market in Banking: The Basel Convergence and . . ." and chapter 2, "The New Capital Adequacy Accord" *generally*.

189. *See* chapter 1, note 99, and accompanying text, and chapter 1, notes 431–435.
190. S. Basu, "The Conservatism Principle and the Asymmetric Timeliness of Earnings," *Journal of Accounting and Economics* 24 (1997): 3–37.
191. Holthausen and Watts, *supra* note 137 at 40, citing D. A. Guenther, E. L. Maydew, and S. E. Nutter, "Financial Reporting, Tax Costs, and Book-Tax Conformity," *Journal of Accounting and Economics* 23: pp. 225–48, "Empirical Tax Research in Accounting," *supra* note 120.
192. Holthausen and Watts, *supra* note 137.
193. M. E. Barth, W. Beaver, and W. Landsman, "The Relevance of Value Relevance Literature for Financial Accounting Standard Setting: Another View," *Journal of Accounting and Economics* 31 (2001): p. 77.
194. *Ibid.*, p. 92.
195. Benjamin Graham and David L. Dodd (David Le Fevre), *Security Analysis* (McGraw-Hill, 1934).
196. S. P. Kothari, "Capital Markets Research in Accounting," *Journal of Accounting and Economics* 31 (2001): p. 105.
197. *Ibid.*, p. 113.
198. *Ibid.; See also infra* note 214 to 216 and accompanying text.
199. *See* chapter 4, "Securities."
200. Kothari, *supra* note 196, at 203.
201. *Ibid.*, p. 204.
202. Mark Roe, "Codetermination and German Securities Markets," in Margaret Blair, *Employees and Corporate Governance* (Brookings, 1999).
203. T. E. Lee, "Cash Flow Accounting's Recent History: A Kuhnian Interpretation of a Changing Accounting Emphasis," in *Cash Flow Reporting*, *supra* note 113, at 19.
204. Financial Accounting Standard no. 125.
205. *Ibid.*, par. 109–11.
206. *Ibid.*, par. 327.
207. George Staubus, "Cash Flow Accounting and Liquidity: Cash Flow Potential and Wealth," in T. E. Lee, *Cash Flow Reporting*, *supra* note 113.
208. *Ibid.*
209. *Ibid.*
210. *See* chapter 2, note 75, and accompanying text.
211. *Op. cit.*
212. Accounting Standards Board, "Cash Flow Statements," Financial Reporting Standard 1 (1990).
213. *Ibid.*, par. 51.
214. D. A. Egginton, "In Defense of Profit Measurement: Some Limitations on Cash Flow and Value Added as Performance Measures for External Reporting" (1984), in T. E. Lee, *Cash Flow Reporting*, *supra* note 113.
215. Mark Bradshaw and Richard Sloan, "GAAP versus the Street: An Empirical Assessment of Two Definitions of Earnings," *Journal of Accounting Research* 40, no. 1 (March 2002).
216. D. W. Collins, E. L. Maydew, and I. S. Weiss, "Changes in the Value Relevance of Earnings and Book Values over the Past 40 Years," *Journal of Accounting and Economics* 24 (1997): p. 39.
217. *Op. cit.*, p. 5.

218. *Ibid.*, pp. 25–26.
219. Mark Bradshaw and Richard Sloan, "Wall Street versus the Street: Pro Forma Earnings Fill a Reporting Vacuum," *Investor's Relations Quarterly* (Forthcoming, 2002).
220. SFAC no. 6 and SFAS nos. 109, 121, 142, and 144; The shift is that instead of amortizing into income, firms are encouraged to take the charges. Negative charges have grown 10 percent to 20 percent to 2 percent of expenses.
221. *Op. cit.*

CHAPTER 6

Reform: Sarbanes-Oxley, Its Consequences, and the European Response

THE SARBANES-OXLEY ACT: CORPORATE GOVERNANCE, FINANCIAL DISCLOSURE, AND ECONOMIC CRIME

Overview

The Sarbanes-Oxley Act,[1] signed into law by President Bush on July 30, 2002, may profoundly change corporate governance, regulation of the accounting profession, and the role of securities analysts. Under Title 1 of the act, a new Public Company Accounting Oversight Board (PCAOB) has authority over registered public accounting firms, which will include any firm that audits public companies. The PCAOB will conduct a program of inspections and establish procedures for the investigation and discipline of public accounting firms. The PCAOB is authorized to impose sanctions for failure to supervise and has the authority to suspend or bar public accounting firms and associated persons from Securities and Exchange Commission (SEC) practice, but it remains subject to SEC oversight. Under Title 2 of the act, nonaudit services must be approved by the audit committee (subject to a 5 percent exception). Certain other activities performed by auditors are prohibited including legal services and expert services.

Perhaps the most significant changes are in the arena of corporate governance, mostly contained in Title 3. Each issuer (under subsequent commission rules) shall be required to disclose a code of ethics, and any changes thereto must be disclosed on Form 8K (within two business days). For the first time in U.S. history, the federal law is determining ethics requirements for promulgate attorneys who, under this title, must report evidence of material violations of securities law to the chief legal officer or chief executive officer (CEO), and, if such officers fail to take action, attorneys are required to report such evidence to the audit committee.[2] The single most important provision of the act may be mandating that it be the responsibility of the audit committee to engage auditors.[3] Lead auditors must be rotated, and the audit committee must either include a financial expert, defined by education or experience as a public accountant, or the company must disclose the reasons it has failed to do so. Certain other activities performed by auditors are prohibited, including legal services and expert services, and all other activities must be approved by the audit committee.[4]

Under Section 302 of the act, certification of periodic reports by the CEO and chief financial officer (CFO) must state that, based on the officer's knowledge, the report does not contain any material untrue fact or any material omission (tracking the language of 10b-5) and that the financial statement and other financial information contained in the report "fairly present in all material respects the financial condition of the issuer and results of operation of the issuer." The officers must further certify that internal controls have been designed to ensure that material information related to the issuer and its consolidated subsidiaries is made known to the CEO and that such controls have been evaluated as of 90 days prior to the report.[5] It is also an offense to coerce, manipulate, or mislead an independent auditor.[6] If, as a result of misconduct, an issuer is required to restate due to material noncompliance, the CEO and CFO will be required to disgorge bonuses relating to the period of the restatement.[7] All civil penalties and disgorgement funds are to be added to a fund for victims of securities fraud.[8] Companies must disclose in periodic reports that they have adopted a code of ethics for senior employees or must disclose why they have not adopted such a code.[9] It is unlawful under this title to directly or indirectly extend credit to an officer or director (unless made on market terms or as part of home financing).[10]

Under Title 4, material changes in the condition of the issuer must be disclosed to the public on a rapid and current basis.[11] Under Title 5, analysts' conflicts of interests are prohibited, and analysts cannot receive compensation from corporate finance departments.[12] The act applies to foreign issuers listed in the United States,[13] all auditors of record for issuers listed in the United States, and all working papers related to a U.S. public offering.[14] The SEC and other agencies undertake certain studies including studies of principle-based rather than rule-based accounting standards (conducted by the comptroller general) under Title 2.[15] Under Title 7, these studies are mandated: concentration in the accounting industry,[16] the role and function of credit rating agencies,[17] and a report on violators and violations,[18] enforcement actions,[19] and Government Accounting Office (GAO) study on investment banks and their role in the collapse of Enron and Global Crossing.[20] Other significant provisions of the act include a ban on insider trading during pension blackout periods (Title 3)[21] and a lengthening of the statute of limitations for securities fraud[22] (Title 8). The SEC is mandated to promulgate various other rules (which have been promulgated and discussed in the notes) under Title 3, including rules of professional responsibility for attorneys;[23] improper influence on the conduct of auditors[24] and Section 302 certifications; and, under Title IV, rules for pro forma earnings disclosures and standards for off-balance sheet transactions.[25] Perhaps the most important provision increases appropriations for the SEC by two-thirds for fiscal year 2003.[26]

Under Title 8, "The Corporate and Criminal Fraud Act of 2002," the knowing alteration, destruction, or falsification of any record or document with the intent to impede, obstruct, or influence an investigation may lead to fines and imprisonment of not more than 20 years. There are explicit criminal penalties for schemes to defraud or obtain money under false pretenses in connection with the purchase or sale of a security. The act contains a mandatory review of sentencing guidelines for the U.S. Sentencing Commission for such offenses and a similar review for securities and accounting fraud and related offenses. Under Title 11, a Civil Cause of Action for whistleblowers who allege retaliation is provided for, as are criminal penalties, including imprisonment for a period of up to 10 years.[27] This title also enables the commission to impose officer and director bars (previously the SEC had to sue offenders in federal court).[28]

Perhaps the most forceful provision of the act, contained in Title 9, Section 906, is the criminal penalty for certifying a periodic report (the periodic statements—the 10Ks and 10Qs) that does not fully comply with 13a and 15d of the Securities and Exchange Act of 1934, which demand that the information contained in the statements "fairly presents, in all material respects, the financial conditions and results of operation of the issuer." Whoever certifies a report knowing that it does not comport with the provisions of the section (that is, fully comply) with the reporting provisions is subject to 10 years at Club Fed and a fine of up to $1 million; anyone who willfully certifies any statement that does not comport with the provisions of 906 (a) and (b) is entitled to 20 years at Club Fed and a penalty of up to $5 million.

Certification and Economic Crime: Criminal Penalties for Knowing or Willful Certification under Sarbanes-Oxley

Putting aside the distinction between willfully and knowingly certifying a statement that does not fully comply with the sections of the securities law or fairly present the financial position of the company in all material respects, these violations are criminal, while the 302 certification requirement that a periodic statement does not contain any untrue statement or omissions of material facts is civil in nature. Thus, a statement that was untrue but unrelated to financial reporting would not be considered criminal under Sarbanes-Oxley unless there is a scheme to defraud under Section 804. The 906 criminal statute creates both a lower and different threshold than that required for a conviction of wire fraud. In particular, there is no need to plead with particularity or prove reliance (elements of common law fraud). And, given the scienter requirement under the Private Securities Litigation Reform Act of 1995 (PSLRA), the standard for criminal conviction is identical to those imposed under the PSLRA for class-action lawsuits (except that class action must survive a stay of discovery if the facts are not sufficiently pleaded to indicate scienter).[29] Under 906(a), it is not even necessary that a report be materially misleading. Thus a de minimis failure to comply might result in a jail term. Sections 13a and 15d concern material contracts, officer and director remuneration, and financial statements (balance sheets and profit and loss statements); therefore, in most instances, we are talking about financial statements, although it is arguable that in the case of Enron, for instance, Fastow's recompense in various special purpose entities would be tantamount to undisclosed officer compensation, even if he had the board of director's approval.

It is unclear what kinds of financial statements fail to comply with this section. Since the SEC delegates rules for financial statements to FASB, which promulgates Generally Accepted Accounting Principles (GAAP) and is likely to be the designated body under the act, if it is independently funded, these are the rules that must be complied with. However, in addition, the periodic report must also fairly present the financial condition of the issuer. Thus a statement may comply with GAAP and still subject the certifying officer to criminal liability. This creates a similar construct to the true and fair override required for foreign issuers under Form 20F.

Headline cases do not provide good examples. Although Worldcom's accounting fraud led to the passage of Sarbanes-Oxley,[30] the capitalization of renting provider facilities should definitely have been expensed under GAAP (even though it will certainly be argued otherwise). In Enron, the failure to consolidate the balance sheet of at least one special purpose entity (SPE)—Chewco—which was not capitalized with 3 percent of independent equity as required by FASB rules,[31] is another instance of a clear-cut violation of GAAP, which would consequently result in a failure to comply with Section 12 of the Securities and Exchange Act of 1934. By contrast, the treatment of lease swap arrangements in Global Crossings appears perfectly legal, although this practice may or may not have been ended depending upon the legal enforceability of an SEC interpretive release.[32] In the interim (until SPE rules are in effect), failure to make mention of other partnerships, although technically compliant with GAAP, would violate the "fairly present" requirement of Sarbanes-Oxley. Failure to make nonperiodic disclosure, however egregious, would not result in criminal culpability under the act.

Fraudulent or Misleading Accounting Practices

In a 1998 speech, Arthur Levitt, the SEC chairman, described four of the most popular accounting gimmicks: revenue recognition where companies recognize revenue even if sales are contingent or subject to expenses; big bath restructuring charges; merger—in-process research and development (R&D) in connection with a merger (taking this as a charge and expensing it on the balance sheet reduces future expenses in the profit and loss statement); and cookie jar reserves when management creates inflated reserves and later releases them into income.[33] There are more permutations on reserves and mergers that will be addressed later.

There are several conditions under GAAP that must be satisfied before revenue may be recognized: (1) persuasive evidence of an arrangement, (2) delivery of goods or services, (3) the seller's price to the buyer is fixed or determinable, and (4) collectibility is reasonably assured.[34] Where the buyer has a right of return, specific conditions apply, including that the sale not be contingent on resale, that the buyer assumes risk of damage or theft, and the transaction has economic substance, meaning that the buyer is not a straw man. Channel stuffing, with or without the right of return, occurs when a buyer is induced to order more goods than it would in the normal course of business. In the context of 10b-5 actions, the courts have been reluctant to consider this fraudulent or even improper. The First Circuit has held that "There is nothing inherently improper in pressing for sales to be made earlier than in the normal course,"[35] and the Ninth Circuit dismissed a claim of channel stuffing as "speculation made in hindsight."[36]

One case involving revenue recognition highlights the tendency of firms to recognize revenue without recognizing expenses. The complaint by the SEC against Xerox alleged that Xerox accelerated $3 billion in revenue, inflating its net income by $1.5 billion, and that by 1998 $3 of every $10 in pretax earnings resulted from undisclosed accounting actions.[37] Under GAAP, Xerox was entitled to book the value of the sales of the equipment but was required to capitalize the revenue from the service contracts and the financing income derived from the leases. The SEC described the accounting practice as false and misleading and fraudulent. But, regardless of whether the conduct was fraudulent or a scheme to defraud, if the practices did not comply with the relevant practices regarding financial statements and the financial statements were knowingly certified by the CFO or the CEO, criminal liability would be present.

Merger-related gimmicks can include the cookie jar motif or the in-process R&D variety. Other forms include goodwill write-offs and write downs of tangible assets. After a merger, companies have often taken a charge in excess of what is required and have released the excess into income. Since this is not specifically countermanded by GAAP, we are in a gray area. But a charge against earnings taken with the intent to mislead investors as to earnings, even if technically complying with GAAP, would not be a fair presentation of the financial condition of the issuer. Thus, there would be grounds for criminal prosecution. In *U.S. v. Simon*, Judge Friendly upheld the conviction of three auditors for fraud, even though there was expert testimony that the financial statements complied with GAAP.[38] AOL's capitalization of customer acquisition costs between 1993 and 1995 is a more complex case. This seems to be a clear violation of GAAP, but there was no immediate enforcement action taken by the SEC. Consequently, AOL would have had an argument that the accounting treatment fairly presented the financial condition of the company. But, if it contravened GAAP, which represents rules imposed by the SEC, we might be in a gray area. Cendant marketed a number of membership profits, recording the revenues but delaying the expenses. However, its biggest game came from merger and acquisition costs and the reversal of these costs into revenue. Officers of Cendant were charged with fraud.[39] Waste Management moved operating expenses like interest expense and maintenance and repair to the balance sheet as plant and equipment. This resulted in the first enforcement action against an accounting firm—Arthur Anderson—since 1985.[40] Waste Management also used gains from its exchange of an interest in ServiceMaster to offset $160 million in unrelated expenses.[41]

By contrast, the situation at Lucent was more textured. Lucent reduced the reserve for doubtful accounts and inventory obsolescence, reversed a previously recorded restructuring reserve and released the money into income. It also wrote off $2.4 billion of $4.1 billion of the purchase price of acquired companies as in-process R&D, thereby increasing income in the future. It also changed pension assumptions.[42] Medaphis used percentage of completion contracts recording revenue before products were shipped, lengthened amortization periods, shifted future expenses to a current period as a charge against earnings, capitalized software costs, and included joint-venture income as revenue.[43] Another method commonly employed, and used by Medaphis, is instructing a target company to take charges or reserves and releasing these into income.[44] The SEC had no trouble characterizing this stance as materially misleading and a departure from GAAP but did not term it fraudulent.[45] If these actions were known to the CEO and in the financial statements certified by him, it is quite likely that these actions would now be considered criminal.

Taking charges or reserves has been among the most prominent methods employed to boost earnings. Sunbeam took big restructuring charges and put over $25 million into income. Had it not done so, pretax quarter profit would have been down 7 percent instead of up 26 percent.[46] In May 2001, the SEC found that Sunbeam had created $35 million in bogus restructuring reserves and other cookie jar reserves (such as a litigation reserve). Sunbeam also recorded bill and hold sales as earnings in 1997.[47] The SEC, in contradistinction to Medaphis, alleged that Sunbeam engaged in an illegal scheme to defraud and the statements were materially false and misleading (as opposed to misleading).[48] In December 1998, the SEC sued, alleging that the $20 million had been improperly placed in reserve. In *In the Matter of W. R. Grace*, another administrative action, the SEC alleged that Grace made false and misleading reports by smoothing over the earnings of its wholly owned subsidiary, National Medical Care Inc (NMC). The allegations include false filings, public dissemination of false and misleading statements, failure to maintain adequate books and records, and failure to maintain adequate accounting controls. NMC received unanticipated Medicare reimbursement benefits that were placed in an excess reserve at the behest of Grace management including the CEO. The Grace management directed that the excess reserves be used for future profit planning. The excess reserve was reversed when NMC was spun off and the CEO falsely ascribed this to a change in accounting method. These actions were termed fraudulent and were alleged to constitute a violation of 10b-5.[49]

In a recent action, Microsoft settled with the SEC for cookie jar reserves, even though the term "cookie jar" is not used in the settlement order;[50] there was no allegation of fraud. In the September 1999 quarter, Microsoft had released $110 million into income from reserves. The 906 Certification does not require fraud. If the CEO or CFO knowingly certified a financial statement given this set of facts (although it only enhances the value of the company), that officer would clearly fall within the ambit of the criminal statute.

Legal Gimmicks

There are other, far more egregious practices that seem to be perfectly legal under existing GAAP. When companies with different calendar years merge, revenue from the stub period is often depressed. USRX reported a $7.6 million profit per month when it merged into COMS versus a year earlier when it had reported approximately $230 million per month. COMS may have deferred this revenue to a later quarter. COMS also took a charge of $426 million related to the acquisition of which almost $100 million was a write-off of tangible assets, thereby reducing depreciation and amortization expenses in the future.[51]

Another way companies hide expenses is by taking goodwill write-offs from acquisitions. In July 2001, JDS Uniphase wrote off $44.8 billion from acquisitions and it allocated $38.7 billion to the previous period by a change in accounting method. (Presumably this practice will be ended by the SEC release on change of accounting methods.)[52] A more complex ploy was used by Compaq, which took a revaluation for tangible reserves acquired in an acquisition as negative goodwill (the excess of tangible assets over purchase price). By allocating these costs to assets, long-term depreciation and amortization will be lower, thereby raising earnings.[53] In 2001, FASB changed goodwill accounting rules, eliminating the pooling of interest method for acquisitions and requiring the purchase accounting rules, and also ended automatic amortization, allowing assets to be kept at book value unless impaired.[54] Now more companies will be likely to keep assets at book value, claiming no impairment has taken place.

Other methods that disguise a company's true financial condition include percentage of completion contracts and changing from an operating lease to a capital lease (a disguised sale where the burden of ownership changes), since the present value of the lease payments is recorded as revenue in the initial period, and the determination of lease assumptions by changing the discount rate assumption can boost revenue substantially. This is akin to changes in payments of defined benefit pension plans where changing the rate of return can lead to lowering the amount necessary to pay into plans. IBM increased its profit $195 million in 2000 when it raised the expected rate of return from 9.5 percent to 10 percent.[55] This may be the next big accounting scandal. Companies generally imputed a 9.5 percent rate of return in 2001 while the real rate of return was −6 percent.

Thus there are a number of accounting ploys that can be utilized to inflate earnings, including shifting revenue, charges, and reserves related to restructuring and acquisitions; recording gain on uncertain sales; changing lease and pension assumptions; and changes in accounting. Which ones are criminal? Which ones are likely to result in SEC investigations and civil penalties? It is particularly urgent that Generally Accepted Accounting Principles are more specifically defined, given the new criminal penalties resulting from the certification to "comply fully" with SEC requirements and to "fairly present the condition of the company." However, GAAP is, in many circumstances, overbroad, ambiguous, and susceptible to unlimited interpretations. The loopholes must be closed. Principle-based, rather than rule-based, standards would be absurd, given the criminal penalties that Sarbanes-Oxley certification imposes. That Congress has proposed such a study makes one wonder how much legislators understand or care to understand about financial reporting or white-collar crime.

Cooperation with the SEC

The criminal provisions of Sarbanes-Oxley must be understood within the gestalt of SEC enforcement actions, even though the SEC is not the arbiter of whether criminal prosecution is warranted. SEC enforcement action is likely to affect the decision of U.S. attorneys to indict. The SEC has enunciated four principles that it will use to evaluate a company's cooperation: self-policing, self-reporting, remediation (whether the company properly disciplined those who are accountable), and cooperation (whether the company provided the SEC with all available information).[56] Where there is evidence of criminal wrongdoing, and the Sarbanes-Oxley statute clearly enlarges these instances, the issues of preserving attorney-client privilege, assuring that an attorney is present at all investigations, and asserting the right against self-incrimination will certainly countermand the priority of cooperation. Since the SEC does not determine whether criminal prosecutions will be launched, the prospect of conflicts between the SEC and the Department of Justice and various U.S. attorneys is evident.

The Future under Sarbanes-Oxley

Sarbanes-Oxley expands the definition of economic crime in the sphere of securities, particularly with regard to financial reporting. While scienter is required, criminal intent or even the intent to mislead rather than the intent to fail to comply is not required. There are numerous instances where a CEO might believe that the financial statement conforms to GAAP even if it fails to present the financial condition of the company. Isn't this a highly subjective standard? If CEOs bend over backward to present the financial condition of the company in all material respects, they will cause earnings to be lower and might well find themselves out of a job, but that option might be preferable to the slammer. In the 1990s, any CEO who considered it an essential part of his job to fairly present, in all material respects, the financial condition of the company would not have had great staying power.

As in the Savings and Loan (S&L) crisis, the current financial crisis is sure to lead to many prosecutions under Sarbanes-Oxley. But will these actions really constitute economic crime? Does "scienter" imply mens rea? Here, one must ponder the nature of crime itself. Deterrence alone is a sufficient basis for criminalizing behavior. But what kind of misconduct or intent should be sufficient? Yet the purpose of the legislation is self-evident and best expressed by Voltaire in *Candide* in discussing the underlying philosophy of a provision of eighteenth-century English military law: "In England, it is considered good to hang an admiral from time to time to encourage the others."

THE SEC AND SELF-REGULATORY ORGANIZATIONS (THE NASD AND THE NYSE)

In May 2002, the New York Stock Exchange (NYSE) proposed new listing standards to apply to all listed companies, with certain exceptions. The NYSE amended Section 303A of the listing rules to require all public companies to have a majority of independent directors.[57] The independence standards are more comprehensive than those under European voluntary disclosure codes. The board of directors must make an affirmative determination that a proposed independent director has "no material relationship" with a listed company as partner, shareholder, or officer of a company that has a relationship with the listed company. Certain associations with a firm will result in a five year cooling-off period:[58] A director who was an employee, auditor, or member of a board with an interlocking directorate of which an executive officer of the listed company is a member of the compensation committee of the other company.[59] To empower nonmanagement directors, they are obligated to meet in regularly scheduled executive sessions without management.[60] Listed companies must have a nominating/corporate governance committee under a written charter, composed entirely of independent directors.[61] Listed companies must have a compensation committee composed of entirely independent directors and a written charter that, at a minimum must address corporate goals and directives relating to compensation and the production of annual reports. The compensation committee must review and approve corporate goals relating to compensation.[62] The NYSE rules also stipulate that sole remuneration for members of the audit committee should be directors' fees.[63] Echoing Sarbanes-Oxley, the audit committee, which is required to have a written charter, must, at a minimum, have sole responsibility for retaining and terminating auditors.[64] Each listed company must have an audit function and retain, as necessary, professional advice from lawyers and accountants.[65]

Shareholders must vote on equity-based compensation plans.[66] A permutation on Sarbanes-Oxley's corporate code of ethics[67] is the Corporate Governance Guidelines required by the NYSE, which require articulation of director qualification standards and orientation and training, management succession, director responsibilities and director access to management, director compensation guidelines, and an annual performance evaluation of the board. The NYSE guidelines directly incorporate Sarbanes-Oxley requirements for a code of ethics and disclosure of any waivers.[68] There follows a laundry list of issues for listed companies to address.[69] Listed foreign issuers must disclose any way in which their corporate governance system differs from that of the United States.[70] These original proposals have been superceded by a less revolutionary program discussed in chapter 8. Finally, the NYSE may issue a letter of reprimand to any listed company that violates listing requirements.[71]

The National Association of Dealers (NASD) and the NYSE have both addressed analyst conflict-of-interest questions. The NYSE amended Rule 472. Research department personnel must not be subject to any supervision by investment banking personnel, and research reports may not be subject to approval or review by the investment banking department. Any communication between investment banking and analyst research divisions, which is permitted only to confirm the accuracy of analysts' reports, if in writing, must be transmitted through legal or compliance departments. Any other communication must be in the presence of a member of the legal or compliance departments. Under Subsection 3, research analysts may not provide research summaries, research rating, or price targets to the investment banking department.[72] Other provisions in the NASD/NYSE proposals place restrictions on analyst compensation arrangements. Analysts may not receive compensation from specific transactions, and if they receive any compensation from investment banking revenues, they must disclose the fact in the firm's research report. Firms would also have to disclose whether they had comanaged an equity offering of the issuer in the last 12 months.[73] Firms cannot issue favorable reports as an inducement for investment banking business and would be prevented from issuing favorable reports during a cooling-off period of 40 days during which the firm led or comanaged an initial public offering (IPO) or within 10 days of a secondary offering. Analysts, or household members, may not purchase stock before an IPO and cannot purchase stocks followed by the analyst for a specified period.[74] The rules also require analysts and firms to disclose ownership of securities in the research report. Firms must also disclose the meaning of all ratings such as "buy," "sell," and "hold," which must be consistent with their plain meaning and must disclose the percentage of all ratings assigned to each category.[75] Inside the industry, these rules, particularly the communication documentation required for interface between research and investment banking divisions, is called the Lumberjack Employment Act because of its potential for generating paperwork.

In September 2002, the SEC issued a proposal for rulemaking on the certification of analysts[76] akin to the CEO certification under Sarbanes-Oxley. The analyst would be required to certify that research reports represented the analyst's personal view and that no part of the compensation the analyst received is related to the specific recommendation in the research report; if it was, the analyst would be required to specify the source and amount of the compensation and is obligated to further disclose that compensation may influence the recommendation in the research report. In a public appearance, an analyst must certify in writing that the recommendations accurately reflect the analyst's personal view and that no part of the analyst's compensation is directly or indirectly related to any specific recommendations.[77] If the analyst is unable to so certify, the broker-dealer must keep a record of a statement, and all research reports must state the inability to certify and the reasons therefore for a 120-day disclosure period after the appearance.[78]

THE ROLE OF RATING AGENCIES

Studies already mandated by Sarbanes-Oxley[79] could give rise to new legislation. The SEC created Nationally Recognized Statistical Rating Organizations (NSRO), stating that, "to a limited extent," it had recognized the usefulness "as a basis for stating the dividing line for securities with a greater or lesser degree of market volatility,"[80] and Rule 15c-1 embeds this in law as a means of determining capital adequacy value of various credit instruments. The rating agencies succeeded in procuring for themselves a broad exemption to Regulation FD.[81] Other work that requires the use of NSRO is the determination of which instruments are suitable for money market mutual funds and the use of NSRO investment grade ratings to streamline S-3 regulations.[82] Additionally, the comptroller of the currency of the Department of the Treasury adopted ratings as a means to measure the quality of national bank books bond portfolios.[83] Professor Frank Portnoy has said that "the web of regulation" pertaining to the use of credit ratings by regulators is so complex "that a thorough review would occupy hundreds, perhaps thousands of pages."[84]

Professor Jonathon Macey proposes that the SEC should consider whether rating agencies should be required to disclose to what extent the rating is based on material nonpublic information, the nature of the information, or if there is no basis that the reasonable investor would consider sufficient to make a determination of the value of the security to so disclose.[85] He advocates the use of credit spreads instead of ratings since they are, in his opinion, frequently more reliable. One study has shown that credit ratings, despite access to private information, lag information contained in the price of a security by one year.[86] Regardless of whether this is true, credit ratings are, at best, subjective and ought only to be a supplementary tool of regulators.

Professor Macey also states that where credit ratings are used instead of credit spreads, NSRO should "at the very least be held accountable for their actions." His chief concern is about the regulatory use of ratings since he believes that market participants are sophisticated enough to ignore ratings. In Enron, credit rating agencies did not downgrade Enron's bonds sufficiently because they presumed that the merger with Dynergy would succeed and Fitch, for example, changed the rating from negative to evolving.[87] But, "The real problem with the declining quality of ratings is that market regulators are using ratings as a substitute for regulation. To the extent that ratings are of a poor quality, the quality of these myriad regulatory schemes are compromised. The quality of U.S. financial regulation is being compromised by its pervasive reliance on credit ratings." But it is not only the U.S. system of financial regulation that is being compromised. Credit ratings are used internationally under the new G-10 accord now in progress.[88]

FUTURE REFORMS

NSRO are enshrined in regulation and given a regulatory subsidy without having any definitive responsibilities. The industry is oligopolistic, and the SEC has not been quick to recognize newcomers, either because these are few and far between or because of official stonewalling. Concentration in the accounting industry has posed similar threats. The much-publicized accounting industry lobby certainly had an effect on attempts to change accounting industry standards.[89] The separation of auditing and consulting may also eventually be effectuated. Sarbanes-Oxley uses audit committee oversight and disclosure of additional services as a partial remedy. But, like conflict of interest problems posed by analysts, the provision of auditing and consulting still poses less than subtle hazards. Companies can turn the spigot of consulting services up or down depending upon how compliant accounting firms are on the audit side. Despite all the fanfare, very few companies divide auditing and consulting services. In a survey by the Investor Responsibility Research Center, only 6 firms (as opposed to 9 in 2001) of 1,240 surveyed have chosen different firms to audit and consult their companies and consulting fees amounted to 72 percent of the total paid;[90] thus, auditing may not only be a loss leader but compliant auditing is likely to be rewarded. Perhaps concentration alone is anathema to quality auditing and high standards. Under Sarbanes-Oxley, the PCAOB has authority to regulate accountants and could, possibly without congressional legislation, determine that, as a long-term objective, it would be necessary to break up the Big Four. Under current circumstances, any current accounting practice used by the Big Four and considered acceptable is difficult to alter in the Financial Accounting Standards Board setting. And this is unlikely to change with Sarbanes-Oxley since FASB will be the likely standard setter under the act, and the additional requirements of the act will have the consequence of driving out non–Big Four auditors resulting in a near complete oligopoly (99 percent of public company auditors). However, an earlier draft of the act would have required that non-accountants be included on the board of the standard setter as well as the PCAOB. In this respect, the legislation may still be amended. Whether adequate accounting standards can be agreed upon under the Big Four oligopoly remains to be seen. It is possible that future legislation will make it illegal to perform both auditing and consulting services. The accounting industry successfully fought off the inclusion of such a prohibition in Sarbanes-Oxley, requiring only the audit board sign-off.[91] But, with only four accounting firms, a buddy system is likely to emerge with trade-offs. Surprisingly, accounting firms managed to reach a compromise with the SEC in the 1930s.[92] But the degree of concentration in the industry today makes one wonder whether any compromise, without a full-scale reorganization of the business of accounting, would serve the interests of good regulation.

However, in my view, the principal issue is the introduction of a financial reporting administrative tribunal that imposes specific SEC regulations on financial accounting standards, in the image of Internal Revenue tax courts. The road away from self-regulation of the accounting industry is a long one, and only the imposition of interpretive rules by a regulator will create a level playing field for reporting entities. This is a pressing need for restoring confidence in financial reporting.

Additionally, the Sarbanes-Oxley Act does little to enforce prohibitions on analyst investment banking conflicts of interest. It is not clear that such conflicts will be arrested until brokerage and investment banking are separated into distinct legal entities between which communication is strictly regulated. And whatever happened to expensing options? Most importantly, to the average American, pension reform, particularly with respect to defined contribution plans such as 401(k)s, and their exposure to company stock, is an unfulfilled legislative agenda.

THE UNITED KINGDOM

The response to Enron and other U.S. scandals in the United Kingdom has been set forth in a report to the Department of Trade and Industry (DTI), which considers auditor independence and oversight, changes in company law, particularly regarding the duty of directors, and the adequacy of financial reporting standards.[93] The report notes that existing standards in the United Kingdom require auditors to act with independence and integrity and to consider threats to independence, real or perceived, before taking on work. The Ethics Standards Board, which is part of the Accounting Foundation established in the early 1990s, recently published a paper, "Setting the Agenda for Ethics."[94] The Financial Services Authority (FSA) may also address the issue of auditor independence from the standpoint of the listing authority, but this authority will be limited by the Listing Particulars Directive.[95] The International Federation of Accounting Bodies also issued a paper on threats to auditor independence and the U.K. Accounting Standards Board (ASB) is a member of this organization.[96] The Department of Trade and Industry's discussion with the Ethical Standards Board resulted in certain recommendations, including a two-year cooling-off period before an auditor may join a client firm and a seven-year rotation of auditors, other provisions that auditors can provide, including limitation of services, and other detailed safeguards of control.[97] The report cites a figure of £218 million paid to auditors of public companies and £675 million of nonaudit fees paid almost exclusively to the former Big Five.[98] The report favors greater disclosure of nonaudit work and a requirement that the audit committee approve nonaudit work,[99] catching at least a whiff of Sarbanes-Oxley. Again, like Sarbanes-Oxley, the report rejects the notion of mandatory rotation of audit firms but favors reducing the mandatory rotation of lead auditors from seven to five years.[100] The report strongly supports an enhanced role for the audit committee and supports a special report by the audit committee to shareholders. Here, the role of the audit committee is both less important than in the United States, since it will not appoint the auditor, and more so, in that it will prepare a report to shareholders. However, in the United Kingdom, in practice, shareholders often appoint the auditors from a list provided by the audit committee.[101] The Financial Reporting Council, which is the custodian of the Combined Code, will attempt a revision that will provide further guidance to audit committees.[102] There is further discussion of the attributes needed for members of the audit committee, akin to the financial expert requirement in the United States, and support for the idea of underpinning the responsibility of audit committees in company law (more shades of Sarbanes-Oxley). The role of nonexecutive directors is being considered by the Higgs Committee.[103] While making reference to Sarbanes-Oxley, the report failed to call for an overhaul of regulation of the accounting profession, noting that the Accounting Foundation was relatively new and the Companies Act 1989 contained provisions about auditor responsibility, but the report highlighted independent finance of the Accounting Foundation.[104] In the United Kingdom, there is mandatory review by inspectors of the Institute of Chartered Accountants. Listed companies are visited every year, with a full inspection every three years.[105]

The report notes the difference between U.S. standards and U.K. standards, "with the emphasis here on the need for the accounts to present a 'true and fair view' and standards that emphasize broad principles over legal form." Here is rather a trenchant difference between U.S. and U.K. financial reporting law after Sarbanes-Oxley. Principle-based accounting substantially reduces the chance for criminal convictions for false and misleading accounting principles that are not tantamount to looting or fraudulent schemes.[106] The International Accounting Standard Board (IASB) and the ASB are formulating standards for accounting for executive options, financial instruments, and revenue recognition.[107] While determined to maintain principle-based standards, the report notes that the Financial Reporting Review Panel (FRRP) has already dealt with 350 cases, issued 70 press releases, and has never had its decisions disputed.[108] But the question of proactivity remains since the FRRP only has one staff member. The report recommends that the panel take on more staff and adopt a more proactive approach while rejecting a SEC model. The FRRP should provide specific proposals by year-end 2002 and should consider the impact of European Union (EU) and international standards.[109] The Auditing Practices Board (APB), which is part of the Accounting Foundation, issued a report on aggressive earnings management[110] and plans to update standards on fraud and materiality, issue a new statement of fundamental principles, consider the relation of auditors to the audit committee, and review other standards, such as related parties and quality control.[111] Currently, there are no EU auditing standards, but the ASB is working toward promoting these standards "wherever possible on an international scale."[112]

In the arena of company law, the report endorses the proposal of the *Company Law Review*[113] for mandatory operating and financial review with particular evidence on the importance of intangibles, an area where the United Kingdom is perhaps ahead of the United States, maybe because of the possible reevaluation of intangibles. The report endorses the codification of directors' duties and the statutory right of auditors to information and penalties for not volunteering information of two years imprisonment (shades of Sarbanes-Oxley). Like Sarbanes-Oxley, which called for a study of concentration in the accounting industry, the report calls for a discussion between DTI, H. M. Treasury, and the Office of Fair Trading to discuss whether there are any competition issues in the concentration of accounting firms. As discussed in the U.S. section, the Big Four have an oligopoly. There is no case law that is relevant in all likelihood. The competition (antitrust) perspective and the doctrine of shared monopoly will not provide a means of reducing concentration in accounting. Eventually, this will need to be accomplished through a public oversight board such as the PCAOB under Sarbanes-Oxley.[114]

THE EU PROPOSED DIRECTIVE ON SUPERVISION OF FINANCIAL CONGLOMERATES

In July 2001, the EU Commission published a proposal for consolidated supervision of financial conglomerates.[115] The proposal is intended to implement the Bank for International Settlements (BIS) G-10 recommendations on financial conglomerates.[116] The commission identified the following lacunae in existing regulation: (1) horizontal groups are not necessarily covered; (2) different structures result in different prudential supervision, regardless of underlying similarities; and (3) financial groups covered by different sectoral regulations are not regulated at the conglomerate level, and this can result in multiple gearing of capital.[117] A group is defined by close links or the determination of a supervisor that one or more persons exert a dominant influence over the group.[118] A group is considered a financial conglomerate if over 50 percent of the balance sheet (aggregated or consolidated) is financial[119] or if it has, as a part of the group, an entity that has cross-sectoral activities that are significant,[120] which is determined by a specific ratio.[121] Member states may decide not to include an entity in another jurisdiction for purposes of consolidation. Where individuals hold participations or capital ties or exert influence without holding capital ties or participation (defined as over 20 percent), a supervisor shall consider the extent of consolidation required.[122] Where a firm is headed by a regulated entity or if the firm has as its parent undertaking a regulated entity within the EU,[123] it will be considered financial regardless of the foregoing.

The competent authority shall require regulated entities to have own funds at the level of the financial conglomerate and shall also require internal controls and capital adequacy policies at the level of the conglomerate.[124] Entities may be excluded for the purposes of capital adequacy if they have negligible assets or if they are in a third country where there are legal impediments to the transfer of information.[125] The competent authorities within member states shall require financial conglomerates to have risk management systems and internal controls to measure and identify intragroup transactions on a conglomerate level.[126] Member states are required to enact laws that require each entity to report to the supplementary supervisor of the conglomerate with particular regard to significant intragroup transactions and all risk concentrations.[127] Pending further action, authorities may set quantitative limits on intragroup transactions or risk concentrations.[128]

Competent authorities shall appoint amongst themselves supplementary supervisors. Where there is no agreement, and the conglomerate is headed by a regulated entity, the supplementary supervisor or coordinator shall be the competent authority responsible for regulating that entity. Where the conglomerate is not headed by a regulated entity, the coordinator will be the coordinator who has authorized the mixed financial holding company.[129] However, where the holding company is, generally, in a different business from that of the regulated entity in the same member state, the coordinator shall be the supervisor in the member state in which the parent company is situated and the one in which the regulated entity with the largest balance sheet total in the most important financial sector is located.[130] Where there are no regulated entities where the mixed financial company has been set up, the regulator of the largest balance sheet entity of the most important financial sector business is to be the coordinator.[131] Where there is no explicit parent undertaking, the task of coordinator falls to the regulator that authorized the entity with the largest balance sheet in the most important sector.[132]

In Article 14, "Parent Undertakings outside the Community,"[133] competent authorities shall verify that regulated undertakings, the parent authority of which is outside the EU, are subject to the same supervision at the conglomerate level. Of course, in the United States, they are not. The banking regulators, the SEC, and the Commodities Futures Trading Corporation (CFTC) are all functional regulators. Although, for instance, 23A and B of the Federal Reserve Act govern intragroup transactions between banks and securities affiliates,[134] the securities affiliates of banks are generally subject only to SEC oversight. The futures commissions merchants (FCM) who are affiliates of broker-dealers are subject to regulation by the CFTC; there are few requirements for consolidated supervision of unregulated affiliates of either (except consolidated subsidiaries of banks).[135] In regard to credit institutions, the proposed directive also allows for the possibility that in the absence of equivalent supervision, the competent authorities may require the establishment of a financial holding company that has its headquarters in the EU and require consolidated supervision on that portion of the conglomerate.[136]

The capital adequacy of financial conglomerates is considered in Annex 1 to the proposal.[137] "The extent and form of the capital of the supplementary capital adequacy of the regulated entities of the financial conglomerate" is considered in this annex and may be accounted for by using one of three methods. Regardless of which method is used, the multiple use of own funds as well as any improper intragroup creation of funds is to be eliminated.[138] Under method 1, the solvency ratio of the group is calculated as the difference between the consolidated position of the group and the sum of the solvency requirements of each different sector of the group; under method 2, the difference between (a) the sum of own funds of each regulated and nonregulated entity in the group and (b) the solvency requirements of all regulated and nonregulated entities plus the book value of other participations by entities in the group; or method 3, the difference between (a) the own funds of the parent undertaking and (b) the sum of the solvency requirements of the parent undertaking and the higher of the book value and the solvency ratio of regulated and nonregulated entities to be calculated by proportional share of participations in other entities or a combination of any of these methods.[139] This is indeed a lot of verbiage for what might have been said more simply.

In the Communication of the Commission to the European Parliament (EP) concerning the proposed directive, the commission assesses the aims of the directive: (1) To ensure that conglomerates are adequately capitalized, in particular, to avoid downstreaming where the parent undertaking issues debt and uses the proceeds as equity for its subsidiary; (2) to establish methods for calculating a financial conglomerates solvency ratio; (3) to deal with the issues of intragroup transfers and group exposure to risks; (4) to deal with the suitability and professionalism of management at financial conglomerates; (5) to ensure adequate internal controls and risk management in financial conglomerates; (6) to require member states to ensure that one single authority is appointed for the overview of each financial conglomerate and to ensure coordination; and (7) to introduce minimum steps to avoid unnecessary inconsistencies in the regulation of homogenous financial groups.[140]

The definition of "group" has been limited to parent undertaking and subsidiaries rather than close links, but the commission still wishes to include horizontal structures of which there is no parent undertaking.[141] There remains a broader definition of "group" involving close links to be used for purposes of intragroup risk. The definition of financial conglomerate remains elusive. The EP proposed a lower threshold (40 percent of balance sheet activities) and a quantitative amount of cross-sectoral activities. The Common Position (adopted on September 9, 2002, but addressed in this communication) has attempted to clean up the ambiguous language in Annex 1, which defines conglomerate solvency ratios (capital adequacy) by stating that sectoral risks are to be covered by sectoral capital and that any additional deficit should be covered by cross-sectoral capital at the conglomerate level.[142] Under the Common Position, the regulatory authority will require any group headed by a regulated entity to choose one of the three methods, but a group headed by a nonregulated entity will be allowed to choose any of the three methods. The Common Position requires that the commission evaluate and report on member state rules for intragroup transactions and risk concentrations. It also places the issue of internal control mechanisms and risk concentration in the context of the Basel Committee capital adequacy framework.[143] The Common Position has also altered the appointment of a coordinator, requiring the automatic appointment subject to the Commission criteria, which may be waived by agreement among regulators. Also, there must be a single coordinator. There is a requirement that the coordinator address inquiries to the functional regulators to avoid duplication of reporting, and the exchange of information cannot be waived; however, there is an explicit confidentiality provision inserted in the preamble. Regarding parent undertakings outside the EU, the coordinator is now required to have an obligatory consultation with the Financial Conglomerates Committee. In the absence of equivalence, member states may use alternate methods.

In a broad purposive way, this directive takes an entirely different approach to financial regulation than that which is dominant in the United States and incorporated in Sarbanes-Oxley. *The Economist* reports, "Some have dubbed it the post-Enron directive."[144] As stated above, consolidated supervision is not the forte of the U.S. regulatory system, which principally involves functional regulation.

One broad shortcoming of the directive is that entities located in jurisdictions that are not forthcoming with financial information are excluded from consolidated supervision. This would include any jurisdictions where hedge funds are located and where many unregulated affiliates of banks and investment banks are situated.[145] However, in principle, this directive highlights the different reform-oriented agenda prevalent in continental Europe. Despite various directives in Company Law, including the Fourth, Seventh, and Eighth Directives in Company Law[146] and the adoption of international accounting standards,[147] any consideration of Sarbanes-Oxley type proposals would be premature in Europe. Additionally, the prevalence of large block holding and bank domination of securities markets in continental Europe means that financial reporting is less likely to be transparent and there are fewer, less powerful market participants such as institutional investors to perform arm's length analysis of public information or to become involved in activist proxy contests. If an Enron situation were to occur in continental Europe, it would most likely be dealt with in terms of bank exposure to the private sector, and the role of Citibank and J.P. Morgan Chase and their securities subsidiaries would be monitored in terms of large exposures, intragroup transfers, and capital adequacy considerations. Even in the United Kingdom, with its arm's length liquid securities markets and dispersed ownership of equity, where Sarbanes-Oxley corporate governance and financial reporting measures are under consideration, the FSA, the regulator of banks and securities firms, has little involvement in corporate governance and the role of audit committees, since this is the province of the Department of Trade and Industry.[148] Thus, it is a foregone conclusion that the EU response to the current instability of the world financial system divagates from the U.S. response.

Former SEC Chairman Harvey Pitt, taking into account the extraterritorial implications of Sarbanes-Oxley, expressed concern over the EU directive, which would require equivalence in third-party regulation.[149] The quid quo pro of reducing regulations limiting the impact of Sarbanes-Oxley on EU issuers who limit U.S. selling efforts to sophisticated investors, in exchange for changes in the proposed EU directive, which limit the imposition of equivalence standards and the single coordinator on U.S. companies, is underway. In October 2003, the SEC proposed an alternate approach to capital which would result in consolidated supervision of securities regimes which would lighten the duplicative burden on EU firms.[150]

NOTES

1. Corporate and Auditing Accountability, Responsibility and Transparency Act and Public Accounting Reform and Investor Protection Act: short title Sarbanes-Oxley, Pub. Law no. 107-204, Title I.

2. *Ibid.*, Section 307. There has been much debate over what constitutes material evidence of a violation of securities law. Would this include a violation of stock exchange rules? Are lawyers limited to report material evidence uncovered only within the scope of their employment, or must the attorney for an underwriter, for instance, have to report material evidence of a violation by an issuer? Must a lawyer report evidence only when there is probable cause or must he or she investigate? The forthcoming rules will have to clarify these questions.

3. *Ibid.*, Section 301. Audit committees must now have a financial expert as one

of their members. The head of the Enron audit committee was the dean of the University of Texas Business School.

4. There is an exception for amounts related that are no more than 5 percent of the total. This list of prohibited activities mirrors the prohibitions contained in the Securities and Exchange Commission (SEC), "Final Rule: Revision of the Commission's Auditor Independence Requirements," SEC Release no. 33-7919, 34-43602 (Feb. 5, 2001).

5. *Op. cit.*

6. *Ibid.*, Section 303.

7. *Ibid.*, Section 304.

8. *Ibid.*, Section 308.

9. *Ibid.*, Section 406. *See* SEC Proposed Release no. 33-8138, 34-46701, "Disclosure Required by Section 404, 406, and 407 of the Sarbanes-Oxley Act" (November 4, 2002). Under 406, the SEC adds to the statutory requirement a definition of code of ethics: "A codification of standards that is reasonably designed to deter wrongdoing and promote honest and ethical conduct . . . avoidance of conflicts of interest . . . full, fair, accurate and timely disclosure . . . and prompt internal reporting [sic]." Under 406(b), companies must make immediate disclosure under an 8K form of any change to or waiver of a code of ethics. The SEC adds to the list any waiver applying to a specified officer or a grant of waiver to a specified officer. Section 404 requires an internal control report to be filed by public companies containing the internal controls in place and management's assessment of them. The SEC proposed that such reports specify that transactions were performed in accordance with management's authorization and transactions were recorded in conformity with Generally Accepted Accounting Principles (GAAP), and access to assets was in accordance with management's authorization. The issue of internal controls and procedures for financial reporting is separately addressed and defined as "controls that pertain to financial reporting for external purposes" in conformity with GAAP or other such standards to be issued by the Public Company Accounting Oversight Board (PCAOB). Under attestation to internal controls by an external auditor as required by Section 404(b) of Sarbanes-Oxley, the SEC proposed that such reports be included in annual reports. The SEC has added to the certification procedure requirements that the officers have reviewed the report, that the officers are responsible for establishing and maintaining "disclosure reports and procedures," have designed such systems to make sure that information is made known to them and have evaluated the systems not more than 90 days prior to filing, have disclosed to the auditors all deficiencies and have disclosed any fraud, material or not, that involves management or any employees who have a role in the issuer's material statements (presumably, other fraud does not have to be disclosed). In addition to the requirement of Sarbanes-Oxley that companies disclose whether the audit committee includes a financial expert under Section 407, the SEC proposed that a company be required to disclose the number and names of financial experts. The SEC also proposed that companies disclose whether financial experts are independent and, if not, the reason for the lack of independence. For the definition of "financial expert," the SEC proposed that the company should disclose whether the person has expertise in the industry. It has allowed a definition of "financial expert" that, in lieu of experience as auditor, principal financial auditor, public accountant, or comptroller, has performed similar functions in the judgment of the board. The SEC provides a laundry list to determine equivalency, including other audit committees on which the

person has served and the level and amount of the person's direct experience in preparing financial statements. Significant changes in internal controls must also be disclosed. The SEC also issued a Proposed Rule for "Conditions for Use of Non-GAAP Financial Measures" (SEC Release no. 33-8145), which tightens Form F-20 requirements.

10. *Ibid.*, Section 402; there is now a great deal of discussion about what constitutes a loan. Are advances for litigation expenses a loan or contingent guarantees? Travel advances are a loan. Certain kinds of insurance must be loans. The provision specifically exempts credit cards.

11. *Ibid.*, Section 409. In a release on 8K filings, the SEC created a catch-all that essentially increased disclosure requirements to cover, among other matters, related party disclosures and contingent liability disclosures à la Enron. In general, the proposed release proposes to shorten the filing deadline from 5 or 15 days, to 2 days for events that trigger disclosure under 8K. The current events that trigger disclosure include a change in control, a disposal or acquisition of a substantial amount of assets, a company's bankruptcy or receivership, a change of certifying accountant, the resignation of a director, and a change in the company's fiscal year. This release adds 11 items that would have to be reported in an 8K filing, thereby revolutionizing 8K filings. SEC, Proposed Rule, "Additional 8K Disclosure Requirements and Acceleration of Filing Date," Release no. 33-8106, 34-46084 File no. S7 22-02.

12. *Ibid.*, Section 501.

13. Section 2(a) 7 of the act defines "issuer" to include foreign private issuers who file under Section 12 or 15(d) of the act; thus, any issuer who wishes to maintain listing on a U.S. exchange is covered. The New York Stock Exchange (NYSE) rules will allow foreign private issuers to summarize corporate governance differences, and the SEC has broad rule-making authority under Section 3(a) of the act. It is unclear how the SEC will use its broad exemptive powers. German supervisory boards will have to have union members from other unions to satisfy the independence requirements of the act. Union members from the same union may not be independent under the act.

14. *Ibid.*, Section 106 states that the PCAOB may determine that a foreign firm that plays a substantial role in the auditing process, even if not the auditor, must be treated as a public accounting firm for purposes of registration. A foreign auditing firm that issues an opinion or performs material services is deemed to consent to produce its working papers. This is particularly important for segment reporting, Section 802(a). The working papers of auditors must also be retained for five years.

15. *Ibid.*, Section 207.

16. *Ibid.*, Section 701; this report must be conducted within one year, other reports within 180 days.

17. *Ibid.*, Section 702.

18. *Ibid.*, Section 703

19. *Ibid.*, Section 704.

20. *Ibid.*, Section 705.

21. *Ibid.*, Section 306.

22. *Ibid.*, Section 804, which extends the statute to two years after discovery of a fraud and five years after the violation.

23. *Ibid.*, Section 307. In keeping with the importance of attorneys in U.S. society, the release on Section 307: Proposed Release, "Implementation of Standards of Professional Conduct for Attorney," SEC Release no. 33-8150, 34-46868 (November 21,

2002). The release notes that the SEC already has rules in place about attorney conduct. Rule 102(a) of the SEC Rules of Practice has been the primary vehicle to ensure professional standards and ensure the competence of professionals (including attorneys) who practice before it. The conditions of the release are triggered when an attorney becomes aware of information "which would lead a reasonable attorney to conclude that a material violation [of the Securities laws] has occurred." Aside from a duty to report under Section 307, the rule creates an alternative in that an issuer may form a Qualified Legal Compliance Committee, which must include at least one member of the audit committee and two independent members of the issuer's board. The SEC release goes far beyond Section 307 in what it requires of an attorney whose reasonable belief of a material violation has not been appropriately addressed, and if the violation will result in substantial injury to the issuer, an outside attorney is required to withdraw, report the withdrawal to the SEC, and disaffirm any submission to the SEC that is tainted. In the event an attorney believes that a material violation has already occurred but has no material effect, he is entitled but not required to take this step. In-house attorneys are not required to withdraw but must disavow any tainted submission to the SEC. (Proposed Part 205.3(d)). Proposed Part 205.3(e) addressed the specific circumstances under which an attorney is required to disclose confidential information related to his or her appearance before the SEC. Parts 205.4 and 205.5 deal with the role of subordinate in-house and outside attorneys whose obligation of the rule is fulfilled if they report the evidence of a violation of law to the supervisory attorney. Proposed Section 205.6 concerns sanctions to be imposed and includes cease and desist orders and now includes administrative proceedings that can result in censures and bars from practicing before the SEC. This proposed release would also apply to foreign attorneys to the extent that they "appear and practice before the Commission." The proposed release states that the attorney does not represent the issuer's officers and directors simply because he or she interacts with them. The client is the issuer itself. A defense counsel representing the issuer in an administrative proceeding would not be included within the definition of appearing before the SEC, which involves transacting business with the SEC. Additionally, there is a requirement that an attorney who has evidence of a material violation keep a contemporaneous record. This is certainly good legal advice.

24. *Ibid.*, Section 303. In the Proposed Release "Improper Influence on Conduct of Audits," SEC Release no. 34-46685, (October 19, 2002), the SEC, as directed by Section 303(a) of Sarbanes-Oxley, proposed rules prohibiting officers and directors of issuers and persons acting under their direction from taking any action to fraudulently induce, coerce, manipulate, or mislead auditors in the preparation of financial reports. The proposed rule, 13b2-2(b)(1), gives an expansive definition of "acting under the direction" of an officer or director, distinguishing between supervision and direction. The SEC provides examples of what would be considered improper influence: (1) offering bribes or future financial incentive, (2) providing an auditor with misleading legal analysis (another example of how attorneys may face increased liability), (3) threatening to cancel existing nonaudit services, (4) seeking to have an auditing partner (but not employee) removed because the partner objects to the financial accounting, and (5) making physical threats (that seems self-evident). The SEC seeks comments on whether there should be a precise definition of "engaged in the performance of an audit" since this precondition must be met under Sarbanes-Oxley 303(a) for the conduct to be actionable. The SEC is also asking for comment on the precise language

to define scienter in order to indicate that no purpose or intent is required. *See also infra* note 9 for rules under Sections 404, 406, and 407.

25. *Ibid.*, Section 401(j). The SEC issued Proposed Rule, "Disclosure in Management Discussion and Analysis about Off-Balance Sheet Arrangements, Contractual Obligations, and Contingent Liabilities and Commitments," SEC Release no. 33-8144, 34-46767 (Nov. 2002), which is required by 401(a). These disclosures would appear in a separately captioned subsection in management discussion and analysis (MD&A). Disclosure would be triggered by any obligation under a direct or indirect obligation, retained, or contingent interest transferred to an unconsolidated subsidiary entity or derivatives, to the extent that their value is not fully reflected in the financial statement, or any obligation or liability to the extent not reflected in the financial statement. Under the release, as opposed to the language of Sarbanes-Oxley, obligations must be contractual to give rise to required disclosure. The SEC states explicitly that there must be disclosure of any liabilities, for which "the reasonable possible maximum exposure of loss under the obligation as of the date of the financial statement" is not fully reflected in the balance sheet. Rather than an obligation giving rise to a disclosure requirement if it is reasonably likely to be material to a company, the SEC is adopting a lower threshold that requires disclosure that may have a current or future material effect. The company would also have to disclose the nature and business purpose of the transaction and the significant terms of the arrangements. Also, the company would have to disclose the total assets and liabilities of the entity. Management would also have to discuss the effects of termination of the arrangement and any situation under which termination might occur and the material effects. Section 401(b) requires that issuers in all pro forma financial disclosures in a periodic report including 8K and "in any public disclosure" present such information in a manner that is not false and misleading and that such information be "reconciled with GAAP." In the SEC proposed release under Sarbanes-Oxley, SEC, "Proposed Rule: Conditions for the Use of Non-GAAP Financial Measures," SEC Release no. 33-8145, 34-4678 (Nov. 5, 2002), the SEC proposes a new Regulation G that would require that such oral disclosures that are not subsequently filed in an 8K be filed separately after an oral presentation. There is a limited exception for foreign private issuers (all foreign nongovernmental issuers listed in the United States) to the extent that the release is aimed at investors outside the United States. The foreign private issuer would be required to file the information in a 6K. It is unclear whether analysts in the United States participating by telephone would trigger the provision. The content of the release and the filing would require reconciliation with GAAP, including historic financial comparable data to the extent that providing such data would not be unduly burdensome. Examples given of non-GAAP financial measures include EBITA, or any earnings figure that excludes nonrecurring expenses, sales per square foot, and operating margins. The Proposed Release would also amend item 10 of Regulation S-B and Form 20F. This would presumably also affect the foreign issuer 6K filing resulting in regulations more extensive than those under Regulation G. The SEC insists that no additional liability would be imposed. But pro forma statements give rise to a private right of action under 10b-5 (subject to the safe harbor under the PSLRA for forward-looking statements). The SEC asks in its request for comments whether Regulation G should only be enforceable by the SEC rather than creating a private right of action. To an extent, this is a technical question as to pleadings in securities litigation since 10b-5 liability would presumably still be present in any event.

26. *Ibid.*, Section 601, which raises the 2003 appropriation to $776 million.

27. *Ibid.*, Section 1107.

28. *Ibid.*, Section 1105. Previously, the commission had to sue the alleged offenders in federal court.

29. *See generally*, Lewis Liman, "Selected Issues under the Private Securities Litigation Act: Pleading Scienter, Pleading Particularity," Practicing Law Institute, Corporate Law and Practice Handbook Series, *Hot Litigation Issues in a Down Economy, 2002: The Impact of Sudden Financial Loss* (July 2002), p. 37.

30. *See Washington Post*, July 28, 2002, describing how the bill was dead until Worldcom's accounting issues hit the news.

31. "Report of Investigation by the Special Investigative Committee of the Board of Directors of Enron Corp.," William Powers, chair, Raymond Troubh, Herbert Winokur, Wilmer Cutler Pickering counsel. February 1, 2002, at 3.

32. Appendix A to Commission Statement Regarding Management Discussion and Analysis of Financial Condition and Results of Operation of the Issuer (Release no. 33-8056, 34-45321 [2002]). (Responding to Petition to U.S. SEC for issuance of an interpretive release, An Interpretation of Regulation S-K, item 303, Management Discussion and Analysis of Financial Conditions and Results of Operations, Dec. 31, 2001.)

33. "The Numbers Game," Remarks of Arthur Levitt at NYU Center for Law and Business (1998), available online at <http://sec.gov/news/speech/speecharchive/1998/spch220.txt>; *see also* Mark Olsen, "Detecting Financial Fraud and Understanding Insolvency Risk," Practicing Law Institute, Corporate Law and Handbook Series, *Basics of Accounting and Finance, What Every Lawyer Needs to Know* (August 2002), p. 519.

34. FASB standard no. 48.

35. *Greebal v. FTP Software Inc.*, 185 F.3d 202 (1st Cir., 1999).

36. *Steckman*, 143 F.3d at 1298; *see In re Splash Technology Holdings Inc. Sec. Litig.*, 160 F. Supp. 2d 1059, 1076 (N.D. Cal. 2001) (granting motion to dismiss claims regarding channel stuffing because plaintiff failed to plead specific facts in support of the allegations of channel stuffing).

37. SEC Litigation Release no. 17465 summarizing Civil Action no. 02 CV 2789 (S.D.N.Y.) (April 11, 2002).

38. *U.S. v. Simon*, 425 F.2d 796 (2nd Cir. 1969).

39. *In Re Cendant*, SEC Exchange Act Release no. 34-49233 (2000). *See also* Howard Schilit, *Financial Shenanigans: How to Detect Accounting Gimmicks and Fraud in Financial Reporting*, 2d ed (McGraw Hill, 2002), p. 3.

40. *Gimmicks and Fraud in Financial Reporting*, *supra* note 39, p. 12.

41. *Ibid.*, p. 108.

42. *Ibid.*, p. 24.

43. *Ibid.*, pp. 36–39.

44. *Ibid.*, p. 160.

45. SEC Release no. 34-43570 (Nov. 16, 2000).

46. *Op. cit.* p. 147.

47. *Ibid.*, p. 166.

48. SEC Litigation Release no. 17001 (May 15, 2001).

49. *In the Matter of W. R. Grace*, SEC Release no. 41578, Accounting and Auditing Enforcement Release no. 1140 (June 30, 1999).

50. *In the Matter of Microsoft*, SEC Release no. 34-46017 (June 3, 2002).

51. *Gimmicks and Fraud in Financial Reporting*, *supra* note 39, at 212.

52. SEC Proposed Release no. 33-8098, "Disclosure in Management Discussion and Analysis about Critical Accounting Methods" (May 10, 2002).

53. *Op. cit.*, p. 171.

54. *Ibid.*, at 214.

55. *Ibid.*, at 144.

56. SEC Report (October 23, 2001).

57. New York Stock Exchange, "Corporate Governance Rules Proposals Reflecting Recommendations from the NYSE Corporate Accountability and Listing Standards Committee as Approved by the NYSE Board on August 1, 2002."

58. The length of the cooling off period was hotly contested. Most comments thought three years would have been less onerous.

59. *Op. cit.*, Section 2(a) and (b).

60. *Ibid.*, Section 3.

61. *Ibid.*, Section 4. This committee, the responsibilities of which can be assigned to another committee composed entirely of independent directors, must have a written charter and address issues of standards for directors and provide for an annual evaluation of the committee's work.

62. *Ibid.*, Section 5.

63. *Ibid.*, Section 6. This may be in the form of cash, stock, or other consideration.

64. *Ibid.*, Section 7. There are a host of other requirements including discussing audit report and financial information and preparing SEC proxy statements. The audit committee must also obtain and review an auditor's report on internal controls, address any issues in such report and must investigate any inquiry by a governmental agency within the last five years. The laboring oar, here, is clearly on the auditors rather than the audit committee. The audit committee must also meet regularly, assess hiring policy of former auditors, review with the independent auditor any auditing problems and management response.

65. *Ibid.*, Section 7(c).

66. *Ibid.*, Section 8. Except inducement options, plans related to a merger and tax qualified and excess benefit plans.

67. *See supra* note 9.

68. *Op. cit.*, Section 10. This relates to officers and employees.

69. *Ibid.* These include conflicts of interest, confidentiality, fair dealing, protection and fair use of corporate assets, compliance with laws regarding insider dealing, and encouraging the reporting of illegal or unethical behavior. This last provision echoes the whistleblower provisions of Sarbanes-Oxley. *See supra* note 27.

70. *Ibid.*, Section 11.

71. *Ibid.*, Section 13.

72. NYSE, Listing Rule 472, Communication with the Public.

73. SEC, Release no. 45908, NASD and NYSE Proposed Rule Changes "Self-Regulatory Organizations; Order Approving Proposed Rule Changes by the NASD and the NYSE."

74. For 30 days prior and 5 days after the issuance of a research report.

75. *Op. cit.* The rules apply only to research reports on equity. (*Op. cit.*, footnote 11).

76. SEC, Proposed Rule, "Regulation: Analyst Certification," Release no. 33-8119, 34-46301 (Aug. 2, 2002).

77. Opinion may differ as to what kind of compensation is indirectly related to a specific recommendation.

78. *Op. cit.*

79. *See supra* notes 15 to 17 and accompanying text.

80. 17 C.F.R. part 240 15c3-1.

81. Rule 100b.

82. Securities and Exchange Commission, Form S-3; *see also* Jonathon Macey, "Nationally Recognized Statistical Rating Organizations and Investor Protection," Testimony of Prof. Jonathon Macey before the Senate Governmental Affairs Committee, March 20, 2002.

83. U.S. Comptroller of the Currency, "Purchase of Investment Securities and Further Defining the Term 'Investment Securities' as Used in Section 5136 in the Revised Statutes as Amended of the 'Banking Act of 1935,'" Section 2 (Feb. 16, 1936).

84. Frank Portnoy, "The Siskel and Ebert of Financial Markets? Two Thumbs Down on the Rating Agencies," *Washington University Law Quarterly* (1999): pp. 619–712, at 692.

85. "Nationally Recognized Statistical Rating Organizations," *supra* note 82.

86. George E. Pinches and J. Clay Singleton, "The Adjustment of Stock Prices to Credit Rating Changes," *Journal of Finance* 33 (1978): pp. 29–55, at 39. *See also* David Zivas, "Why the Rating Agencies Get Low Marks," *Business Week*, March 12, 1990, p. 4, cited in "Nationally Recognized Statistical Organizations," *supra* note 82.

87. Statement of Ralph G. Pellechia, submitted to the Senate Governmental Affairs Committee (March 20, 2002).

88. *See* chapter 2, "The New Capital Adequacy Accord."

89. *See* chapter 4, notes 26 to 28, 53, 61 and 62, and accompanying text and chapter 5, notes 127 to 132, and accompanying text.

90. Gretchen Morgensen, "On Reform, It's Time to Walk the Walk," *New York Times*, October 6, 2002, Section 3, Money and Business, p. 1.

91. *See supra* note 4 and accompanying text.

92. *See* chapter 5, notes 108 to 111, and accompanying text.

93. "Coordinating Report on Auditing and Accounting," Interim Report to the Department of Secretary of State of Trade and Industry and the Chancellor of the Exchequer (July 2002), Executive Summary, Section 1.

94. *Ibid.*, 3.2–3, *see also* Ethics Standards Board of the Accounting Foundation, "Setting the Agenda for Ethics" (May 28, 2002).

95. *Ibid.*, 3.4.

96. *Ibid.*, 3.6. The European Commission published recommendations on auditor independence in January 2002.

97. *Ibid.*, 3.8. Reference is made to the auditor independence rules published by the SEC in November 2000; *see also* chapter 4, note 30.

98. *Ibid.*, 3.12. Citing Finance Director Magazine Survey of the Financial Times-Stock Exchange (FTSE) 100 Companies, January 2002.

99. *Ibid.*, 3.23.

100. *Ibid.*, 3.33–3.34.

101. *Ibid.*, 4.9.

102. *Ibid.*, 4.11.

103. *Ibid.*, 4.15 et seq.

104. *Ibid.*, 5.9.

105. *Ibid.*, or the Association of Chartered Accountants. The Securities Practice Section is not mandatory, but American Institute of Certified Public Accountants (AICPA) members have mandatory inspections. The new U.S. Public Company Accounting Oversight Board will have more all inclusive standards.

106. *See infra* "Fraudulent or Misleading Accounting Practices."

107. *See* chapter 4, note 70.

108. *Ibid.*, 6.7.

109. *Ibid.*, 6.12.

110. In June 2001.

111. *Op. cit.* 7.3.

112. *Ibid.*, 7.7.

113. The Steering Group presented its final report to the Secretary of State on July 26, 2001; accompanying text. The government published a white paper, "Modernising Company Law" (Cm 5553) on July 16, 2002. This contains its responses to the review's major recommendations and its proposals to reform company law. *See* chapter 1, note 351.

114. *See supra* note 1 and accompanying text.

115. "Proposal of the European Parliament and the Council on Supplementary Supervision of Credit Institutions, Insurance Undertakings, and Investment Firms in a Financial Conglomerate," O.J Eur. Comm. C-238 (July 31, 2001), p. 227, COM/2001/0213 final, pursuant to a commitment by the Lisbon Council and considerations by the Financial Services Action Plan. The final version is Directive 2002/87/EEC (December 16, 2002); O.J. Eur. Comm. L.035 (February 11, 2003), pp. 1–27.

116. *See* chapter 2, note 78, and accompanying text.

117. *Op. cit.*

118. *Ibid.*, Article 2, par. 9.

119. *Ibid.*, Article 3, par. 1.

120. *Ibid.*, Article 2, par. 13 9(c) and (d).

121. *Ibid.*, Article 3, par. 2. The ratio of the smallest financial services firm to the largest calculated by the solvency ratio should exceed 10 percent; but the competent authorities may decide to exclude a firm on the border of regulation, to lower the ratios or to use different criteria with reference to income structure or off-balance sheet activity.

122. *Ibid.*, Article 4, par. 4.

123. *Ibid.*, Article 4, par. 2 or every regulated entity linked by a relationship within the meaning of Article 12(1) of 83/349/EEC.

124. *Ibid.*, Article 5, par. 2.

125. *Ibid.*, Article 5, par. 4.

126. *Ibid.*, Article 6, par. 2.

127. *Ibid.*, par. 3.

128. *Ibid.*, par. 5.

129. *Ibid.*, Section 2, Article 7, par. 1, par. 2(a) and (b).

130. *Ibid.*, ii.

131. *Ibid.*, iii.

132. *Ibid.*, iv.

133. *Ibid.*, Section 3, Third Counties, Article 14, Parent Undertakings outside the Community.

134. *See* chapter 4, notes 166–168.

135. *See* chapter 3, "Net Capital Rules."

136. Proposed Conglomerates Directive, *supra* note 115, Article 25, Amendments to 2000/12/EEC, par. 9, inserting Article 56a.

137. *Ibid.*, Annex I Capital Adequacy I Technical Principles.

138. *Ibid.*, par. 2.

139. *Ibid.*

140. "Communication of the Commission to the European Parliament on Common Position of the Council on the Adoption of a Directive on the Supplementary Supervision of Credit Institutions Insurance Undertakings and Investment Firms in a Financial Conglomerate and Amending [other directives]," SEC 995/2002 final (September 20, 2002).

141. *Ibid.*, 3.2.

142. Thresholds for deduction have been raised from 10 percent to 20 percent; the techniques to be used by financial conglomerates may also be utilized by sectoral groups regarding their capital holding in a different financial sector.

143. *See* chapter 2, "The New Capital Adequacy Accord."

144. "A Bit of Give and Take: Another Transatlantic Regulation," *Economist*, Oct. 19, 2002.

145. *See* chapter 3, "Net Capital Rules." U.K. and European banks and investment banks have many unregulated affiliates. While bank regulators tend to look at all aspects of bank activity, if only informally, securities regulators are less likely to do so. *See* chapter 2, note 75, and accompanying text.

146. *See* chapter 1, notes 104 to 108 and 433 to 454, and accompanying text.

147. *See* chapter 1, note 454, and accompanying text.

148. *See* chapter 1, 351, and accompanying text.

149. Harvey Pitt,

> I believe any proposed relief should focus on foreign exchanges that limit their U.S. activities to offering foreign securities to sophisticated U.S. investors. Our primary goals are protecting investors and market integrity, while encouraging competition and a level playing field. Our regulations are designed to achieve these goals regardless of the laws applicable in the country of the market participant. By ensuring that each market participant acts in a manner consistent with these goals rather than judging the regulatory system in the participants' home countries, the SEC allows the largest possible number of qualified market participants to have access to U.S. markets. In considering requests for exemptive relief, reciprocity is critical—we must take into account any contrary regulatory approach that leaves U.S. market participants at a disadvantage to their foreign counterparts.
>
> In that context, I'd like to say a few words about the Proposed Directive on the consolidated supervision of financial conglomerates which, as you know, would establish minimum requirements for group-wide supervision of "financial conglomerates" and "mixed financial holding companies" doing business in the EU. The Proposed Directive has the noble intent of facilitating more effective prudential oversight of cross-sector groups. But, questions surrounding its potential extraterritorial impact have generated considerable concern at the SEC and among U.S. securities firms. If, for example, EU authorities charged with making "equivalence" determinations take the position that the SEC's supervision of securities firms at the holding company level is not equivalent to the EC's standards, the likely result would be to increase the cost to U.S. firms of doing business in Europe, and place them at a competitive disadvantage with European-based firms.
>
> At a time when we are carefully evaluating the impact of U.S. rules and regulations on foreign entities, in an attempt to move to more global markets, the EC would do well to ward against the possible extraterritorial imposition of standards on U.S. firms by the EC in the

form of "equivalence" determinations. To the extent that "equivalence" signals an effort to move towards an approach based on reciprocity, I welcome the effort. But to the extent "equivalence" is really a thinly-veiled means of having a "co-ordinator" in the EU evaluate the quality of the U.S. regulatory regime, that approach will be counter-productive and will not enhance investor protection. Our staff has been discussing the issue of equivalence and reciprocity with EC representatives, and how our respective approaches can best address the need for group-wide supervision of financial conglomerates in today's global markets. We are optimistic those discussions will be productive, and I look forward to continuing this dialogue, with the goal of reaching a prompt, sensible and mutually satisfactory outcome.

(Speech before the Institute of Chartered Accountants of England and Wales, October 10, 2002).

150. *See* chapter 3, notes 147–151.

CHAPTER 7

The Curious Case of Japan: Capital Market Rigidity and Regulatory Failure

In "The Curious Case of Benjamin Banaeker" by F. Scott Fitzgerald, Benjamin Banaeker gets younger and younger until he finally disappears; Japan is also disappearing, but it is doing so by getting older and older. It is estimated that by 2050, Japan's population will be 50 percent of what it was at its height. The absolute number of people in the 20- to 24-year-old category will fall by 35 percent over the next 20 years.[1] A 1 percent rise in gross domestic product (GDP) in Japan is nothing to sneeze at on a per capita basis (the United States would have to achieve nearly 3 percent growth to equal per capita increase). However, Japan has not achieved a 1 percent growth rate on a consistent basis. Although it continues to run a structural trade surplus with the rest of the world (about $100 billion a year), Japan has contracted in several recent years by 2 and 3 percent. Japan's budget deficit, so complex to calculate because of the opacity of accounting and bureaucracy in Japan that its magnitude is a question of debate, appears to be running at about 130 percent of GDP; thus far, about 60 trillion yen, nearly $600 billion (already making it six times the size of the Savings and Loan [S&L] crisis per capita), has been expended bailing out the banking sector. Yet, the crisis in nonperforming loans (NPL) shows no signs of abating. Ironically, Japan's weakness has now become a matter of concern to the United States, which has resorted to *giaitsu* (foreign pressure) to affect Japanese financial policies as it once did and halfheartedly continues to do in the trade sphere. Ultimately, Japan is not a capitalist market society in the narrow way the term is employed in Anglo-American capital markets. It is also a nation in transition without a political rudder. The consequences to the international financial system could prove profound.

Concerns about Japan's trade surplus with the United States have abated significantly although Japan continues to run a large surplus with the United States. In 2000, Japan-U.S. trade reached its zenith of $212 billion with Japan running an $81 billion surplus.[2] But in 1999, Japan accounted for only 20 percent of the trade deficit and in some years has been replaced by China as the nation with the largest trade surplus vis-à-vis the United States.[3] The long history of bilateral negotiations with Japan includes anti-dumping measures, the Market-Oriented and Sector Specific talks (MOSS), the Semi-Conductor Talks, the Structural Impediments Initiatives, and the Framework Agreement. In a book entitled *No More Bashing*, Fred Bergsten, the director of the Institute for International Economics, and colleagues have determined that these bilateral talks have had minimal impact and that U.S.-Japan policy should focus on engagement within the framework of multilateral institutions, particularly the World Trade Organization (WTO).[4] They argue, inter alia, that Japan's shrinking economy has been perceived as less of a threat to the United States. In my view, the failure to address the structural dimension of the trade deficit with Japan, and with the various Japanese affiliates and nations with which Japan has a trade surplus, reveal the weaknesses of global capitalism. We aren't all on the same page. Japan's economy is founded on different principles than that of Anglo-American capitalism. But this difference is accounted for by the international financial system with its various readjustment mechanisms, with the proviso that fragility and uncertainty over time are undesired byproducts. Japan's aging population makes it desirable that Japan run a trade surplus and consequently a current account surplus so that portfolio income will accrue to the aging part of the population through long-term appreciation of the yen and portfolio investment vis-à-vis the individual, but the magnitude of the surplus is unsustainable, and its consequences counterintuitive. It has been argued by the historian Ferdinand Braudel that Spain's accumulation of gold led to a long deflationary cycle.[5] Japan seems to be facing a similar prospect in a much-abbreviated period of time. Consider that Japan's woes began with asset inflation, which, at one point, made the Imperial Palace grounds worth five times as much as the state of California. This asset inflation turned to deflation beginning in 1991 when the interest rate was raised. Since then, it has been one muddle after another. Japan's experience is a cautionary tale of what lies ahead, on a less pronounced scale, for the United States.

THE *KEIRETSU*

Although overlaid with the basics of an American style financial system in the postwar years, including the separation of banking and securities firms,[6] the *Keiretsu* remains the overarching structure in the Japanese financial system.

The Japanese capital market is characterized by the existence of the *Keiretsu*, loosely organized groups of companies descended from the earlier *Zaibatsus* that dominate listed companies on the Japanese stock markets. The *Keiretsu* (cross-holdings) increases the price of Japanese equity stock and reduces the cost of capital. Because nearly two-thirds of the corporate equity in Japan is held by other corporations, a considerable adjustment of about 15 percent of Japanese stock market capitalization may be accounted for by intercorporate share ownership.[7]

But Japanese portfolio investment is not an insubstantial factor in the Japanese economy and, like the recent upsurge in bond issues, suggests a movement away from the preexisting structure of cross-holdings and bank monitoring. Still, the extent of the transformation of the Japanese economy to an arm's-length capital market should not be exaggerated. Although a considerable body of knowledge suggests that the role of the *Keiretsu*, and consequently of relational financing, is overstated,[8] recent research suggests otherwise.[9]

The Role of Institutional Investors as Monitors

The principal question formulated by a comparative study of U.S. and Japanese capital markets is whether the organization of Japanese capital markets enables a more or less efficient and/or a successful organization of financial and corporate structure. Beyond consideration of the cost of capital to the extent that it derives from savings rates and interest rate differentials, the roles played by institutional investors in the United States and Japan result in incomparable capital market structures. Japanese institutional investors are able to monitor the behavior of financial firms in which they invest, principally through the role of the long-term or city bank, under what is called the main banking system.[10]

Japanese financial institutions are allowed to take large positions in both the debt and equity of the same firm. Some commentators suggest that the differing interests of shareholders and debt holders in the Japanese corporation are in this way minimized, thereby reducing the difference between the going concern value of a firm and its liquidation value.[11] U.S. commercial banks have less than 1 percent of outstanding corporate equity while Japanese commercial banks have 20.5 percent; U.S. life insurance companies have 3 percent of U.S. corporate equity, while Japanese life insurance companies have 13.3 percent.[12] Consequently, it may be that overlapping debt and equity claims by Japanese financial institutions reduce agency costs. The inference is that Japanese firms because of lower agency costs enjoy greater leverage; thus, the same amount of equity can contribute to greater corporate opportunity.

A series of articles have shown that Japanese firms with main bank ties perform better after the onset of distress than those without such ties.[13] Anecdotal evidence suggests that Japanese banks will lend money to such companies at favorable interest rates and will encourage them to sell their shares in the main bank so as to raise capital (the market for such share prices will not be reduced because other corporations within the same *Keiretsu* will maintain the share price). Studies also suggest that corporations with main bank ties are less influenced in their investment patterns by liquidity than are similar firms without such main bank ties.[14]

However, Japanese capital markets are becoming distinctly more open, as arm's-length transactions between borrowers and lenders replace close-knit *Keiretsu* relations;[15] bank monitoring appears to be on the wane, as well-capitalized companies are capable of issuing their own highly rated bonds.[16] It may also be that implicit agreements by banks to reduce financial expenses such as interest do not exist. Banks have evolved elaborate security collateral and pledge agreements to ensure their control over collateral.[17] The rate at which Japanese firms have changed their main banks is disputed,[18] yet the rate of defection is inconsequential when compared with that of U.S. firms. Bank-firm ties are representative of *Keiretsu* ties in general and specifics of bailouts of distressed companies will be considered in this context in the next section.

Commercial bank cooperation and affiliation may produce financial market ineffectiveness. The existence of stable shareholding enables large portions of new issues to be placed within the *Keiretsu* and the bulk of shares listed on Japanese exchanges are never traded.[19] Financial groupings can be viewed as entrenchment mechanisms defending incumbent management against hostile takeovers. And bank monitoring in Japan may be viewed as a lax form of monitoring.[20] Additionally, banks and securities firms that were separated as a matter of law were frequently affiliated, thus cumulating stakes.[21]

The main banking system may enable Japanese firms to engage in an inefficient empire building policy of hoarding free cash flow that could otherwise be more effectively used by shareholders.[22] Nevertheless, certain aspects of Japanese financial monitoring may do more than serve as a mechanism for managerial control, if, as has been surmised, banks supplement their legal rights under security agreements with an informal monitoring process.[23]

The application of this theory to Japan might rationalize the elaborate structure of cross-holding as a dispute resolution mechanism. Aside from the many intermediate and high-level meetings among firms with the presidents' clubs coordinating action,[24] and the implicit undertaking not to compete within the firm and to prefer intra-*Keiretsu* trading to trading outside of the *Keiretsu*,[25] the relationships among *Keiretsu* members may effectively form an organization that acts as a social norm to facilitate better creditor relations. Although banks may be tempted to act only from a profit motive when distress looms,[26] this tendency may be lessened by the fact that other members of the president's group, who together will own a controlling interest in the bank, will be able to provide commercial rather than pure banking expertise, and thus inform decisions of banks in various situations.

Although representing only about 10 percent of the industrial firms listed on the Tokyo Stock Exchange as of the late 1970s, firms formally affiliated with one of the six *Keiretsu* groups controlled between 43 percent and 56 percent of total sales in natural resources, primarily metal, chemical, and industrial machinery sectors. Financial institutions affiliated with these groups represented 40 percent of total bank capital companies, 53 percent to 57 percent of total insurance companies, and 55 percent of real estate business. In distribution, 67 percent of sales were accounted for by formal *Keiretsu* companies, primarily through general trading companies *(Sogo Shoshas).*[27] The more flexible definition indicates an increase in affiliations between 1970 and 1990.[28]

There has been a tendency for the reliance on bank financing in Japan to decrease, and this would seem to suggest that reliance on the *Keiretsu* structure has decreased.[29]

The *Keiretsu* is characterized by the internalization of transactions. Outside directors are 21 times more likely to come from affiliated firms than from outside the *Keiretsu.*[30] Internalization to own-group firms, defined as top 10 shareholders, is over 25 percent for all six *Keiretsus* and over 50 percent in the three former *Zaibatsu* groups.[31] Preferential trading within groups is not as high as might be expected, aside from the *Sogo Shoshas'* (trading companies) domination of distribution.[32] In general, firms are about three times as likely to trade within groups (defined as 9 to 20 companies). This figure, while not pronounced, excludes *Sogo Shoshas* and vertical suppliers.[33] Connected with the loosely linked definition of the *Keiretsu* are the tight connections between suppliers and customers (i.e., vertical integration).[34]

Thus, in Japan, stakeholders in a corporation have several overlapping claims. They are simultaneously shareholders, debt holders, and suppliers. Consequently, the residual claimant—the shareholder—will have information not usually available to the U.S. shareholder. Agency problems in Japan are therefore less frequent than in the United States. In assessing the comparative ownership patterns of Japanese firms, it is possible to go beyond the distinction made by Williamson between arm's length and relational contracting,[35] and to consider whether the efficiency of Japanese corporate financing is enhanced because of overlapping legal claims owned by each stakeholder.[36] Certainly, transactional costs in restructuring are reduced. The going concern value of the firm, rather than its liquidation value, is more likely to be retained.[37] This approach to corporate governance is not without costs and may result in wasteful allocation of capital to declining firms.[38] But circumstantial evidence suggests that withdrawal of capital has been orderly and systematic in Japan.[39] In any event, multiple claims (as supplier, shareholder, debt holder) by shareholders would tend to reduce investment in declining industries and may be as effective in shifting capital out of declining industries as leveraged buyouts are in the United States.

The importance accorded balance sheets in the U.S. financial markets, where claimants have single arm's length claims (i.e., shares or bonds), may have created a process of capital budgeting that diminishes investment intangibles.[40] Intangible productivity-enhancing investments include specialized information, education and training, and systems for coordination and integration necessary to achieve superior performance in terms of speed, quality, flexibility, and innovation.[41] Profitability is also demonstrated when a company cannibalizes its resources, that is, replaces an existing product or process with another that is currently worth less, but may in the end be worth more. Examples include replacing old equipment when cost savings do not justify capital expenditures and introducing a new product that decreases sales of existing products.[42] The reorganization of most large corporations into a set of stand-alone business units makes profit and cash flow statements for each business unit available to top managers and their advisors.[43] Thus, each individual profit center would have to report to the central management structure. This tends to increase the importance of profit because ultimate management is uninvolved in the decision-making process of each individual unit and may be unimpressed by anything other than the bottom line.[44] Japanese firms are far less diversified than U.S. companies, and diversification into unrelated areas is also rarer in Japan (7 percent versus 20 percent). But, in 1984, Japanese companies invested 44 percent of their own paid-in capital in satellite firms, and the figure was higher still in Japan's automobile industry.[45]

Thus, informational networks of suppliers, customers, parents, subsidiaries, affiliates, and captive-affiliated companies within the *Keiretsu* provided Japan with an international advantage in innovation until the 1990s and in terms of internationally traded goods continues to do so. The evidence that the *Keiretsu* structure facilitates adjustment in declining industries is weak.[46] What we can ascertain in a loss-sharing situation is the pattern of risk management utilized by the Japanese *Keiretsu* structure. The continued infusion of capital into declining industries may represent one economic function of the *Keiretsu*,[47] but the efficiency of the *Keiretsu* as an ex ante risk-sharing insurance contract has little factual support.[48]

Unlike the U.S. stock market, in which significant price rises are the result of significant trading, Japanese markets may be bid up significantly by very thin trading.[49] The evidence suggests that Japanese brokerage houses will, in many instances, lose significant amounts of money on trading, and that their trading is in large measure intended, or necessary, to ensure the liquidity of the market. Some major companies' stocks may not even be traded for a several-day period.[50]

FINANCIAL REGULATION IN JAPAN

The separation of banking and commerce and the separation of banking from investment and securities is entrenched in Japanese law under Section 65 of Japan's Securities and Exchange Act of 1948, and bank ownership of commercial firms is limited by the anti-monopoly law of 1947.[51] However, these restrictions failed to take hold in Japan because prohibitions that are explicit in U.S. law about attribution of ownership to affiliates and subsidiaries are not present in the restrictions on bank ownership in Japan. Affiliates of major banks operate under no restriction with regard to investments in security firms.[52] These informal linkages create a structure that is similar to the traditional *Keiretsu*, enabling companies that are cross-owned to carry out strategies based on cross-ownership and informal close relationships between companies.

The roles and categories of banks are stipulated by the Banking Law of 1981, which formally separated banks from other financial institutions such as securities firms and insurance firms and categorized them according to the type of business specialization.[53] Although capital markets have developed in Japan, bank lending in Japan in 1994 was 105 percent of nominal GDP compared with 38 percent in the United States where disintermediation is well ahead.[54] Interest rates on deposits have been gradually liberalized since the mid-1970s and are now fully deregulated except for current accounts.[55] The Financial Systems Reform Bill, which passed the Diet in 1992, allowed banks, trust banks, and securities companies to establish subsidiaries to engage in other businesses—trust and securities businesses for banks, securities businesses for trust banks, and banking and trust businesses for securities firms.[56] Beginning in 1993, reciprocal entry for banks into securities activities and for security firms into banking was allowed.[57] Thus, in many respects, by 1993, Japanese financial regulation was more futuristic than U.S. regulation and presaged many of the changes later wrought by U.S. legislation under Gramm-Leach-Bliley and still remains more expansive.

Any doubts about the extent of formalistic deregulation, if not the transparency of the Japanese financial system, should be removed by Big Bang. Unveiled with big fanfare in 1996, the package had the stated objectives of enhancing the international competitiveness of Japanese financial intermediaries and the status of the yen as an international currency, to smooth the flow of funds between Japan and foreign currencies, increasing efficiency via the creation of a free marketplace, increasing the transparency and reliability of markets in order to create a fair marketplace, and maximizing user benefits in the form of investment returns, choice of products, quality of service provisions, and so on.[58] (This sounds like the preamble to the U.S. Constitution or Tokyo Rose or both.)

However, the laws promulgated under the Big Bang involved considerable increases in flexibility in the kind of products banks could sell, introduced cash management products, initiated the process of commission deregulation in securities markets, and established the bank-holding company structure.[59] But, the most important aspect of the legislation was the "prompt corrective action" language that would apply to banks' portfolios of nonperforming loans, empowering the newly created Financial Services Agency to take prompt corrective action against noncomplying banks. This provision was actually subject to delay, not being enacted until April Fools' Day 1999.

There are four groups of initiatives under Big Bang. Under Group 1 measures designed to expand user choice is a lifting of the ban on derivative transaction.[60] This section includes provisions for money market funds and banks' ability to sell all non-equity products and liberalization of cross-border transactions.[61] Group 2 is the introduction of the holding company structure and the licensing regime applicable to securities,[62] removal of restrictions on nonbanks issuing bonds, and liberalization of foreign exchange business.[63] Group 3 issues involve settlement of securities. Group 4 measures are designed to ensure a fair market and involve the strengthening of disclosure requirements including mark to market evaluation of financial instruments.[64] In 1998, Japan instituted consolidated accounting for financial institutions.[65] As of 2002, firms are supposed to record their assets at market, and now all subsidiaries over which the parent company has "effective control," as opposed to the 50 percent ownership required previously, are to be consolidated.[66]

However law in one nation is not exactly the same as the nearly identical law in another nation. The Japanese Commercial Code, like the Model Business Corporation Act, is modeled on the Illinois Business Corporation Act of 1933 and both were enacted in 1950; yet, it functions entirely differently.[67] As the result of the enactment of the law, shareholder rights were greatly expanded and the board of directors was introduced.[68] The greatest distinction in the development of the law is the noninvolvement of lawyers in the evolution of the law where changes are initiated principally by a small group of bureaucrats.[69] Many of the early changes involved restrictions on minority shareholders and their right to call meetings. There were several amendments relating to the *sokaiyam*, special mobsters who ask embarrassing questions at meetings.[70] The 1993 Amendments to the Commercial Code liberalized shareholder derivative suits.[71] It made the stake only 8,600 yen and provided for attorneys' fees as well as time and expenses. In the United States, this would have been very encouraging, but there is no plaintiff's bar in Japan. There are other changes in the offing that address corporate governance.[72] Yet Japanese corporate governance must be understood in light of the fact that only 22 percent of Japan's directors are not employees of the firm versus 65 percent in the United States.[73]

Japan is a nation in which administrative guidance, rather than the rule of law, predominates. For instance, the process of securities regulation is not characterized by the theme of disclosure. If the relevant authority, which has changed, is unsatisfied with an offering, it is unlikely to see the light of day.[74] The Securities Exchange and Surveillance Commission (SESC) was established in 1992 and hived off from the Ministry of Finance (MOF) in 1998 and placed under the Financial Supervisory Authority. In 2000, the SESC was moved again, this time placed under the supervision of the newly created Financial Services Agency. Private rights of action under Japan's Securities Exchange Law have been virtually nonexistent. Instead, the MOF's role had been virtually dispositive.[75] However, this has begun to change.

The SESC is divided into two sections: general inspections of corporations and special investigations of a criminal nature. It is entirely an investigative body that passes on the product of investigation to the Financial Supervisory Authority, the Financial Services Agency, the Financial Reconstruction Agency, or the Ministry of Finance (MOF), depending on the nature of the offense. Actual revocation of licenses is the province of the Japan Securities Dealers Association.[76] If it finds evidence of criminal behavior, it can refer the case to the prosecutor's office, which it has done 31 times since 1992; most of the cases involved insider trading. Sections of the Securities Exchange Law addressing fraud or misrepresentation have been the subject of almost no attention.[77] Of over 300 cases of the general inspection section, most focus on loss compensation or solicitation with downside guarantees. Almost absent are fraud, misrepresentation, or similar cases.[78] Order 4(1) of the Securities and Exchange Law (SEL) prohibiting "false representations or representations which cause misunderstandings of material facts"[79] have been employed only twice. The SESC continues to find trading that "neglects the interests of the investors" (churning) and issues no sanctions.[80]

Private securities litigation has exploded in Japanese terms: In 1997, the four major securities houses were involved in 225 cases.[81] Instead of finding securities fraud, courts have tended to find a duty of care, the breach of which is a violation of Article 709 of the Civil Code.[82] The cases having generally undergone an analysis, which takes into account the complexity of the investment product, the knowledge of the broker, and the investor's ability to understand the nature of the investment. There is a sharp distinction between public and private law in Japan and there is no private right of action under the securities law, but the Public Law gives rise to a duty under the Civil Code.[83] The duty of care has been articulated to include three separate duties: (1) the duty not to provide conclusive evaluations regarding the profitability of an investment; (2) a duty not to solicit clients about investments that in light of their circumstances expose the clients to excessive risk; and (3) a duty to explain the investment and the risk it entails. While the duty not to provide conclusive evidence is inherent in Section 42 of the SEL, courts have dispensed with the statutory basis under public law[84] and focused exclusively on the duty to explain.[85]

The Law concerning the Sale of Financial Products was enacted in May 2000.[86] The law seems designed to catch complex financial instruments. In Section 3, it requires material facts to be disclosed, including whether changes in currency, interest rate risk, or market price will lead to a loss of principal and the period for exercising rights (such as in equity warrants).[87] Additionally, the duty to explain is codified in that the following factors are prescribed: (1) the knowledge and condition of the party solicited, (2) the method and period of time of the solicitation, and (3) the appropriateness of the solicitation.[88]

The Consumer Contract Act was promulgated in May 2000.[89] In pertinent part, the law states the following:

(1) With regard to material fact, to represent other than the truth [resulting in] mistake that the content of said representation is true; (2) to provide conclusive evaluations regarding future prices, future sums of money to be received by the said consumer, or future changes in uncertain items; (3) Consumers may rescind an offer or acceptance of consumer contracts if said consumer mistakenly believes in the non-existence of facts if the [business] in the course of soliciting the conclusion of the customer contract represents to the consumer that the contract will be in consumer's interest as to material facts and items . . . and intentionally fails to convey negative facts disadvantageous to the consumer.[90]

Thus the failure to provide negative information requires scienter, but conclusive evaluations or misrepresentations do not. Yet, the definition of materiality speaks of the price and terms of the transaction and the quality of rights, goods, and services,[91] reminding one that this act is hardly specific to securities law.

The recalcitrance of the Diet to enact a private right of action under Public Securities Law is not remedied by this act, and it is too early to see how cases under the act play out. But, it is important to recall that the SESC has 112 people on its staff;[92] so the whole program of securities regulation and enforcement in Japan ought not to be overstated. Perhaps, even more importantly, there are barely any cases on material misrepresentations and none on material misstatements or misrepresentations by issuers. All the above would be construed as conduct violations in the United States or the United Kingdom where the emphasis in the law is on issuer misstatements, misrepresentations, and omissions of material facts. Is it the case that no one in Japan reads prospectuses? If this is the case, the current development of law does not seem to provide the groundswell for an improvement of financial disclosure and fair value corporate accounting. All of which evidences the fact that Japan does not have an equities market in the same way as the United Kingdom or the United States or even France or Germany would comprehend the term.

Unlike the United States, Japan actually does not have enough lawyers. Although many attend law schools, the pass rate for the bar exam hovers at about 1 percent. In fact, the pass rate has been a subject of trade discussions in the Clinton Framework.[93] There is a ceiling of 1,000 lawyers admitted to practice each year for the whole of Japan.[94] In 1997, 477,000 civil cases were filed in Japan compared with over 15 million in the United States; Japan has 16 lawyers per 100,000 while the United States has 340; but Japan's volume of cases is surprisingly small even when compared to Germany and France.[95] As a consequence, litigation is insufficient to establish precedents or reveal deficiencies in the law for legislators to address. For instance, in the United States, the S&L crisis led to 1,850 indictments and 1,600 convictions, whereas Japan's massively larger crisis has led to about 100 indictments.[96] In some of the more colorful scandals, in 1995, it was revealed that the head of Daiwa's New York office had engaged in 30,000 fraudulent trades over 11 years amounting to $1.1 billion in unreported losses. It was also revealed that the

MOF had known about the problem for one month before informing U.S. regulators.[97] In 1997, the Tokyo Prosecutor's Office discovered that the big four brokerage houses had paid more than $100 million to a mobster to avoid embarrassing disclosures; the scandal spread to Mitsubishi, Toshiba, and Hitashi among others.[98] The prosecutor's office found evidence of collusion among these firms and the MOF, including illegal financing in the United States. The MOF offices were raided and two minor officials were arrested. Eventually, there were several resignations and a suicide, 44 reprimands, and 17 pay cuts. Everyone got off lightly.[99] However, the Ministry of Finance has lost power to the Bank of Japan and the Financial Services Agency although this turf has been fiercely contested.[100]

Stocks and asset prices began plummeting in Japan in response to rising interest rates and regulation on real estate lending.[101] The first banks affected were *Jusen*. These had been created in the 1970s and were roughly equivalent to S&Ls; in the second half of the 1980s *Jusen* had started lending to real estate developers after their traditional business was squeezed by commercial banks. Only 685 billion yen in public funds were used to clean up the *Jusens*, but commercial banks were forced to pony up 1.45 trillion yen and took losses of 1.17 trillion. The Agricultural Coop Banks lent 5.5 trillion yen but took a loss of only half a trillion yen. The commercial banks were outraged. The MOF had lost out to the Agricultural Ministry. As Bergsten et al. describe the situation, "The MOF, the overseer of the apparently mighty Japanese banks, did not have a strategy or the political power to restructure the financial system."[102]

These initial losses underscore a distinctive feature of the Japanese financial crisis. Although, unlike the situation in the United States or the United Kingdom, equity shares are a part of bank capital and have a major impact on overall capital, the fall in land prices had a larger impact on the Japanese economy than did the fall in share prices[103] and, in my view, continues to be more of a burden to commercial bank balance sheets than the declining value of equity shares, which have largely been realized. Generally, insolvency and foreclosure law are unsettled in Japan; the rights of junior secured lenders are particularly murky. Junior lien holders, in the United States, for instance, often play a vital part in assigning market value to real property assets. There are five insolvency laws in Japan that represent a hodgepodge of remedies that are difficult to enact.[104] In April 2000, the new Civil Rehabilitation Law came into effect.[105] The law allows the pre-filing management to remain in possession. A court-appointed supervisor is responsible for rejecting or accepting the petition. In the Tokyo area, a qualified CPA is appointed as an investigator to check the debtor's financial information, and, although creditors committees can be formed, few are in practice.[106] In principle, foreclosure is permitted,[107] subject to the right of the debtor for an injunction if the debtor can demonstrate the creditor's interests will not be harmed and the right of the debtor to a determination of the cash value of the collateral and to pay such amount.[108] When a supervisor is appointed, the supervisor may set aside certain preferential transactions.[109] One important difference between this law and previous laws is that the supervisor can retain jurisdiction over the proceeding for up to three years.[110] Another recent development to slightly benefit creditors is a decision by the Supreme Court that allows mortgage lenders to seek eviction of tenants illegally occupying property that has been sold at public auction.[111]

While there are four proceedings for corporate reorganization, they are generally considered too cumbersome to utilize. But a bigger problem is that Japan's attorney law indirectly grants attorneys a monopoly on debt collection, but the shortage of attorneys capable of assisting in the debt collection and foreclosure process is one of the reasons Japan's banks have not more aggressively pursued foreclosure of nonperforming loans.[112] Furthermore, there is evidence that organized crime serves as a substitute for formal legal mechanisms. The prevalence of private orderings of this kind dampens the enthusiasm for reform.[113]

THE BANKING CRISIS

Even more critically, banks were not put under pressure to realize losses and their portfolios deteriorated. What is particularly bizarre is that the United States had enacted the Federal Deposit Insurance Corporation Improvement Act of 1991 (FDICIA)[114] only about two years earlier and had proved extremely successful in cleaning up the S&L mess by creating the Resolution Trust Corporation. If anything defines the bright line between U.S. and Japanese capitalism, it is the Japanese unwillingness to see the efficacy of this kind of crisis resolution. Credit cooperatives failed, then small banks, then large banks. In November 1997, one of the big four securities firms and one of the 20 large banks failed in the same month.[115] Around the beginning of 1998, the government pushed through major legislation raising about 30 trillion yen for bank recapitalization and, at the end of March, all major banks and three regional banks received 2.1 trillion yen to recapitalize. At the same time, it abandoned all pretense of realistic accounting and allowed banks to value land at high market valuations and stocks at high book value, abandoning any pretense of fair-value accounting.[116] At about this time, the Bank for International Settlements (BIS) standard on market risk was coming into effect[117] creating an unprecedentedly enormous gap between international party line and economic accounting reality. Notwithstanding the current state of Japan's bankbook, Japanese banks wrote off 56.6 trillion yen in bad loans between 1991 and 1998.[118]

In the spring of 1998, it was rumored that Long Term Credit Bank (LTCB) would fail (it seemed that the market realized what government auditors had failed to realize—that LTCB had hidden large losses in subsidiaries). Within months, LTCB applied for nationalization.[119] In June, the cabinet decided on two pieces of legislation: first, it raised the bank capitalization fund to 60 trillion yen and, second, it decided to establish the Financial Services Agency, giving it the job of performing prompt corrective action in remediating nonperforming bank loans.[120] It was nearly a year before the prompt corrective action procedure became law.[121] The Financial Services Agency originally had a reformist leader, Hakuo Yanagisawa. Since the agency's formation in 1999, he has had five successors, but after a 14-month absence he returned to duty in July 2000.[122] Total loans outstanding were 455 trillion yen in 2001. One hundred fifty-one trillion fall into category two or lower (80 trillion net of collateral). Category three, four, and five are 34 trillion combined. Five largely nontradable sectors account for 85 percent of the bad debt: construction, wholesale trade, retail trade, finance, insurance, and real estate.[123]

However, other observers are not so sanguine. In June 2001, the *Nikkei* carried a report on 605 firms that had filed for bankruptcy and found that 70 percent of the loans were classified as category one or two.[124] In 2000, Goldman Sachs issued a report putting the level of risky loans at 237 trillion yen, or about 50 percent of GDP (equivalent to about five trillion dollars for the United States) and those in category three and below at 170 trillion yen.[125] The IMF (International Monetary Fund) Country Specific Report on Japan cited the higher private-sector figures,[126] prompting Financial Services Authority (FSA) complaints.[127] In April 2001, an emergency economic package was announced that called for the writing off of nonperforming loans within two years and new NPLs within three years and reducing equities on balance sheets through a Banks' Shareholding Acquisition Corporation.[128] That is wishful thinking.

THE BUDGET DEFICIT

Meanwhile, Japan has embarked on a campaign to spend its way out of recession, although its earnestness in this endeavor has been called into question. The government debt has risen from 59.3 percent in 1992 to 118.2 percent as a percent of GDP in 2001, making it the worst among G-7 countries.[129] The announced size of the package is usually deceptive since the government is trying to impress the public.[130] The government debt is lower, net of government assets and including social security, as low as 50 percent. However, all the Internationales (the IMF, the BIS, and the Organization for Economic Cooperation and Development [OECD]) argue for excluding social security since pension liabilities are equal to the social security fund. Furthermore, the OECD says there are implicit liabilities for civil service pension funds that are not budgeted and that should cause gross and net debt figures to rise by 150 percent. In 2000, all the rating agencies downgraded Japan's government debt.[131] One could spend several long weekends tracing the use of proceeds and the bridges to nowhere. The Koizumi government made a promise to cap new government bond issues at 30 trillion yen, which equals a 10 percent cutback or a 0.7 percent reduction in GDP spending, which is roughly equivalent to what the United States accomplished between 1993 and 2000.[132]

The Bank for International Settlements believes that government debt is on an upward path toward unsustainability,[133] which arises when interest payments to new bonds have to be financed by issues of new bonds, which cannot be sustained by taxes, or when bondholders demand higher interest rates to refinance the debt. I am not so sure. Japan's bondholders are a pliant bunch. Consider the amount on deposit in Japanese banks. An even more passive capital base is the Postal Savings System, which as of March 1998 had 231 trillion yen in savings.[134] Koizumi has vowed to privatize postal savings, but he may have difficulty since the government may rely on the passivity of depositors. Bergsten says the problem could be exacerbated with capital flight, but the yen's strength as an international currency is greatly exaggerated, about as exaggerated as reports of Mark Twain's death. Furthermore, in addition to the 460 billion dollars worth of official reserves,[135] Japan probably has untold amounts of hidden dollar reserves, and despite the received wisdom of economists in the early 1980s about the impossibility of a managed exchange rate, Japan, at great cost to itself, has, in fact, had a hand in managing its exchange rate. Secretary of Treasury Paul O'Neill was probably quite correct when he says that China's measly $230 billion won't get them far, but Hong Kong has an additional $110 billion in reserves, and Japan's $460 billion in cold hard cash is nothing to sneeze at, and there is a lot more. Asian countries as a whole possess more than a trillion dollars, mostly denominated in dollars, in official reserves.[136] In addition to undisclosed government reserves, the system of administrative guidance that still obtains in Japan enables the government to make use of dollars and dollar-denominated assets in private hands in the event of a crisis. However, it is far more likely that a crisis will develop in the other direction with yen appreciation.

JAPANESE POLITICAL ECONOMY

A rare glimpse into the Japanese administrative mindset was available twice in international arenas. In September 1997, Japan proposed an Asian Monetary Fund, which was to be capitalized with $100 billion. The idea was to quickly disburse funds without regard to conditionality and quota limitations. The proposal was blocked by the United States and China.[137] Meanwhile, the United States, in a series of reports, was arguing for greater conditionality.[138] Japanese Finance Minister Kiichi Miyazawa, in response to the Meltzer Commission Report,[139] described as "unrealistic" the idea of limiting IMF lending activities to short-term emergency credits, and in March 2000, MOF Vice Minister Hirohiko Kuroda called for the IMF to limit the inclusion of structural reform conditionality in its assistance packages.[140] In the competition as to who would succeed Michael Cadmessus as director of the IMF, Japan put forward a protest candidate, Eiseuke Sakakibara, who not only promoted government-led capital channeling but had been disciplined for his role in the MOF financial scandal.[141] Bergsten et al. postulate that this indicates how weak the potential field of candidates in Japan is and that the candidature was in protest of the European stranglehold of the directorship.[142] I disagree. In my view, this represents an essential strain of Japanese politics, which is not entirely satisfied with market-oriented economics, and which has been responsible for the constant derailing of bank reform and the topsy-turvy leadership struggle for the Financial Services Authority. Any other explication of the political economy of Japan would lead one to believe that it is falling into autarchy under the sway of dimwits. In reality, there is a struggle between free marketers who are realists and traditionalists who favor a system of administrative guidance. The Koizumi government seems to represent a victory of the former over the latter, but this may prove temporary given the unreality of the government's plan for banking reform.

Japan is ultimately a producer-driven society in which consumers are given short shrift, despite all the Nintendo games and robots. They are shoved into metros in the morning and return to small quarters in the evening. Consumer prices are extremely high in Japan. A 1999 Ministry of Trade and Industry (MITI) survey found that the average price of industrial goods was 67 percent higher in Japan than in the United States, 57 percent higher than in Germany, and 200 percent higher than in Korea.[143] Another report found that prices in Japan were 74 percent higher than in the United States while the next most expensive country, Norway, was only 32 percent higher.[144] Naturally, a certain amount of this can be attributed to agricultural subsidies: Japanese people spend 23 percent of their income on food compared with 14 percent for people in the United States, despite the fact that Americans eat out twice as often.[145] Japan remains the only country without an independent telecommunications regulatory commission. However, within the retail sector, the repeal of the Large Scale Retail Store Law[146] has resulted in many openings, and in the transportation field, the government announced a phased relaxation of fare-setting for taxis, railways, buses, ships, and aviation.

But the biggest impediment to lower consumer prices is the anticompetitive behavior of Japanese firms through cartelization or the *Keiretsu* structure.[147] In one instance, the agricultural department of a prefecture organized a bid rigging.[148] Even more onerous to the consumer is the role of the vertical *Keiretsu*, which utilizes one of many forms of vertical restraints including resale price maintenance, exclusive dealing or distribution, tied sales, reciprocity agreements, territorial restrictions, or refusals to deal.[149]

The World Trade Organization states the following:

> Distribution *Keiretsu* are not found equally in all sectors; they are concentrated in specific sectors, such as cosmetics, electrical appliances, and automobiles, all of which are characterized by product differentiation, specialty goods, or occasional purchases,

and important market segmentation. Outside the automobile sector, where the affiliation ratio is exceptionally high, keiretsu distributors cover at most about half of the total market (50 percent in the cosmetic sector and 40 percent in the electrical appliance sector). Although manufacturers cannot legally prevent affiliated dealers from dealing in competing products, such deals are likely to be discouraged by additional burdens on after-sale servicing and sales-promoting activities, as well as by other advantages extended or pressures exerted by *Keiretsu* manufacturers.[150]

Where there are monopoly or oligopoly situations, there are oligopoly profits, and studies indicate that lower borrowing costs and more stable, if lower profits are associated with *Keiretsu* affiliation;[151] although Japanese banks are dumping shares, they are dumping non-*Keiretsu* shares.[152] In fact, trading companies—*Shogo Shoshas*—may be a repository of hidden wealth.[153]

Japan's bilateral trade imbalance with the United States is compounded by the surplus of Japanese-Asian affiliates with the United States. Although this is difficult to measure, it was estimated at 21 billion in 1995 and had grown 240 percent between 1985 and 1994.[154] This is a consequence of many factors, chief among which is the U.S. penchant for spending and the Japanese penchant for saving, the wealth effect in the United States, where stock ownership is more common, as well as demographics, cartelization, and high land and building costs.

The contrast between Japanese and U.S. household portfolios is stark. In 2000, Japanese households held 56.6 percent of their financial assets in currency and bank deposits and 15 percent in equities, whereas U.S. households held only 14 percent of their assets in cash and bank deposits in 1997 and 50 percent in stocks and bonds.[155] In 1997, Japanese gross fixed investment as a share of GDP was the highest in the OECD and 68 percent higher than in the United States in the middle of its capital-spending boom.[156] Brookings Institute Fellow Edward Lincoln extrapolates that, in 1997, Japan had a 2.5 percent annual rate of home acquisition, whereas, in the United States, there is an 8.5 percent annual turnover, which expresses the relative liquidity of the U.S. residential real estate market. Although the cost of land has fallen from its dizzying heights, many banks have yet to sell and realize the loss on land held as collateral on nonperforming loans.[157] In 1998, the government increased its loans to small businesses to 30 trillion yen (248 billion at then prevailing exchange rates).[158] By the late 1990s, return on capital in the United States was 59 percent higher than in Japan. At the end of the 1990s, the return on capital to the corporate sector in Japan was between 2 and 3 percent.[159]

CONCLUSION

The U.S. trade policy of constructive engagement has been misguided. Now the game is played out. It is perfectly acceptable for the hegemon in the world order to run a continued trade deficit but not a current account deficit. The trade deficit must be balanced by a foreign portfolio or foreign direct investment. Throughout the post-war period until the mid 1990s, this was the case for the United States. Deluded by high productivity growth (U.S. productivity has run ahead of Japan, throughout the 1990s averaging 2.5 percent per annum versus 1.5 percent per annum for Japan, turning the tables for the 1980s),[160] U.S. policy has failed to take note of the threat created by the instability of the Japanese financial system, which is so reliant on running perennial trade surpluses. However, with respect to investment, even if the source of funds was foreign savings, the United States easily matched Japan in the 1990s. In the United States, capital spending accounted for one-third of total GDP growth in the 1990s versus its traditional share of one-sixth,[161] and this imbalance had dramatic consequences; however, it paled in comparison to Japan's imbalance between capital spending and consumer spending. In Japan in the early 1990s, capital accumulation led to an economic slowdown from which Japan has yet to recover. Japan is only gradually emerging from its reliance on export-led growth. It has yet to truly liberate the consumer sector and can only do so by breaking up the vertical *Keiretsu*, an action unlikely to happen in the near future. A possible halfway measure that Japan could adopt is a form of contingent liabilities modeled on Ginnie Mac and Fannie Mae, government guaranteed mortgages, but perhaps Japan's moment to take on further contingent liabilities has passed, regardless of their low cost.

In 1997, Japan actually declared the recession over and introduced a 3 percent consumption tax. This may well have led to the failure of Long Term Credit and the Asia Crisis. But, in 2000, the Bank of Japan, celebrating its liberation from the Ministry of Finance, raised interest rates to 1 percent, ending the 0 interest rate policy. For these reasons, together with Japan's unwillingness to deal with its banking crisis, it is misleading to suggest that Japan has actually employed Keynesian deficit spending as intended. As of this writing, Japan's trade surplus is more than 20 percent greater than last year. In June 2002, rating agencies again downgraded Japan's debt so that it is now on a par with Latvia, and the government is cutting corporate taxes and introducing a new consumption tax. It is not clear which side will emerge victorious in Japan's internal struggle for identity.

In essence, a false economy was created by the U.S. trade deficit. This deficit brought about the collapse of the Japanese financial system in the early 1990s. Rather than fully realize this collapse, the Japanese government has sought to prolong the current regime by failure to take prompt corrective action and by supporting the dollar and maintaining a structural trade surplus. At the same time, the United States, in believing that it had curtailed the budget deficit and made productivity gains, failed to resolve the issue of the current account deficit. Now this deficit can only be resolved through expropriation of foreign assets or a new international monetary regime and attendant trade and investment regimes.

Developments in 2003

Japan had the highest GDP growth rate of G-7 countries in 2002 and a respectable per capita GDP growth rate in 2003; nonetheless, a burgeoning budget deficit and an inability to deal with financial sector rigidities, especially the write-off of nonperforming loans, continues to plague the Japanese economy and may become a source of instability in the future. Developments in 2003 can be characterized as "more of the same" in the slow development of a market-based financial structure. Major developments included the formation of the Industrial Revitalization Corporation of Japan (IRCJ) to aid Japanese corporations in restructuring, another special round of inspections leading banks to raise external capital, the incorporation of the Japanese Post (a stage on the way toward privatization), and the amendment of the Securities and Exchange Law to include a "fit and proper" test on the principal shareholders of securities companies. The IMF makes six general recommendations: (1) Strengthen banks' NPLs by extending the use of forward-looking expected loss estimates and limiting the use of deferred tax estimates; (2) improve bank capitalization, particularly systemically important banks, and require these banks to bring in new management and raise the minimum capital requirement for domestic banks to 8 percent; (3) require banks to adopt corporate governance reform consistent with Basel, including outside directors and a board audit committee; (4) encourage banks to set up separate subsidiary "work out" companies and develop the market for distressed debt by having the new IRCJ and the Resolution and Collection Corporation act as a catalyst; (5) increase the authority of the FSA; and (6) reduce the government involvement in the financial sector by restricting the activities of the Postal Savings, insurance schemes, and government lending agencies.[162]

As of early 2003, banks had written off an aggregate of 90 trillion yen since 1992, about eight or nine times as much as U.S. banks wrote off in the early 1990s. However, an unacceptable level of nonperforming loans remains.[163] Still, after rising from 1997 to 2001, the ratio of nonperforming loans to total loans has been declining since the second half of 2002.[164] In general, Japanese banks remain capital deficient. Deferred tax assets now represent half of tier-one capital.[165] The government rescue of failed banks continued with the recapitalization of Resona Bank with public funds and involved salary cuts and the departure of 70 members of senior management. The shareholders elected a new nonexecutive director and outside directors.[166] Commercial Codes revisions that took effect in April 2003 allowed corporations the options of choosing a specific governance structure with a majority of outside directors.[167]

NOTES

1. Edward Lincoln, *Arthritic Japan: Explaining the Slow Pace of Growth* (Brookings, 2001).

2. U.S. Department of Commerce (2000), cited in Fred Bergsten, Takatoshi Ito, and Marcus Noland, *No More Bashing: Building a New Japan United States Economic Relationship* (Institute for International Economics, 2001), p. 114.

3. *Ibid.*, p. 35, noting that the bilateral deficit with China may be overstated; Gary Hufbauer and Kimberly Elliot, "America's Access to China's Markets: The Congressional Vote on PNTR," Economics Policy Brief 00-03 (Washington Institute for International Economics, 2000).

4. *Ibid.*, at 263–66.

5. Ferdinand Braudel, *The Mediterranean World in the Age of Phillip II*, translated from the French by Sian Reynolds (Harper and Row, 1972–73).

6. *See infra* notes 51–53 and accompanying text.

7. J. McDonald, "The Mochai Affect: Japanese Corporate Cross-Holding Ownership," *Journal of Portfolio Management* 16 (fall 1989): pp. 90–95.

8. *See*, for example, R. Komiya, *The Japanese Economy, Trade Industry, and Government* (University of Tokyo Press, 1990); Masahiko Aoki, *Information, Incentives, and Bargaining in the Japanese Economy* (1988), p. 123, citing Bank of Japan Monthly Report (February 1984), at 138; David Meerschwam, "The Japanese Financial System and the Cost of Capital," in *Trade with Japan: Has the Door Opened Wider?* (Paul Krugman, ed., 1991); Jeffrey Frankel, "Japanese Finance in the 1980s: A Survey," in *Trade with Japan*, at 225.

9. Michael Gerlach, "Twilight of the Keiretsu: A Critical Assessment," *J. Japan. Stud.* 18 (1991): p. 74.

10. T. Hoshi, A. Kashyap, and D. Scharfstein, "The Role of Banks in Reducing the Costs of Financial Distress in Japan," *Journal of Financial Economics* 27 (1990): p. 60.

11. Stephen Prowse, "Institutional Investment Patterns and Corporate Financial Behavior in the United States and Japan," *J. Fin. Econ* 27 (1990): p. 43. *See also* M. Jenson and W. Meekling, "Theory of the Firm: Managerial Behavior, Agency Costs, and Ownership Structure," *Fin. ECW* 31 (1976): p. 30.

12. Federal Reserve Board Flow of Funds Account (September 1987), Japanese Securities Research Institute, "Securities Markets in Japan" (1988). Cited in Drowse, at 45.

13. T. Hoshi, A. Kashyap, and D. Scharfstein, *supra* note 10, at 70.

14. T. Hoshi, A. Kashyap, and D. Scharfstein, "Corporate Structure, Liquidity, and Investment: Evidence from Japanese Industrial Groups," *Q. J. Econ.* 106 (1991): p. 33. But *see also* Paul Sheard, "Main Banks and Internal Capital Markets in Japan," *Shoken Keizai* 157 (1986): p. 255.

15. T. Hoshi, A. Kashyap, and D. Scharfstein, "Bank Monitoring and Investment: Evidence from the Changing Structure of Japanese Corporate Banking Relationships," in *Asymmetric Information Corporate Finance and Investments*, ed. R. Glenn Hubbard (University of Chicago, 1990), p. 105.

16. *Ibid.*, at 113.

17. Mark Ramseyer, "Legal Rules in Repeated Deals: Banking in the Shadow of Defection in Japan," *J. Legal Stud.* 20 (1991): pp. 91, 103.

18. *Ibid.*, at 98, footnote 18, citing the fact that every five years, 15 percent of the firms listed on Section 1 of the Tokyo Stock Exchange switch main banks, citing Akiyoshi Horiuchi, "The Function of Financial Institutions" (1987); and 33.2 percent change such connections over 10 years, citing Yoshiro Miwa, "Main Banks and Their Functions," (*ibid.*). But the evidence regarding bank ties also suggests an increase in

stability as the rates of defection from main banks have declined from 17 percent in 1962–67, to 15 percent during a five-year period in the late 1960s and early 1970s, and have decreased still further to 11 percent from 1978 to 1983. Recent data suggest that publicly traded Japanese companies increased their borrowing by 29 trillion yen between 1980 and 1989. The issuance of stocks and bonds accounted for 43 trillion yen for these companies, while new capital produced or retained earnings increased 24 trillion yen during this period (Gerlach, "Twilight of the Keiretsu," *supra* note 9, at 99 citing Nikkei Business [January 15, 1990]). However, U.S. firms also increased their borrowings substantially in the 1980s, and it was only because of the growth of the market value of equity that the debt/equity ratio did not alter significantly.

19. Eric Berglof and Enrico Perotti, "The Japanese Financial *Keiretsu* as a Collective Enforcement Mechanism," Massachusetts Institute of Technology Japan Program 91–09 (1991).

20. John Coffee, "Liquidity versus Control: The Institutional Investor as Corporate Monitor," *Colum. L. Rev.* 91 (1991), at 1294: 1277, 1300–02.

21. *See infra* notes 51–53 and accompanying text.

22. *Op. cit.*, at 1299, and Michael Jenson, "Agency Cost of Free Cash Flow, Corporate Finance, and Takeovers," *Aei. Econ. Rev.* 76 (1986): p. 323.

23. Ramseyer, *supra* note 17. (The conflict between the legal and the relations orientations of Japanese finance may be expressed in terms of the dichotomy between implicit and explicit contracts that has been utilized to explain corporate contractual relations in the United States. [Oliver Hart, "An Economist's Perspective of the Theory of the Firm," *Columbia L. Rev.* 89 (1989): p. 1757.] If complete or comprehensive contracts were to specify the payoffs and actions for every conceivable state of events, there would be no conflicts. However, when contracts are incomplete, contracting parties may attempt to mitigate conflicts by certain ex-ante contractual arrangements. The alternative to unconstrained bargaining is to delegate to one of the parties the right to make decisions not specified in the contract. The residual control rights are residual property rights. S. J. Grossman and O. Hart, "The Cost and Benefits of Ownership: A Theory of Vertical and Lateral Integration," *J. Pol. Econ.* 94 [1986]: p. 691.)

24. Michael Gerlach, *Alliance Capitalism: The Social Organization of Japanese Business* (1992), pp. 137–50.

25. *See infra* note 30 and accompanying text.

26. Ramseyer, *supra* note 17.

27. Gerlach, *supra* note 24, at 88. These percentages exclude financial and industrial firms in smaller city groups, such as Daiwa, as well as many companies affiliated with the Industrial Bank of Japan, the largest bank in Japan, which was government owned. As of about 1990, Toshiba alone has 200 subsidiary companies and another 600 grandchild companies. A looser classification system, based on stable capital affiliation, finds that 577 of 986 stocks listed in the first section of the Tokyo Stock exchange had identifiable affiliations with one of the Big Six Groups. These companies accounted for 69 percent of total assets of all first-section firms and 76 percent of the total sales.

28. *Ibid.*, at 95. (Under the looser definition [*Keiretsu Kenayu*], 577 firms in the first section of the Tokyo Stock Exchange had *Keiretsu* affiliations, an increase of over 200 companies from those quoted in the 1970 volume. Total assets and total sales accounted for by these companies as a share of first-section firms increased from 66 percent to 69 percent and from 71 percent to 76 percent, respectively. Under the more formal

criterion, defined as membership in the President's Council of the Big Six *Keiretsu*, membership expanded rapidly, gaining 56 new participants, an increase of 41 percent over a 23-year period ending in 1980. Perhaps the most telling characteristic of the *Keiretsu* is the established and still increasing stability of their top 10 shareholders. Of all Japanese companies' top 10 shareholders, 7,311 remained stable during two-year intervals in the early 1970s. This number had increased to about 87 percent in the mid-1980s. [*Ibid.*, at 96.] [Other figures about stable shareholding for a two-year period show an 81 percent stability among the top 10 shareholders in the *Keiretsu* firms and 83 percent for non-*Keiretsu* firms, while the comparable statistic for the United States was 23 percent (results are from a survey of 250 large corporations in each country).] [*Ibid.*, at 92–93.])

29. Furthermore, extremely strong companies, such as Toyota and Matsushita Electric, have no external debt and are therefore able to avail themselves of capital market financing at extremely advantageous rates. Recent data suggest that publicly traded Japanese companies increased their borrowing by 29 trillion yen between 1980 and 1989. The issuance of stocks and bonds accounted for 43 trillion yen for these companies, while new capital produced or retained earnings increased 24 trillion yen during this period. Gerlach, *supra* note 24, at 99, citing Nikkei Business (January 15, 1990). However, U.S. firms also increased their borrowings substantially in the 1980s, and it was only because of the growth of the market value of equity that the debt/equity ratio did not alter significantly. But securities and other capital markets are largely mediated by institutions through a complex set of strategic relationships with corporate users of capital. The relationship between banks and securities houses is quite significant, despite the limitations imposed by the Securities Act of 1948. Among Sumitomo Group's top 20 companies, for example, all but 4 relied on Daiwa securities as their lead underwriter as of 1989, and all but 1 of these companies had been doing so for the past two decades. Daiwa, in turn, is linked to Sumitomo Group by virtue of the fact that its two leading shareholders and reference banks are Sumitomo Bank and Sumitomo Trust. (Gerlach, *supra* note 24, at 103.) Banks and insurance companies continue to be net purchasers of securities and together control nearly one-half of publicly traded shares in Japan. (*Ibid.*, citing Nikkei Business [January 15, 1990] and Securities Market in Japan 10 [1990]). The degree of direct financing, including funds raised for investment trust, is nearly 90 percent as of 1987. However, it is not clear that this figure would be significantly different for the United States. The interlinking between banks and securities firms has been particularly close because the capital adequacy requirements of the G-10 agreement necessitated a short-term boost in bank capital. (*See* chapter 1, "The EU Single Market in Banking. . . .") During the six years from 1984 to 1990, Japan's 23 largest banks raised 13.5 trillion yen in equity capital, a substantial portion of all equity capital raised, and nonfinancial firms, in order to maintain their stable shareholdings in banks, also utilized 30 percent to 40 percent of their own new capital to acquire bank equity issues. (*Wall Street Journal* [March 18, 1991]). By contrast, U.S. banks, which have required capital, have relied on the free market for securitization of assets and international capital markets where, until 1986, they successfully raised perpetual and long-term debt through floating rate notes on the eurobond market.

30. Gerlach, *supra* note 24, at 166 and 179.

31. *Ibid.*, at 168.

32. The *Sogo Shoshas* tend toward reinforcing *Keiretsu* ties, particularly for in-

dustries in decline. For example, in the Mitsubishi Group, as of 1983, the group trading company handles 55 percent of sales for Mitsubishi Heavy Industries, and 75 percent for Mitsubishi Aluminum and Mitsui Shipbuilding (*ibid.*, at 184, citing a 1983 study of Okumura Hiroshi).

33. Gerlach, *supra* note 24, at 187–88.

34. Core firms in Nissan Suppliers Association provide over 90 percent of its input, and, out of 150 suppliers in Toyota's Suppliers Association, only 3 departed over a 12-year period (Banri Asanuma, "Manufacturing-Supplier Relationships in Japan as a Concept of Relation-Specific Skill," *J. Japan. Int'l Econ.* 3 [1989]: p. 130). Preferential trading has specific implications in the international arena. It has been argued that distribution by *Sogo Shoshas* make penetration of Japanese markets difficult for foreign companies. Preferential trading carries over in foreign direct investment. The tendency of Japanese firms to trade within the *Keiretsu* has been transplanted overseas. It is probably augmented by the role of *Sogo Shoshas* in foreign trade. Evidence suggests that a much higher proportion of Japanese firms trade within their corporate group than do similar American firms. (Robert Lawrence, "How Open Is Japan?" in *Trade with Japan: Has the Door Opened Wider?*, pp. 9–40.) In 1986, intrafirm trade accounted for 48.5 percent of U.S. exports to Europe and 32 percent of U.S. imports from Europe, but intrafirm shipments accounted for 75 percent of U.S. imports from Japan and 72 percent of U.S. exports to Japan. Intrafirm shipments from U.S. exporters accounted for 36.9 percent of U.S. exports to Europe while Japanese exports to the United States were dominated by intrafirm shipments of Japanese exporting firms—-66.1 percent of all U.S. imports from Japan. This pattern suggests the international vertical integration process moving downstream internationally from producers to their markets, according to Professor Robert Lawrence (*ibid.*). In 1986, Japanese affiliates in the United States shipped 58.4 percent of all U.S. exports to Japan back to their Japanese parents. By contrast, U.S. affiliates in Japan imported from their parent companies only 13.6 percent of all Japanese imports from the United States (*ibid.*, at 9, 15–17). On President Bush's 1992 trip to Japan, Japanese promises to buy $20 billion per year in auto parts from the United States in order to reduce the merchandise surplus with the United States were criticized because most of these purchases would come from Japanese firms. The merchandise surplus of Japan and the corresponding U.S. deficit with Japan would also be reduced. While an unfair trade issue may exist, the point to be underscored here is that intracorporate finance is bound up with intragroup trade, leading inexorably to unfair trade issues.

35. Oliver Williamson, *The Economic Institutions of Capitalism: Firms, Markets, Relational Contracting* (New York: Free Press; London: Collier Macmillan, 1985).

36. *See* Carl Kester, "Banks in the Board Room: The American versus Japanese and German Experiences" (Harvard Business School Research Colloquium, May 27–28, 1992).

37. Jensen, *supra* note 22.

38. Carl Kester, *Japanese Takeovers* (1991), pp. 169–235.

39. *Ibid.*

40. Carliss Baldwin and Kim B. Clarke, "Capabilities and Capital Investment: New Perspectives on Capital Budgeting," prepared for the Council on Competitiveness and Harvard Business School (1992).

41. *Ibid.*, at 5.

42. This study cites several other studies that show that cannibalism can make

companies more competitive, including R. N. Foster, *Innovation: The Attacker's Advantage* (New York: Summit Books, 1986); C. H. Ferguson, "American Microelectronics in Decline: Evidence Analysis and Alternatives" (Ph.D. diss., Massachusetts Institute of Technology, 1987); and C. Y. Baldwin, "How Capital Budgeting Deters Innovation and What Companies Can Do about It" (Research-Technology Management, 1991).

43. Baldwin and Clarke, *supra* note 40.

44. In those patent areas recognized by the U.S. patent office in which the United States still maintains a strong position, a majority (over 80 percent in one study) are marked by deterioration vis-à-vis Japan. J. Davidson Frame and Francis Narain, "The United States, Japan, and the Changing Technological Balance," *Res. Pgl.* 19 (1990): pp. 447–55. Japanese firms tend to concentrate basic R&D (research and development) in parent companies but allocate marketing responsibility to satellite firms. Japan's six major computer and communications equipment firms had 329 majority-owned subsidiaries and 48 affiliated companies, and total investment in these subsidiaries and affiliates averaged 194.8 billion yen. Michael Gerlach, "Economic Innovation and Corporate Finance in Japan," 13 (1992) (unpublished).

45. Michael Gerlach, "Economic Innovation and Corporate Finance in Japan," 13 (1992) (unpublished) at 10. (In Japan there is no counterpart to the U.S. venture capital market, and the market for initial public offerings is a fraction of the U.S. market. Consequently, users were involved in the origination of 26 percent of R&D projects versus 1 percent in the United States. [Edwin Mansfield, "Industrial R&D in Japan and the United States: A Comparative Study," *Am. Econ. Rev.: Papers and Proc.* 78 (May 1988), at 228.] Suppliers in Japan are also more heavily involved in basic component engineering [73 percent of outside purchases in Japan are of supplier-proprietary parts, versus 19 percent in the United States and 46 percent in Europe]. [Gerlach, at 26; M. Aoki, "The Japanese Firm in Transition," in *The Political Economy of Japan*, ed. Kozo Yanamura and L. Yasuba, vol. 1 (1987).])

46. Robert Zielinski and Nigel Holloway, *Unequal Equities: Power and the Stock Market in Japan's Stock Market* (Kodansha International, 1991), at 107–10, 123.

47. *Ibid.*

48. *See* Williamson, *supra* note 35, and Grossman and Hart, *supra* note 23. The application of the implicit contract theory as a risk sharing by the Japanese *Keiretsu* is attributable to I. Nakatani, "The Economic Role of the Financial Corporate Grouping," in *The Economic Analysis of the Japanese Firm*, ed. M. Aoki (1984), pp. 227–58. The ability of the Japanese financial system to make adjustments in depressed and declining industries is questionable. The example of the aluminum industry provides some indication of the pattern of adjustment. Paul Sheard, "The Role of Firm Organizations in the Adjustment of a Declining Industry in Japan: The Case of Aluminum," *J. Japan and Int'l Econ.* (1991). Although loans were made by 11 major parent firms for a total of 275 billion yen, these loans were made in many cases to finance existing deficits, and capital injections were usually made in conjunction with a writing off by the parent company of equity claim. *Ibid.* In the case of Sumitomo Aluminum Smelting, this company underwent share reductions each year between 1982 and 1985 and was dissolved in 1986. Between 1982 and 1986, Sumitomo Chemical injected 57 billion yen in share capital into SAS, and in the same period wrote off 61 billion yen in losses as a result of SAS's share capital write-down (Zielinski and Holloway, *supra* note 46, at 123). There are also numerous instances of loss sharing mechanisms that

do not show up directly in corporate accounts. Zielinski and Holloway, *supra* note 46. Banks played a major role in adjustment of the industry by providing interest rate reduction to the aluminum smelting firm. It was reported that in 1978, Nippon Light Metal's three main banks implemented interest rate reductions representing an annual interest subsidy of some 900 million yen. General trading companies also perform essential functions in facilitating risk-sharing in corporate groups. *Ibid.*, at 124. In the case of one smelting company, it was found that three closely associated trading companies provided a total of 32 billion yen in low interest off-balance sheet financing in 1981. Confidential documents unearthed by one researcher suggest that a complex formula exists for risk-sharing among group members, allocating nearly all the loss to banks and insurance companies. *Ibid.*, at 128.

49. *Op. cit.*, at 120.

50. Though there is a considerable turnover, only about a quarter of the shares are traded on the Tokyo Stock Exchange (TSE), and the rest remain in stable holdings. Consequently, a very large share price rise can occur on very slim trading. For example, the Industrial Bank of Japan saw a share price rise of 8 percent on August 7, 1989, creating $7 billion in shareholder wealth on a mere $25 million worth of trading. Only 3.7 percent of its 2.3 billion shares outstanding are considered floating shares. *Ibid.* The fact that shares are so slimly traded on the TSE may make the Japanese financial system more susceptible to economic shocks than a true capital market system. There are many sources of financial news in Japan. *Ibid.* However, the information they supply could never equal that accessible to insiders within the *Keiretsu* group. Investment trusts have consequently underperformed the Nikkei average.

51. Securities Exchange Act §65, Law no. 25 of 1948 provides that a Japanese bank may not engage in investment banking under Section 11 of Japan's Anti-Monopoly Act regarding the prohibition of private monopolies and the maintenance of fair trade (§ 11a, Law no. 54 of 1947). Banks may not own more than 5 percent of a nonbanking firm. Originally the Anti-Monopoly Act placed a maximum level at 10 percent, but this was reduced to 5 percent by Law no. 63 of 1977. Banks were given until December 1987 to divest excess holdings. Ramseyer, *supra* note 17, at 99, footnote 21, and Coffee, *supra* note 20, at 1294.

52. *Ibid.*, Coffee, *supra* note 20; Ramseyer, *supra* note 17. For example, about 1990, Mitsubishi Bank, together with its affiliates, owned more than 78 percent of the outstanding shares of Ryoko Securities, through its parent and 29 affiliates. (*Ibid.*)

53. Yutaka Tajima and Misako Inagaki, "The Impact of Globalization on Japanese Banking Law," in Barry Rider, Tajima Yutaka, and A. K. Fiona Macmillan, *Commercial Law in a Global Context: Some Perspectives in Anglo-Japanese Law* (Kluwer Law International, 2000), p. 37. This law amends the Banking Law 1927 and includes a special provision for credit limit on large-scale loan extensions. The law allows banks to conduct five activities: (1) banking, (2) ancillary business supplementary to traditional banking, including guarantees in compliance with Article 10(2) and securities custodian business, and (3) securities business including government bonds and private placement arrangements, (4) other business stipulated in Article 12 including trust business and corporate bond registration, and (5) peripheral business, such as leasing and investment services. Someone had been studying the development of U.S. banking law. There are, naturally, a host of other relevant laws including the Long-Term Credit Bank Law of 1952, the Foreign Exchange Bank Law 1954, the Mutual Saving Bank Law 1951, and the Revised Trust Bank Law 1954 (based on the original 1922 law).

54. *Ibid.*, at 40.

55. *Ibid.*, at 41.

56. Additionally, Shinpan companies registered with the Ministry of Trade and Finance can provide credit under the Installment Sales Law of 1961, *ibid.*, at 45.

57. Law Amending Laws in Relation to Financial and Exchange System Reform (June 19, 1992), promulgated June 26, 1992.

58. Maximillian Hall, "Japan's Big Bang: the Likely Winners and Losers," *Journal of International Banking Law* (1999): p. 204. The measures were designed under five headings: (1) those designed to expand user choice; (2) those designed to improve the quality of service and competition; (3) those designed to help preserve financial stability; (4) those designed to ensure the establishment of a fair market; and (5) those designed to help preserve financial stability. The measure was intended to bring securities-related reforms, enable further asset securitization, liberalization of capital movements, liberalization of foreign subsidiary rights to do business, promotion of holding company structure, enhanced consumer protection structure, liberalization of foreign exchange rules, relaxation of rules separating short- and long-term financing, and enhanced supervision through prompt corrective action. This required amending 22 financial laws including the Securities and Exchange Law, the Securities Investment Trust Law, the Banking Law, and the Insurance Business Law. In 1997, cash management accounts were introduced for the first time and the business scope of banks was extended to include all nonequity business, and the gradual process of deregulating securities commissions began.

59. *Ibid.*

60. Including trading of options on stock exchanges and securities derivatives (these had been traded in other markets such as Singapore); banks are allowed to engage in OTC (over the counter) trading.

61. *Op. cit.* at 211 appendix.

62. This will involve a graded approach to licensing and liberalization of scope of business for bank securities affiliates, diversification of securities business for securities firms, and total deregulation of brokerage commissions.

63. *Ibid.*

64. *Ibid.*, at 213.

65. Akiyoshi Huriuchi, "Cash Flow Accounting," in Takeo Hoshi and Hugh Patrick, *Crisis and Change in the Japanese Financial System* (Boston: Kluwer Academic, 2000), pp. 233, 243.

66. *Ibid.*, p. 195. Japan utilizes a current cost method accounting system that has drawn scads of criticism. "Japanese Banking in a Global Context," *supra* note 53 at 34, also citing Nihon Keizai Shimbun, July 18, 1996, in comparison with the fair value Anglo-American model. There is to be "enhancement of the external audit process" and a review of the definition of securities. Rules concerning the conflict of interest, manipulation, and insider trading are to be broadened. Inspection and penalties for violation of securities laws are to be reviewed. A consumer credit protection law is to be considered, and measures on the misuse of consumer information translated as consumer privacy are to be considered. "The Likely Winners and Losers," *supra* note 58 at 213.

67. Mark West, "The Puzzling Divergence of Corporate Law: Evidence and Explanations from the U.S. and Japan," *University of Pennsylvania Law Review* 150 (2001): p. 527.

68. *Ibid.*, p. 546.
69. *Ibid.*, p. 568.
70. *Ibid.*, p. 576.
71. *Ibid.*, p. 579.
72. *Ibid.*, p. 585.
73. Michael Gibon, "Big Bang Deregulation and Corporate Governance: A Survey of the Issues," in *Crisis and Change in the Japanese Financial System, supra* note 65, pp. 291, 304.
74. This is a view that emerged strongly among U.S. lawyers who had practiced in Japan in a working group I conducted for the International Law Committee of the Association of the Bar of the City of New York in 1994.
75. Andrew Pardieck, "The Formation and Transformation of Securities Law in Japan: From the Bubble to Big Bang," *UCLA Pacific Basin Law Journal* 19 (fall 2001): p. 1.
76. *Ibid.*, p. 13.
77. *Ibid.*, p. 15.
78. *Ibid.*, p. 16.
79. Securities Exchange Law of 1948 Section 42 prohibits acts enumerated in the accompanying regulations including Order 4(1), which prohibits "false representations or representations which cause misunderstanding of a material fact."
80. *Op. cit.*, p. 23.
81. *Ibid.*
82. *Ibid.*, p. 36.
83. *Ibid.*, citing Osaka District Court Decision June 13, 1995, Hanrei Taimuzu 890 (1995) and Tokyo Appellate Court Decision July 10, 1997, Hanrei Taimuzu 984 (1997). The Judiciary Looks to Public Law for Relevant Standards, Osaka District Ct. Decision September 14, 1994, Hanrei Taimuzu 875 (1994) and Osaka District Ct. Decision May 30, 1997, Kinyu Shoji Hanrei no. 1030 (1997).
84. *Ibid.*, p. 39, citing Nara District Court Decision October 5, 1995, Hanrei Taimuzu no. 911 (1996) and Hiroshima Appellate Court Decision May 31, 1996, Hanrei Jiho no. 1594 (1997).
85. *Ibid.*, citing Tokyo Appellate Court Decision July 10, 1997, Hanrei Taimuzu 984.
86. *Ibid.*, The law came into effect in 2001. Law no. 101 of 2000.
87. *Ibid.*, p. 70, citing Section 3 of the Financial Products Law.
88. *Ibid.*, p. 72.
89. Consumer Contract Act Law no. 61 of 2000.
90. *Ibid.*, p. 77, citing Section 4.
91. *Ibid.*, p. 77, citing Section 4(4) 1–2.
92. *Ibid.*, p. 86.
93. *Ibid.*
94. International Monetary Fund, "Japan: Economic and Policy Developments," Country Report 01/221 December 2001, p. 93.
95. Judicial Reform Council of Japan (2000) cited in Curtis Millhaupt, "Laws, Judicial Systems, and Economic Growth: The Uneasy Case of Japan" (World Bank Summer Research Workshop on Market Institutions, July 12–17, 2000).
96. *No More Bashing, supra* note 2 at 72.
97. *Ibid.*, at 74.

98. *Ibid.*, at 71.

99. Peter Hartcher, *The Ministry: How Japan's Most Powerful Institution Endangers World Markets* (Harvard Business School Press, 1998).

100. *See infra* note 122.

101. *No More Bashing, supra* note 2 at 67. Tax provisions regarding real estate were changed, as were the ceilings on bank lending.

102. *Ibid.*

103. Yoshinori Shimzu, "Convoy Regulation, Bank Management, and the Financial Crisis in Japan," in *Japan's Financial Crisis and Its Parallels to the U.S. Experience*, Special Report 13, Mikatani Ryoichi and Adam Posen (Institute for International Economics, 2000).

104. Two of these procedures addressed corporate liquidation: Bankruptcy (enacted 1921) and Special Liquidation (enacted 1938). The others addressed reorganization: Composition (enacted 1921); Corporate Arrangement (enacted 1938); and Corporate Reorganization (enacted 1952). The law on composition has been repealed, and the corporate arrangement proceedings are almost never used ("Legal Issues: Japan," Nakashima, Ohno, and Tsunematsu, 2001).

105. Civil Rehabilitation Law, Law of April 1, 2000; 906 cases were filed the first year compared with only 231 cases under the existing law—the Composition Law.

106. *See generally*, Masafumi Kodama, "The New Japanese Reorganization Procedures," Katama Law Office (Osaka, Japan: 2001).

107. A secured creditor may execute a private or a public sale. In the case of real estate, a holder of a registered mortgage may take a civil execution process for a public sale; a creditor who has a registered mortgage by assignment may execute a private sale. "Legal Issues: Japan," *supra* note 104.

108. *Ibid.*, Under the Corporate Reorganization Law, foreclosure is generally prohibited. The law also contains simplified procedures for approval of a plan of reorganization by creditors.

109. *Ibid.*, Under CLR Article 54, a supervisor is appointed when the court considers it necessary.

110. "Financial Issues: Japan" (PriceWaterhouse Coopers, 2001).

111. Supreme Court Decision of November 24, 1999. Previously, the position had been that the mortgage holder had no priority over creditors for repayment and had no right to evict illegal occupants (Supreme Court Decision of March 1991), "ABS Market in Japan: Review of FY 1999," Review by IBJ Securities (Mizuho Securities, April 2000), p. 3.

112. *No More Bashing, supra* note 2 at 69 and "Legal Issues: Japan," *supra* note 104.

113. Curtis Milhaupt and Mark West, "The Dark Side of Private Ordering: An Empirical Analysis of Organized Crime," 67 *U. Chicago L. Rev.*, 41, 59 (2000).

114. Federal Deposit Insurance Corporation Improvement Act of 1991. Pub. Law 102-232 (Dec. 19, 1991). 12 U.S.C. Sec. 1811.

115. *Op. cit.*, Yamaichi, the securities firm, was forced to admit that it utilized illegal offshore accounts and accounting periods and made large payments to corporate racketeers.

116. *Ibid.*, at 76.

117. *See* chapter 2, notes 43 and 44.

118. Ueda Kazuo, "Causes of the Japanese Banking Problems in the 1990s," in Takeo Hoshi and Hugh Patrick, *Crisis and Change in the Japanese Financial System* (Kluwer, 2000), pp. 59, 77.

119. *No More Bashing*, *supra* note 2, at 77.
120. *Ibid.*
121. *Ibid.*
122. *Ibid.*, at 72.
123. *Ibid.*, at 79.
124. Gillian Tett, "Financial Times," April 20, 2001, cited in *No More Bashing*, *supra* note 2 at 79.
125. *No More Bashing*, *supra* note 2 at 80.
126. International Monetary Fund, "Japan, Country Specific Report, Annual Review 2001."
127. *No More Bashing*, *supra* note 2 at 80.
128. *Ibid.*, at 81.
129. *Ibid.*, at 98, citing Organizations of Economic Cooperation and Development, "Economic Outlook" (1999).
130. *Ibid.*, at 96.
131. *Ibid.*, at 97.
132. *Ibid.*, at 99.
133. Bank for International Settlements, "Annual Report" (2000), at 20.
134. Thomas Cargill and Naoyoki Yoshino, "The Postal Savings System, Fiscal Investments, and Loan Programs and Modernization of the Japanese Financial System," in *Crisis and Change in the Japanese Financial System*, *supra* note 118.
135. As of October 8, 2002, International Monetary Fund, Japan, "International Reserves and Foreign Currency Liquidity" at <http://www.imf.org/external/np/sta/ir/jpn/eng/curjpn.htm> (last visited November 2, 2002).
136. *No More Bashing*, *supra* note 2 at 203.
137. *Ibid.*, at 200–201.
138. *See* chapter 2, notes 255–258.
139. *See* chapter 2, notes 255 and 258.
140. *No More Bashing*, *supra* note 2 at 205.
141. *Ibid.*, at 207.
142. *Ibid.*
143. *Ibid.*, at 151, citing Japan, Ministry of Industry and Trade, "2000 Report on WTO Consistency of Trade Partners by Major Trade Partners."
144. *Ibid.*
145. *Ibid.*, at 129.
146. *Ibid.*, at 138.
147. *See infra* notes 30 to 34 and accompanying text.
148. *Op. cit.*, at 145.
149. *Ibid.*, at 146.
150. World Trade Organization, "Japan Trade Policy Review," (1995), pp. 92–93, cited in *No More Bashing*, p. 148.
151. Masarhiro Kawai, Juro Hashimoto, and Izumidi Shigemi, "Japanese Firms in Financial Distress and Main Banks," *Japan and the World Economy* 8 (1996), pp. 175, 194.
152. *Arthritic Japan*, *supra* note 1.
153. This is only a surmise but the oligopolistic nature of *Shogo Shoshos* suggests as much.

154. Edward Lincoln, *Troubled Times: U.S. Japan Trade Relations in the 1990's* (Brookings Institute, 1999), p. 112.

155. *Arthritic Japan, supra* note 1 pp. 22–23. In 1990, per capita income was 3.5 million yen and, by 1999, this figure had risen almost 12 percent to 3.8 million yen. (*Ibid.*, p. 68).

156. While plant and equipment investment in the United States has fluctuated between 9 and 12 percent of GDP (gross domestic product), it has ranged from 15 to 20 percent in Japan. Lincoln, *Arthritic Japan*, pp. 70–71. Also, there is corruption. Japan consumed nearly as much iron and steel as the United States (81 million metric tons as compared to 84 million for the United States, an economy twice its size). It is not clear whether this consumption is the result of making Japan earthquake proof or a half-century of collusion among steel companies, construction companies, and politicians. *Arthritic Japan, supra* note 1, at 74.

157. *Arthritic Japan, supra* note 1 at 117.

158. *Ibid.*, at 179.

159. *Ibid.*, at 199.

160. *No More Bashing, supra* note 2 at 42.

161. *Ibid.*

162. International Monetary Fund, "Financial System Stability Assessment," prepared by the Monetary and Financial Systems and Asia Departments (August 5, 2003), box 2, "Key Policy Recommendations."

163. *Ibid.*, at 12.

164. *Ibid.*, at 69.

165. *Ibid.*, at 19. In the United States, the only other country that permits the inclusion of deferred tax assets, these are limited to 10 percent of tier-one capital. If Japanese banks deducted tier-one capital, their average tier-one to capital would fall from 5 percent to 2 percent.

166. *Ibid.*, box 5, "Government Rescue of Resona Bank."

167. *Ibid.*, at 30.

CHAPTER 8

Evolving Trends in Corporate Governance and Disclosure in the United States and the United Kingdom

THE UNITED STATES

Since the advent of Sarbanes-Oxley, broad-ranging changes have occurred in corporate governance and disclosure in the United States. While it is impossible in this chapter to give full scope to these changes, suffice it to say they have been driven by Securities and Exchange Commission (SEC) and New York Stock Exchange (NYSE) rules; the debate within the Financial Accounting Standards Board (FASB); SEC studies on principle-based accounting and fund management; third-party liability for banks involved in Enron; criminal prosecutions; SEC enforcement actions; securities class-action suits that have been increasing in number and size of awards; compensation scandals arising; old ones being adjudicated like Tyco; and a new environment fueled by revelations about Richard Grasso's $140 million pay package. Without qualification, the most important changes are the increased monitoring role played by directors, officer certifications with criminal penalties, a system of checks and balances that brings the traditional gatekeepers—lawyers and accountants—within the purview of the system, and generally expanded whistleblower protection, which work together in a new compliance environment. Thus the nature of the publicly listed company in the United States is in transition. It is too early to tell how the Public Company Accounting Oversight Board (PCAOB) will operate in practice although there has been significant public debate about ethics in accounting and the expensing of options, but the broader challenge of the financial standards themselves and how they are applied remains unaddressed.

LEGAL REQUIREMENTS AND RESPONSIBILITIES OF THE AUDIT COMMITTEE UNDER SARBANES-OXLEY

The regulation of audit committees under Sarbanes-Oxley represents a foray of the federal government into corporate governance, an activity that until now had been largely a matter of state regulation. While officers have been within the purview of the securities laws, directors have been subject to federal securities regulation only in connection with their own sale or purchase of securities (except in certain instances, particularly in connection with registration statements) or as the result of material misstatements of information. Directors may have an affirmative duty to disclose material information under certain circumstances, and recklessness in the conduct of their duties may lead to liability under the Private Securities Litigation Reform Act (PSLRA). But changing the norms of corporate governance may prove even more important than the new liability environment to which it gives rise.

Under Sarbanes-Oxley Section 301, U.S.-listed companies must have audit committees that are independent and include at least one financial expert or disclose the reason why they do not. In order to meet the definition of independence, the SEC has promulgated a rule requiring that directors must not receive any fees—including consulting, or advisory, legal, or accounting fees—from the company or its subsidiaries. No compensation can be made to the immediate family of an audit committee member or to an entity in which an audit committee member is a partner, member, or officer occupying a position comparable to that of an officer or director; and an audit committee member must not be an affiliate of such a company (a 10 percent shareholder or executive officer).[1] The NYSE proposed even more stringent rules, which require a five-year cooling-off period in the event that an audit committee member or immediate family member has been employed in a professional capacity by the firm's internal or external auditor, or if the company of which the audit committee member is an executive officer accounts for more than 2 percent of the gross revenues of the listed company.[2] The National Association of Dealers Automated Quotations (NASDAQ) proposed rules that define independence as excluding anyone who has, in any of the previous three fiscal years, received a payment in excess of $60,000, except as a member of the board of directors, excluding employee benefits or investments if the proposed director or family member was an executive officer.[3]

Under Sarbanes-Oxley Section 407, companies must disclose whether the audit committee has among its members at least one financial expert, and if not, why not. A financial expert under the final SEC rules is a person who has

- an understanding of Generally Accepted Accounting Principles (GAAP);
- the ability to assess the general application of GAAP in connection with the accounting for estimates, accruals, and reserves;

- experience in *either* preparing, auditing, or analyzing financial statements that present a breadth and level of complexity of accounting issues that are reasonably comparable to those that the issuer's financial statements can reasonably be expected to raise or actively supervising individuals engaged in these activities.

These attributes must have been acquired through

- education or experience as a principal financial officer, comptroller, public accountant, or auditor, or person performing similar functions;
- actively supervising such a person;
- experience overseeing or assessing the performance of companies or public accountants with respect to the preparation, auditing, or evaluation of financial statements;
- other relevant experience.[4]

The safe harbor provides that this designation will not impose any greater duties or liabilities than would otherwise affect the member of the audit committee, nor will it affect the duties or liabilities of other members of the board. This definition safely incorporates Anderson partners and chief executive officers (CEOs) as well as many financial analysts and investment bankers (explicitly named in the SEC release) with no formal training in accounting but excludes accounting professors who run training programs for auditors. The independence and financial expert rules must not be expected to serve as a quick fix for the problems of corporate governance relating to financial statements. We should recall that the archetype of dysfunctional audit committees, Enron's, included Robert Jaedecke, who was a professor at Stanford Business School, and the only limitations on independence involved Enron donations to charitable institutions where board members were employees.

The listing of securities by a foreign private issuer exempts foreign private issuers if

- the foreign private issuer has a statutory board of auditors pursuant to home-country laws or listing requirements;
- the board of auditors is separate from the board of directors or composed of one or more members of the board of directors and one or more members who are not also members of the board of directors;
- has listing or home-country laws that have different standards of independence from issuer or management, has no executive member of the issuer on the board of issuers;
- the board of auditors has responsibility for the appointment and retention of auditors, to the extent permissible by law;
- the audit committee requirements relating to retention of advisers and funding and the complaint procedures relating to audits apply to the board of auditors.[5]

Responsibilities of the audit committee include the following:

- appointment, compensation, retention, and oversight of any work done by registered public account firms engaged for purposes of preparing an audit report or any other audit; reviewing or attesting services; and review of nonaudit work to determine whether these services are prohibited under Sarbanes-Oxley;
- adopting procedures for the receipt, retention, and treatment of complaints regarding accounting and internal control and for confidential anonymous submissions;
- having authority and proper funding for the retention of independent counsel and outside advisers as it deems necessary;
- under Section 204, receiving reports from outside auditor on all critical accounting policies and alternative treatment of financial information, within GAAP related to material items discussed with management, including ramifications of the use of alternative treatments and the treatment preferred by the outside auditor and all other material written communication.[6]

Additional NYSE rules would require the following:

- at least annually, obtain and review a report by the independent auditor on the firm's internal controls, which must describe any issues raised by the internal audit or by any inquiry or investigation by a government or professional authority within the last five years and any steps the firm has taken to deal with such issues, and must assess auditors' independence;
- discuss with management and internal auditors the quarterly and annual statements, including the company's disclosure under management discussion and analysis;
- review earnings press releases, financial information and quarterly financial statements, financial information and earnings guidance given to analysts and credit rating agencies;
- discuss policies with respect to risk assessment;
- meet separately or periodically with management, internal auditors, and independent auditors;
- review with independent auditors any audit problems;
- set clear hiring policies for employees or former employees of the independent auditors;
- report regularly to the board of directors.[7]

A related provision requires that each listed company have an independent audit function that reports regularly to the audit committee. Additionally, companies must have corporate governance guidelines that address, inter alia, responsibilities of directors and director access to management. A little-noticed provision requires director orientation and continuing education.[8]

The audit-committee powers with regard to appointment of auditors have recently been exercised by certain companies in such a way that management has only learned of the appointment of the auditor after the fact. Other companies, no doubt, continue to rubber-stamp management choices. But 56 percent of companies will submit their choice of auditor to a shareholder vote, according to a Deloitte and Touche survey. The survey also indicates a greater involvement by audit committees in reviewing financial statements. In April 2003, 71 percent of full audit committees reviewed 10Qs before filing, compared to 46 percent in September 2002, and 85 percent had already established whistle-blower procedures.[9] Companies are thus getting up to speed with the requirements.

None of this indicates how effective audit committees will be in their newfound Sarbanes-Oxley roles. Absent from the discussion has been any thoroughgoing analysis of what kind of accounting violations audit committees should be on the lookout for. Certainly, Sarbanes-Oxley and NYSE-detailed rules, if followed to the letter, will provide better oversight, but even so, they do not imply an active dialogue on accounting policies. Some hint of what audit-committee members must focus on is given by the requirement that audit-committee members have an understanding of estimates, accruals, and reserves. Does this imply some knowledge of matching income and expenses or estimating contingent liabilities? Does it imply a familiarity with the SEC releases on revenue recognition and the case law of channel stuffing?

In Worldcom, according to an internal report, there is no evidence that the outside auditor was aware of the mischaracterization, and no degree of vigilance on the part of the audit committee would have revealed that more than $9 billion had been capitalized rather than expensed. In Enron, we do not find anything particularly egregious about the waiver of the code of ethics. We do, however, find the audit committee's and the board's lack of interest in the underlying transactions that they approved to be astonishing. The decision to blow out liabilities should be met with skepticism on the part of any reasonably astute businessman, much less a professor of accounting. Even given the 97/3 rule, the extent of the liabilities to be included in these Special Purpose Entities ought to have been a matter of concern.

The Worldcom report highlights that director vigilance by itself would do little to cure financial fraud. But as part of a system of checks and balances, particularly in insisting on the best internal controls as proposed by auditing experts, these new responsibilities might prove effective. The final report of Richard Breedon, the court-appointed Worldcom monitor, issued a series of recommendations to improve corporate governance that goes well beyond the NYSE rules. These recommendations, unanimously approved by Worldcom's board of directors, include separating the offices of chairman and CEO; requiring all directors other than the CEO to be independent; requiring the full board to meet eight times a year; and substantially raising directors' compensation.[10] These changes will also raise, at least in terms of best practice, the standards expected of audit-committee members.

Under NYSE rules, the audit committee must review the internal audit function. One internal control memo by a big four accounting firm suggests certain criteria for analyzing internal control through an accounts approach at the consolidated level and lists several factors (other than size of accounts) to be considered, including volume of activity; homogeneity of transactions; the extent to which account balance is subjectively determined; changes in accounts characteristics; and separation by organizational structure or business unit. Components of each account for a sample manufacturing firm include financial statement close; cash receipts and disbursements; sales and accounts receivables; estimated commitments and contingencies; warranty reserve and exposure; plant depreciation and amortization; obsolete inventory reserves; currency adjustments; purchase and pay for assets; pension liabilities; last-in-first-out (lifo) calculations, and so on, which include categories of routine, nonroutine, and estimates. While such detailed checklists are useful, there is no apparent correlation between the number of boxes checked and the accuracy of financial statements. In this regard, the implementation of the detailed rules approach adopted by the NYSE may not enhance audit-committee oversight.

Sarbanes-Oxley, particularly those provisions involving audit-committee responsibility, represents an unprecedented foray by federal regulation into corporate law. Before Sarbanes-Oxley, federal securities law was focused on the acts of officers and did not usually, except in instances of self-dealing, consider the duties of directors. State law, which has generally found that directors owe a fiduciary duty to the corporation, has zealously guarded the business judgment rule, absent self-dealing (violating the duty of loyalty). According to the Delaware Chancery Court in *Smith v. Van Gorklam*, acts amounting to gross negligence invited judicial review of corporate transactions.[11] But directors were insulated from much of this additional liability by statutes that allowed shareholders to adopt legislation to insulate directors from claims arising from breach of the fiduciary duty of care,[12] although misleading disclosure to shareholders in the context of shareholder actions such as proxy fights or merger votes may conceivably give rise to liability. But in May 2003 the Delaware Chancery Court, in a memorandum opinion, allowed a derivative action against Disney, arising out of allegations relating to Michael Ovitz's employment contract, to proceed.[13] The court noted the following:

> It is rare when a court imposes liability on directors for a breach of the duty of care, and this Court is hesitant to second guess the business judgment of a disinterested and independent board of directors. But the facts alleged in the new complaint do not implicate merely negligent or grossly negligent decision making by corporate directors. Quite the contrary; plaintiff's new complaint alleges that the Disney directors failed to make any business judgment and failed to make any good faith attempt to fulfill their fiduciary duties to Disney and its stockholder.[14]

As Chancellor William Chandler and Vice-Chancellor Leo Strine stated in a paper last year, new expectations created by Sarbanes-Oxley may "generate new types of state corporate law cases" against directors. The authors conjecture the following:

> One form that these cases may take could involve claims that directors are breaching their fiduciary duties by not complying with the reform . . . [that state law] ought to embrace the substance of a feature of the Reforms . . . [or] an allegation that directors breach their fiduciary duties by exposing the corporation (and therefore its stockholders) to an injurious sanction (e.g., delisting) that may be imposed if the Reforms are not adhered to.[15]

I would not go so far as various editorials and corporate lawyers have gone, to suggest that the recent decision involving Disney represents a quantum leap in state corporate law. It is more likely that a paradigm shift in directors' liability will occur—if ever—as the result of failure on the part of audit committees to disclose or act upon evidence of a material violation of securities law, particularly with reference to financial statements. That federal class actions, rather than state law derivative actions, will become the vehicle for the mainstay of actions against directors indicates the degree to which Sarbanes-Oxley federalizes corporate law. Until recent financial scandals, few class action suits under PSLRA have named outside directors, and those who were named were alleged to be responsible for misstatements.[16] The wave of corporate scandals has dramatically changed the landscape, as directors at Enron and elsewhere face personal liability in situations in which directors and officers (D&O) insurers may dispute the policy coverage. In most instances, indemnification by the company will reimburse directors, but directors of insolvent companies may face real personal liability; D&O insurers are claiming the right of rescission in the event of material restatements. The operative question, in terms of director's liability in federal class action suits, is what kind of director negligence rises to the level of recklessness required to show scienter under PSLRA.

But the enhanced role of audit committees must not be seen in a vacuum. Legal scholars such as Professor John Coffee view the wave of corporate scandals as resulting, in large measure, from the failure of traditional gatekeepers, particularly lawyers and accountants, to perform their professional responsibilities to the corporation with diligence. Sarbanes-Oxley Section 307 requires lawyers to report up the line "whenever it would be unreasonable for a reasonable and prudent attorney to fail to conclude that the evidence makes it reasonably likely that a material violation of the securities law has occurred, is likely to occur or is ongoing"; all such violations that involve financial statements, whether or not via a qualified legal compliance committee, chief legal officer, or CEO, will eventually make their way to the audit committee. When the PCAOB has set forth ethical obligations for auditors, there will be instances when auditors will report directly or indirectly to the audit committee. Also, if faced with material evidence of interfering with a whistleblower or an auditor, the audit committee must report to the board of directors. In particular, the Section 204 review of alternative accounting treatments discussed with management and the auditor's preferred treatment will require the audit committee to make decisions in the event of any conflict between the auditor and management or even if the audit committee disagrees with management and the auditor. The enhanced responsibilities of the audit committee make it evident that the audit committee will have much more significant knowledge of the financial reporting regime of the company and with knowledge comes responsibility and potential exposure to liability. If the board of directors, after a proper investigation, fails to take appropriate action (which would probably include dismissing any officer engaged in violation of the securities law, after an investigation in which the offending officer is given a chance to make an affirmative defense), it will risk exposure to liability. It is unclear whether halfway measures would suffice, or what—absent adjudication—the audit committee (with legal advice) would determine to be a material violation of the securities law, or whether the SEC must be informed. If a misleading or fraudulent financial statement or pro forma statement has been issued, the audit committee or the full board, in order to avoid liability, will, in the authors' view, require that the violation be reported to the SEC. In either event, public disclosure would be the safest course of action.

The Sarbanes-Oxley approach to corporate governance is a system of checks and balances in which, for instance, the audit committee hires and fires the auditors and reviews pro forma disclosures; chief financial officers (CFOs) and CEOs certify financial statements; lawyers report up the line; and accountants are subject to the ethics requirements of the PCAOB. While directors might face increased liability as an unintentional consequence, the clear intent of the act is to change the norms of corporate governance rather than to spread liability. The only problem is the medium in which these players act: GAAP. The tortuous logic of accounting standards is bound to continue to cause confusion. GAAP has ambiguous standards relating to big bath restructuring, cookie jar reserves, write-offs in connection with a merger, mismatching of earnings and expenses, and voluminous standards for derivatives. The crux of Sarbanes-Oxley is to limit the possibility of false and misleading financial statements, but nebulous and overly detailed accounting rules allow auditors and management to pick from a Chinese menu of options for stating earnings.

Without more clearly defined standards, audit committees will have no means of determining which accounting standards are appropriate and which are misleading or fraudulent. The SEC's release, pursuant to Sarbanes-Oxley, on principles-based accounting, together with the Federal Accounting Standards Board's decision to seek convergence with International Accounting Standards (IAS), offers some hope that GAAP standards will eventually become more coherent. In the meantime, audit committees should attempt to work diligently through the tangled web of GAAP standards to ensure that financial statements are as accurate as the current reporting system will permit.

THE STATE OF CIVIL AND CRIMINAL DISCLOSURE ACTIONS

Theoretically, the SEC has almost 200 administrative actions pending that could conceivably involve fraud in financial reporting. However, given the state of confusion in interpreting accounting standards, it is not clear how many of these actions involve aggressive accounting. The check-the-box mentality has led to special practice groups within the big four that are charged with finding loopholes in each new accounting rule. Lawyers who structure transactions, particularly mergers and acquisitions, off-balance sheet transactions, and long-term contracts are mindful that the substance of the transaction is unimportant in achieving the right result in terms of earnings. We ignore such a state of affairs at our peril.

A growing awareness of the rapacious behavior of corporate officers has resulted from coverage of corporate scandals. Certain officers have been indicted, notably from Enron[17] and Worldcom.[18] The SEC has also filed a wide range of actions against both Enron[19] and Worldcom.[20] Private litigation rages on against Enron and Worldcom,[21] but shareholders and pension plan participants will end up with pennies on the dollar. Meanwhile, who knows how much money Kenneth Lay or Jeffrey Skilling have socked away. Independent compensation committees under NYSE and NASDAQ rules will only slightly stem the tide in executive compensation, and requiring shareholder approval for executive compensation would be unlikely to have serious impact.[22]

Various analysts have either been subject to Section 20 bars on involvement in the securities industry such as Jack Grubman, and others such as Frank Quattrone have been prosecuted; the extent of punishment is actually quite mild. Brokerage firms participated in a settlement with New York Attorney General Elliot Spitzer and the SEC,[23] and banks have settled with the SEC for their role in disguising Enron's financial condition.[24] In the wake of its report on mutual fund discounts[25] and announcement of new initiatives about market timing,[26] the SEC, along with Spitzer, has extended its ambit and has filed criminal charges against a mutual fund executive.[27] A recent SEC settlement with Putnam[28] has been severely criticized by Spitzer:

> The commission's first failure is one of oversight. The mutual fund investigation began when an informant approached our office with evidence of illegal trading practices. Tipsters also approached the commission, which is supposed to be the nation's primary securities markets regulator, but the commission simply did not act on the information.
>
> The commission's second failure was acting in haste to settle with Putnam even though the investigation is barely 10 weeks old and is yielding new and important information each day. Whether the commission recognizes it or not, the first settlement in a complex investigation always sets the tone for what follows. In this case, the bar is set too low.
>
> The Putnam agreement does contain a useful provision mandating that the funds'

board of directors be more independent of the management companies that run its day-to-day operations. It also talks of fines and restitution, but leaves for another day the determination of the amount Putnam should pay.

Most important, the agreement does not address the manner in which the fees charged to investors are calculated. Nor does it require the fund to inform investors exactly how much they are being charged—or even provide a structure that will create market pressure to reduce those fees. Finally, there is no discussion of civil or criminal sanctions for the managers who acted improperly by engaging in or permitting market timing and late trading.

S.E.C. officials are now saying that they may be interested in additional reforms. But by settling so quickly, they have lost leverage in obtaining further measures to protect investors. After reviewing this agreement, I can say with certainty that any resolution with my office will require concessions from the industry that go far beyond what the commission obtained from Putnam.[29]

The SEC probe widened, and as of this writing, Morgan Stanley agreed to pay a $50 million fine. Morgan Stanley steered clients toward preferred mutual funds in exchange for millions of dollars in commission payments from those fund companies. Morgan Stanley did not tell investors about the practice or the higher fees.[30] The mutual fund investigation has also spread to Schwab.[31] The mutual fund industry is the second leaky pipe in the pipeline between an investment in public companies that separates investors from their money.

The Savings and Loan (S&L) crisis led to 1,850 indictments and 1,600 convictions.[32] The prosecution of Mike Milliken and Ivan Boesky sent a message that insider trading would not be tolerated. To an extent, the profits made on the sale of options by corporate officers who knew that they had overstated earnings is a particular case in point of market manipulation that is not altogether distinguishable from insider trading. But such practices are so prevalent that legislation is unlikely to have an immediate impact. Health South is the first case brought under Sarbanes-Oxley Section 906, criminal officer certification provisions. It is likely that legislation in some ways analogous to Sarbanes-Oxley will be enacted to govern the mutual fund industry.

The Shape of Things to Come

The inequity of executive compensation has been highlighted in the instance of the CEO of American Airlines who failed to disclose his compensation package when dealing with the unions and Richard Grasso's $140 million pay package. The future of self-regulation is now in doubt. The expensing of options, which is inevitable under some formula, is just one battle to containing the rapacious greed of corporate management. Sarbanes-Oxley is a tool in this fight. Compensation committees will now be independent.[33] Under recent proposals, shareholders will be able to vote on executive compensation[34] and small changes will enable public pension funds to play a larger role in corporate governance.[35] (Public pension funds tripped over one another in trying to get the best sound bite describing the insufficiency of the changes.)[36] But nonpublic fund managers will toe management's line while corporate chieftains wield power over pension fund investment. Moreover, the skepticism about these piecemeal reforms underscores a more self-evident truth: current corporate governance and disclosure is broken. Empowering audit committees is a step in the right direction. The question of executive compensation like all other questions relating to corporate governance will remain on the agenda for the foreseeable future. But until corporate books are no longer routinely cooked, progress will not be meaningful. The SEC has taken a small step in its release on principle-based accounting,[37] which suggested that various accounting pronouncements such as statements of concepts and statements of positions and Emerging Issues Task Force (EITF) pronouncements be interpreted in a hierarchical order. This is the beginning of an orderly system of accounting standards, which in my view, will result in an administrative court with jurisdiction over financial reporting. Accountants and lawyers work for corporations. Government may impose duties on them, but until government undertakes regulation of accounting standards complementary to those which the PCAOB will implement in auditing practices and ethics standards, equity markets will remain crapshoots in which management, brokers, and fund managers profiteer. Yet, as keen observers may remark, we are in the initial stages of a revolution in the management of investments in public companies.

THE UNITED KINGDOM

Introduction

Since the U.S. Sarbanes-Oxley Act was promulgated, the SEC has issued rules under it, including officer certification of financial statements; as these rules apply to all companies listed in the United States, the future of the U.K. principles-based approach is in doubt. Companies tend to focus their attention on the most onerous regulatory regime, and the extraterritorial reach of Sarbanes-Oxley cannot be overstated. It dictates rules for attorneys in the event of company misconduct, rules for hiring audit committees, and the form of officer certification. NYSE and NASDAQ rules on independent directors are now echoed in the Higgs Report, as are Sarbanes-Oxley enhanced audit-committee responsibilities. It is a foregone conclusion that U.K. law will be overshadowed by U.S. law in the preparation of annual statements. In a permutation of Gresham's law, stronger regulation drives out weaker regulation; the application of Sarbanes-Oxley to U.K. public companies listed in the United States will inevitably filter down to affect the market for financial reporting for the rest of U.K.-listed companies.

This leaves British regulators and lawmakers in a difficult position. Ultimately, they may be led by the market. A convergence is taking place in such instances as a new proposal making mandatory the officer's financial report (the U.K. version of management discussion and analysis). Still, a principles-based regime is ultimately incompatible with a rules-based regime. What is this vaunted principles-based approach really about? In general, a principles-based approach makes it more difficult to obtain criminal convictions for violations of law or to instigate private rights of action. Violation of a principle is grounds for exclusion from the club. In the parlance of the Financial Services and Markets Act 2000 (FSMA), Financial Services Authority (FSA) disciplinary procedures include censure; loss of authorization to conduct investment business; and officer and director bars. But, as we shall see, even these remedies are rarely imposed.

The sheer plethora of reports issued by the various instrumentalities of the Department of Trade and Industry (DTI) (with one from the FSA) boggles the mind. The reader may well wonder what may be the point of recording these various musings. Absent actual legislation, they provide only the equivalent of tea-leaf readings about the future form of financial regulation in the United Kingdom. In my view, they also illustrate the schizophrenic response of a regulatory regime pushed to the brink by the forces of modernization and globalization. The current regime of regulators aided by experts and market participants inevitably faces this onslaught by fragmentation, which creates the impression of schizophrenia. The voices of gradualism and those of regulatory modernization are engaged in a pitched battle played out in conflicting reports with different emphases.

After due consideration, this part has been organized along functional lines. This entails considerable overlap, as each report affirms aspects of other reports. The first section considers the vantage point of company law; within it the spotlight is turned successively on the current enforcement regime; on the steering group report on company law and the DTI White Paper; on the Higgs Report on independent directors and the Smith Report on audit committees; and on an FSA U.K. Listing Authority (UKLA) report that focuses on the role of European Union (EU) directives. The second section deals with accounting: first a background; then the regulatory regime for the United Kingdom and the reorganization of regulation of the accounting profession; lastly, the proposed rules for auditor independence, rotation of auditors, and standard setting. Inevitably, there is an overlap. The Coordinating Committee on Accounting Reform weighs in with a proposal to criminalize false or misleading financial statements. The third section, entitled "If You Haven't Had Enough Reports: Recent Developments," is self-explanatory; it relates back to the previous two. The fourth concludes that the skein of principles versus rules, which runs throughout, will need to be addressed, and that the current unwillingness to criminalize accounting fraud or provide for statute-based private rights of action creates a serious impediment to the future of U.K. equity markets. Currently, an EU Directive on Insider Trading and Market Manipulation[38] has been promulgated, but this directive is very general and may be followed by more prescriptive legislation. Analysts are subject to the Conduct of Business Sourcebook, which sets out principles for the fair presentation of financial information,[39] and which will be subject to the Market Abuse Directive and its provisions relating to analyst disclosure.[40]

Of the many differences between U.K. and U.S. corporate governance, the most salient issue is absence in the United Kingdom of the private right of action. Although there are private rights of action for misrepresentation and for false and misleading statements in connection with the sale or purchase of a security, these actions rarely, if ever, result in class actions. U.K. class actions are limited by the rules relating to class actions and by rules governing contingency fees charged by attorneys. This is essential in differentiating between the United Kingdom and the United States. Although the PSLRA severely curtails class-action lawsuits, requiring that scienter be pled with particularity to defeat a motion to dismiss, there have been several hundred class-action suits in the United States each year. The United Kingdom does not afford such a remedy. Furthermore, in order to bring an action for tort for negligent misstatement, a potential claimant must show a special relationship between the company and the claimant. The High Court held that the duty of care imposed on directors does not extend to those buying shares.[41]

Thus, despite the legal apparatus afforded by U.K. law that makes it (along with New York law) the choice par excellence for the governing law and choice of law in international contracts, U.K. securities law affords few private remedies. There are limitations to the desirability of the private right of action: insurance premiums go up, and existing shareholders are disadvantaged vis-à-vis exiting shareholders. The principal advantage of the private right of action is that it supplements the enforcement of the law by the statutory authority. In fact, there has been much criticism of the SEC for its inability to enforce the law. In the instance of the FSA the situation is that much more dire. There is a compensation scheme under the FMSA,[42] as there is under Sarbanes-Oxley; however, this provision of the FMSA has yet to be employed. There has also yet to be a case of disciplinary action for market abuse adjudicated by the FSA, although it is promised that such administrative proceedings are working their way through the administrative apparatus of the FSA,[43] and a private right of action for damages arising from market abuse remains only a theoretical possibility. The tribunal inaugurated by the Financial Services and Markets Act has now made one procedural ruling. It is possible that it has made secret rulings since this is an option granted it under the legislation.

Modernizing Company Law? Steering Group Report and White Paper

The final report of the Steering Group on Company Law was presented in 2001 and included draft legislation. In July 2002, the DTI presented to

Parliament a White Paper in which it accepted most of the recommendations of the steering group.[44] The White Paper was mindful of the conflicts of interest of institutional investors, by pressure on a fund from corporate finance departments within a financial group, and agreed in principle that it would be a good idea to require institutional investors to disclose how they had voted in proxies.[45] The White Paper also agreed with the steering group about the codification of directors' duties but did not accept the recommendation about the duty of directors of an insolvent company to its creditors.[46] Although the White Paper does not specify the final form to be taken, it endorses the codification of civil remedies for directors' breach of fiduciary duties. Remuneration of directors will also be required to be disclosed and approved by shareholders. (In this respect the proposal is more advanced than U.S. law.) The White Paper agreed with the report that the Combined Code should remain as a code of best practices rather than a statutory code.[47] The operating and financial review (OFR) will become mandatory for public and certain private companies that meet two of the three criteria: annual turnover of £50 million (and private companies with an annual turnover of £250 million); a balance sheet of more than £25 million; and more than 500 employees. The report and White Paper note that this comprises 1,000 companies, which represent 0.1 percent of all companies.[48]

The White Paper also determined that the responsibility for the form and content of annual reports should devolve to a new rule-making body; that auditors' statutory role should be made to encompass the OFR; and that auditors should have a statutory right to information. But the question of auditors' liability remains open.[49] Also endorsed was the report's recommendation that annual financial statements be available within four months of the end of the financial year (the U.S. proposal is significantly more timely) and that quoted companies should make preliminary announcements over the Internet as soon as practicable.[50]

The White Paper explicitly rejects rules-based accounting and criminal liability for the preparation of financial statements:

> One of the strengths of UK accounting standards is that they steer clear of a "cook book" of rules that invite only a narrow interpretation of standards . . . [The principles-based approach] is widely seen as producing meaningful accounting. Imposing criminal penalties would serve to create pressure to move toward the "cook book" approach to compliance.[51]

Here the explicit link between criminal penalties and rules-based accounting is admitted. The unwillingness to criminalize financial reporting standards is diametrically opposed to Section 906 of the Sarbanes-Oxley Act, which provides for penalties of up to 20 years for knowingly certifying a financial statement that does not, in all material respects, represent the financial condition of the company.[52]

The White Paper proposes overhauling the existing framework for establishing accounting standards, oversight of auditors, and company law review. Firstly, it proposes to create a statutory Company Law and Reporting Commission with which the secretary of state of the DTI would be required to consult with in regard to secondary legislation under the new Companies Act. It also proposes a new standards board to replace the Accounting Standards Board (ASB) and to be responsible for detailed reporting requirements for financial as well as nonfinancial information required under the new OFR, which would have a direct legal effect.[53] There would also be a new reporting review panel (RRP) with a broader remit, having responsibility for financial as well as nonfinancial disclosures, and a new Private Companies Committee.[54]

The standards board would be responsible for setting disclosure standards for the OFR, such as detailed comparative information for past years or risks and rewards of future opportunities.[55] The Company Law Review had recommended that the standards board have responsibility for making rules under the Combined Code, an approach rejected by the White Paper. However, the new standards board will have responsibility for making rules for companies to disclose whether or not they have complied with the Combined Code (this distinction seems unnecessary). The new RRP will enforce these rules.[56] Currently, the Financial Reporting Review Panel (FRRP) can apply to the court to force companies to comply with its decisions, but the broader remit of the new RRP will allow it to apply to the court for noncompliance with nonfinancial information requirements.[57]

Independent Directors and Audit Committees: The Higgs and Smith Reports

While the Higgs Report[58] merits a paper unto itself, it is discussed here in the context of principles versus rules; it represents some of the best of what the principles-based approach has to offer while, in its crucial aspects, incorporating a rules-based approach. Building on the Combined Code and the comply-or-disclose standard, it proposes changes that clarify the roles of independent directors and of remuneration, audit, and nominating committees and provides appropriate descriptions. It also proposes a role for a senior independent director who should be available to shareholders if there are concerns not vetted through the normal channels.[59] Higgs also provides that a "small group of business leaders and others" will be set up to determine how to bring more candidates, possessing improved qualifications, to the role of nonexecutive independent director;[60] it further proposes an induction course for new directors and continued training. Guidance for the appointment of a new chairman is also set forth. Nonexecutive directors are also required to ensure that, in the event of resignation, their differences with board policy or decisions are recorded (if they cannot be resolved) in the minutes of the board-of-directors meeting.[61] (This is not as rigorous as SEC rules, which require disclosure within two days.)[62] One of the report's more descriptive provisions is a rule of thumb that independent directors should work as such (for an individual company) for between 15 and 30 days each year.[63] The Higgs Report is also quite specific in setting forth suggestions regarding liability insurance and the management of cases against directors.[64] All nonexecutive directors should, under the report's recommendations, attend the annual general meeting (AGM) and be ready to respond to shareholder questions.[65] Nonexecutive directors should also meet with major shareholders (institutional investors in most instances).[66] Currently, 87 percent of FTSE 100 companies have separated the roles of chairman and CEO, but the Higgs Report goes further, suggesting that no former CEO should become chairman.[67] In any event, nonexecutive directors should meet without the chairman or executive directors.[68]

With respect to independent directors, the Higgs Report specifies that at least half of the directors (excluding the chairman) should be independent directors. Here a rules-based approach is explicitly endorsed. Independence is defined as excluding anyone who

- is a former employee, until five years has elapsed since the employee last worked for the company or had any other material connection with it;
- has had a material business with the company, or with another company that has such a relationship with the company, within the last three years;
- has received additional compensation from the company apart from a director's fee—this includes participation in share option related schemes or membership in the company's pension fund;
- has close family ties with the company or its advisers, directors, or senior employees;
- holds cross-directorships or significant links with other directors;
- represents a significant director; or
- has served on the board for more than 10 years.

In stringency this definition vies with NYSE- or NASDAQ-proposed rules and far surpasses the SEC's final rules defining independence.[69]

The all-important audit committee must be composed entirely of independent directors. At least one member of the committee must have significant relevant and recent financial information. These rules are far less restrictive than the definition of "financial expert" under Sarbanes-Oxley.[70] However, in my view, this is far more desirable than the simplistic auditing background required under Sarbanes-Oxley, in that it is far more relevant. (It is the opinion of at least one distinguished panel of lawyers that this section of Sarbanes-Oxley, which is a comply-or-explain standard, will result in explanations rather than compliance.[71]) The nominating committee, which must be composed of a majority of independent directors, will also be mandated under the new Combined Code.[72]

Also issued in January 2003 was a report, under the aegis of the Financial Reporting Council, on Audit Committee Combined Code Guidance (the Smith Report).[73] The Smith Report specifies that the best practice of the proposed amended Combined Code goes beyond what is required, although the report contains guidance that every audit committee should meet.[74] The audit committee's responsibilities include monitoring the financial statements of the company, reviewing the internal controls of the company, and (unless there is a separate risk-management committee undertaking this function) making recommendations about the appointment of an external auditor and monitoring the external auditor's independence, objectivity, and the supply of non-audit services.[75] These last two responsibilities are interrelated; they have been the subject of considerable regulation in the United States under SEC rules and Sarbanes-Oxley.[76] The audit committee is to meet with internal and external auditors without the presence of management, and the board should make funds available to the audit committee to engage independent legal and accounting advice.[77] Companies are also encouraged to consider additional remuneration for members of the audit committee for their additional responsibilities.

The Smith Report goes further than the Higgs Report in stressing the financial qualifications of at least one member of the audit committee. Although the terms "significant," "recent" and "relevant experience" are used, this description is qualified by "for example as an auditor or a finance director of a listed company."[78] In addition, training in understanding financial statements and changes in accounting practice and company law is proposed. Whistle-blowing is specifically addressed by suggesting arrangements to meet with staff in confidence. However, the criminal provisions relating to interference with auditors or whistle-blowers present in Sarbanes-Oxley are not suggested. Although the audit committee does not engage the auditor, it will be responsible for reviewing the terms of engagement of the auditors. Although the audit committee submits reports on controls, the numbers and attendance at audit committee meetings are to be reported, and—going beyond Sarbanes-Oxley—the chairman of the audit committee is to be present at the AGM to answer questions by shareholders on matters within its ambit.[79] In certain respects, these arrangements are more comprehensive than those under U.S. law, particularly with respect to the role of the chairman of the audit committee at the AGM and the consideration of additional remuneration to members of the audit committee. Aside from not directly engaging the auditors, as required by Sarbanes-Oxley, the audit committee under the Smith Report would be as formidable as U.S. audit committees with the exception of the environment created by Sarbanes-Oxley, which provides for criminal penalties for interference with auditors' work and whistle-blowing and for CEOs and CFOs who knowingly or willfully certify financial statements that do not present, in all material respects, the financial condition of the company.

The FSA Weighs In: Review of the Listing Particulars Regime and the EU Dimension of Listings

In the *Review of the Listing Particulars Regime*,[80] the FSA UKLA provides a revealing chart in which the UKLA is in the center of a group of overlapping circles including accounting and auditing, company law, and EU directives. While the first two issues have been covered here, new EU directives are presumed to be a factor in the future of securities regulation in the United Kingdom. The new Proposed Mutual Recognition of Prospectuses Directive (MRPD) is considered a Maximum Harmonisation Directive.[81] Most of the current requirements are laid out in the Consolidated Admission and Reporting Directive (CARD) (2001), which will be replaced by the Prospectus Directive. CARD allows the national authority to impose requirements in addition to those imposed by the directive; however, the new MRPD will alter this approach. There is no super-equivalency provision in the MRPD allowing national authorities to tinker with the harmonization of disclosure requirements. Currently, such super-equivalent disclosure provisions include directors' remuneration and directors' dealings.[82] The discussion paper on the listing regime also notes that a standard-setting body will take responsibility for disclosure under the Combined Code.[83] The government also intends to make rules to monitor compliance with the Combined Code.

The *Review of the Listing Particulars Regime* also discusses the "Guidance on Price Sensitive Information" to determine when price-sensitive information can be disclosed to advisers without breaching the guidance, and notes that (thus far) the Proposed Market Abuse Directive has required disclosure of all price-sensitive information. The new SEC rule requiring disclosure of certain information, such as a material adverse change, loss of a major customer, or the resignation of a director[84] moves the U.S. regime closer to a continuous disclosure regime, but in the United Kingdom such information would have to be disclosed immediately.

Review of the Regulatory Regime of the Accounting Profession

In October 2002, the DTI issued a *Review of the Regulatory Regime of the Accounting Profession*.[85] The document questions whether the focus of an accounting board that regulates the standards of the accounting industry should continue to be on the accounting profession, or whether it should be limited to the audit function of listed companies—an approach that is similar to the PCAOB created by Sarbanes-Oxley. The *Review* also proposes the possibly more radical course of moving the regulatory role to an independent accounting board like the PCAOB and altering funding arrangements for the Accountancy Foundation. The arrangements for all the ethical, disciplinary, and auditing standards work are currently divvied up in such a way that, although

I would like to place in this text the account and the amusing flow chart that are part of the review, they would befuddle even the most conscientious of readers. Consequently, these different bodies are largely, to the extent practicable, set forth in this footnote.[86] It would be difficult to explain any purpose for this arrangement other than to assure both minimal regulation and minimal liability for the accounting profession. This structure must also be viewed in the context of the Financial Reporting Council (FRC) and the FSA, particularly the UKLA, which is the FSA's subsidiary.[87] In the prospect of cleaning up this labyrinthine maze, the DTI *Review* suggests a structure with the Accounting Foundation at the top and two spokes, one of which is the Auditing Practices Board with a subsidiary ethics panel and the other of which is the Investigation and Discipline Board. It suggests that the Accounting Foundation Board, which appoints the members of the Ethics Standards Board, the Auditing Practices Board, and the Investigation and Discipline Board, be linked to the FSA, but notes that the DTI has responsibilities for company law and that this would create an inconsistency.[88] Unfortunately, there's the rub. The FSA should be the responsible party, but given its prudential role of the supervision of banking, this would result in too much concentration of power in a single governmental entity. The *Review* also suggests the possibility of concentrating the Accounting Foundation under the FRC (which is not the same as the FRRP, which is its subsidiary).[89] The funding of the Accounting Foundation, which is currently sourced from the self-regulatory accounting bodies, is also called into question.[90] This report postdates the DTI White Paper on Company Law. Although it addresses issues not covered by the White Paper, the net effect of the *Review* undercuts provisions of the White Paper relating to the oversight of the accounting profession.

On January 29, 2003, the DTI released the final Report on the Regulation of the Accountancy Profession (RRAP).[91] The RRAP establishes an independent regulator at the apex of a hierarchy, the New FRC Council, which includes quasi-self-regulating agencies that are in part funded by the accounting industry.[92] The function of setting standards for audit review should be transferred to an independent regulator. The FRC would take on the functions of the Accounting Foundation, and the Professional Oversight Board would determine the framework of auditing standards.[93] Within this structure, at a lower level of the hierarchy, the Accounting Practices Board (APB) would take on the functions of setting auditing standards. The audit inspection unit would report to the Professional Oversight Board, which would have a wider remit than the existing review board and would also assume the secretary of state of the DTI's responsibility for the recognition of professional bodies, and the new ASB would set accounting standards. The FRRP would enforce these standards and the Professional Oversight Board would regulate the profession generally. The secretary of state of the DTI would appoint the chair and vice-chair of the new FRC and there would be open advertisement for all positions. The report also recommends that there should be a strong principle of lay majorities for the FRC and all subsidiary boards.[94] The RRAP also recommends that due consideration be paid to the International Organization of Securities Commissions (IOSCO) audit practice principles enunciated in "Principles for Auditor Oversight" in order to harmonize standards. These new agencies would have dominion over listed companies, pension funds, and public charities.[95] While the FSA has concurrent powers to remove auditors, it does not have the power to remove audit firms from the right to practice.

The annual costs of running the Professional Oversight Board should be broadly shared between the government and the accountancy profession, with the exception of cases brought before the new Investigation and Discipline Board (IDB).[96] Thus, the regulatory structure would be as shown in figure 8.1.

The FRRP would retain control over the investigation of financial statements, with a broader remit to review all financial information published by listed companies, and would do so on a risk-based approach. The FSA is to play a major role in determining which companies to investigate, and the RRAP recommends that the FSA and the FRRP reach a memorandum of understanding (MOU).

Currently, the Joint Monitoring Unit (JMU) of the Institutes of Chartered Accountants of England, Ireland, and Wales and the Association of Chartered Certified Accountants (ACCA) conducts audits of auditors. These functions are to be transferred to a new independent disciplinary board (the IDB). This new regime for the discipline of auditors is rigorous and exceeds the current U.S. regime.[97] However, as the U.S. PCAOB develops, one might expect further changes to achieve convergence and harmonization, particularly in light of the development of international accounting standards.

Figure 8.1
Reformed Independent Regulator

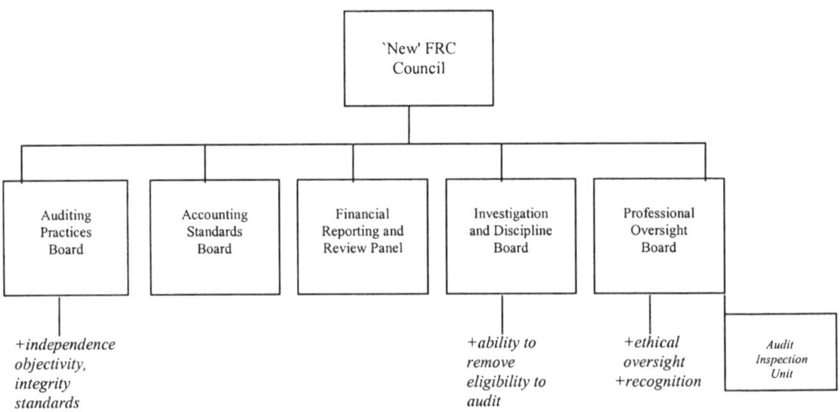

*Current FRC subsidiaries, not part of review's remit.
Source: *Review of the Regulatory Region of the Accountancy Profession: Report to the Secretary of State for Trade and Industry, January 2003.*

Standards for Auditors: The Coordinating Group Report, July 2002 and January 2003

The response to Enron and other U.S. scandals in the United Kingdom has been set forth in a report to the DTI that considers auditor independence and oversight, changes in company law (particularly regarding the duty of directors), and the adequacy of financial reporting standards.[98]

The report endorses the codification of directors' duties and the statutory right of auditors to information, and penalties for not volunteering information include two years' imprisonment (shades of Sarbanes-Oxley). Here, the report is diametrically opposed to the viewpoint of the White Paper on Reforming Company Law.[99]

On January 29, 2003, the secretary of state for the DTI announced the final Report of the Coordinating Group on Auditing and Accounting Practices (CGAA). The January report of the CGAA reflects the avatar of the art of political compromise, even if its turgid, long-winded style is a necessary outgrowth of its content. In general, the report endorses the Higgs and the Smith Reports, discussed above, and principles-based regulation based on the comply-or-explain principle of the Combined Code. However, it endorses the notion of a completely independent body to supervise the accounting profession and an enhanced role for the FSA. Yet, mysteriously, any discussion of criminal penalties with regard to false and misleading financial statements has been omitted. It reiterates the mandatory rotation of lead audit partners every five years and other mandatory rotation of audit firms or retender for audit services. It creates a strong presumption against the provision of internal audits by the external auditor and creates a high review standard against the provision of non-audit services, including legal, information technology (IT), and financial information technology systems,[100] and supports a two-year cooling-off period before a former auditor may join a client firm as an employee or director.[101] The CGAA also endorses a stronger role for audit committees and more detailed disclosure regarding non-audit services.[102]

The new independent body should develop detailed rules to guard against incursions on auditor independence arising from auditors' fears of losing a key client. Audit firms should disclose instances in which fees from one client are greater than 5 percent of total revenue[103] (this situation will be very rare for the big four). Auditors should make information available about their processes and procedures for managing auditor independence, and the monitoring unit should specifically provide this information, as well as aggregate statistics on the effectiveness of its audits.[104] Such reports should be published as nonstatutory documents, but should be placed on a statutory footing if the first round of reports is deemed inadequate by the DTI.[105] Quite significantly, the CGAA endorses the IAS exposure draft for the expensing of share options. (This debate continues to rage in the United States at the time of writing.) The CGAA also endorses new rules on accounting for financial instruments,[106] revenue recognition,[107] and measures to account properly for off-balance sheet financing.[108]

The International Context and Principles-Based versus Rules-Based Accounting

On May 27, 2002, the European Parliament and Council issued a regulation on the adoption of International Accounting Standards by 2005.[109] By the end of 2002, the commission was to decide upon the "applicability of the international accounting standards in existence upon entry into force of this regulation." Article 4 requires consolidated accounting for company accounts for those companies traded on a regulated exchange within the EU.[110]

The FASB and the International Accounting Standard Board (IASB) have reached an agreement to work toward convergence of accounting standards by 2005, the date by which EU member states are required to implement international accounting standards for most public companies.[111] Given the divergences between their standards, and the distinction between principles-based accounting, which characterizes the EU (including the United Kingdom), and rules-based accounting, employed by the FASB, this is wishful thinking. In October 2002, FASB issued a paper expressing an interest in applying a principles-based approach to financial reporting.[112] Sarbanes-Oxley mandated a study by the SEC of principles-based accounting. In a sense, principles-based accounting principles are a more extreme example of the internal risk-based approach of the new capital adequacy agreement and increase the instability of the world financial system.

But chapter 4 of the CGAA report represents a radical departure from the principles-based system of accounting standards. While adhering to principles-based accounting, the CGAA remarks on the study being conducted pursuant to Section 108 of Sarbanes-Oxley, to be completed by July 2003, on principles-based accounting. The report also quotes with approval the statement of Sir David Tweedie, chairman of the IASB:

> If companies and auditors use a principle based approach as a way to skew reality, are unwilling to use judgment, or demand greater detailed application of rules to avoid lawyers second guessing auditors in court, then standard setters are compelled to respond, inevitably, by creating additional rules.[113]

The CGAA does not pick up on Tweedie's view that it may be companies themselves that desire such rules to avoid litigation and restore investor confidence. My own view is that accounting rules require explication through specific rules that are determined by means of stare decisis in administrative courts modeled on the U.S. tax court. Placing the FRRP on a more solid statutory footing beyond its current right of judicial appeal and enabling it to enforce accounting standards by enunciating rules for the interpretation of financial standards would go a long way toward achieving this result. Thus far, in the near 20 years since the FRRP has had this power, it has not had to apply to the court to enforce its rulings.[114] Without a judicial record on appeal resulting from adversarial proceedings, rules for interpretation of accounting standards will remain vague and subject to manipulation.[115] As discussed above, the FRRP proceedings are largely undocumented.[116] Nonetheless, this rather dramatic about-face in the CGAA report indicates the future path of regulation in the United Kingdom and toward convergence; however, in the final analysis, it will more likely be U.S. rules-based International Standards that will win, pointing toward harmonization rather than convergence.

IF YOU HAVEN'T HAD ENOUGH REPORTS: RECENT DEVELOPMENTS

Two recent consultation papers published by the DTI, *Review of the Regulatory Regime of the Accounting Profession: Legislative Proposals*[117] and the *Operating and Financial Review: Working Group on Materiality*,[118] demonstrate the attempt by the DTI to soft-pedal accounting and corporate governance reform.

The first of these papers provides for the FRRP to be funded by fees collected from regulated companies and additional DTI fees. It suggests that the FRRP be designated a recognized body to which the DTI delegates its responsibility for the oversight of company financial statements. It also calls for a public oversight board within the mandate of the DTI; requires the accounting professional bodies to recognize the audit standards adopted by the FRRP; and allows the independent disciplinary body to apply to courts for subpoenas of witnesses and the production of documents. The paper does not specify what punishments are to be meted out, nor define the standards to be employed. It does not discuss the mandate of the public oversight board or the independent disciplinary body.

The consultation paper on *Materiality* is concerned with a definition of materiality and a proper context for defining materiality. The paper enumerates three components that directors "might apply" in arriving at judgments of materiality:

- the concept of materiality in the context of the OFR;
- the set of principles that directors might apply in arriving at their judgments on materiality; and
- the process that directors might go through in arriving at such judgments and thus deciding what should be included in their OFR.[119]

These three components morph into six principles:

- The starting point for directors:
  - knowledge and experience;

- skills and competencies;
- good faith, honest judgments.
- The starting point for the OFR:
  - objective of the OFR;
  - purpose and values of the business;
  - taking a broad view.
- The scope of the information in the OFR:
  - balance between historic review and focus on the future;
  - quantitative and qualitative information;
  - facts and events, probabilities, risk and opportunities.
- Identifying the information for the OFR:
  - nature and size of items;
  - significance of issues;
  - variability and volatility.
- Reporting in the OFR:
  - measuring and describing;
  - consistency from year to year;
  - consistency with other information and reports.
- The approach to disclosure in the OFR:
  - balanced judgments;
  - confidential information [and when it needn't be disclosed];
  - future possibilities.[120]

Although there is a significant body of case law in the United Kingdom on fraudulent and misleading statements, the above definition of materiality makes no effort to track or incorporate these concepts, thereby requiring, when these definitions become statutory duties in the OFR, that courts interpret the meaning of these standards. How a director's skill set relates to materiality is a case of apples and oranges. These definitions, which cobble together all the concepts that have been used to find liability, are explicit. But if they serve merely to add to the definition of "true and fair view" without affecting the common law on directors' liability (which, absent privity or fraud, is virtually nonexistent),[121] such statutory principles will prove counterproductive.

CONCLUSION

Clearly the future of U.K. corporate governance, disclosure, and regulation of the accounting profession is a work in the making, as the various instrumentalities of government and the private sector seek by indirection to find direction out. Therefore it is a propitious moment for a critique. The U.K. regulatory regime sits at a unique vantage point, poised between the European principle-dominated corporate governance and accounting regime and the U.S. rules-obsessed prescriptive regime emphasized by Sarbanes-Oxley. The FASB rules for accounting for derivative instruments, for instance, are amazingly complex.[122] In an ideal world, the United Kingdom could intermediate between these regimes, informing international corporate governance and the implementation of international accounting standards in the EU. Unfortunately, adherence to the vaunted principles-based system of accounting and disclosure is the odds-on favorite to win. The new legislation is likely to be fragmented and unsuccessful in its attempt to negotiate the extremes of rules and principles, and the interest of investors will be ill served in an era in which restoring investor confidence and the race to the top are the new mantras. The ill-conceived agenda of gradualism will do irreparable harm to London's status as the center of European capital markets.

Despite the Higgs Report recommendations on independent directors and the enhanced role of the audit committee envisioned by the Smith Report, the principles-based approach in corporate governance, disclosure requirements, and the regulation of the accounting profession represent a serious impediment to the future of the U.K. financial system. As all the documents issued by the DTI suggest, there is a pride in the maintenance of what is essentially a system overlaid with self-regulation, harking back to the days before the passage of the Financial Services Act 1986 and before the end of the independent listing authority and self-regulation of broker-dealers in the Financial Services and Markets Act 2000. One stand-alone provision of U.K. law has received a great deal of press. Shareholders at annual general meetings can make nonbinding resolutions regarding executive compensation. In 2003, shareholders used this power only once: to reject the compensation package for the CEO of Glaxo Smith Klein.[123]

While the criminalization of securities laws poses possible threats, and penalties under Sarbanes-Oxley may be extreme, there is no reason why certain kinds of accounting fraud intended to mislead investors should not be proscribed by the criminal code. Another disadvantage of the principles-based approach is that a new private right of action, which is painted by the various reports in the most broad-brush terms, is fairly meaningless without a definitive statutory basis. Such a basis could be provided through existing statutes under the FMSA if tied to failure to disclose noncompliance with the voluntary code. But legalizing of contingency-fee arrangements for lawyers and a class-action statute would also be required.

In the domain of accounting, it is quite clear that some new regulatory structure is necessary. Insistence on principles-based accounting, however, makes unlikely the prospect of either private rights of action or the criminalization of accounting fraud becoming a broad-based deterrent to financial fraud. With 2005 fast approaching, the U.K. regulatory structure could play a role in mediating between the extreme version of rules-based procedures in the U.S. GAAP—which in fact allows loopholes,[124] such as those for off-balance sheet financing (since corrected by both the FASB and rules promulgated pursuant to Sarbanes-Oxley)—and the vague principles-based approach employed in the rest of the EU and, to a lesser extent, in the United Kingdom itself. However, the principles-based mindset, which is an outgrowth of the tradition of self-regulation, may seriously undermine U.K. equity markets if their continued pre-eminence depends on investor confidence. The CGAA reaffirms its earlier view that there has to be a proactive element to enforcement and allows for the possibility, if not the inevitability, of detailed accounting rules. But the snail's pace with which the United Kingdom chose to enact the Criminal Justice Act 1993, creating criminal penalties for insider trading, reflects both an initial ambiguity about white-collar crime and a gradual willingness "to let the punishment fit the crime" and "make each prisoner pent . . . a source of obvious 'merriment.'"

NOTES

This chapter is based on two articles that appeared in the December 2003 issue of the *International Journal of Disclosure and Governance*, vol. 1, no. 1: "Editorial: The Audit Committee under Sarbanes-Oxley" and "Disclosure and Governance in the U.K.: Between Scylla and Charibdas," published by Henry Stewart Publications, London, U.K. <http://www.henrystewart.co.uk>

1. Securities and Exchange Commission (SEC), "Standards Relating to Listed Company Audit Committees," Final Rule, SEC Release no. 33-8820, 34-47654 (April 9, 2003).

2. New York Stock Exchange (NYSE) Rulemaking: SEC, "Self-Regulatory Organizations; Notice of Filing of Proposed Rule Change and Amendment No. 1 Thereto by the New York Stock Exchange, Inc. Relating to Corporate Governance" (Release no. 34-47672; File no. SR-NYSE-2002-33) (April 11, 2003).

3. National Association of Dealers (NASD) Rule Making: SEC Self-Regulatory Organizations; Notice of Filing of Proposed Rule Change and Amendment No. 1 Thereto by the National Association of Securities Dealers, Inc. Relating to Proposed Amendments to NASD Rules 4200 and 4350 regarding Board Independence and Independent Committee (Release no. 34-47516; File no. SR-NASD-2002-141) (March 17, 2003).

4. "Disclosure Required by Sections 406 and 407 of the Sarbanes-Oxley Act of 2002," final rule release nos. 33-8177, 34-47235 (January 24, 2003).

5. The SEC has clarified, for the purpose of the rules, that the nonmanagement supervisory board constitutes the board of directors. The SEC has also issued a no conflicts clarification, such as home-country rules that prohibit the board of directors from delegating responsibilities to the audit committee or vesting such powers with a government entity, in situations where the Sarbanes-Oxley-designated audit committee should perform such duties to the extent permitted by law.

6. SEC Release, *supra* note 1.

7. NYSE release, *supra* note 2.

8. *Ibid.*

9. Deloitte and Touche, "Audit Committee and Governance Survey" (April 2003).

10. The Breedon Report also calls for an Internet site where shareholders can vote on resolutions without approval at the annual meeting and set a maximum pay package, including options and other remuneration, for the chief executive officer (CEO).

11. 488 A.2d 858 (Del. 1985), in which directors approved the sale of a company in two hours, without seeing the final version of the contract of sale.

12. *See*, for example, Del. Code Ann. Title 8, 102(b)(7).

13. *In Re. Walt Disney Company Derivative Litigation*, Del. Chancery Court, Consolidated C.A. no. 15452 (May 28, 2003).

14. *Ibid.*, at 2. Five other cases have also ruled against outside directors in cases alleging breach of fiduciary duty on procedural grounds: *Telxon v. Meyerson*, 802 A.2d 257 (Del. June 7, 2002); *Saito v. McKesson HBOC* (reversing grant of summary judgment), *Saito v. McKesson HBOC, Inc.*, 806 A.2d 113 (Del. June 11, 2002) (reversing decision limiting access to books and records by shareholders); *Levco Alternative Fund Ltd v. Reader's Digest Association, Inc.*, 803 A.2d 428 (Del. August 13, 2002) (reversing denial of motion for preliminary injunction); *MM Cos. v. Liquid Audio, Inc.*, 813 A.2d. 1118 (Del. January 7, 2003) (reversing final judgment dismissing challenge to board decision to adopt defensive measures that changed the size and composition of the board during a proxy contest); *OmniCare, Inc. v. NCS Healthcare, Inc.*, 818 A.2d 914 (Del. April 4, 2003) (reversing denial of summary judgment).

15. W. Chandler and L. Strine, "The New Federalism of the American Capital System: Preliminary Reflections of Two Residents of One Small State" (unpublished version).

16. R. Thompson and H. Sale. "Securities Fraud as Corporate Governance: Reflection upon Federalism," Vanderbilt University Law School Law and Economics working paper no. 02-27 (2003). Outside directors named are often alleged to have been involved in insider trading.

17. *See United States v. Andrew S. Fastow*, U.S. District Court, Southern District of Texas, Houston Division, CR no. H-02-889-M, October 1, 2002; *United States v. Andrew S. Fastow, Ben F. Glisan, Jr., and Dan Boyle*, U.S. District Court, Southern District of Texas, Houston Division, Civil Action no. H-02-0665, April 30, 2003; *United States v. David W. Delaney*, U.S. District Court, Southern District of Texas, Houston Division. Civil Action no. H-03-4883, October 29, 2003.

18. Sealed complaint, *United States v. Scott D. Sullivan and David F. Myers*, S.D.N.Y. 02 MAG. 1511; *State of Oklahoma v. Worldcom, Inc., Bernard J. Ebbers*, District Court of Oklahoma County, State of Oklahoma, Case no. CF 2003-4689, filed August 27, 2003.

19.

- "Former Enron Chairman and Chief Executive Officer Agrees to Stipulation and Order Requiring Production of Documents" (SEC Litigation Release no. 18449, SEC Release no. 18372, Nov. 7, 2003).
- "SEC Charges Former Chief Executive Officer of Enron North America and Enron Energy Services with Violating Federal Securities Laws" (Litigation Release no. 18435, Oct. 30, 2003).
- "SEC Charges Former Chief Accounting Officer of Enron North America with Fraud" (Litigation Release no. 18403, Oct. 9, 2003).
- "SEC Files, Subpoena Enforcement Action against Kenneth L. Lay; Former Enron Chairman and Chief Executive Officer Refuses to Produce Documents on Fifth Amendment Grounds" (Litigation Release no. 18372, Sep. 29, 2003).

- "SEC Charges Ben F. Glisan, Jr., Enron's Former Treasurer, with Securities Fraud" (Litigation Release no. 18335, AAER Release no. 1852, Sep. 10, 2003).
- "SEC Settles Enforcement Proceedings against J.P. Morgan Chase and Citigroup" (Press Release no. 2003-87, Jul. 28, 2003).
- "Citigroup, Inc." (Administrative Proceeding Release no. 48230, AAER Release no. 1821, Jul. 28, 2003).
- "SEC Charges J.P. Morgan Chase in Connection with Enron's Accounting Fraud" (Litigation Release no. 18252, AAER Release no. 1820, Jul. 28, 2003).
- "SEC Files Amended Complaint Charging Five Enron Executives with Fraud and Insider Trading Relating to Enron's Broadband Subsidiary" (Press Release no. 2003-58, May 1, 2003).
- "Kevin A. Howard, Michael W. Krautz, Kenneth D. Rice, Joseph Hirko, Kevin P. Hannon, Rex T. Shelby, and F. Scott Yeager" (Amended Complaint) (Litigation Release no. 18122, AAER Release no. 1771, May 1, 2003).
- "Statement by SEC Chairman William H. Donaldson re: Suit against Merrill Lynch and Four Merrill Lynch Executives for Aiding and Abetting Enron Accounting Fraud" (Mar. 17, 2003).
- "Statement by Enforcement Director Stephen M. Cutler, Remarks to Announce the Filing of *SEC v. Merrill Lynch, et al.*" (Mar. 17, 2003).
- "SEC Charges Merrill Lynch, Four Merrill Lynch Executives with Aiding and Abetting Enron Accounting Fraud" (Press Release no. 2003-32, Mar. 17, 2003).
- "Merrill Lynch and Co., Inc., Daniel H. Bayly, Thomas W. Davis, Robert S. Furst, Schuyler M. Tilney" (Litigation Release no. 18038, AAER Release no. 1742, Mar. 17, 2003).
- "A. Howard and Michael W. Krautz" (Litigation Release no. 18030, AAER Release no. 1738, Mar. 12, 2003).
- "SEC Charges Fastow, Former Enron CFO, with Fraud" (Press Release no. 2002-143, Oct. 2, 2002).
- "Andrew S. Fastow" (Litigation Release no. 17762, AAER Release no. 1640, Oct. 2, 2002).
- "SEC Charges a Former High-Ranking Enron Official with Fraud" (Press Release no. 2002-126, Aug. 21, 2002).
- "Michael J. Kopper" (Litigation Release no. 17692, AAER Release no. 1617, Aug. 21, 2002).
- "Subpoena Enforcement Action against Andrew S. Fastow" (Litigation Release no. 17270, Dec. 13, 2001).

20. Following is a partial list of the SEC actions:

- *SEC v. WorldCom Inc.* (Litigation Release no. 18277, AAER no. 1834, August 7, 2003).
- *SEC v. WorldCom Inc.* (Litigation Release no. 18219, AAER no. 1811, July 7, 2003).
- *SEC v. WorldCom Inc.* (Litigation Release no. 18210, AAER no. 1810, July 2, 2003).
- *SEC v. WorldCom Inc.* (Litigation Release no. 18147, AAER no. 1785, May 19, 2003).
- *SEC v. WorldCom Inc.* (Litigation Release no. 17866, AAER no. 1678, November 26, 2002).
- *SEC v. David F. Myers and Buford Yates, Jr.* (Litigation Release no. 17842, AAER no. 1665, November 15, 2002).
- *SEC v. WorldCom Inc.* (Litigation Release no. 17829, AAER no. 1658, November 5, 2002; Complaint).
- *SEC v. Betty L. Vinson and Troy M. Normand* (Litigation Release no. 17783, AAER no. 1650, October 10, 2002; Complaint).
- *SEC v. David F. Myers* (Litigation Release no. 17753, AAER no. 1635, September 26, 2002; Complaint).

- *SEC v. WorldCom Inc.* (Litigation Release no. 17594, AAER no. 1586, June 28, 2002).
- *SEC v. WorldCom Inc.* (Litigation Release no. 17588, AAER no. 1585, June 27, 2002; Complaint).

21. *In re* Enron Securities Litigation (Southern District of Texas, Houston) Civil Action Consolidated no. H-01-3624 (April 8, 2002), *see generally*, <http://www.enronfraud.com> (last visited Jan. 31, 2004). *In re* Worldcom Securities Litigation S.D.N.Y. Master File 02-3288 (Oct. 11, 2002), *see generally*, <http://www.worldcom stockfraud.com> (last visited Jan. 31, 2004).

22. These requirements are contained in the Proposed Governance Rules of the NYSE and NASDAQ (National Association of Dealers Automated Quotations). *See supra* notes 2 and 3.

23. *See* e.g., SEC Lit. Rel. 18115 as to Merrill, Lynch, Pierce, Fenner, and Smith; Lit. Rel. 18109 as to Bear Stearns and Co.; Lit. Rel. 18112 as to UBS Warburg; Lit. Rel. 18116 as to Lehman Brothers.

24. The following is a list of SEC-related actions *in re* Enron. These do not include criminal proceedings:

- "SEC Charges Former Chief Accounting Officer of Enron North America with Fraud" (Litigation Release no. 18403, Oct. 9, 2003).
- "SEC Files, Subpoena Enforcement Action against Kenneth L. Lay; Former Enron Chairman and Chief Executive Officer Refuses to Produce Documents on Fifth Amendment Grounds" (Litigation Release no. 18372, Sep. 29, 2003).
- "SEC Charges Ben F. Glisan, Jr., Enron's Former Treasurer, with Securities Fraud" (Litigation Release no. 18335, AAER Release no. 1852, Sep. 10, 2003).
- "SEC Settles Enforcement Proceedings against J.P. Morgan Chase and Citigroup" (Press Release no. 2003-87, Jul. 28, 2003).
- "Citigroup, Inc." (Administrative Proceeding Release no. 48230, AAER Release no. 1821, Jul. 28, 2003).
- "SEC Charges J.P. Morgan Chase in Connection with Enron's Accounting Fraud" (Litigation Release no. 18252, AAER Release no. 1820, Jul. 28, 2003).
- "SEC Files Amended Complaint Charging Five Enron Executives with Fraud and Insider Trading Relating to Enron's Broadband Subsidiary" (Press Release no. 2003-58, May 1, 2003).
- "Kevin A. Howard, Michael W. Krautz, Kenneth D. Rice, Joseph Hirko, Kevin P. Hannon, Rex T. Shelby, and F. Scott Yeager" (Amended Complaint) (Litigation Release no. 18122, AAER Release no. 1771, May 1, 2003).
- "Statement by SEC Chairman William H. Donaldson re: Suit against Merrill Lynch and Four Merrill Lynch Executives for Aiding and Abetting Enron Accounting Fraud" (Mar. 17, 2003).
- "Statement by Enforcement Director Stephen M. Cutler, Remarks to Announce the Filing of *SEC v. Merrill Lynch, et al.*" (Mar. 17, 2003).
- "SEC Charges Merrill Lynch, Four Merrill Lynch Executives with Aiding and Abetting Enron Accounting Fraud" (Press Release no. 2003-32, Mar. 17, 2003).
- "SEC Charges Fastow, Former Enron CFO, with Fraud" (Press Release no. 2002-143, Oct. 2, 2002).
- "Andrew S. Fastow" (Litigation Release no. 17762, AAER Release no. 1640, Oct. 2, 2002).
- "SEC Charges a Former High-Ranking Enron Official with Fraud" (Press Release no. 2002-126, Aug. 21, 2002).

- "Michael J. Kopper" (Litigation Release no. 17692, AAER Release no. 1617, Aug. 21, 2002).
- "Subpoena Enforcement Action against Andrew S. Fastow" (Litigation Release no. 17270, Dec. 13, 2001).
- "Merrill Lynch and Co., Inc., Daniel H. Bayly, Thomas W. Davis, Robert S. Furst, Schuyler M. Tilney" (Litigation Release no. 18038, AAER Release no. 1742, Mar. 17, 2003).
- "A. Howard and Michael W. Krautz" (Litigation Release no. 18030, AAER Release no. 1738, Mar. 12, 2003).
- "SEC Charges Fastow, Former Enron CFO, with Fraud" (Press Release no. 2002-143, Oct. 2, 2002).
- "Andrew S. Fastow" (Litigation Release no. 17762, AAER Release no. 1640, Oct. 2, 2002).
- "SEC Charges a Former High-Ranking Enron Official with Fraud" (Press Release no. 2002-126, Aug. 21, 2002).
- "Michael J. Kopper" (Litigation Release no. 17692, AAER Release no. 1617, Aug. 21, 2002).
- "Subpoena Enforcement Action against Andrew S. Fastow" (Litigation Release no. 17270, Dec. 13, 2001).

25. Staff Report, "Joint SEC/NASD/NYSE Report of Examinations of Broker-Dealers regarding Discounts on Front-End Sales Charges on Mutual Funds" (March 2003).

26. "SEC Chairman Donaldson Releases Statement Regarding Initiatives to Combat Late Trading and Market Timing of Mutual Funds," Press Release 2003-136 (October 9, 2003).

27. *See* SEC Press Release, October 16, 2003, and *In the Matter of James Patrick Connelly, Jr.*, SEC Release 33-8304, 34-48643; Investment Act, Release no. 2183; Investment Co. Act 4026209; Administrative Proceeding File no. 3-11303 (October 16, 2003).

28. "SEC Institutes Administrative Proceeding against Putnam Investment Management LLC in Connection with Self-Dealing in Putnam Mutual Funds by Two Managing Directors and Other Putnam Investment Professionals." Securities and Exchange Commission; Investment Advisers Act of 1940 Release no. 2185/October 28, 2003; Investment Company Act of 1940 Release no. 26232/October 28, 2003; Administrative Proceeding File no. 3-11317.

29. Eliot Spitzer, "Editorial: Regulation Begins at Home," *New York Times*, Nov. 17, 2003.

30. "Morgan Stanley Agrees to Pay $50 Million Fine," *New York Times*, Nov. 18, 2003.

31. Kenneth Gilpin, "Mutual Fund Investigation Turns to Charles Schwab," Nov. 17, 2003.

32. Fred Noland Bergston, Takeshito Ito, and Marcus Noland, *No More Bashing: Building a New Japanese-U.S. Relationship* (Institute for International Economics, 2001) at 72.

33. NYSE rules, *supra* note 2.

34. *Ibid.*

35. SEC, Proposed Rule, "Security Holder Director Nominations," Release nos. 34-48626, IC-26206 (October 14, 2003).

36. Stephen Labaton, "Big Pension Funds Object to Proposal on Proxy Rules," *New York Times*, Oct. 3, 2003.

37. SEC, Staff, "Study Pursuant to Section 108(d) of the Sarbanes-Oxley Act of

2002 on the Adoption by the United States Financial Reporting System of a Principles-Based Accounting System" (July 25, 2003).

38. Directive 2003/6/EC of the European Parliament and of the Council of January 28, 2003, on insider dealing and market manipulation (market abuse); Official Journal of the European Union L.096, 12/04/2003 P. 0016–0025.

39. These principles include integrity, skill, and care. Principle 7 requires clear, fair, and not misleading communication with clients; Principle 3, management and control; and Principle 8 deals with conflicts of interest, COB 7.1 conflict of interest and material interest and Chinese wall principles, COB 2.4. Additionally, chapter 9 of the United Kingdom Listing Authority (UKLA) Listing Rules requires that price-sensitive information be disclosed to the market. Guidance on the dissemination of price-sensitive information is contained in the Price Sensitive Information Guide, which is appended to the UKLA Guidance Manual. *See generally,* Financial Services Authority (FSA), "Investment Research: Conflicts and Other Issues," Discussion Paper no. 15 (July 2002).

40. Art. 6(5) of the Directive on Market Abuse (Article 6.5 of—*supra* note 38) is concerned with fair presentation of research and other relevant information and would require the disclosure of conflicts of information that would impair the quality of information. *See generally,* the Committee of European Securities Regulators (CESR), CESR's Advice on Possible Level 2 Implementing Measures for the Proposed Market Abuse Directive, consultation paper, reference no. CESR/02/089b (July 5, 2002).

41. *Caparo Industries v. Dickman* (1990) 2 WLR 358.

42. Financial Services and Markets Act 2000 Part 15, 2000 Chapter c.8.

43. Comments of the UKLA Director (Practicing Law Institute, *European Securities Regulation* [seminar, London, December 9–10, 2002]). But *see* ref. 24 above and accompanying text, where Iceland Group was censured for violating the "Guide on Price Sensitive Information."

44. "Modernising Company Law," CM 5553, presented to Parliament by the Secretary of Trade and Industry by command of Her Majesty ("the White Paper").

45. *Ibid.*, § 2.42 et seq.

46. *Ibid.*, § 3.8–3.9.

47. *Ibid.*, § 3.26–3.31.

48. *Ibid.*, § 4.36.

49. *Ibid.*, § 4.47.

50. *Ibid.*, § 4.50.

51. *Ibid.*, § 4.44.

52. *See* J. Friedland, "Sarbanes-Oxley: Certification, Financial Reporting, and Economic Crime," *Company Lawyer* (December 2002): pp. 384–88.

53. *Op. cit.*, § 5.6.

54. *Ibid.*, § 5.6.

55. *Ibid.*, § 5.9.

56. *Ibid.*, § 5.11–5.14.

57. *Ibid.*, § 5.21.

58. Department of Trade and Industry (DTI), D. Higgs, "Review of the Role and Effectiveness of Independent Directors" (January 2003).

59. *Ibid.*, par. 7.4–7.5.

60. *Ibid.*, par. 10.32.

61. *Ibid.*, par. 2.31. It is also proposed that a company secretary will be available to the nonexecutive directors.

62. *See* chapter 4, note 105, and accompanying text.

63. *Op. cit.*, par. 12.11.

64. *Ibid.*, note at 73, par. 14. These include guidance on the code for provisions relating to the position of a nonexecutive director that will be relevant for liability purposes; instructions to the Lord Chancellor's Department regarding active case management for cases against directors; indemnification of directors in advance; and guidance by the Law Society and other relevant groups on insurance for directors.

65. *Ibid.*, par. 15.10.

66. *Ibid.*, par. 15.16–15.18.

67. *Ibid.*, par. 5.3 and 5.7. Over three-quarters of FTSE 100 companies have a chairman who was not formerly the CEO.

68. *Ibid.*, par. 8.8. By contrast, NYSE rules require nonmanagement directors to have regularly scheduled meetings without management.

69. SEC, "Standards Relating to Listed Company Audit Committees, Final Rule," Release no. 33-8820, 34-47654 (April 9, 2003). While this rule is stringent regarding independence in terms of fees, employment, and payments, it does allow material business relations.

70. Pub. Law 107-204; 116 Stat. 745 (2002), at § 407.

71. Practicing Law Institute, *European Securities Regulation* (seminar, London, December 9–10, 2002).

72. "Higgs Report," *supra* note 58, par. 10.9

73. Financial Reporting Council, *Audit Committee Combined Code Guidance: A Report and Proposed Guidance by an FRC Appointed Group*, chaired by Sir Robert Smith (January 20, 2003).

74. *Ibid.*, par. 1.1–1.3

75. *Ibid.*, par. 2.1.

76. *Supra* note 70, § 210; 17 C.F.R. 210.2; *see also* SEC, "Strengthening the Commission's Requirements regarding Auditors' Independence," Final Rule, Release no. 34-47276 (January 29, 2003b).

77. *Op. cit.*, par. 3.10–3.14.

78. *Ibid.*, par. 3.16.

79. *Ibid.*, par. 6.3.

80. FSA, "Review of the Listing Particulars Regime," Discussion Paper no. 14 (July 2002).

81. *Ibid.*, par. 1.8.

82. *Ibid.*, par. 3.16.

83. *Ibid.*, par. 3.16.

84. *See* chapter 4, note 105, and accompanying text.

85. DTI, "Review of the Regulatory Regime of the Accountancy Profession: A Consultation Document" (October 2002).

86. The Companies Act 1985 states that every company shall appoint auditors. The Companies Act 1989 gives effect to the Eighth Directive on Company Law and requires that all auditors be statutory auditors with professional qualifications and subject to the requirements of a recognized statutory board. The Accounting Standards Board (ASB) took over the responsibility of setting auditing standards in 1990. Prior to the establishment of the Accountancy Foundation, the Auditing Practices Board,

legally an entity of the six accounting bodies, was responsible for nonstatutory independent regulation of the six chartered accountancy bodies in England, Wales, Scotland, and Northern Ireland, a responsibility that in the late 1990s was assumed by the Accountancy Foundation. The Accounting Foundation consists of five limited companies that employ a staff of 18, only 8 of whom are chartered accountants. The Review Board of the Accounting Foundation sometimes considers ethical matters, which are also the province of the Ethics Standards Board and the other ethics group. The Auditing Practices Board continues the work of its predecessor and is responsible for setting auditing standards. The Ethics Standards Board is responsible for developing ethical standards, but there is also a Cumulative Committee of Accounting Bodies (CCAB) ethics group. The Investigation and Discipline Board will take over the present joint disciplinary scheme operated by the Institute of Chartered Accountants of England and Wales (ICAEW) and the Institute of Chartered Accountants of Scotland (ICAS), but its role will be extended to cover all CCAB bodies except the ICAI. "Review of the Regulatory Regime of the Accountancy Profession," § 3–6.

87. The chair is appointed by eight nominating bodies. The FRC is chosen by the Secretary of State of the DTI and the Governor of the Bank of England (which now no longer regulates banks); the chairs of the ASB and the FRRP (Financial Reporting Review Panel) are automatically members. The chair and the board of the FSA are appointed by the Treasury.

88. "Review of Accountancy," *supra* note 85, § 8.4. These boards should have a majority of nonaccountants.

89. The Accountancy Foundation and the FRC are nonstatutory bodies, although the FRRP is authorized to carry out enforcement procedures under the Companies Act 1985.

90. *Op. cit.*, s. 10.

91. "Report to the Secretary of State for Trade and Industry: Review of the Regulatory Regime of the Accountancy Profession," (January 29, 2003), URN 03/589.

92. *Ibid.*

93. *Ibid.*, par. 1.11.

94. *Ibid.*, par. 3.25.

95. *Ibid.*, par. 5.17.

96. The Report on the Regulation of the Accountancy Profession (RRAP) suggests that power for the Investigations and Discipline Board (IDB) to remove eligibility to audit could be achieved through a modification of s. 25 of the Companies Act 1989.

97. U.S. SEC rules strictly bar the payment of any fee to independent directors but allow other business relationships. Exchange rules may impose additional criteria for independence. *See* § (2003a).

98. "Coordinating Group Report on Auditing and Accounting," Interim Report to the Secretary of State for Trade and Industry and the Chancellor of the Exchequer (July 2002), Executive Summary, section 1.

99. *See supra*, notes 44–52.

100. *Op. cit.*, par. 1.41–48.

101. *Ibid.*, par. 1.61.

102. *Ibid.*, par. 1.51–58.

103. *Ibid.*, par. 1.65–66.

104. *Ibid.*, par. 1.69 and 1.72.

105. *Ibid.*, par. 3.6.

106. Exposure Draft of IAS (International Accounting Standards) 32.

107. Exposure Draft of IAS 39.

108. The SEC has already issued rules, pursuant to Sarbanes-Oxley, *supra note* § 401(a): SEC, "Disclosure in Management Discussion and Analysis about Off Balance Sheet Arrangements and Aggregate Contractual Obligations," SEC Final Rule, Release nos. 33 8102, 34-47264 (January 2003c).

109. Regulation of the European Parliament and the European Council, Interinstitutional File 2001/0044 (May 27, 2002). Companies applying another set of internationally accepted accounting standards traded on the exchanges of a nonmember state may, at the option of a member state, have until 2007 to conform to the regulations (art. 11).

110. Under art. 10, companies listing only debt securities shall have until 2007 to comply.

111. *See* conclusion, Chapter 1, note 2.

112. FASB, "Principles Based Approach to U.S. Standard Setting," no. 1125-001 (October 21, 2002). Examples given include accounting for derivatives and capitalization of interest. In these instances, the principles-based approach, in my view, inevitably leads to more disparate accounting treatment.

113. CGAA Report, *supra* note 98, par. 4.5, citing D. Tweedie, "Renewing Confidence in the Markets," *Bank of England Financial Stability Review* (December 2002).

114. DTI, "Modernising Company Law," *supra* note 44, par. 5.22 (1999).

115. *See generally*, L. Spacek, "The Need for an Accounting Court," *Accounting Review* 33 (July 1958): p. 361.

116. *Ibid.*

117. DTI, "Review of the Regulatory Regime of the Accounting Profession: Legislative Proposals" (March 2003).

118. DTI, "Operating and Financial Review: Working Group on Materiality" (June 23, 2003).

119. *Ibid.*, § 22.

120. *Ibid.*, § 23.

121. *See supra*, note 41.

122. Three paragraphs define derivative instruments and there are nine exceptions, which are subject to guidance from the Derivative Implementation Group (DIG). The DIG identified 19 issues relating to scope exceptions. Paragraphs 12–15 of Rule 133 discuss derivatives embedded in other instruments and consider boundaries and definitions. There is extensive guidance in Appendix A and B to the rule, including 36 issues relating to the "clear and closely connected" exception. There is also an exception for embedded instruments, the fair value of which cannot be reliably estimated. There are special rules for hedged instruments, involving a plethora of conditions to be met and exceptions. The special accounting of hedged instruments is considered in about four paragraphs, which determine the effect of the hedging. The guidance in Appendix A amounts to 40 paragraphs and that in Appendix B to 60. The DIG identifies 21 issues.

123. "Fat Cats Feeding," *Economist* (Oct. 9, 2003).

124. Enron never in fact complied with the famous 97/3 rule, which required 3 percent of outside equity in order to avoid consolidation of subsidiaries.

The Powers Report ("Powers") acknowledged that Enron understated its obligations. As a consequence of the failure to consolidate, Enron indicated it had overstated its income by approximately $500 million and understated its liabilities by $2 billion.

The Chewco and LJM1 restatement reduced net income by nearly $500 million over four reporting years (principally in the last three years) and reduced shareholder equity by nearly $2.2 billion and increased debt by $2.7 billion ("Report of Investigation by the Special Investigative Committee of the Board of Directors of Enron Corp.," William Powers, chair, Raymond Troubh, Herbert Winokur; Wilmer Cutler Pickering counsel [February 1, 2002, at 3]).

For the Chewco Partnership, $11.4 million in equity was required, but the money was advanced by Barclay Bank and secured by pledges of collateral characterized as reserves (Powers). The existence of the cash collateral was fatal to the 3 percent requirement, since the $6.6 million could not be both collateral and equity (Powers, at 50). Wilmer Cutler and Pickering, which prepared the report for Enron's Board of Directors, seem to be obsessed with understanding the motivation for the failure to fund the 3 percent, almost in the same way as a criminal lawyer is fascinated by a particularly complex murder. Although Enron ultimately decided to give up the ghost on LJM1, it might not have done so if Chewco had not failed. The Powers Report is ambivalent about the legality of the Special Purpose Vehicle used in that partnership (Powers, at 52–53). In the LJM1 deals, the report says, "There are plausible, more innocent explanations of some of the repurchases, but a sufficient basis remains for further examination."

Conclusion

> When the capital development of a country becomes a byproduct of the activities of a casino, the job is likely to be ill done. The measure of success attained by Wall Street, regarded as an institution of which the proper social purpose is to direct new investment into the most profitable channels in terms of future yield, cannot be claimed as one of the outstanding triumphs of laissez-faire capitalism, which is not surprising if I am right in thinking that the best brains of Wall Street have been in fact directed towards different objectives. . . .
>
> These tendencies are a scarcely avoidable outcome of the successful organization of "liquid investment markets." It is usually agreed that casinos should, in the public interest, be inaccessible and expensive and perhaps the same is true of stock exchanges.
>
> (John Maynard Keynes, *The General Theory of Employment, Interest, and Money*, 1935)

Since the market as casino has once again become an apt metaphor, Keynes's prescription for raising the barrier to entry to equity markets should be considered anew. While a securities transaction tax would only serve to place sand in the wheels of finance, given the premium placed on liquidity and the sense of security involved in derivative instruments, hedges, and portfolio insurance, there are other means of achieving this result. The diversification provisions of the Employee Retirement Income Security Act (ERISA) could be interpreted to require a balancing of debt and equity; of course, small investors have become involved in capital markets in ways that Keynes could not even imagine, particularly as debtors making use of equity linked mortgages and commercial paper. Perhaps, the use of such instruments should be restricted to more sophisticated investors or, at least, to more conservative underwriting by financial institutions.

Like the changes in U.S. corporate governance and a more gradual revolution in financial reporting, the impetus for the European Union (EU) is broadly political and economic in that the removal of tariff and nontariff barriers (including monetary union) in a custom union leads to increased trade and greater economic efficiency. This has been a mantra of the postwar economic establishment since the World Trade Organization (WTO) was proposed, and the General Agreement on Tariffs and Trade (GATT) became part of the tripartite Bretton Woods Agreement.

The prospects for the euro as future reserve currency are limited, but the precipitous rise of the euro creates a possibility of *Herstaat* (currency risk), which could lead to a breakdown of payment systems in the United States and internationally. Regardless of how the United Kingdom votes in the referendum to join the euro, London will continue to be the financial center of Europe with its cadre of investment banks, exchanges, and market professionals, and the FSA will be the regulator par excellence, providing public and private exchange of world-class caliber rivaled only by New York. However, the importance of International Accounting Standard Board's (IASB) accounting standards cannot be overstated. The development of an integrated European securities market is essential for the growth and further integration of EU capital markets. Enabling Continental public companies to access capital markets for equity may enable credit expansion in the eurozone. But Europe, like Japan, will continue to be plagued by its shrinking demographics.

The structural trade surplus that is essential to the Japanese economy is unlikely to continue at its current level given the widening trade deficit of the United States. Japan, China, South Korea, and Taiwan, in particular, will come under increasing pressure to develop consumer markets. Japan is hampered by the weakness of its legal framework, and it is difficult to see how its financial and corporate accounting systems can be modernized in a medium-term scenario. Although Japan is unlikely to default on its government debt, its growth will be further impaired by its lack of flexibility in this arena. The failure to write off nonperforming loans will continue to make capital scarce for the foreseeable future. Until Japan musters definitive political will, it will be stymied in its attempt at complete economic recovery.

Internationally, intragroup risk transfer in conglomerates, highly leveraged fund counterparty risk, and contagion in the unregulated derivative instruments market pose the most substantial short-term risk. There are no serious studies on intragroup exposures. One doubts whether, in the United States, the Commodities Futures Trading Corporation (CFTC) and the SEC even share information; and there is no real attention paid to unregulated affiliates of broker-dealers since liquidation is the intention in the event of failure.

The European Directive on the Regulation of Financial Conglomerates only begins the international process. One also ought to be wary of the internal risk-based approach since, although the methodology involves great technical improvements over the 1988 Accord, an internal approach is an incentive to cheat. Furthermore, the methodology fails to define an impaired loan, leaving this for obvious political reasons to the national supervisors.

It is inconceivable that confidence in capital markets can be restored in the medium term without a complete overhaul of Generally Accepted Accounting Principles (GAAP) and IASB rules (particularly in the most important market, the United States). The Financial Accounting Standards Board (FASB) and the IASB have reached an agreement to work toward convergence of accounting standards by 2005, the date by which EU member states are required to implement international accounting standards for most public companies.[1] Given the divergences between their standards, this is wishful thinking. However, another issue arises when considering the distinction between principles-based accounting, which characterized the EU, including the United Kingdom, and rules-based accounting, which FASB employs. In October 2002, FASB issued a paper that expressed an interest in applying a principles-based approach to financial reporting.[2] Sarbanes-Oxley mandated a study by the SEC of principles-based accounting.[3] In that context, and insofar as criminal liability for false and misleading certification is concerned, I criticized such an approach as making the elements of criminal intent far more difficult to prove. In a sense, principles-based accounting principles are a more extreme example of the internal risk-based approach of the new capital adequacy agreement and increase the instability of the world financial system. However, in the context of public company reporting, they lead to increased vagueness in what constitutes a legal norm for financial reporting.

Unlike the U.S. Internal Revenue Code, GAAP and IASB standards are a hodgepodge of convenience, fraud, and genuine common sense. There is no underlying logic, and there is no court of competence that has jurisdiction. The Sarbanes-Oxley Act will greatly enhance the quality of financial reporting over time. However, systematic improvement will only occur when GAAP is the subject of a case-by-case appellate process where the application of rules can be properly adjudicated. This might be within the province of administrative courts with the right of appeal to federal court. The administrative process for financial reporting should be predicated on the successful model of the tax court as established by the Internal Revenue Code. Additional legislation restricting equity-linked mortgages by Fannie Mae and guaranteed first mortgages by Ginnie Mac and cracking down on consumer loan portfolios by banks is unlikely to be forthcoming without an intervening financial comeuppance. Deregulation of banking under Gramm-Leach-Bliley led to conflicts of interest in connection with Enron and Worldcom.

The Investment Company Act of 1940 and ERISA should be amended to facilitate large block holding by mutual funds and pension plans. The best corporate governance system benefits from both liquidity and control. More importantly, conflicts of interest in private mutual fund management of 401Ks should be eliminated, so fund managers, individually and in concert, can serve on corporate boards. The inherent conflict of interest between brokerage/ analysts and investment bankers has hopefully been resolved. Expensing share options by the IASB and the virtual certainty of FASB taking similar action will go some way toward reducing agency costs, but much more remains to be done in rationalizing executive compensation and incentives.

The Federal Reserve has for too long targeted broad money—M3, the measure of the money supply—as the relevant measure, when, in many instances, total credit is a more relevant gauge of an overheated economy. By failing to tackle asset inflation by raising interest rates and utilizing the other tools in its arsenal—bank assets, in particular, consumer loans, equity linked mortgages, and exposure to commercial real estate—the Federal Reserve Board (FRB) has failed in its mandate; as recent scandals such as Salomon Brothers, Citibank, and Chase Morgan regarding analyst conflicts and Enron-related loans demonstrate, it has failed to supervise financial institutions on a consolidated basis. Provisions of existing law may not be satisfactory to accomplish this objective. The FRB has not been proactive, in the aftermath of Glass Steagall abolition, in monitoring the not-so-subtle hazards that arise from the combination of banking and investment banking, which has proven every bit as hazardous as the combination of brokerage and investment banking. In addition, the FRB should exercise some power over the capital adequacy of securities firms (which it may bail out under the Federal Deposit Insurance Corporation Improvement Act of 1991 [FDICIA]). Such a reconstituted Bank of the United States would best serve as a guarantor of the safety and soundness of the U.S. financial system.

There is now a consensus among economic historians that the Depression, per se, resulted, in part, from the Smoot-Hawley Tariff, which deepened the recession created by the stock market crash and the subsequent raising of interest rates by the United States, France, and England to maintain national gold reserves. How can the United States and Asia negotiate an exit from the cul-de-sac created by the international balance of payments? The EU and the rest of the world are almost an irrelevance to this imponderable since they have no serious balance of payment deficit or surplus. The pas de deux of the United States and Asia, particularly China and Japan, without a solution, will upset the apple cart in the not too distant future. The Smoot-Hawley Tariff revisited looms close to the horizon. The need to finance increasingly huge trade deficits has led to the instability of U.S. capital markets and consumption-driven growth. The boomlet in capital spending in IT was only a red herring. More to the point are the equity-linked mortgages, consumer debt, and a giddiness in profits and earnings reflecting a demand for U.S. financial instruments—equities and corporate and treasury bonds, in particular. Consumer debt, for instance, has mushroomed from 70 percent of GDP in 1999 to 83 percent of GDP in 2003.[4] The huge amount of dollar denominated assets held by Asian governments means that a devaluation of the dollar vis-à-vis Asian currencies is unlikely, unless foreign governments are forced to liquidate dollar denominated instruments to stave off domestic financial crises. Then competitive devaluation would be in play and *Herstaat* risk and intermarket risk could result.

It is shocking that there has not been more discussion on the consequences and remedy of the U.S. net investment position and the current account deficit. To hamper this outcome, my proposition is the creation of a World Trade and Finance Organization (WTFO) charged with the redressing of the current account imbalances. The International Monetary Fund (IMF) and the WTO would amend their charters to subordinate to the new organization, which would begin operation in 2006 and retroactively begin to address the current account imbalances, in essence, by requiring the United States to export up to an additional $250 billion per year in goods and services or to make foreign direct or portfolio investment. This would be paid for pro rata by the United States as well as foreign governments that have trade surpluses with the United States and wish to maintain these surpluses. The credits would be provided in the form of guarantees of up to 50 percent of the previous year's surplus by the United States, through an expanded export-import bank, and 50 percent by an import agency. The question of which goods and services would be produced and provided by the United States would be subject to consultation with the importing nation and mediated by the WTFO. Dollar reserves could be utilized for this purpose, and it is possible that convertibility would need to be limited. This would also require an industrial policy, on the part of the United States, not considered since the National Recovery Act. In essence, the plan would involve elements of the Marshall Plan, except the putative beneficiaries would be providing funds, and the real beneficiary would be the United States. In practice, the volume of trade would drop and the dollar would weaken, dropping demand for imports. But the ultimate goal of the plan would be to develop a consumer market in Asia that would be an end user of U.S. exports, including intangibles such as patents and intellectual property, perhaps at a readjusted value. Part and parcel of the proposal would be the harmonization of accounting rules, since reliance on a foreign governmental entity as a counterparty under the proposal would imply reliance on its accounting system.

Unfortunately, increasing the amount of goods shipped to China and providing the means for the Chinese to purchase goods is unlikely to improve the long-term outlook for the stability of the financial structure. However, if the Chinese government converted some of its dollar reserves into higher wages for workers in the public sector, the spillover effect would go a long way toward improving the domestic consumer sector, even if the long-term U.S. interest rate were raised, the dollar exchange rate lowered, and Chinese exports to the United States suffered in the process.

Currently, Japanese banks have enormous portfolios of nonperforming loans. Bankruptcy and foreclosure proceedings must be streamlined in legislation.

Currently, under Japanese law, in most instances only the first lender would be repaid, and any decision to foreclose requires the consent of all the creditors. Legislation will be necessary to enact reforms that are similar to Anglo-American property laws (including equity of redemption and public auctions). Assets will then end up in the hands of value investors, which is what occurred in the United States in the early 1990s.

Although Japan is characterized by large block stakeholdings and bank monitoring, the long-term success of the Japanese financial system will require improved corporate governance, including independent directors, and improvement of the auditing and financial reporting system, particularly standardization of financial reporting and market based—rather than historical cost—accounting. The United States, as the largest importer of goods from Asia, would be in a position to dictate financial liberalization and the sale of dollar reserves, if it used the threat of high tariffs as a stick.

Whether or not the U.S. external debt stablizes, the well-being of the international financial system necessitates a restructuring of the Bretton Woods system. The harmonization of international financial and corporate accounting will dominate the landscape of international capital markets in the decade to come. However, the United States is of necessity the lead player in the numbers game. Progress in this arena will serve to provide a foundation for continued growth very much as the disclosure regime of the Securities and Exchange laws has done for 70 years.

NOTES

1. *See* chapter 1, note 454, and accompanying text.

2. Financial Accounting Standards Board (FASB), "Principles Based Approach to U.S. Standard Setting," no. 1125-001 (October 21, 2002). Examples given include accounting for derivatives and capitalization of interest. In these instances, the principles based approach, in my view, inevitably leads to more disparate accounting treatment.

3. *See* chapter 6, note 15.

4. Eduardo Porter, "Debt Heavy May Be Too Jittery about Rates," *New York Times*, Jan. 31, 2004, at C1.

Index

About the Author

JOHN H. FRIEDLAND is Managing Director of the Lawland Corporation, New York City, and Managing Editor of the *International Journal of Disclosure and Governance.*